Voices of Glasnost

BOOKS BY STEPHEN F. COHEN

Rethinking the Soviet Experience: Politics and History since 1917

Bukharin and the Bolshevik Revolution: A Political Biography, 1888–1938

The Soviet Union since Stalin *(co-editor)*

An End to Silence: Uncensored Opinion in the Soviet Union *(editor)*

The Great Purge Trial *(co-editor)*

Sovieticus

STEPHEN F. COHEN
KATRINA VANDEN HEUVEL

Voices of Glasnost

Interviews with
Gorbachev's Reformers

W · W · NORTON & COMPANY · *NEW YORK* · *LONDON*

Copyright © 1989 by Stephen F. Cohen and Katrina vanden Heuvel. All rights reserved. Printed in the United States of America.

THE TEXT *of this book is composed in Times Roman, with display type set in Times Roman. Composition and manufacturing by the Haddon Craftsmen, Inc. Book design by Marjorie J. Flock.*

Library of Congress Cataloging-in-Publication Data
Cohen, Stephen F.
  Voices of glasnost: interviews with Gorbachev's reformers / by Stephen F. Cohen and
  Katrina vanden Heuvel.—1st ed.
  p.   cm.
  Includes index.
  1. Glasnost.   2. Interviews—Soviet Union.   I. vanden Heuvel,
  Katrina.   II. Title.
  DK287.C64   1989
  947—dc20   89–32441

ISBN 0-393-02625-6

W. W. Norton & Company, Inc., 500 Fifth Avenue, New York, N.Y. 10110
W. W. Norton & Company Ltd., 37 Great Russell Street, London WC1B 3NU

2 3 4 5 6 7 8 9 0

Contents

Photographs appear following page 156

Preface

M OST OF US in the West get our knowledge and perceptions of
the Soviet Union from television and newspaper reports. This
book of candid interviews with fourteen Soviet public figures
offers readers a more direct kind of access to the historic reforms known
as perestroika, or restructuring, that have been underway in that country since Mikhail Gorbachev became its leader in 1985. It is, so far as we
know, the first book of this kind, at least by Americans.

All of the people in *Voices of Glasnost* are what have become known
in Moscow as *perestroishchiki*—outspoken proponents, some of them
even architects, of Gorbachev's most radical reforms. As the Soviet
press frequently characterizes the ongoing struggle over change, they
are on "the barricades of perestroika." To give a merely formal example
of their involvement, ten of the people in this book were elected to the
newly created Congress of People's Deputies in the Soviet Union's first
quasi-democratic national elections, in 1989, and most of the others
were candidates or activists in the process. As readers will understand,
Gorbachev's policy of glasnost, or openness, has also made audible the
voices of people who oppose or who are skeptical of his leadership, but
they are not the subject of this book. Finally, all of the people interviewed here are intellectuals of one kind or another, and most of them
belong to the Gorbachev generation—men and women who began their
careers during the first period of post-Stalin reform, in the 1950s, under
Nikita Khrushchev.

In other respects, however, *Voices of Glasnost* brings together a
diverse group of Soviet reformers, ranging from politicians and a poet
to journalists, scholars, and an actor. Even the political figures among
them have had different "fates," as Russians often refer to their lives.
They include the Politburo member who is almost certainly Gorbachev's staunchest supporter in the top leadership, as well as three other
full or candidate members of the Central Committee who are or who
have been advisers to Gorbachev, but also a once high-ranking political

figure who was expelled from the Communist Party in 1975 and read-mitted only in late 1988, after years as a "half-dissident." Nor do these voices of glasnost speak in a single voice. Even though all but one of them (Yevgeny Yevtushenko) are party members, they disagree about important issues, from the nature of the Soviet system today to the desirability of various policies already adopted or being considered by the Gorbachev leadership. What could be more fundamental, for exam-ple, than the dispute between Georgi Smirnov and Yuri Afanasyev over whether or not any kind of socialism exists in the Soviet Union?

Readers should also know something about the making of this book. In 1987 we decided to conduct lengthy interviews with leading advo-cates of Gorbachev's reforms in various areas of Soviet life in order to get firsthand accounts of the meaning of perestroika in politics, culture, economics, and the media. As Russian-speaking observers of Soviet affairs and frequent visitors to Moscow, we already had access to all of the people in this book except Aleksandr Yakovlev, the Politburo mem-ber, and Smirnov, director of the Central Committee's Institute of Marxism-Leninism. For access to those very high-ranking officials, we turned to Valentin Falin, then head of the Soviet press agency Novosti, and his deputy Vladimir Milyutenko. We take this opportunity to thank them for their assistance. We also want to emphasize that no one involved with the book put any restrictions on the questions we asked or on how we edited the answers. Indeed, no Soviet participant or official has seen the interviews prior to their publication here.

The tape-recorded interviews took place between June 1987 and April 1989, mostly in Moscow. All of the participants except one (Yevgeny Velikhov) were interviewed at least twice and most of them several times during the period of almost two years. Each initial inter-view lasted three to five hours and focused on the participant's autobi-ography, general understanding of perestroika, and opinions about reforms in his or her own profession. Follow-up interviews dealt with subsequent events and subjects that we had neglected to raise. All of the discussions were conducted in Russian except those with Yevtushenko and Georgi Arbatov, who preferred to speak English and gave us per-mission to edit their remarks for style. The Russian transcripts were translated by our friends Nina Bouis, Anna Gelpern, Mikhail Sheve-lyov, and George Shriver. We are grateful to them, especially to Anna Gelpern, who did most of the translations and helped us in other ways as well.

The original transcripts of the interviews were, of course, much longer than the versions in this book. In editing them, we tried to preserve everything of interest both to general readers and to scholars, leaving out only those parts that were unduly digressive or repetitious. We also decided to omit many of our own comments, which were far more extensive than appear below. Indeed, our original idea was to publish chapters more akin to conversations or dialogues than to traditional interviews. But reading the transcripts and faced with the need to create a book of manageable length, we decided that it was more important to preserve the Soviet voices, which turned out to be unusually interesting and diverse, than our own.

For much the same reason, we did not approach or edit the interviews in the adversarial or prosecutorial spirit that has so characterized American–Soviet relations over the years. Some readers may feel that we should have challenged the Soviet participants more often or sharply, but that was not our purpose. We wanted to give Western readers the opportunity to hear these voices of glasnost and makers of Gorbachev's new Soviet "revolution" without bias or distraction. Readers do not need our help in forming their opinions about one of the most important political developments of our time.

S.F.C.
K.v.H.

Moscow
May 1989

Voices of Glasnost

Introduction: Gorbachev and the Soviet Reformation

By Stephen F. Cohen

A HISTORIC POLITICAL DRAMA has been unfolding in the Soviet Union since Mikhail Gorbachev became its leader in March 1985. In the face of large and deeply rooted obstacles, Gorbachev and his supporters are trying to carry out a full-scale political, economic, and social reformation, or what they call *perestroika,* in one of the world's largest, most authoritarian, and most conservative countries. Among other reforms, they are proposing to introduce a substantial degree of free market relations, private economic enterprise, rule of law, liberal political values, local self-government, and democracatic procedures in a nation that has had virtually no experience with any of these practices and indeed has long regarded them as un-Soviet. All things considered, Gorbachev's proposed reformation is unprecedented in modern history. It is also, given the Soviet Union's superpower role in international affairs, probably the most fateful struggle underway in the world today.

The emergence of a Soviet leadership devoted to radical reform confounded most Western scholars and media commentators, who had long believed that the Soviet Communist system lacked any capacity for real change. Scholarly axioms and popular stereotypes can be tenacious. For two years, if not longer, many Western observers dismissed Gorbachev's policies as merely "technocratic" measures that would not affect the nature of the system, or even as deceitful propaganda. The torrent of remarkable changes inside the Soviet Union since 1985 has finally persuaded most serious observers that Gorbachev's program is both authentic and radical, but even those of us who study Soviet affairs still lack analytical concepts adequate to cope with the ongoing process of change. Unable to find new ways to think about the subject, some observers simply cling to their old convictions that the Soviet system is unreformable by prematurely concluding that perestroika will fail.

Three important questions have been obscured by the vexed Western reaction to the Soviet Union under Gorbachev. What is perestroika, how did it originate, and what has it achieved since 1985? Here too Western experiences and preconceptions can do little but mislead us. Gorbachev's reforms are not, for example, an effort to rid his country of socialism in favor of what we know as capitalism, but an epic quest for a new kind of Soviet socialism. The pursuit of technological modernization and economic efficiency are driving forces behind perestroika, but so too is the belief that genuine socialist values and practices, which are still associated at least loosely with the founding father Lenin, were lost during Stalin's despotic rule from 1929 to 1953. By any Western or modern-day Marxist criteria, Gorbachev's advocacy of a mixed economy and "socialist market" do not constitute a return to capitalism. Instead, for Gorbachev and his most fervent supporters, perestroika is a crusade for a "humane socialism." Many of them, including people in this book, even speak of "socialism with a human face," the aspiration identified with the Prague Spring crushed by Soviet tanks in 1968.

Those of us who are not socialists may find it difficult to sympathize with this kind of undertaking, or to believe that it is possible, but we should understand that successful reforms in any country must arise and evolve within the prevailing political culture. They must promise the nation a renewal of established values, not their repeal. As Aleksandr Bovin says below, a society cannot jump out of its own history. For the great majority of Soviet officials and ordinary citizens, who were born well after the Russian Revolution of 1917, some kind of socialism, however ill-defined and unsatisfying over the years, remains the only legitimate and imaginable way of life. That is why we must take seriously Gorbachev's declarations that perestroika means a "renewal of socialism" and "more socialism." It also is why the final words spoken in Tengiz Abuladze's film *Repentance*, a powerful condemnation of Stalinism and a major political event when it opened in 1986, have become a refrain in so many Soviet criticisms of the existing system: "Of what use is a road if it doesn't lead to the Temple?"

The Russian word *perestroika* translates literally as "restructuring," but as conceived by the Gorbachev leadership it means the de-Stalinization of the Soviet system. If the major reforms already legislated since 1985 are actually implemented in the years ahead, they would greatly reduce and in some respects abolish the absolutist state

controls Stalin imposed on society sixty years ago. Therein lies perestroika's potential as a historic reformation and recreation of Soviet
socialism.

Gorbachev's reforms are a belated but direct response to the extraordinary history and size of the present-day Soviet state that is the
enduring legacy of Stalinism. It took shape in Stalin's revolution from
above of the 1930s—in the forcible collectivization of 25 million peasant households, the draconian drive for industrialization and urbaniza-
tion, and mass deportations and police terror that eventually victimized
tens of millions of people. In an all-out campaign to transform every
area of Soviet life, from economic production and distribution to consumer services, culture, and politics, the Stalinist regime created a vast,
nationwide system of state commands, control, and administration.
Centered in enormous Moscow ministries, its countless republic, regional, and local branches, agents, procedures, and documents en-
snared virtually every kind of enterprise, vocation, and citizen. Even the
once dominant Communist Party, crushed by Stalin's terror in the late
1930s, was engulfed by the process of rampant statism, or what Soviet
writers now call "bureaucratic statization."

The subsequent history of this statist system has been less traumatic
but no less remarkable. The structure of its bureaucratic controls over
society survived not only Stalin's death in 1953 but Nikita Khrushchev's de-Stalinization efforts of the 1950s and early 1960s. The Soviet
state grew even larger during the long conservative reign of Leonid
Brezhnev, from 1964 to 1982. Brezhnev's policies, which emphasized
"stability of cadres" and shunned significant reform, further nurtured
the myriad of ministrial bureaucracies at the center and across the
country. By mid-1985, according to official figures that do not include
collective farm administrators, the Ministry of Defense, the Ministry of
Internal Affairs, or the KGB, the Soviet state employed 17.7 million
functionaries. Through some 800,000 "organizational links," it administered—or to be precise, sought to administer—several hundred thousand state-run industrial, agricultural, and trade enterprises and the
prices of countless goods and services, while issuing millions of annual
commands, instructions, and prohibitions in every area and at all levels
of Soviet life. When Gorbachev's *perestroishchiki* talk about "liberat-
ing" society from this "thicket" of state controls and "banomania,"
they are not speaking metaphorically.

More specifically, what Gorbachev calls perestroika is based on five
kinds of major reform, each of which would expand society's freedom
of activity by diminishing the realm of the state. One is glasnost, or

openness, which means a substantial reduction of state- and party-imposed bans and other forms of censorship in the mass media and in political, intellectual, and cultural life generally. The second is managerial decentralization, which seeks to free thousands of nationalized industrial and agricultural enterprises from the clutching directives of planning agencies and ministries in Moscow. The third reform is economic privatization, which would reduce the size of the state economy itself by turning over some portion of its functions to newly created cooperative and individually owned businesses. The fourth reform, economic marketization, follows from the previous two. It would compel many state enterprises to compete among themselves on the basis of efficiency and profitability, as well as with private firms. Finally, there is Gorbachev's "democratization" program, which would sharply reduce the number of party-state appointed officials by permitting multi-candidate elections to the new national parliament, the network of governmental soviets at every level across the country, at workplaces, and even inside the Communist Party.

As Gorbachev's supporters have written repeatedly, all of these reforms are designed to "destatize" the "Stalinist command-administrative system." When pressed to spell out the dimensions of their proposed "de-statization," they promise eventually to abolish fully half to two-thirds of all state bureaucratic positions. Like everyone who engages in politics in the Soviet Union, Gorbachev and his allies think and speak in the context and idiom of the Soviet historical experience. Therefore, for them perestroika as de-statization is synonymous with a "process of decisive de-Stalinization." That they have articulated this understanding of perestroika so candidly, persistently, and coherently should dispel notions that Gorbachev is some kind of centrist positioned between the party's radical and conservative factions and that his policies are makeshift measures without any overall conception. Like any successful national leader, Gorbachev understands, as he often says, that "politics is the art of the possible." But as his speeches and deeds since 1985 make clear, he is himself the visionary leader of the exceedingly radical reformation known as perestroika.

The advent of the Gorbachevian reformation still puzzles many Western experts whose conceptions of Soviet history and politics had excluded such a development. They did not believe, for example, that there was an anti-Stalinist tradition in the Soviet experience capable of inspiring an alternative to the existing order or that radical reformers, even if they existed at lower levels, could rise to high echelons of the

Communist Party, much less emerge as its leadership. For these experts, the Gorbachev phenomenon remains a kind of inexplicable accident, an aberration without roots in the Soviet system and thus without any real prospects of success. A brief look at the origins of perestroika suggests a different way of thinking about its possibilities.

The basic ideas behind perestroika are not new, and the movement to translate them into official policy did not begin with Gorbachev. Their remote antecedents are to be found in Lenin's New Economic Policy (NEP), which in 1921 abandoned the party's extremist Civil War measures in favor of much more conciliatory ones. Until NEP was abolished by Stalin's revolution from above in 1929, it evolved into a whole series of related policies that anti-Stalinist reformers have long viewed as an embryonic model of socialism. Unlike the encompassing statist and terror-ridden Stalinist system that followed, NEP's characteristic features, though not democratic, strongly resembled those Gorbachev now ascribes to perestroika. They included a more limited and liberal form of one-party rule; official tolerance of considerable economic and social pluralism; a market economy composed of state, cooperative, and individual enterprises; intellectual and cultural activities relatively unrestricted by heavy-handed censorship; and broader parameters of debate and open conflict in sanctioned political institutions, including the Communist Party.

Perestroika is not and could not be simply a replication of the policies of the 1920s, when the Soviet Union was a predominantly backward, illiterate country of 125 million peasants. Nonetheless, NEP is perestroika's ancestral forerunner and the primary source of its ideological legitimacy. As Gorbachev and his reformers have made clear, the "lessons of NEP" are an essential part of their "renewal of socialism." Indeed, the lineage between NEP and perestroika is personified in the especially fulsome rehabilitation of the Bolshevik leader Nikolai Bukharin, who after Lenin's death in 1924 was the leading Politburo theorist and defender of NEP, first against the party's left opposition and then unsuccessfully against Stalin in 1928–29. Condemned as an "enemy of the people" at the notorious 1938 Moscow purge trial and executed on Stalin's orders, Bukharin was fully exonerated by the Gorbachev leadership in February 1988 and is now being honored as a forefather of perestroika.

The latter-day origins of perestroika lie, however, squarely in the first period of post-Stalin reform, from 1953 to 1964, led by Nikita Khrushchev. Because he was deposed by his Politburo colleagues and his role excised from official history for more than twenty years, many

Western scholars have concluded that Khrushchev failed as a leader. They see in this only ominous signs for Gorbachev. But it makes little sense to evaluate a leader's record only by how his career ended. Khrushchev held office longer than has any American president except Franklin Roosevelt, and during those years he had many achievements as well as failures. His reform policies were limited and often ill prepared, and as a leader he was an erratic, conflicted figure—an anti-Stalinist shaped and constricted by his own Stalinist past, a man receptive to progressive ideas but frequently lurching back to retrograde ones, the patron of a new generation of which he was also wary. And yet, Khrushchev was a historic Soviet leader. Without the reforms he introduced, which changed the Soviet Union in fundamental and lasting ways, it is hard to imagine the rise of Gorbachev's full-scale reformation twenty years later.

Consider the most important ones. Under Khrushchev, Stalin's twenty-five-year mass terror was ended, millions of people freed from concentration camps and exile, the political police's Gulag empire radically curtailed, much of the truth told about the crimes of the past, and an irreparable blow dealt to the Stalin cult and its oppressive array of ideological and policy dogmas. As a result, personal despotism was ended and the Communist Party, with a form of collective leadership at its head, restored to primacy in the political system. Equally important, long-term investment was greatly increased in areas involving people's everyday needs—housing, consumer goods and services, and welfare—so that most Soviet citizens lived considerably better as a result of Khrushchev's years in power. No less ramifying, censorship was reduced sufficiently to produce the Khrushchev "thaw"—a first though lesser experiment with glasnost—which revived intellectual and cultural life, gave the intelligentsia a much larger role in political affairs, and marked the emergence of public opinion as a significant factor. Nor should we forget that having repudiated a number of Stalin's Cold War dogmas, Khrushchev was, along with President Dwight D. Eisenhower, the cofounder of what later became known as detente.

Great reforms anywhere are not a single event but a multi-chapter process that unfolds fitfully over decades, if only because they always encounter powerful opposition and widespread conservative resistance. Though the analogy is imperfect, Franklin Roosevelt's New Deal was a perestroika of American capitalism that began in the 1930s and continued, with major advances and setbacks, well into the 1960s, and whose last chapter may not yet have been written. Viewed in this way, the changes introduced by Khrushchev constituted the first chapter in

the reformation of the Soviet Stalinist system—the beginning of perestroika, even though the word was not yet in use. However partial and
though eventually stopped by his successors, Khrushchev's reforms
created a precedent to inspire another chapter and a foundation upon
which to build.

Still more, his struggle against neo-Stalinist elites and popular sentiments gave birth to an anti-Stalinist movement inside the modern-day
Soviet Communist Party. Its inaugural event was the historic Twentieth
Party Congress in February 1956, where Khrushchev delivered his
stunning exposé of Stalin's mass crimes. The speech became the charter
document of the anti-Stalinist movement. Though not published in the
Soviet Union until March 1989, its contents became widely known at
the time. In response to Khrushchev's leadership during the next eight
years, anti-Stalinist reformers emerged in every area of the Soviet system, so much so that the movement grew much larger than its founding
father and acquired a political life of its own, particularly in the realm
of socialist ideology and programmatic thinking. With only a few exceptions, and despite his complaints about excessive bureaucracy,
Khrushchev's policies did not seek to remove Stalinist state controls
over society, but they inspired many ideas that proposed to do so and
that survived his downfall. Suffice it to say that almost every ideological
perspective and policy proposal now associated with Gorbachev's perestroika can be found, in one form or another, in discussions that began
in newspapers, mass journals, and specialized publications under
Khrushchev.

In short, the anti-Stalinist movement born under Khrushchev eventually grew, after many years of bitter political defeat and agony, into
the perestroika movement led by Gorbachev in the 1980s. Its history is
embodied in the first post-Stalin generation of young men and women
who began their careers in the Khrushchev 1950s and early 1960s,
becoming heirs to the reformist tradition he founded. A remarkable
number of those people stand in the forefront of Gorbachev's reformation. They are, to use a Soviet expression, "the vanguard of perestroika." They include most of the people in this book, who
characterize themselves as "children of the Twentieth Party Congress,"
which means, of course, Khrushchev's political offspring, as well as
Mikhail Gorbachev, who began his own career as a young party politician in 1955. Here, too, it can hardly be said that Khrushchev failed.
Nor should it surprise us that by mid-1989 his official rehabilitation was
well underway in Moscow.

To complete this interpretation of the origins of perestroika we must also call into question the Western view that overlooks or minimizes political diversity long existing inside the Soviet Communist Party. Political reactions to Khrushchev's reform policies were so diverse, and conflicts over them so great, that something akin to rival "parties" took shape inside the one-party Communist system. Precise language may be lacking here. They were not political parties in the Western sense. And because intraparty factions had been banned by Lenin and murderously eradicated by Stalin, nor were they formal entities. But they were more than merely inchoate tendencies. As time went on, each acquired distinctive ideas derived from Marxism-Leninism, a loose network of association and communication, institutional affiliations, and even publications. However we term these rival ideological and policy movements—crypto-parties, groupings, or "parties"—an awareness of their crimped, shadowy existence from the mid-1950s to the mid-1980s is necessary to understand Soviet political history from Khrushchev to Gorbachev.

At least three movements had formed inside the Communist Party by the time Khrushchev was overthrown in 1964: an anti-Stalinist "party" calling for a more far-reaching relaxation of state controls over society; a neo-Stalinist one charging that Khrushchev's policies had gravely weakened the state and demanding that it be rejuvenated; and a conservative "party" mainly devoted to preserving the existing post-Stalin status quo by opposing further major changes, whether forward or backward. During the next twenty years, these "multiparty" conflicts were waged in largely muted and subterranean ways. The conservative majority headed by Brezhnev ruled the Soviet Union, with some concessions to the neo-Stalinists, for almost two decades. The reform movement barely survived, but in 1985, along with Gorbachev, it came to power. Since that time, the polarizing conflicts engendered by perestroika, and the open polemics released by glasnost, leave no doubt that a de facto multiparty political situation is raging in the Soviet one-party system. In fact, by 1988 calls for a de jure multiparty system were being openly discussed in the Soviet press, including proposals that the Communist Party reconstitute itself into at least two parties to accommodate its own friends and foes of perestroika.

This is not the place for a detailed account of how anti-Stalinist reformers survived the long harsh winter of Soviet conservatism under Leonid Brezhnev. The great majority of those who did not abandon their convictions worked quietly, usually without promotion, at lower or middle levels in party, state, or soviet institutions. The fates of other reformers are represented by many of the people interviewed or discussed in this book. A few were sent into ambassadorial exile. Many more took refuge in academic institutes or cryptic journalism. Artists often had their best work banned until 1985. Some reformers became persecuted dissidents or emigrés. And a few, like the agricultural innovator Ivan Khudenko, died at the hands of local authorities. The full story of their saga remains to be told.

Nor can we explore here all the reasons why the party's reform movement headed by Gorbachev emerged victorious in the spring of 1985, though several important factors should be mentioned. By the late 1970s, the statist administrative system inherited from Stalin had brought the Soviet Union to what Gorbachev has described as a "precrisis." Among other indications, the economy had virtually stopped growing and technology lagged badly behind Western advances; consumer shortages, popular cynicism, alcoholism, workplace indifference, bureaucratic corruption, mafia-like crime, rural decay, ecological abuses, and social injustices had become widespread; and infants were dying in great numbers while adult life expectancy was declining. Censorship maintained public silence about most of these problems and their magnitude, but they were generally known to the ruling elites, including many high officials who were deeply concerned about their country's well-being at home and standing abroad. The growing welter of "precrisis" problems shook their confidence in longstanding Stalinist dogmas, particularly about the state-run economy, and made them more receptive to reformist solutions.

Meanwhile, a larger process that can be called de-Stalinization from below had been underway for many years. Far-reaching and autonomous social changes—among them, acclimation to city life and the spread of urban culture, the maturing of generations with much more education and exposure to the West, and the proliferation of professional groups and other middle-class strata—had made the Soviet Union profoundly unlike the "society of cogs in the Stalinist machine" of the 1930s, as Soviet writers now characterize that era. This inexorable process of de-Stalinization from below further exacerbated the inadequacies of the fifty-year-old Stalinist bureaucratic system. It could no longer effectively control an economy or society of such complexity. By the end of the 1970s, large segments of both had escaped the state's control, while the remainder responded with declining productivity. Despite the state's efforts to maintain a Red orthodoxy, as a Soviet scholar has aptly remarked, the economy developed its own "black market" and society its "black pluralism." Nor were party and state elites, with their greatly enhanced levels of education and professionalism, immune to all these social changes. This too gave the reform "party" a much larger constituency than it had had before.

By the early 1980s, the main obstacle to a new chapter of reform from above was the generation of aged officials who had begun their careers under Stalin in the 1930s. Now in their seventies, they had ruled the Soviet Union since Khrushchev's overthrow, with Brezhnev at their head. Having survived so many historical traumas, and identifying with the administrative system that had raised them so high and awarded them lifetime bureaucratic peerages, they were profoundly conservative. Brezhnev's death in November 1982 triggered the politics of leadership succession, but he was only one of scores of ailing septuagenarian influentials who passed from the scene in an inevitable procession. Thus the way was cleared for a reform movement swept along on a tide of generational change.

The choice of Yuri Andropov to succeed Brezhnev as general secretary marked the resurgence of the reform "party" in two important respects. Although already aged and ailing, he was known to be the most reform-minded senior member of Brezhnev's Politburo and a man with ties to younger reformers dating back to the 1960s. Andropov's selection showed that even the aged oligarchy, faced with growing problems and reformist sentiments, felt the need for at least some kind of limited change. It also enabled more radical reformers, with Andropov's help, to reenter or approach the center stage of Soviet politics. Andropov's death in February 1984, and the last stand of the Stalin generation under his seventy-two-year-old successor Konstantin Chernenko, who died in office thirteen months later, only slowed the resurgence of the reform movement. It was already gathered and waiting for Gorbachev, then the youngest member of the Politburo.

The man who has led the Soviet Union since 1985 is not, therefore, an aberration but the leader of a political movement, however embattled, with a long history in the Communist Party. One question cannot yet be answered with certainty. When did Gorbachev, who rose steadily in the conservative party apparatus over a period of almost thirty years, put himself at the head of the radical reform "party"? Many Western scholars believe that he recognized the need for a full-scale anti-Stalinist reformation only a year or more after becoming general secretary, when he discovered the full extent of the country's problems. Though not conclusive, there is evidence that points to a different interpretation of his political biography.

It suggests that even as a Moscow University student in the early 1950s, and then as a provincial party secretary in Stavropol, Gorbachev was already reform-minded. That soon after being promoted to Moscow in 1978 and appointed a Politburo member, he began to seek policy advice informally from well-known radical reformers. Certainly, by the early 1980s his speeches sometimes echoed their ideas, and when he took office in March 1985 representatives of the reform "party" soon appeared as his formal or informal advisers. Gorbachev no doubt learned much in office that altered his thinking, but it seems likely he was already committed to the de-Stalinization, or perestroika, of the Soviet system. If so, his cautious conduct during his first year or so in office is not baffling. A leader who wishes to introduce great reforms in a conservative country must also be a clever politician. As Gorbachev resumed the reformation begun by Khrushchev, surely he had learned that from the fate of his predecessor.

In 1989, a large number of articles appeared in the Western press commenting on the fourth anniversary of Gorbachev's rise to power. Focusing on the most serious shortcomings and disruptive consequences of his policies, many commentaries read like obituaries of perestroika. They left the impression that it had failed or soon would do so. "Perestroika isn't working," *Newsweek* reported. It seemed only a matter of time before Gorbachev's opponents would "topple him or eliminate his reforms."

As those articles pointed out, the Soviet economy remained in bad shape. The GNP had grown barely 1.5 percent in 1988, while food and other consumer shortages were even more acute in some areas than they had been in 1985. Too much disposable income chasing too few commodities had fueled inflation. And the state budget deficit had swollen due partly to an abortive campaign to curtail vodka sales and to the enormous costs of the 1986 Chernobyl nuclear disaster and 1988 Armenian earthquake. Meanwhile, Gorbachev's democratization and glasnost policies had spawned a multitude of raucous "informal" organizations challenging established political authority from the capital to provincial towns. Even more ominous, they had unleashed pent-up nationalist aspirations and ethnic hatreds in the vast multinational Soviet federation. Mass protests, some of them violent, erupted in several republics, from Estonia, Latvia, and Lithuania to Armenia, Azerbaijan, and Georgia. All this and more, including the possibility of greater unrest in Eastern Europe, convinced many observers that powerful Soviet elites and public opinion, already indifferent to perestroika, had turned against Gorbachev's reforms, frustrating the adoption of effective measures and thwarting ones already enacted.

None of those developments should be minimized, and still graver threats to perestroika may lie ahead. But they should not be taken as a full picture or basis for a reasoned analysis of Gorbachev's years in office. Given the epic dimensions of perestroika as a reformation—or, as the leadership proclaims, "a revolutionary political, economic, social, and psychological transformation"—its initial failures and traumas were predictable. A more balanced evaluation of them can be found in the interviews below and in the Soviet press, which openly acknowledges their gravity as the "unavoidable costs of change and democratization." Nor is there reason to think that Gorbachev expected his reforms to unfold quickly or painlessly. He has spoken candidly about the "risks" of perestroika and the enormous obstacles it faces, and about his own leadership mainly in terms of making a long process of change "irreversible," rather than of being able to see it through to the end.

In an economy as large, rigid, and problem-infested as the Soviet one, the transition to a new system will take years and involve serious dislocations. Moreover, many economic reformers insist that higher growth rates during the transition would be a negative indicator if there is to be a real shift from quantity to quality of production. As for the proliferation of unofficial political organizations, some of their behavior no doubt exceeds what Gorbachev would prefer, but they are largely the anticipated result of his own policies of "democratization" and "socialist pluralism." In any event, he has said little to discourage and much to encourage their activities. Nationalist unrest, with its potential to destabilize the Soviet Union, is a different matter, but here too it seems that only its intensity, not its existence, may have surprised Gorbachev and his advisers. And while demonstrations and ethnic conflicts in several republics have endangered his policies, thus far his leadership has contained them with remarkably little use of the coercion at its disposal.

Despite many generalizations in the Western press, no one knows exactly how the disappointments and disorders since 1985 have affected mass attitudes toward Gorbachev's perestroika, not even Soviet pollsters, who are now officially encouraged to study public opinion. The Soviet Union is an exceedingly diverse country, and the various reforms collectively known as perestroika mean different things to different segments of the populace. Clearly, in a nation whose citizens have long relied on a cradle-to-grave welfare state that may provide relatively meager benefits but demands little hard work or personal responsibility in return, there is widespread resistance to the kind of new social contract Gorbachev is proposing. Sixty years of deeply engrained Stalinist dogmas are also a major obstacle. Many people dislike cooperative and individual enterprises—some of them have been torched or looted—as well as other innovations that "betray our socialism." In addition, as the leadership admits, "people are fed up with shortages and with standing in lines." After more than four years, popular belief in the necessity or feasibility of perestroika will be hard to sustain if it does not soon begin to satisfy peoples' needs.

But it is a mistake to exaggerate the consumer demands of most Soviet citizens, whose living standards and expectations are far below those in the West, or to overlook the legions of enthusiastic perestroika supporters in every walk of life. They include many of the most entrepreneurial city and village dwellers, capable workers, peasants, managers, scientists, technicians, teachers, and artists, idealistic junior officials, and democratic-minded members of the party's rank and file. Crudely stated, Gorbachev is counting on his country's best and brightest citizens. To assume that the Soviet Union lacks such people in large numbers would be both unwise and contemptuous. All that can be said with certainty, as the Soviet press regularly reports, is that perestroika has "polarized" much of public opinion, while the rest remains undecided or apathetic.

Nor should powerful political opposition to perestroika be interpreted out of context. That it exists at middle and very high levels in the party and state apparatuses is evidenced by what has and has not happened since 1985—by Gorbachev's inability to alter the composition of either the Politburo or the Central Committee decisively in his favor; by compromises he has had to make in reform legislation; by bureaucratic "sabotaging" of policies already adopted; by frank admissions on the part of Gorbachev's supporters that publications such as the famous Nina Andreyeva letter published in a Central Committee newspaper in March 1988 are manifestos of "the anti-perestroika forces"; by similar speeches at the Nineteenth Party Conference in mid-1988; and by constant complaints about high-level efforts "to stop perestroika on the pretext of saving socialism." Indeed, at a Central Committee meeting on April 25, 1989, several provincial party bosses blamed perestroika, and thus by implication Gorbachev, for most of the country's problems, including social unrest, economic disorder, rising crime rates, disarray in the Communist Party, desecration of Soviet history, and a plague of "ideological AIDS."

And yet, if equally or more powerful pro-perestroika forces did not also exist in those same high places, Gorbachev could not have survived four years of radical changes, turmoil, and opposition. At that same Central Committee plenum where his policies were so sharply and openly assailed, for example, he nonetheless forced the retirement of a large number of its other members who had strong reasons to resent his leadership. As with most national leaders, Gorbachev's authority at home depends partly on his foreign policies, which have been unusually successful. Jettisoning longstanding Soviet national security dogmas for "new thinking," he managed to bring a Cold War American president to five summit meetings, including one in Moscow; negotiate a treaty abolishing a whole category of U.S.-Soviet missiles in Europe; end the disastrous nine-year Soviet war in Afghanistan and the twenty-five-year cold war with China; improve relations with Western Europe, Japan, and even Israel; and win for himself extraordinary international popularity. In the final analysis, however, Gorbachev has endured politically because he leads a reform movement at home, a "party" within the Communist Party, with a long historical tradition, a compelling program, and many official and rank-and-file followers in the "bloodless civil war," as Soviet writers have called it, raging over perestroika.

Above all, premature obituaries of perestroika dismiss or discount its remarkable accomplishments since 1985. In four years, the equivalent of one American presidential term, Gorbachev legislated virtually his entire program for a Soviet reformation. Additional laws, enabling acts, and probably constitutional changes will still be needed, but the general political, economic, social, and cultural features of perestroika, including their philosophy and stated goals, are now ratified in state and party documents. For the first time since 1929, the Soviet government is officially committed to creating a system and kind of socialism radically unlike Stalinism. Would any serious observer give low marks to a first-term American president with such a legislative record on the grounds that it had encountered problems and not yet been fully implemented?

Of perestroika's several components, Gorbachev's economic reforms have been the least successful not only because the structural problems are so large but because change must be implemented by recalcitrant ministerial and other bureaucracies—or at least with their acquiescence. Many forms of "sabotage" are underway in that conservative labyrinth stretching from the capital to the localities. Various agencies are simply ignoring new laws designed to free state enterprises from Moscow's tutelage, contriving new directives in the guise of reform, denying licenses to aspiring cooperative and individual firms or suffocating them with excessive taxation and regulations, devising technicalities to deprive peasants of their new right to lease land, and imposing more restrictions on local markets. For these and other reasons, including the leadership's fear of ending state subsidies and deregulating consumer prices, a flourishing market sector may be years in the making. Even so, fundamental economic reforms are underway in the Soviet Union for the first time since the 1930s. The formation of non-state property, particularly cooperative property, is on the rise with official backing. And increasing numbers of managers, workers, peasants, and small business people are exercising the rights given to them by Gorbachev's legislation.

Gorbachev's glasnost policies, on the other hand, have already been implemented with spectacular success since 1985, largely because they faced many fewer bureaucratic obstacles and had many more eager supporters. Soviet censorship continues to operate in formal and informal ways, but it has been dramatically reduced. Thousands of previously banned historical and contemporary subjects, forms of popular culture, ideas, authors, books, articles, and archive documents now flood the mass media. Moscow newspapers, journals, artistic unions, and theaters began the assault on "forbidden zones" and taboo subjects, but national television and radio programs have caught up and are carrying glasnost to the provinces, where bureaucratic opposition is more entrenched. Despite important limits on free speech, there is an ongoing explosion of public information and opinion. The decades-long coverup of everything from Stalin's genocidal policies and current abuses of power to economic, social, and ecological calamities is over. As a result, Soviet political, intellectual, and cultural life has become extraordinarily rich and interesting. It is said, "People can't eat glasnost," but glasnost is an essential component of Gorbachev's perestroika, and many Soviet citizens consider it one of his greatest achievements.

The ongoing public trial of Stalinism is an especially important part of glasnost. Brezhnev's conservative restoration stopped partial revelations about the past initiated by Khrushchev and rehabilitated the Stalinist period as a "heroic and positive" era. Under Gorbachev, the whole criminal history of Stalin's twenty-five-year rule is being told in the mass media, from the murderous assault on the peasantry during collectivization to the massive political terror that continued until the despot's death. The Soviet press now confirms that tens of millions of innocent men, women, and children perished in the holocaust caused by Stalinism. An authoritative account published in 1989 revealed for the first time, for example, that "almost 20 million people" were arrested just from January 1, 1935, to the German invasion on June 22, 1941; 7

million were shot and the rest dispatched to forced labor camps, where most of them died. All this is being related with graphic details of famine, deportations, torture, executions, slow death in the camps, and orphaned children. Killing fields and mass graves used fifty years ago by Stalin's police, the NKVD, are even being uncovered near many cities. Nor has the Gorbachev leadership avoided its official responsibility. It has rehabilitated the original Communist elite slaughtered by Stalin. And faced with millions of other fraudulent cases against ordinary citizens, it has simply declared them to have been "falsified," exonerating most of the victims *en masse* and setting up special commissions to help surviving relatives.

Without truth-telling and historical justice of this magnitude, Gorbachev's proposed reformation stands no chance. Only a full national process of moral reckoning can free the Soviet socialist idea from the Stalinist past and its "barracks socialism." As the nation is being told by the mass media, "Stalinism lives on today" not only in the system's institutions and administrative controls over society but in widespread popular dogmas and habitual submission to bureaucratic authority. Unless those legacies are exorcized, the leadership's call for perestroika "from below" will fall on too many hostile or fearful ears. Gorbachev's anti-Stalinist campaign unfolded cautiously until 1987, but since then it has grown into a fervent crusade. Clearly, he and his supporters are determined, as one remarked, "to drive a stake through this vampire's heart once and for all." Little now remains of the once glorious official history of the Stalinist 1930s and 1940s, which are being portrayed as a "catastrophic tragedy" imposed by an illegitimate regime that treated people like "cogs in a bureaucratic machine." Until Gorbachev became leader, such criticisms were routinely punished as political crimes. Now they are guiding tenets in the leadership's program, ideology, and dialogue with the nation. In the context of Gorbachev's proposed reformation, that too is a historic achievement.

Finally, there are the large-scale political reforms that Gorbachev terms "democratization." Legislation adopted since 1985 promises in effect to create a new kind of Soviet political system featuring "a state based on the rule of law." These reforms call for turning the former rubber-stamp Supreme Soviet into a real national parliament; transferring governmental power from party and state bureaucracies across the country to the thousands of local soviets whose deputies are to be chosen in multi-candidate elections; forming a more just and humane legal and penal system that also would protect civil liberties against bureaucratic caprice and other abuses of power; and giving considerably more sovereignty to the fifteen national republics that make up the Soviet Union.

Most of these ambitious democratic reforms still are only on paper, but not all of them. Since 1985, along with the spread of glasnost, a far-reaching process of liberalization has taken place in the Soviet Union. Hundreds of political prisoners have been released, the criminal code partly depoliticized, and the KGB and regular police force exposed to some public scrutiny. Restrictions on religious worship and foreign travel have been considerably reduced, and a number of once persecuted dissidents have become active in sanctioned politics. Encouraged by Gorbachev's endorsement of "socialist pluralism," thousands of unofficial fronts, associations, and clubs have emerged around the country to compete with the Communist Party and other established organizations, thereby ending the one-party state's sixty-year monopoly on political life. With them have come, at national and grassroots levels, a multitude of new political activists and leaders. Insurgent groups demanding democratization have formed even inside the 20 million–member Communist Party and its 36 million–member junior counterpart, the Young Communist League, or Komsomol. Indeed, political glasnost has begun to penetrate the party's Central Committee, whose voting and uncensored proceedings were made public in 1989 for the first time since the 1920s.

Above all, perhaps, the country has held its first national multi-candidate election since 1917. In a complex process lasting from March to May 1989, the nation elected a new 2,250-member Congress of People's Deputies. Leaving aside 750 members from various public organizations, approximately 75 percent of the deputies were chosen in multi-candidate district elections preceded by hotly contested and widely publicized campaigns. Among the losing candidates were many powerful state officials, party bosses, and other dignitaries. Among the winners were many unorthodox political figures, including young grassroots activists, radical intellectuals, the maverick party politician Boris Yeltsin, and the former dissidents Andrei Sakharov and Roy Medvedev.

The Soviet system is still far from being democratic, but Gorbachev's policies have moved farther and faster in that direction than almost anyone imagined possible. Some Western observers interpreted the defeat of so many party and state officials in the 1989 elections as a defeat for Gorbachev's leadership. That was not the case. As with "democratization" more generally, the introduction of multi-candidate elections was his reform. And as he and his allies rightly claimed, the results were a popular referendum in favor of perestroika and a major blow against its opponents. Here too there is hardly any reason to conclude that Gorbachev's reformation has already failed.

My effort to give a more balanced evaluation of Gorbachev's reforms since 1985 should not be taken as an argument that perestroika is certain to succeed. Despite what has already been accomplished, the process of change still could be stopped and even reversed. To do so at this stage would probably require considerable repression, but in a country with a long despotic tradition, that too is conceivable. No one can foresee the future of a full-scale reformation that has just begun, that faces so many enormous obstacles, and that will need so many years to unfold—not even the people interviewed below, participants in these historic events. As for those of us in the West who study the Soviet Union, we have barely begun to find ways to think about all the dimensions and complexities of perestroika, or even the language to describe them. At best, only a few generalizations and unanswerable questions about the future are possible.

Just as revolutions always bring forth counterrevolution, reformations are always opposed by powerful forces of counterreformation. The struggle over perestroika is being waged at every level of the Soviet system and in every area of Soviet life—not just between the ruling officialdom and the people but within those party and state bureaucracies and society itself. Given the vast dimensions of perestroika and all the vested interests it threatens, there is no reason to expect this "civil war" to diminish or be decided conclusively in the foreseeable future. Moreover, even if perestroika is largely implemented over a long historical period, its opponents are likely to win some major battles along the way, as happened during the decades-long history of the New Deal. All that can be said with any confidence is that the struggle will go on, and many of us will not live long enough to witness the eventual outcome.

That is also why constant Western speculation about Gorbachev's own position, which fluctuates between announcing his "consolidation of power" and predicting his downfall, is pointless. No one can know what lies ahead, not even Gorbachev; too many unpredictable and incalculable developments, manmade and otherwise, are possible. It is enough to understand, as Machiavelli put it, that a great reformer is always an endangered prince. Even as his reforms begin to succeed, deepen, and become more radical, supporters often grow less staunch, conservative enemies more numerous, and the risks he must take still greater. Nor should we overlook the fact that, for the first time since

Lenin, a Soviet leader is relying more on the force of his ideas and program than on the power of an *apparat*. Thus far, Gorbachev's high-level opponents have tried to emasculate his radical policies rather than to remove him, perhaps because they lack a credible leader of their own. But even in the best of political circumstances, so long as he stands at the head of a Soviet reformation, Gorbachev will always be an embattled leader.

Indeed, programmatic alternatives challenging his radical reforms have already appeared in the official Soviet press. Not surprisingly, they come from the other longstanding "parties" inside the Communist Party. One demands conservative solutions to the country's problems instead of a reformation—for the most part, limited economic changes without the Gorbachevian "excesses" (as they are derisively called by his opponents) of glasnost, anti-Stalinism, and democratization. The other anti-Gorbachev challenge comes from the party's neo-Stalinist, openly counterreformist wing, which clamors for a revival of despotic state power, reimposition of social order and ideological orthodoxy, and restoration of Cold War policies toward the outside world. Considering the enormity of the Soviet Union's problems and the fact that glasnost has made them known to virtually every citizen, it seems unlikely that the conservative center, or a muddle-through leadership, could now govern the country effectively or for any length of time. The real choice, as a pro-Gorbachev editorial in *Izvestia* emphatically declared in April 1989, is either "a Stalinist kind of 'order' or democracy with its inevitable costs."

Whatever the balance of forces, the struggle over perestroika will be fought not only in Moscow—over the actual power of the new national "parliament," for example—but also on crucial battlefields in the provinces. One pits the fledgling cooperative economic movement against hostile local authorities and popular suspicions of even this "socialist" form of private enterprise. The number of registered cooperatives grew dramatically between January 1988 and January 1989, from 13,921 firms employing 155,880 people to 77,548 with 1.4 million employees, but they remain a tiny fraction of the economy. In the more congenial environment of Moscow, for example, in April 1989 they provided only 2.2 percent of the city's consumer goods and services. Unless the cooperative movement, including small manufacturing enterprises and banks, can overcome the array of barriers in the provinces, where most citizens live, there will be no flourishing Soviet marketplace, substantial nonstate property, or economic reformation.

The same is true of Gorbachev's political reforms, which are closely related. As in the West, the lives of Soviet citizens are most directly affected by local government—in their case, local Communist Party secretaries and soviet executive committees. But it is there that official opposition to all of Gorbachev's reforms is most broadly and deeply entrenched. Unlike Peter the Great and Stalin, with whom he is mistakenly compared, Gorbachev cannot root it out with centralized state power. Even if he had the capacity to do so, which he does not, it would undermine his own program to de-Stalinize the Soviet system by reducing the reach of the state. That is why he is counting on perestroika "from below."

Gorbachev is hoping that "democratization," and particularly the broadening process of multi-candidate elections, will eventually oust or overwhelm local soviet and party conservatives. The results of the 1989 national election may have confirmed his assumption that a majority of ordinary citizens, party members and nonmembers alike, will rally behind perestroika if they are given a democratic opportunity to fight its bureaucratic opponents. More than 87 percent of the winning candidates, including those who defeated powerful party bosses, were Communist Party members. But provincial soviet and party elections, which are only beginning, are a different battleground. If nothing else, local authorities will find many more ways to manipulate the electoral process, and insurgent candidates and voters much less glasnost to protect them. If Gorbachev's supporters are right in speaking of an ongoing civil war, even fiercer battles will have to be fought in the provinces.

In the final analysis, however, the largest obstacle confronting Gorbachev's proposed reformation is not any specific elite or group. It is Russia's long tradition of bureaucratic state power over society that began centuries before the Revolution and reached a new apothesis in the Stalinist system. Has the grip of that powerful statist tradition been considerably weakened by social and political developments in recent decades? Has a Soviet civil society matured sufficiently to take on the self-governing and other initiatives from below necessary if Gorbachev's perestroika is to succeed? Those crucial questions are being passionately debated in the Soviet press. But as readers will see from the interviews that follow, no one really knows the answers.

ALEKSANDR YAKOVLEV

Perestroika or the "Death of Socialism"

ALEKSANDR NIKOLAYEVICH YAKOVLEV *is widely considered to be the staunchest Politburo supporter of Gorbachev's radical reforms and the "architect of glasnost." Some insiders even describe him as perestroika's leading ideologist. A longtime party politician with strong intellectual credentials and several books to his name, Yakovlev worked in the Central Committee apparatus from 1953 to 1973, occupying powerful posts until suddenly being sent to Canada as Soviet ambassador. His ten-year stay in Ottawa was a form of political exile for having offended the increasingly conservative Brezhnev leadership. In 1983, Yuri Andropov, the new general secretary, brought him back to Moscow to head the Institute of World Economics and International Relations, a prestigious Academy of Sciences think tank that housed many reform-minded intellectuals. Yakovlev's rise to power was meteoric under Gorbachev, with whom he had spent ten days in Canada in May 1983. By 1985 he was chief of the Central Committee's Department of Propaganda; by 1986, a member of the Central Committee Secretariat; and by 1987, a full member of the Politburo as well. Until the fall of 1988, when he became chairman of the Central Committee Commission on International Policy, Yakovlev's main responsibility involved ideological, intellectual, and cultural affairs, including the media, where glasnost began in 1985 and spread rapidly. As is the case with several people in this book, many prominent editors and other reformers appointed in the Gorbachev period had longstanding ties to Yakovlev, who is reported to be the most reliable and powerful protector of the liberal intelligentsia. In his other role as foreign policy-maker, Yakovlev was often at Gorbachev's side during the Soviet leader's five summit meetings with President Reagan. Yakovlev's earlier writings gained him a reputation of being anti-American, but his recent statements, like those below, are char-*

*acterized more by a "realistic" concern that the United States still is not
ready to respond fully to Gorbachev's new policies.*

IT IS DIFFICULT, if not impossible, for me to answer your question
about how my life experiences brought me to my present position as a
member of the Politburo and secretary of the Central Committee. I've
never given much thought to it. I did not seek a political career.

I was born in 1923 in a tiny village about fifteen kilometers from the
ancient city of Yaroslavl. My father was a peasant who received a
fourth-grade education at a church school. For those times that was a
very high level of education. I still have his bible, inscribed to Nikolai
Yakovlev for diligence and good schoolwork. In 1917 he served in the
Russian army and then fought in the Civil War. Later he became the
first chairman of the collective farm in our region. My father had a
profoundly peasant mentality. He loved the forest very much, for example. And to this day I too love it. In the city I can get lost within three
blocks, but even in the depths of a forest I can find the exact place I
started from.

My mother was a housewife, and there were a lot of children in our
family. She had much less education; she only went to school for two
months. After that she was hired as a nursemaid. She was illiterate, a
downtrodden peasant woman, and a religious believer to the end of her
days. She couldn't read or write, but she was a woman with common
sense. Her entire life was taken up with worrying about and caring for
her family.

So without the Revolution your life would have been very different?

Without question. I remember the harsh system of farming and how
my father and mother worked from sunrise to sunset. That kind of life
was a dead end. Because of the Revolution, after fighting in World War
II from 1941 to 1943, when I was badly wounded, I managed to graduate from a Yaroslavl pedagogical institute in 1946. I aspired to an academic career, not a political one, so I applied for postgraduate study.
But I was not accepted. They said I was late submitting my application,
but I think there were bureaucratic reasons. I was from the provinces,
and the application had to be approved in Moscow.

They suggested instead that I study at the Higher Party School,
which I did. I had become a party member in 1944. Then I worked on a
provincial newspaper and applied again for postgraduate study. This
time they assigned me instead to a regional party committee. While

working there I again applied to graduate school, but I was transferred instead to the Central Committee, here in Moscow, as a staff instructor. I applied three times to the Academy of Social Sciences while working for the Central Committee. Finally my superior, Pyotr Pospelov, who was a Central Committee secretary at the time, got sick of my applications and let me go to the Academy. When I graduated, my fellow townsmen in Yaroslavl proposed that I become rector of the pedagogical institute I had graduated from, and I agreed. But at the last moment I was told to return to the Central Committee.

It was only after my ambassadorship in Canada, in 1983, that I accepted with great pleasure an academic appointment as director of the Academy of Sciences Institute of World Economics and International Relations in Moscow. Nikolai Kosolapov, my assistant sitting here with us, also worked at the institute. He'll confirm that I was happy there. They say it was the first time in the history of the institute that its party committee had ever elected a director unanimously. I would have been content to work there to the end of my days. But again things turned out differently. So you see, I did not set out to make a political career. I was always drawn toward scholarly, or rather scholarly publicistic, activity. And in this respect I think my work at the institute was my most fruitful. I wrote and edited a great deal.

In the United States quite a few academics and intellectuals want to get into politics.

I know the psychology.

Should we conclude from your autobiography that you are an intellectual taken prisoner by politics?

If the stars take a different configuration, I would be happy to go back to work at the institute.

Tell us something about growing up in the Stalin years. For example, here in Moscow they say that at a meeting with representatives of the Soviet press, Mikhail Gorbachev said that he, you and your fellow Politburo member Yegor Ligachev had relatives who suffered from Stalin's repressions.

He didn't say "repression." He said that each of us had problems at that time. Once in 1937 they came to our house, but my father wasn't home and he stayed away for three days. But if he had been home . . . Well, you know. But people are wrong nowadays when they sometimes say that was a time of universal cowardice. My father was warned, for example, by the military commissar of the district. He told my father, "Why don't you just disappear somewhere for three days or so?" In the Civil War he had been commander of my father's squadron. The old bond of wartime friendship and brotherhood remained between them, so he warned my father.

Some writers who are about your age, people who fought in World War II, say that your generation was raised as a Stalinist one and therefore that the post-Stalin era has been difficult and traumatic for people your age. They see some connection between today's perestroika and a feeling of repentance on the part of your generation.

This is a very complex question. In what sense can we be spoken of as a Stalinist generation? We were only teenagers. How were we responsible for the terrible things that happened? And to judge the level of consciousness of seventeen and eighteen year olds of that time by our present level of personal and political knowledge is foolish. In general, I am categorically opposed to analyzing any events apart from their historical context.

We believed very strongly and sincerely in what then existed. As to whether there were grounds for such faith, I would say yes and no. Yes, because of the enthusiasm which inspired our people at that time. In general, we young fellows went off to war with an absolute, one hundred percent faith in Stalin. And I will tell you that the moral state of Soviet society—from the point of view of attitudes, honesty, decency, and good conduct—was on the whole very high.

Now they say there was universal fear in those times. Terrible violations of legality, repressions, happened. But I keep thinking, what was this? For whom was there fear? Clearly, it did exist, particularly among those people hit or touched by the repressions. But I remember that at Komsomol meetings after the war, and at party meetings, people bore themselves patriotically and bravely.

My mother, for example, despite her deeply religious faith, was the greatest agitator for Soviet power. We had a custom of family get-togethers, and it remains to this day even though my parents are gone. My three sisters would come with their husbands and children, and I with my children, to our parents' home. A conversation would begin among these twenty people who were very close to each other. We would sometimes complain, "This thing isn't right, and that thing isn't right." My mother would listen and then say something like this: "Ach, all of you! Do you know what it used to be like? Do you know I had nothing to wear? That we had only enough to eat until March, until Lent? That I had to work from sunrise to sunset? But you all, excuse me, you've become fat and lazy." And so I say there was real popular enthusiasm during the Stalin years. The Soviet people put out an enormous effort. Yes, all sorts of terrible things happened. Yes, the humane aims of socialism were not realized. But we sincerely believed in it all.

You must understand that those were very complex, contradictory times. You know, for example, that today there are very different points of view about collectivization. One reason is that though much of it was forced and there were many stupidities, it took place in different ways and with differing results in different parts of the country. In our district it was relatively painless. For example, only one man was deported as a "kulak," and even he later returned to the district. He had a son who was serving in the army, and it seems that under the law the family of someone who was in the army could not be dekulakized. And so in our district there was no dekulakization. Many people there joined the collective farms willingly.

You say "willingly," even though your own press now emphasizes the mass coercive aspects of collectivization?

Yes, willingly. Moreover, after collectivization in our district—and again I am only talking about our district—people began to live considerably better. Perhaps not immediately. I can't say from my own recollection what it was like in 1933, because I was only ten years old. I know things were worse elsewhere. But I had milk and our mother gave us enough to eat. I haven't done any sociological research into this, but I know that later, when I was older, on the eve of the war, people began to dress and eat better. I even remember that our collective farm was run democratically. No outsider interfered in its business. The peasants would curse and argue for days over where to sow and what to sow. Occasionally, the district agronomist would ask the peasants to sow something somewhere, but they didn't pay any particular attention to him. So, you see, in our history things happened in various ways.

You must also understand the psychology of that time. Very little time had passed since the Revolution. The political culture was still low, but the historical sweep and scope of what had been achieved was enormous. Even today that's how I see things. Otherwise what would there be to live for?

Does this mean you think it would be better not to reopen such painful and controversial historical questions, as is now happening?

No, that's never been my opinion. I think it's now necessary to choose our priorities. I think that we have to focus on perestroika and particularly deal with all the economic problems of food, housing, and consumer goods that we discussed at the June 1987 meeting of the Central Committee and have emphasized ever since. That doesn't mean we shouldn't be concerned with historical questions. Certainly we must draw important conclusions from them.

What is your own feeling about all the controversial works about history that have been published since 1985?

It's normal. I don't see anything wrong with it. What concerns me is that everything be carefully documented and that there be no emotional inventions.

Given the nature of Soviet history, that's a hard thing to do.

Maybe it is hard for an author. I don't know. But if I undertook to write about our history, I would be guided by such considerations because writing history entails great responsibility. One must have a factual basis for what one writes.

But your country's past includes so many tragic events that previously your historians did not write about. And many basic historical documents still are not available. Even today, it is mainly writers, rather than professional historians, who are telling the truth about Soviet history. The historian Yuri Afanasyev recently said, "Why should the playwright Mikhail Shatrov, the poet Yevgeny Yevtushenko, and others be writing our history, and not we historians?"

Well, if a historian wrote one thing yesterday, and today he writes something else, even if it is the truth, no one will believe him. According to the bible, if you have once lied, who will believe you? It seems we may have to wait for a new generation of historians, one that won't be tied to the past. That will take time. In such matters there's a very good saying: "If you hurry, you'll make people laugh."

Let's turn then to perestroika itself. The word seems to encompass so many kinds of change. What does it actually mean? For example, sometimes Gorbachev says perestroika is a revolution, sometimes he says it is radical reform. But in both Marxist and non-Marxist thought revolution and reform are very different things.

I don't attribute great importance to any kind of abstract schemes or labels. No definition can fully capture such a phenomenon. Even such a weighty word as "revolution" doesn't mean there is a revolution in every respect.

Perestroika is our quest to achieve a qualitatively new condition of Soviet society—politically, economically, culturally, morally, spiritually. It is a quest to bring the Soviet Union to the forefront in all of these respects. It is the renewal of socialism, a striving to reveal the truly democratic and human face of socialism. To achieve this, radical reforms must be carried out in all spheres—in our economy, social structure, psychology, and our politics, where we need democracy.

Aren't you worried that you will frighten your citizens by calling perestroika a revolution? Won't this remind them of all the revolutionary upheavals and traumas of the past and cause them to fear rather than support your calls for perestroika?

I must answer this question on two levels. On the theoretical plane, we have never asserted that the revolution in our country, which began in 1917, has ended. It has taken various forms at different stages. And today it continues in another way. Perestroika is the continuation of the revolution. Second, our people can't be frightened by the word "revolution." In the Soviet Union, people understand revolution somewhat differently than do people abroad. Moreover, our calls for perestroika are based on profound dissatisfaction among the masses themselves with our past and present. Level-headed Soviet people extrapolate their understanding of perestroika as revolutionary changes on the basis of their personal experience. You are extrapolating from books and impressions, correct and incorrect ones.

Much of the debate about perestroika in the Soviet press revolves around the legacies of Lenin and Stalin, around distinctions between what many Soviet writers, and you yourself, call Leninism and Stalinism. How does this discussion relate to the specific reforms now underway?

Perestroika requires a revival of genuine Leninism. Only now do we realize the full dimensions of Stalin's abandonment and distortion of Lenin's ideas, principles, and practices. When Stalin broke with Lenin's New Economic Policy [NEP] at the end of the 1920s, he broke with Lenin's conceptions of socialism. Democracy, civil peace, and individual economic initiative were replaced by commands, repression, and bureaucracy. The administrative-command system created under Stalin in the 1930s and 1940s allowed the state to swallow up civic society and dominate it through bureaucratic structures. The result was excessive concentration of power, which led to abuses of power and, by the 1970s, to economic stagnation, even an economic crisis—declining growth and then no growth at all. All this was dressed up in an array of theoretical and ideological dogmas. These delusions lasted half a century, and we are still paying the price.

Now we are freeing ourselves from these delusions and returning to

Leninist thinking about socialist practices, ideals, and humanism. We are rejecting the authoritarian structures inherited from the past, along with obsolete, ossified, deformed ideas and practices. We are seeing ourselves as we really are and this is already a great spiritual achievement of perestroika. We know that we can no longer live in the old ways. And though Lenin did not live long enough to work out all the conceptions of socialism that we need, we are returning to his basic perceptions. In this sense, Lenin is a living adviser in our analysis of present-day problems.

Why weren't these kinds of radical reforms begun earlier, after Stalin's death in 1953, under Khrushchev, for example?

A society acts according to its possibilities at a given time. We believe in such historical laws. I don't think, for example, that given our low level of development and prosperity in the past, we could have spoken about democracy then in the same broad way we do now. You can't expect an infant to act like an adult. But today we think that the time has come when we are sufficiently developed, educated, and experienced to make correct decisions and to move toward more democracy.

Were we ready to do this earlier—in particular, after the Twentieth Party Congress in 1956? I personally think we were. Sometimes people are like a sponge: They absorb everything but they don't digest anything. At that time we took everything in, but we weren't able to assimilate it.

My personal point of view is that objectively Soviet society was ready for fundamental changes in 1956 and this was reflected in certain reforms begun then. But I don't think the leadership was ready. It remained stuck in the past. Today the situation is different: the leadership is ready for these changes.

Speaking of those years, what is your opinion of Nikita Khrushchev's leadership from 1956 to 1964, and the relationship between that period of reform and perestroika today?

It's difficult for me to avoid being subjective on this point. I wasn't merely an observer in those years but to some extent a rank-and-file participant in the party's work. Looking back, some things appear differently than they did twenty or thirty years ago.

The changes and reforms begun in that period were absolutely necessary. Much of what was initiated at that time, under Khrushchev, has become an integral part of our life. Many reforms begun then brought the country enormous benefits. Take, for example, the housing construction program. Three quarters of Moscow as it looks today was built since World War II, which in effect means since 1956. Another great achievement of the party at that time was its first serious attempt to analyze the Stalin cult as a phenomenon and to understand its consequences. And these are only two examples of what was achieved under Khrushchev.

There were negative things as well. In undertaking perestroika today, both the party and the people have much more experience with various kinds of reform than they had thirty years ago. In 1956 the way processes of change are interrelated was not fully understood. As a result, not everything was done in the best way and much wasn't carried through to completion. In addition, particular features of Khrushchev's personality had an adverse effect on the situation. Now we are faced with the task of analyzing that period of our history in a full and balanced way. Not in order to stick this or that epithet on Khrushchev, but to understand our past, present, and future development.

Many of your supporters, including several people interviewed for this book, see perestroika as a continuation or renewal of the Twentieth Party Congress.

I wouldn't put it exactly that way. The resolutions of the Twentieth Congress and the policy that existed at that time consisted of 90 percent negation of the past and only 10 percent looking ahead into the future, and that only in a very general way. Now we have a different situation. We are criticizing the past in ways that allow us to draw practical lessons for the present and the future. For example, when we talk about the stagnation of the 1970s and early 1980s, it's from the point of view of lessons and constructive activity that will give our socialism a second wind.

Recently you said that these ideas about the need for domestic reform were adopted quickly in 1985, after Gorbachev became general secretary, because reformist ideas already existed "in higher echelons of the party."

Yes, reform ideas have existed in all strata of society, and in the party as well, since the 1950s and 1960s. But people didn't all have the same reform in mind. Moreover, circumstances in the 1950s and 1960s and those today are not the same. Nor are the solutions. The content of reformist ideas is different. The ideas of perestroika were nourished in different fields for a long time, sometimes a very long time, even too long. These ideas have been developed over the years by scholars, cultural figures, and people engaged in political activity. Such ideas have been discussed in the press and in private conversations. All this was the background to the growing understanding that it was impossible to live in the old way and that many serious changes were necessary.

This explains the rapid acceptance—on the whole—of the ideas of perestroika and its overall strategy. Not simply acceptance, but the active support of the people. But now the most complicated part has begun—the actual implementation of perestroika.

If the ideas of perestroika were being developed and were circulating before 1985, does this mean that Gorbachev played no special or essential role in turning them into policy?

Of course he did. Circumstances had been demanding changes. The time for change had already come, it was knocking at the door, but Gorbachev understood earlier than others that the door had to be opened. His special political abilities and education made things move faster. And you must understand that it wasn't until 1985 that we learned just how bad things really were, particularly in our economic and financial affairs.

Be more specific about the reforms you want to carry out, about the actual components of perestroika. Glasnost is probably the best known among Americans, so let's start there. Does glasnost mean, in plain language, an end or at least a radical reduction of censorship in the Soviet Union?

Without glasnost there is no perestroika, no democracy, no socialism. Glasnost is the strength, courage, and willingness to look truth in the face, at home and abroad. We have emerged from self-delusions, from a silence designed to cover up negative phenomena and abuses of power. Daringly and radically, we are changing our thinking and our practices, as you know from reading our press. And as you know, as a result of glasnost there is a tremendous demand to increase the print runs of newspapers, magazines, and journals. Everyone wants to subscribe to the best ones. But we don't have the paper at this time, which shocks me. Here, too, is economic mismanagement. We have cut the export of paper and reduced paper supplies to bureaucratic offices, but we are at least 50,000 tons short. What a situation!

But you are wrong. Glasnost really has nothing to do with censorship. A great many myths have been created about censorship. I was involved in this work more than twenty years ago, when I worked in the Department of Propaganda, and I am involved now. Believe me, I know all about it. For example, according to the Western press, because of censorship many films weren't allowed to be shown. But censorship had nothing to do with this. It does not look at films. If the censorship looks at anything, it would be screenplays in order to be sure those scenarios do not contain military secrets.

Well, who banned all the Soviet films now being released as part of glasnost?

Something different happened to each film. Take the Ukrainian film by Kira Muratova, *The Long Goodbye*, which is now being shown. Someone in Odessa didn't like it. And to this day I haven't been able to find out who it was. The same thing happened to Aleksei German's film *Roadchecks*. Someone in Leningrad didn't like it.

What about books? For example, Anatoly Rybakov's novel Children of the Arbat, *about the Stalinist terror, was announced in the 1960s and again in the 1970s, but it wasn't published until 1987. Surely that was censorship.*

I checked into this carefully. When the book was first listed as forthcoming it had the seal of the censorship stating that it contained no military secrets. The censorship had not the slightest objection to it. But there is another aspect. If we speak about this particular book from the point of view of Soviet laws and regulations, it shouldn't even be published now. I will tell you why. No historical documents have been discovered, nor do they exist, attesting to Stalin's participation in the assassination of Sergei Kirov [the Leningrad party boss whose murder in December 1934 set off the Great Terror]. Under our regulations, if something is published on a Soviet historical subject, the Institute of Marxism-Leninism must rule as to whether it corresponds to historical truth. Rybakov depicts Stalin as having organized Kirov's assassination. We are talking about the factual aspect of the matter. Fact, not literature.

A commission was established under Khrushchev to investigate Kirov's assassination, but its findings have not been published.

It did not find documentary evidence corroborating that version of events. There is no proof of Stalin's role in the assassination.

Do you really mean that a Soviet writer even of historical fiction must submit his work to the Institute of Marxism-Leninism, or any historical institute, to verify the historical facts? Your objection to Rybakov's novel is also surprising because many Soviet writers believe that you personally supported its publication.

There is something you should understand. I believe that historical works of imaginative literature, novels on historical themes, should correspond to historical truth. I understand that if a novel is written about Cicero or some other ancient figure, it's difficult because there are inadequate documents. Or let's say about Khan Batu or Genghis Khan, about whom there are novels based on general conceptions and imagination, not on documents.

But Rybakov writes about Stalin and Kirov, and there are still many people alive who knew both of them. This history is still alive and throbbing. How it still throbs. It's still painful, it's still bleeding. For a writer to describe this whole business without sufficient documentary evidence is to undertake a very great responsibility.

My personal point of view is that works on modern and controversial historical subjects such as the 1930s should be written on the basis of actual history, established facts, not on the basis of an author's imagination. Everything must be verified. Soviet readers have an interest in this and expect the truth. And in this respect I have no evidence to confirm the version of Kirov's assassination presented in Rybakov's novel.

But it is a completely different question as to whether or not the novel should be published. If it does not violate morality and is valuable in artistic respects, why would it not be published? In principle, I am against bans. Rybakov has taken this responsibility upon himself, together with the editorial board of the journal that published it.

Maybe you don't understand the question. Are you saying that if a Soviet novelist wants to write a historical novel—just to make money or to entertain readers, as often happens in the West—he would first have to verify all his facts?

The novelist can do whatever he pleases, but when the name of his character is Ivanov or Sidorov—not Stalin—it is different. When actual historical persons are named, there are living people who may be affected. For example, there was a novel completed by Aleksandr Bek in the early 1960s, *The New Appointment*, that wasn't published here until 1986 because of the wife of a former state minister named Tevosyan. She threatened to go to court on the grounds that Bek had slandered her late husband by using him as a model for the novel's main character, a Stalinist minister.

You insist on historical truth, but that kind of truth is often very complex and hard to establish. For the Soviet novelist Pyotr Proskurin there is one Stalin, for Rybakov there is another Stalin, for Aleksandr Chakovsky yet another. Historical truth is not just a matter of events and evidence but also the interpretation of events and evidence.

Of course. And of an author's sensibility.

Let's return to your point that glasnost is unrelated to censorship. Do you mean that it was not a system of censorship but merely certain individuals or institutions that prohibited all these works and subjects in the past?

Absolutely. The censorship in the past and today is concerned only with the protection of military and state secrets, so in this respect there has been no need to limit the censorship. That there was a serious deficiency in glasnost in the past—a lack of open public discussion and disclosure of problems—is a different matter. Many editors and other individuals who were responsible for whether or not some work was published, whether or not certain information was made public, might have made excuses by referring to the censorship and its supposed bans. But in and of itself the censorship never had the right to prohibit something unless it involved military secrets.

But your own media today speak about previous "forbidden zones." Who created these "zones" and all the taboos now being removed by glasnost?

This phrase "forbidden zones" leads me to think that there's a misunderstanding of language here. It's not that the censorship had forbidden something. Take the case of Kazakhstan. The republic's leader Dinmukhammed Kunayev was a member of the Politburo, a very powerful and prominent political figure of long standing. He would simply raise a stink about a few outspoken newspaper articles and after that no editor in Kazakhstan would print anything critical or outspoken.

It was all very simple, much simpler than you imagine in your country. Our newspaper Literaturnaya gazeta recently tossed off an ingenious phrase. According to a well-known Russian saying, "Life isn't as simple as it seems at first glance." Literaturnaya gazeta remarked, "In fact it is much simpler."

Clearly, not everybody likes glasnost, particularly the new role of the Soviet press.

The press has exposed a great many problems, revealed many abcesses, destroyed the immunity of many local fiefdoms. Some people don't like this, so they attack glasnost and particularly the press. But to accuse glasnost or the press is like accusing a physician for diagnosing a serious disease. There is no alternative to glasnost, which is the realization of Lenin's idea that under socialism man should know absolutely everything so as to make conscious judgments about everything. Absolutely everything, about the past and the present.

In this respect, glasnost has a gamut of functions. The press must help the pioneers of perestroika throughout the country. Glasnost means keeping people informed, and it means the people monitoring public affairs. When we say, for example, that the executive committee of a district soviet must work openly, we mean that the people who live in that district must be able, through glasnost or openness, to supervise and oversee what the executive committee and district authorities in general are doing—and to pass judgment. We are giving this much greater importance than before, in connection with democratization. When we say that people should be involved fully in the affairs of society and government, we mean not only through elections but through their knowledge of what the authorities are doing. Let's say I'm the chairman of the executive committee of a city soviet—I am obliged to tell everything I do, and thus I am under popular supervision and control. And while this is not a full guarantee, it is at least a serious guarantee that I will think about what I am doing and that I will not allow abuses of power because I will not be able to hide them. Everything will be in full view. That is what glasnost is. And we are now publishing more and more things to keep people informed.

In that sense, glasnost is something much broader than merely the absence of censorship. I would say that glasnost, or the lack of it, begins first of all with individuals. Will an author speak out loudly or barely make a peep? Will he go into the essence of matters or slide superficially and unthinkingly over the surface? Will he defend his point of view or at the first sign of some influential's disagreement abandon it? Will he take a position of his own?

There are also editors, directors of publishing houses and scientific institutes, members of various artistic or academic councils, editorial boards, and so on. They too have a personal choice. How will they behave if an author speaks out bravely, in an unusual way, or expresses a controversial point of view and defends it tenaciously? An editor can support an author or just play it safe, especially since his salary doesn't depend on the choice. If an editor refuses to back up an author, he can say it's a personal disagreement. But that would risk damaging his personal relations with the author. So he might make vague allegations that such and such isn't permitted "from above."

Readers, powerful and powerless, also have to make a choice. If a reader disagrees with an author, does he write an article in reply, engage in an open and public discussion, or does he organize a slander campaign against the author? Does he write a letter to the militia or the KGB demanding that this person be called to account? Of course, in all these cases the personal choice will be determined to a considerable degree by the overall political and psychological atmosphere as well as by existing practices.

I want to emphasize that glasnost is a process and one that cannot be introduced by decree or by the flick of a switch. On the social level it is the development of a democratic process, of democratic institutions, and of a state based on the rule of law and orderly legal procedures. On the personal level, it is the development of the individual himself, of his moral fiber, so that personal choices can be made on the basis of high moral criteria, not on the basis of primitive egotism, opportunism, or even worse considerations.

Of course, certain slips or lapses into past practices and habits are possible. And there's also the problem of groups trying to take advantage of glasnost.

Glasnost is said to be only one component of a larger process of "democratization" in the Soviet Union, which Gorbachev and you have said repeatedly is an essential part of perestroika. In June 1988, the Nineteenth Party Conference passed a series of resolutions calling for many political reforms. They include permitting multi-candidate elections, transferring some real power to the soviets throughout the country, separating the powers of the executive and legislative branches of government, and enacting legal reforms that will bring about "a state based on the rule of law." Should we assume therefore that the conference was a truly important event?

It was a tremendous step forward. I hope that the conference will become known in history as the conference of the democratization of Soviet society.

Let us assume, for the sake of discussion, that all these political reforms will actually be enacted and that a democratized Soviet political system emerges sometime in the future. Will such a Soviet democratic system be like the American democratic system or will it be different?

Certainly it will be different. After all, democracies with the same kind of social and economic system—the United States, England, and France, for example—are different. Since we have a different kind of social and economic system, it is logical to expect that our democracy will be different. Of course, there will be some common aspects—pluralism of opinions, multi-candidate elections, nominations and voting, and other technical aspects of democracy. But the differences will be more substantive and important, though I don't rule out the possibility that we can learn from each other.

First of all, in our socialist country, democracy will be at the disposal of the people as a means to solve its problems and achieve its goals. So far as I can judge, this is not a primary task of American democracy. Secondly, we interpret democracy more broadly than you do. We don't limit it to participation in elections. We want to put it into practice in our everyday life, including at the workplace. For us, it is the way to overcome people's centuries-old alienation from political and economic power—and this alienation still exists in our socialist system—and to give people the chance to make their opinions felt in all kinds of decisionmaking. Of course, this is a future perspective, but we intend to move precisely in this direction. Finally, I think that as our reforms develop and as we continue to put our socialist principles and values into practice, the constitutional aspects of our democracy will be more dynamic than they are in America. Our constitution will be developing and changing, along with our society. I think that some of those changes will bring us closer together, for example, in the area of human rights. But for the foreseeable future, yes, we will be very different.

But please understand that there is nothing to fear here, no reason for confrontations or hysterics. After all, we have different historical experiences, different cultures, different social systems, and much else that is different. And this is good and normal. It enriches and moves mankind forward.

To be more specific, between March and May 1989, Soviet voters elected a newly created Congress of People's Deputies, whose 2,250 deputies then elected a smaller Supreme Soviet, which is supposed to function as a real parliament. The elections, and the campaigns leading to them, were the first major stage of the political reforms enacted by the Nineteenth Party Conference as well as the country's first multi-candidate elections in more than sixty years. Being in Moscow at the time, we found the electoral process to be very interesting but also rather complicated, with 750 deputies to the Congress being chosen by complex electoral assemblies in what are called social organizations, which include national entities ranging from the Communist Party and various professional unions to the Society of Inventors, and the other 1,500 by direct vote in residential districts and larger territories. Many of your own legal and political scholars were pleased that the new electoral process worked so well, but others were critical of some of its aspects. What is your own evaluation?

I can answer that question as a member of the party leadership, as a person who was elected a deputy from the party by a plenum of the Central Committee, and as a voter in my own district. The month-long election campaigns were a serious test of our society's democratic maturity. As for the actual elections, the party rightly hoped that voters would give a decisive "yes" to its program for further development of perestroika—for the creation of a democratic and truly humane, moral system.

On balance, I think it was a very unusual, important, and positive experience for us—a major step toward democracy. I agree that some problems emerged. Speaking as an ordinary voter, it sometimes was difficult to understand the actual programs and specific proposals of candidates. Though there were many discussions and debates on television and in newspapers, there may not have been enough information about and from the candidates. Voters need ample information. In this respect and others, we are still learning democracy and its political culture. We have to continue along and explore this road to popular sovereignty, self-government, and a socialist democracy that differs in positive ways from bourgeois democracy.

We are struck by Gorbachev's special emphasis on the need for what he calls "a state based on the rule of law." The Soviet Union has had several constitutions, a legal system, and a great many laws since it was created more than seventy years ago. Why is this area of political reform now so important?

Again, partly because we weren't ready for these kinds of reforms in the beginning—we weren't ready culturally, economically, or theoretically. Also, you must remember that we were the first socialist state in the world, in history. The international environment was very different. And then there were the outrageous violations of socialist legality under Stalin, which many people came to accept as a norm. So we are talking about raising people's legal consciousness. The law must be supreme in all areas of life, and everyone must be unconditionally equal in the eyes of the law. This is clear in theory, but we still have many violations in practice. Many party bosses, bureaucrats, and managers operate on the basis of different norms. And here I must add that we are now conscious of how many abuses are created by the preponderance of bureaucratism in our economic, political, cultural, and scientific life. Perestroika cannot succeed if people continue to be alienated from the system, if bureaucratic administration remains the dominant method of government and management, if undemocratic structures from the past dictatorially block people's initiative. Bureaucratism is a kind of legalized lawlessness. It is a condition in which common sense and the real interests of the individual and of society are sacrificed to the unlimited power of bureaucrats and office routine.

Only democracy, glasnost, and people's independence can effectively oppose this kind of bureaucratism, and all that is possible only given the rule of law. Sometimes we lack it quite literally. There are articles in our constitution, for example, declaring that certain offenses are to be prosecuted by law, but it turns out that in some of these cases there are no such laws. It seems that they just forgot to adopt them. So in this area of a truly legal state, we need more and better than we had yesterday. It will take time, but Columbus did not arrive in America with the American Constitution in hand.

Will this kind of democratization take a very long time?

To create a socialist state in a free and open society, we will have to go through the school of democracy. We must learn, for example, the political culture of discussion and of tolerating the widest possible range of conflicting views, within the context of socialism. The struggle against intolerance is one of the most important prerequisites of democratization. Given our historical legacy, this struggle will take generations. Over the years, we have developed so many habits of rejecting each other's opinions and tastes. This has caused great harm, especially in cultural life. We still have too much autocratic, totalitarian thinking. My opinion is the only right one and yours is wrong, and so on.

In this context, what is your view of the so-called informal groups, fronts, clubs, and similar organizations that are now playing a vocal role as a result of democratization?

Thousands of these spontaneous groups have already sprung up in the Soviet Union. We view them as positive manifestations of citizens' initiative. How else can the different views and interests of social groups be expressed? One goal of socialism is to ensure a pluralism of views so that different interests can be unified and harmonized. Unfortunately, some of these groups go to extremes. We welcome, for example, expressions of national feelings, but we condemn chauvinistic, malicious, arrogant forms of nationalism, which turn one nationality against another. Some of this has also arisen.

From what you say and from what other Soviet leaders have said, it seems clear that despite what you call democratization, the Soviet Union will continue to be a one-party system. But as your own press has pointed out recently, the Soviet Communist Party itself has had little, if any, democracy within its own ranks over the years. Now the Gorbachev leadership is calling for the democratization of the party itself. How will this happen? What kind of democratic mechanisms or procedures are needed inside the Communist Party?

The party is reforming itself as well, but at this time it is impossible to answer your question fully or in detail. Much will have to be suggested by life itself, as we go along. We don't want to create a priori schemes in some office and then try to make everything conform to them. We have had enough of that kind of thing. But I can tell you that we have reached general and clear principles about the need to democratize the party.

First, we recognize that the party cannot play its proper leading role in society, or increase its authority in society, without there being a strong process of democratization both inside the party and in society. Second, we recognize that the party's democratization is a precondition for society's democratization. Indeed, this process must be even more advanced within the party, so that the party can lead the democratization of society. The party must test the new democratic approaches on itself. Third, it is clear which of these approaches and measures must now be applied in the party. The number of elections must be expanded, and there must be multi-candidate elections. There will be limitations on how long party officials can hold elective office. There must be a separation of the functions of the party from those of soviet and economic institutions. The structure of the party apparatus is already being changed, reduced, and brought under the control of the proper party committees. Fourth, we have a major new practice decided by the Nineteenth Party Conference. At each level, the head of the party organization, the party secretary, will also be chairman of the soviet of people's deputies. This means he will have to be approved, voted on, by the soviet. If the voters deny him their confidence, probably it will mean he isn't worthy of being the party secretary. This seems like a good idea to us, but we'll see as it is put into practice. Finally, as the conference also indicated, there will be even more glasnost inside the party, as well as a simplification of rules and procedures.

All of these points, as they are introduced, will constitute the mechanism of party democratization you ask about. Maybe there will be other changes in the party. Certainly there will be a pluralism of views. Just look at what a spectrum of opinions within the party was expressed at the conference in June 1988. We have laid a good foundation, and now we must learn from life itself. Probably the next party congress will consider many proposals for changes in the party's by-laws.

Can you be more specific? Take the case of a regional or local party boss, a party secretary—a powerful figure—who abuses his powers, acts undemocratically, or generally behaves badly. The Soviet press reports many such cases in the past and even today. What happens to such a party secretary today?

First of all, a distinction must be made between a party committee and people in general. After all, decisions about a party committee are made by the members of that organization.

All right. How do local Communists rectify the situation?

Either they criticize that secretary or they elect someone else. Nowadays, at meetings, at regional and district conferences, for example, there is such criticism that—oy-yoy-yoy!—many party secretaries simply resign their posts. "I don't want to be under such pressure, such criticism," they say. Many simply can't take it. And when this criticism is supplemented by demagogy, it really gets bad. Nowadays there are a great many new leaders being elected.

You say they will elect someone else if they don't like a party secretary. But where will the new candidate or candidates for party leadership and other executive positions come from? Who will nominate them?

There's no standard procedure here, nor can there be one. I attended several cultural union congresses where new leaders were elected. And in each case the process was different. At the Artists Union Congress, several candidates were proposed by the party group there and additional ones directly from the floor. Even with the filmmakers two candidates were proposed, but as it turned out they refused. Mikhail Ulyanov, the actor, withdrew his own name. He stood up and said, "No, I won't do it."

We've heard two versions of what happened in 1986 at the Filmmakers Union Congress and at the Theater Workers Union Congress, which were important events in the development of glasnost and cultural reform. We asked Ulyanov, who became chairman of the Russian Theater Workers Union, how these remarkable rebellions against the old leadership took place. He said from above: "They decided above and we implemented it."

But Elem Klimov, who was elected the first secretary of the Filmmakers Union, gave us a different version. He said it was a revolt from below. What is the truth?

You shouldn't view it as a revolt either from above or from below. In the Filmmaker's Union, as in society as a whole, unresolved problems had piled up and were simply knocking at the door. It wasn't necessary to try to influence developments, but matters did not proceed in an anarchistic way either. Sometimes the discussion had the flavor of bickering and intrigue, the settling of personal scores—as was the case at the Writers Union Congress later in 1986. But you can't avoid that kind of thing. In my opinion, the settling of personal scores is a general phenomenon among intellectuals. They like to snap and nip at each other a little, and they do so with great pleasure.

How can the accounts of Ulyanov and Klimov both be right?

They are both right and wrong. Nothing was dictated from above other than simply a new policy, a new attitude, a new general mood or approach. But people weren't told to do this or that. Let's take, for example, Klimov's election as first secretary of the Filmmakers Union. We here did not decide in advance who should be elected. It was decided by the union. After all, there was more than one candidate.

But you decided that there would be changes there.

Why do you say that? They decided. I chaired the meeting and asked who the candidates were. I nominated Klimov. Another person nominated someone else. And a third nominated a third. Then the discussion began.

But you are a very influential person. Surely the delegates were swayed by your nomination of Klimov.

I know influence works that way in your country because you are a very disciplined people. But we don't have that degree of discipline here. We Slavs are a very anarchistic people. If I had nominated someone else, I'm convinced I would have been the only person voting for that candidate.

At the Russian Artists Congress, a very large number of candidates were nominated. The artists discussed matters for a long time, argued, and ended up with what they viewed as a compromise. They elected the president and the first secretary together as a twosome—like your president and vice-president. I asked myself what I should do. But it didn't matter to me who was elected. Let them live; let them decide.

At that time you had primary responsibility in the Central Committee Secretariat for cultural affairs, but you didn't care who ran those important unions? In the past, the Soviet leadership has cared greatly.

It was absolutely all the same to me. It's a cultural union that serves artists. So let it serve them. I may be naive or excessively idealistic, but I don't think the Writers Union needs a lot of help. They can elect who they want. If someone has no contact with other professional organizations or with party or government bodies, who in the Writers Union is going to support such a candidate? Even the most fervent anarchist would say we need someone who has contacts, who has influence, a person of significance. I believe in people's sober good sense. It's fine to make a lot of noise, but when it comes down to deciding questions, practical considerations usually gain the upper hand. Sure, there were extreme left and right speeches at the various congresses. But when the secret balloting came, the governing bodies were elected neither by the right or the left but by the center. That's all there is to it.

But you are talking now about cultural unions, not party organizations. Can such a situation really develop inside the Communist Party itself?

Oh yes. Not long ago, in one of the districts of the Kirov region, the higher regional party committee proposed a candidate for the district party committee bureau. The district bureau discussed this and decided to propose its own candidate. Then the regional committee proposed a second candidate. And what do you think happened at the district conference? A third candidate was proposed. Totally unexpectedly. Then this third candidate protested that he was already too old to be on the district committee; he was fifty-six—younger people were needed. Nevertheless he was elected by a majority, that is, nominated directly at the conference. There have been other incidents like this elsewhere.

So you see there are variations. But often there is only one candidate, because he is thought to be suitable.

And that is democracy?

Of course. But we must look at two sides or aspects of democratization inside the party. First is the official, formal aspect, governed by the party rules. These are not fixed or frozen. The rules have evolved, together with the party. Changes were adopted by the Twenty-Seventh Party Congress in February 1986, and the rules will continue to evolve.

The other aspect is the way things are actually done in various party organizations and in relations between them. Everything depends on specific individuals. For example, the party rules do not limit the number of candidates to only one, but they also don't say there have to be several. Party members can and must decide this for themselves, and the same goes for many matters of internal party procedure.

There is, of course, the obvious and very powerful force of established and generally recognized practice. People do a great many things in life without even thinking about why they act one way rather than another. They think it's always been done this way; that's all there is to it. We are now introducing new ways of doing these things.

The same situation also exists in relations between various levels within the party. Our main principle—democratic centralism—is good in that it leaves broad scope for interpreting its specific content. How it should be put into practice depends on the general historical conditions, tasks, and level of development of society and the party as a whole. I have no doubt that future generations of Communists will also have to decide this for themselves. I personally consider this a great plus.

That is democracy: decisions made at local party meetings, with secret ballot or by open voting, whether there is one candidate, or two, or three. We are holding widespread elections to district and lower party committees. We will have to see how those elections go. Until now, such elections have occurred mostly when someone has died or been transferred to another post.

You seem to be saying that the Soviet political system, even inside the party, will be different in different parts of the country. In some places there will be several candidates and in other places not?

Why not? It's absolutely fine. That is what democracy is. Let them decide.

But what sort of political system will that be if in one place there are several candidates and in another only one? You will have several different systems.

Well, and what of it? What's so frightening about that? Absolutely nothing. Let them decide.

And will this kind of let-them-decide democracy prevail even here in Moscow, at the center?

Yes, at the center too. Why not?

Things have been very different in the past.

The party rules do not forbid this. Nowhere is it said there can be only one candidate, though in the past there was usually one candidate. But now people themselves should decide about their leader and then they will be responsible for the person they elected and bear collective responsibility.

But if there are different opinions on the most important issues even among Communists, even inside the party, how can there be the kind of obligatory party line that was so important in the past?

The party rules say that opinions can be discussed and taken into account as long as there has not been a decision by the majority. You and I can shout, raise a fuss, accuse each other, and debate. Then we vote. Say there are five people here, and there is a motion saying such and such. And three people vote for it, two against. After that the two are obliged to submit to the decision of the majority. That's all. Otherwise we will expel you from the party. Unconditional implementation of the decision of the majority. That is what is called democratic centralism.

But before the voting everyone has the right to fight for his or her own point of view?

Of course. What's the problem? At party meetings in the past things were sometimes that way, though not to the same extent as now. When I worked on a regional party committee they really let us have it. Oy-yoy-yoy! It was like sitting on hot coals. You'd think you were going to faint dead away.

Won't you have to reconsider and even abolish the resolution against groups and factions inside the party, which was adopted under Lenin's leadership at the Tenth Party Congress in 1921?

There is no need for a new resolution on this matter today. As for the way the 1921 resolution was actually used in the past, there is simply no way to annul what happened. You can't replay the past. Moreover, there must not be organized groups or factions within the party that would carry on an organized struggle against the party's officially adopted line.

I consider this principle correct today as well. I don't want to overemphasize it. We are not talking about the banning of various points of view in the party but about the impermissibility of organized struggle within the party against its adopted course. The experience of many parties, not only communist parties, attests to the fact that when such a thing happens a party undergoes an internal crisis, sometimes becoming incapable of effective action for a long while. Decisions, once made, should be implemented by all.

Differences of opinion—and they are inevitable—lead to two possible results. One is conflict; the other is a constructive consensual solution. We consider the second path the optimal one.

It's still not clear: Is the 1921 resolution against factions still relevant today?

No, there's no need for it. We don't have any factions.

Though economic reform isn't a subject we will pursue at any length with you, aspects of it are strongly related to your political reforms and also to opposition or resistance to perestroika more generally. In particular, we are interested in your new emphasis on the role of the market in the Soviet economy.

When we speak of the market we don't mean what the West means by this idea—unlimited competition, the creation of prices on the free market, unemployment, and other negative social consequences. But we accept the idea of a socialist market. It is time to put an end to the dogma, which formed under Stalin, that socialism and the market are incompatible. Commodity-money relations do exist, and we think these relations must play a larger and healthier role in Soviet economic life. They should not be subjected to artificial prohibitions. Prices should be formed not on the basis of subjective-utilitarian considerations but on the basis of the cost of production, the real value of a commodity. Prices should convey accurate information about a product. Today they do not. For example, we subsidize bread so that the retail price is lower than the cost of producing it. And meat and other things, too. Why? Because we want people to have bread and meat and milk at cheap prices and not the way it is in the West. We want the Soviet market to be formed as a result of the activity of state enterprises, expanded cooperatives, and individual economic activity. They will be competitive elements of the socialist market.

How much private enterprise, cooperative enterprise, and market do you envision, say, ten years from now?

We're not even trying to plan or force that. We want things to develop, so to speak, normally.

What happens to state planning and control, which has been so centralized in Moscow for the last six decades?

An individual state enterprise will make its own plans. It will decide that out of the profits so much is needed for its production fund, amortization, and social fund. That it will need to build so much housing and so many child care centers for workers' families. The labor collective itself will plan all this. Its plan will be examined and undoubtedly there will be debates. Some will say no, wait, why haven't you taken into account this or that? All this will be done in a way that's more complex than it is now. Today Gosplan [the State Planning Commission] does everything. And this machine somehow miscalculates it all. Obviously there will be some sort of national control figures—some things have to be supplied to the state and some goals have to be met. We can't let certain things slip. So much steel and metal is needed, let's say, so many miles of railroad and means of transport to ship certain things. There are some serious areas such as defense without which the state cannot exist. Gosplan will make corrections, by economic methods, by legal methods, that's all.

Even now, as late as 1989, you, Gorbachev, and other Soviet leaders have said repeatedly that the economic reforms are not going well. In some respects, it seems that the economic situation in the country is even worse than it was before the Gorbachev leadership took over in 1985. Some of your leading reform economists, such as Nikolai Shmelyov and even Leonid Abalkin, who helped draft the reforms, have argued that the leadership has adopted too many half-measures and that much greater boldness is needed in this area.

I agree that the economic reforms are not going as well as they might have. After four years we cannot be satisfied with the economic results of perestroika. Command and bureaucratic methods still dominate the economy. But real economic reforms are underway. Some of our people are much too impatient. As the nineteenth-century novelist Saltykov-Shchedrin wrote, they like to run ahead of progress. They can be just as harmful as inveterate conservatives. After all, politics is the art of the possible. We are living in the romantic and heady times of perestroika, but we must be realists. Like weightlifters, we can lift only what we can cope with at the time.

Moreover, economic perestroika affects the lives and interests of tens of millions of people. It is only natural, therefore, that it should encounter resistance, inertia, an unwillingness to give up undeserved privileges, and so forth. We can't use bulldozer methods against this resistance, especially since we are renouncing the Stalinist command system and calling for democracy. People have to be persuaded to change. We can't carry out perestroika with the methods of the past, simply by imposing orders from above.

You must also understand the complexity of all this. So much has been neglected in the country over the years. Everything relates to something else. One set of reforms requires another. New economic practices lead to the necessity of political changes, which in turn call for legal reforms. Even with our desire and willingness to carry out these reforms, they can't be realized in a few weeks or months. Everything must be thought through carefully, every measure, or mistakes will be made. You know, for example, about the good and necessary struggle we undertook against alcohol consumption, but which was conducted in ways that produced harmful excesses. In a country as large as ours, irresponsible experimentation is impermissible, whether in the economy or elsewhere. That is the firm conviction of the Soviet leadership. Our formula is to move ahead with perestroika consistently, insistently, and purposefully, but in realistic ways, without jumping over stages. But once a decision has been taken, we will do our utmost to fulfill it.

Of course, the economic situation became more complicated after 1985 because the old and the new were coming into conflict. It may become even more complicated as we approach the problems of reforming prices, wholesale trade, and the financial system. All this lies ahead. It is like repairing a house or an apartment. Living becomes better only after the reconstruction is complete. By the way, when you hear people say we should act even more boldly in our reforms, imagine trying to introduce comparable changes in your own country. Then you will have a sense of what is and is not possible.

Your media regularly report, Gorbachev has frequently said, and you have suggested in our discussion that there is considerable opposition to all these political and economic reforms. Who is opposed to perestroika— which groups, classes, or people? How serious is the opposition?

Look, perestroika involves a revolution of mind-sets, so it is natural that there is a broad range of attitudes toward it. Some people are enthusiastic, even impatient proponents of perestroika. Others understand that it will have to be their life's work. And still others are skeptical, even hostile to perestroika. Conservatism exists in many areas—in politics, theory, ideology, and everyday life. There are many deeply rooted prejudices against the economic reforms—against land leasing, cooperatives, and individual enterprise. And this will continue to be the case in the future. There will be people who will turn their backs on perestroika because their personal comfort is threatened by social justice, whose spiritual comfort is disturbed by the discarding of obsolete concepts and dogmas. Many people are frightened by democracy and

glasnost and blame our intelligentsia and young people for all our problems. The fond practice of reaching for the administrative handle to
stifle initiative will survive for a long time, as will nostalgia for past
customs. But the perestroika of minds, of consciousness, is an ascent
toward the truth that will continue, as will our ruthless evaluation of
past tragedies and mistakes.

All things considered, I think the main problem is inertia and habits
developed over decades. It is very difficult to abandon certain methods
of political and economic leadership. If I have long held certain views
and I sincerely believe in them, then I will cling to them. If the secretary
of a party district committee is used to governing by command, things
are easy. "Listen, Ivan Petrovich, do this, start the sowing." And Ivan
Petrovich begins the sowing. The party secretary is content and Ivan is
content. And don't assume that only bosses like command methods.
Times have been such that subordinates and workers do too. When the
guy on top says, "Do this," the guy on the bottom doesn't have to think.
He does it and goes home, and at home he has a dacha, a wife, or not a
wife, whatever, it's simple and it's easy.

But if his superior suddenly says, "You know what, dear fellow, you
should think it out for yourself," he will respond: "What's wrong with
you? Have you gone out of your mind?" That's the whole problem. We
are talking about the inner restructuring of people, not machines. This
person doesn't like it and that one doesn't like it. One doesn't want to
work, another doesn't want to think, a third is too used to this kind of
life. And some of our new slogans aren't very popular either. "Don't
steal." Well, but why not, my friend? And "Work! Don't drink!" But of
course he wants to have a drink. Another doesn't want to work. The
third doesn't want to think. That's the whole problem, not that some
group is resisting. Everyone professes to be for perestroika. I say I am
willing to change, you're the one who's not willing. I look at others and
not at myself. That is the problem.

You mean there is no real political opposition to perestroika?

I don't think there is. It is almost impossible because the working
class, the peasants, and the intelligentsia are overwhelmingly for perestroika. The Central Committee has received hundreds of thousands of
letters expressing firm support for perestroika. I think the great majority of the people are with us. What would political opposition consist
of? What would it look like? Presumably, it would involve an alternative platform, political forces, and political action. But no one here

today puts forth any alternative to perestroika. Any proposal can be discussed today, and I can assure you it would be discussed even at the Politburo level. But who would call for an end to perestroika and a return to the times of stagnation? There is an anti-perestroika minority, but it is losing its ability to profit from the old stagnant ways. Such a minority might be able to attract some people by operating under the slogans and banners of perestroika. We saw this in Nagorno-Karabakh, in the dispute between Armenians and Azerbaijanis, where militant nationalism paraded under the banner of perestroika. And of course there are other kinds of petty political resistance. But to do nasty things behind people's backs, to lurk in corners, that isn't real politics.

In this connection, we must ask you about persistent reports, in the West and here in Moscow, that you and your fellow Politburo member Yegor Ligachev represent two different Politburo points of view on the scope and tempo of perestroika.

You understand, of course, that Politburo decisions always are and must be confidential. We never characterize publicly the opinions of other Politburo members. If we did so, we could not have truly free, open, fruitful discussions at Politburo meetings, or an atmosphere of camaraderie and constructive Politburo work.

That is why when I read in the Western press alleged reports of the personal views of this or that member of the Politburo, I know they are pure inventions or speculation. As for rumors in Moscow, most of them actually originate in the West, are transmitted through foreign radio broadcasts, and then become overladen here with various local fantasies and pseudo-specifics. Then they return to the West as so-called first-hand reports.

Are there serious discussions in the Politburo? There certainly are, on all important questions. Sometimes these discussions are sharp and turn into heated and lengthy debates. But these discussions are neither for nor against perestroika. They are about how to achieve it, how to move forward. Discussions like that are normal and natural.

Speaking of different opinions in the leadership, we were impressed by the Central Committee's decision to make public its voting, in March 1989, for its own 100 deputies to the Congress of People's Deputies. Disagreements and voting in the Central Committee having been largely secret since the 1920s, many Soviet citizens were virtually stunned to read in Soviet newspapers that 12 of 641 votes were cast against Gorbachev, 78 against Ligachev, and so forth.

Publicizing such things is better than allowing rumors about them to flourish. Moreover, people now can see and understand that voting should be a normal process everywhere, including at Central Committee meetings.

And what was your personal reaction to the fact that fifty-nine people voted against you?

Again, it was a normal and natural development.

Returning to the larger question of political opposition, what about what your press derisively calls "the bureaucrats"—bosses, managers, and other officials? According to Soviet estimates, there are 18 million of them.

It varies. How does perestroika threaten an economic manager who is really willing to work? He is for it. But there is another kind of manager who won't admit that he can't cope but who knows it himself. Of course he is against perestroika, but he doesn't want to get out of the way.

If so many people are in favor of perestroika, it shouldn't be very hard to put it into practice.

You have to understand a striking observation Lenin once made. "The greatest ideals," as he put it, "are not worth a brass farthing if they are not linked with people's interests." To a large extent the trouble in the past was an alienation of practices and ideals from people's real interests. That's the whole problem. And the task of perestroika is to reunite the ideals of socialism and people's real interests.

In this respect, the struggle against dogmatism is a very serious matter. The socialist idea began as a great social hypothesis, but under Stalin and later it degenerated into primitive dogmas, sacred cows, arrogance, pseudosciences, and self-serving hymns. There have been so many prohibitions and restrictions that we have had to do away with. And we've had too many self-proclaimed interpreters of what is and what is not socialism. Some of them have interpreted socialism to suit their own personal interests. When we break with their conceptions, they accuse us of capitalism, revisionism, and all sorts of sins. Many tenets of Marxism were dogmatized and canonized. Any canonization of Marxism is the destruction of Marxism. That is my profound conviction. Our task today is to restore Marxism to its true meaning—development and dialectics. Only then will it be a genuine theoretical doctrine and not a religion.

Did Soviet Marxism-Leninism become a religion?

I wouldn't say it became a religion, but for a long time it acquired a semi-religious quality. People said, This position is right and that one is wrong. But what if circumstances change? As Lenin said, Marxism is the study of reality, a method for gaining knowledge of reality—scientific study. And nothing more. So when they write articles saying that this law must operate under socialism because Marx said such and such about capitalism—that doesn't interest me except from a purely intellectual perspective. But not from the point of view of drawing political conclusions. I am interested in conclusions based on the study of reality. And if we draw a theoretical conclusion on the basis of reality, that will be Marxism.

It is hard not to think that you are minimizing the extent of opposition to perestroika. The history of most countries shows that such great reforms usually meet enormous opposition of various kinds, not just social inertia but actual political opposition. If that does not happen in the Soviet Union, it may be the first time or one of the first times in history.

It is possible because as a people we were inwardly ready for perestroika. Not only the people, but also the party. In the party we had already discussed all of this quite actively. Look, in March 1985 there was the change of leadership, the election of Mikhail Sergeevich Gorbachev, and less than a month later he gave a report on the need for all of this to the April plenum of the Central Committee. These ideas could not have fallen from the sky. They were alive, and alive, it turned out, at a high level, in the upper echelons of the party.

And everyone was in favor, even in favor of democratization?

No, of course not. If previously I could say, do this and that quickly by ordering someone about, today I have to reason with him, prove something to him. It takes more time, and more nerve.

And yet there are reports even here in Moscow that there has been opposition to Gorbachev's democratization program from members of the Central Committee.

No I wouldn't say so.

What about statements, including some by Gorbachev himself, that the state ministries don't like the economic reforms? Surely, they are a formidable bastion of opposition, especially since the ministries themselves must implement such reforms and thus have many opportunities to delay or even sabotage them? Indeed, didn't this happen with the 1965 reform?

Not all the ministries and ministers dislike economic reform. Moreover, if a minister doesn't like a reform and doesn't implement it, let him get out of the way, let someone take his place who does like it and will implement it. That is what we are doing. It is an organizational question, not a political one.

Well, it's hard to distinguish between organizational factors and political ones. But let's take expressions of opposition to perestroika even among intellectuals, for example, in the Russian Writers Union, which seems to be on the conservative side. You will recall that in 1987, the novelist Yuri Bondaryev called for some kind of new Battle of Stalingrad against internal forces that threatened to destroy Russian values. Presumably, he meant forces associated with perestroika and glasnost.

Yes, I remember, and to this day I don't understand what he had in mind. Bondaryev is an honest person, but like many people he doesn't like it when he or his work is criticized, as often happens now with glasnost.

By the way, one of our most important achievements since 1985 is that we have closed the breach that had opened up between the political leadership and the intelligentsia, which had felt the absence of glasnost most acutely. In 1985 we offered our hand to the intelligentsia. Perestroika is impossible without the intelligentsia because perestroika is also the intellectualization of society, so to speak. That is one reason why, in my opinion, hostile attitudes toward the intelligentsia are immoral. At the same time, however, the intelligentsia must act responsibly, without arrogance or condescension, without petty quarrels over who is the most talented and cleverest, without intragroup squabbling.

But isn't it true that Bondaryev and many other prominent writers and publicists represent the kind of traditional Russian nationalism that you criticized in your famous 1972 article, the one that caused an uproar and brought you considerable personal grief? And isn't this kind of nationalism, with its conservative instincts and emphasis on "eternal values," ideologically opposed to the kinds of changes represented by Gorbachev's conception of perestroika?

Look, the past has also bequeathed us many complex nationality problems. Perestroika must include a restructuring of nationality and ethnic relations in the Soviet Union. Our democratization process, as I told you, will continue to develop. Political reforms must include issues of sovereignty, autonomy, and the development of national cultures and language. There will be a Central Committee plenum on this. I firmly believe that we must broaden the rights of the republics that make up the Soviet Union so that people will feel themselves to be masters of their own republic and region. At the same time, however, we must act responsibly. We must not give conservative forces an opportunity to say that perestroika is allowing the nationalities to get out of hand. To say, "Well, you see where your glasnost and democracy are leading!" And we do hear this.

Yes, but it was Russian nationalists who struck out at you in 1972 and who do so even now.

Anyone is free to hear what he wants to hear. There are aspects of that kind of nationalism which don't coincide with the interests of perestroika, but I wouldn't exaggerate the threat. Anyway, in my 1972 article I didn't criticize only Russian nationalism. I criticized nationalism in all of its extreme forms, whether it be great power chauvinism, local nationalism, or anti-Semitism. Frankly, all kinds of nationalism are repugnant and alien to me. I don't understand it when people are at odds over nationality issues. That sort of thing is disgusting. It is unacceptable for civilized people in a civilized society. The moment I start thinking I am superior because I am a Russian, I cease to be a real human being, because that is where humanity ends. I hate all forms of chauvinism. We know where it leads—to bloodshed.

Let's make this question more specific. Take the example of the Pamyat [Memory] Society, one of the informal or unofficial movements that have appeared and are active at meetings, in the streets, and elsewhere. Many Soviet supporters of perestroika think that the Pamyat Society is a dangerous threat because of its very aggressive Russian nationalism. They say it has strong neo-Stalinist, anti-Semitic, even quasi-fascist overtones, and that it seems to have many members or supporters.

This is a very complex phenomenon. The party took the initiative in introducing perestroika, in moving toward democratization. Then the Pamyat Society appears and while raising some perfectly proper questions—such as the preservation of monuments, combatting public drunkenness and ecological concerns—suddenly attacks the party, saying that things should be done differently. And all this is mixed together with some sort of reactionary ideology, involving denunciations of Masonry, anti-Semitism and so on. What will all this lead to? Pamyat's leaders are trying to arouse philistine sentiments among a broader segment of the population—cynical, philistine sentiments. And when they wave banners saying, "We are for perestroika," a person who doesn't make careful distinctions thinks: "Well, if that's perestroika, who needs it? Who wants that kind of perestroika?"

Most of the people who take part in the Pamyat Society have honorable intentions. Who could be opposed to restoring historical monuments or preserving the ecology? No one. The entire Central Committee is in favor of ecology and sobriety. It was the Central Committee that first posed these questions, not the Pamyat Society. Its leaders are people whose ideas are a strange mixture of crude, prerevolutionary Russian pogromism and illiteracy. They use well-known techniques of demagogy. But when we profess democracy, what can we do except let people express themselves, say what they think? We have to fight blowhards, demagogues, speculators, but we have to do so openly, and with glasnost. Let them come before the public, and let the public see what they are.

What if the Pamyat Society, to take the example we are discussing, decides it must form a new political party because the Communist Party is against the Russian nation? Is that also acceptable under glasnost and democratization?

Who would join such a party? Two or three crude Russian pogromists? That's not a party. Anyway, I don't believe in hypothetical cases, in "what-ifs." The subjunctive mode has no significance for evaluating either the past or the future.

Such pogromist or neo-Stalinist attitudes seem to exist inside the Communist Party as well. For example, in September 1987 the newspaper Moskovskaya pravda *published articles by two party members with opposing conceptions of perestroika. One was entitled "We Need the Whip," the other, "No Going Back to the Past."*

Well, what can you do? One person thinks one way, another thinks another. Such people exist.

Is the party secretary who wants to bring back the whip an opponent of perestroika?

I don't think he's an opponent of perestroika, but he thinks that it can be carried out by administrative means. But we think that the driving force of perestroika is the development of democracy. That is where we part ways with this comrade.

Are there many such people?

I don't know. No one has counted, but I think so because those habits of power do exist.

We haven't really explored the question of popular discontent with perestroika, which may also be a form of opposition or resistance. In frequent visits to Moscow we have often heard people say something like this: After almost four years, perestroika is still just something for the intelligentsia. The intelligentsia has glasnost. Ulyanov can do his plays, Klimov his films, and Yevtushenko can publish his poems. And Aleksandr Yakovlev, who oversaw the development of glasnost, is also an intellectual. But ordinary Soviet people, they say, have gotten nothing from perestroika. Is this a fair judgment?

Yes and no. To expect real material changes in only a few years is impossible and naive. Why the devil would we need such a thoroughgoing restructuring of the system, such revolutionary changes, if everything could be fixed in only three or four years? Things don't work that way. The new leadership didn't have full storehouses and granaries, or any extra reserves. Everything was empty. But there have been some significant results. The production of meat and milk has increased, though it is not sufficient. In industry we think it is good that we are not fulfilling the plan because now we have a system of state quality control rejecting inferior goods. We think it is better to have one refrigerator that works well than three that work poorly. And this helps people because they won't have to run around trying to get it repaired. In one year of perestroika, we commissioned more new housing than in the previous fifteen years, though tens of millions of people still need better housing. So it's not enough, but we have done a lot since 1985.

In this respect, perestroika is at a turning point. From now on it will be judged by the way it solves vital everyday problems of food supplies, housing, consumer goods and services, and the rest. We must repay all those neglected debts of the past. Otherwise, perestroika will disappoint and offend the people.

But there is a real danger in the expectations of too many people that perestroika will come as a kind of miracle. That someone up here will say "perestroika," clap his hands three times, and a fairy godmother will suddenly appear to solve all these problems. The future depends on all of us, on the people, alone.

You talk about the many problems and obstacles, but compared to some very worried supporters of perestroika, you seem to be an optimist.

Long ago, under Emperor Cyrus of Persia, there was a river called Diala, in what is now Iraq. Once he was crossing this river on a white horse and the horse drowned. Cyrus was so angry that he banned the river. It's the only case in history when a river was punished. He had 360 canals dug to lay waste to the river. For a thousand years the river flowed down a different channel, but today it flows in its former channel. Thus, if you take what you consider to be a correct position, and if it really is so, then no matter how many canals are dug around it, the correct position will prevail. So yes, I am an optimist.

Gorbachev often says, as do you, that perestroika must be made "irreversible." What do you mean? Is anything in politics "irreversible"?

Let's be specific. There cannot be a repetition of the situation that existed before in the Soviet Union. You know Gorbachev's declaration—"Not one step backward." But if you are asking me a hypothetical question, then there could be some sort of zigzag, some expressions of dissatisfaction by some people. In a democracy, why shouldn't that be possible? And our dogmatists will hold fast to their conceptions for a long time. They will continue to believe that it is possible to reverse perestroika.

Isn't Gorbachev's call to make perestroika irreversible an allusion to the reforms that were initiated in 1956 and 1965 but were stopped and reversed?

As I have told you, my personal view is that society was ready at that time for fundamental changes, but the leadership wasn't. It remained mired in the past. Today the situation is different—the leadership is ready for these changes.

Maybe so, but let's put the same question in a different way. Gorbachev says repeatedly that there is no alternative to his program of perestroika for the Soviet Union. And yet Marx, Lenin, and most serious students of history know there are always alternatives in politics—political forks on the historical road, so to speak. In this sense, if perestroika fails, what is the alternative for the Soviet Union?

There can be no alternative. Otherwise I wouldn't be sitting here. I cannot even admit such a possibility. If I even allowed myself to think that maybe perestroika couldn't be carried out, I would immediately submit my resignation and take up something else.

What are you saying? Either perestroika succeeds or—what?

Or the death of socialism.

Is the situation really that serious here in the Soviet Union?

Of course it is. Here and in the world more generally, because without socialism there is no other alternative at the present moment or for the foreseeable future.

We want to end our discussion with you by talking briefly about international affairs and particularly Soviet–American relations. You now play a special role in this policy area, so perhaps you will begin by telling us something about the primary responsibilities of a member of the Politburo and of the Secretariat. From the time you joined the Politburo in 1987 until recently, your own primary responsibilities involved ideology, culture, the media, and related issues. It was then that people began calling you "the architect of glasnost." In the fall of 1988, however, when the Central Committee apparatus was reorganized into six new standing commissions, you became chairman of the Commission on International Policy. And yet, even before that change, you seemed to be deeply involved in international affairs, traveling with Gorbachev to his meetings with President Reagan, meeting with foreign visitors to Moscow, and so forth.

Each Politburo member who is also a secretary of the Central Committee has a sphere of special responsibility. Mine, for example, as you point out, changed recently. But no member of the Politburo and the Secretariat is locked into a sphere. Work of the Politburo and the Secretariat is structured in such a way that every member can express interest and speak out on any question of domestic and foreign policy. He can raise any issues on his own initiative. And he can introduce amendments to any documents presented for discussion. All of our work and discussion are conducted in this free and collegial way.

Given the two areas for which you have had special responsibility, perhaps you can explain why the process of glasnost has been slower and less broad in matters of Soviet foreign policy than in domestic policy. Indeed, glasnost began to affect public discussion of foreign policy in a significant way only in 1988.

When we discuss our internal affairs, it affects only us. So we can conduct the discussion anyway we see fit, as candidly as we wish. But when discussion turns to our foreign policy, it affects other countries as well, and we have to take this into account. Nonetheless, as we reevaluate the past and as our understanding increases, glasnost is spreading into foreign policy. After all, this is part of what we call "the new thinking" in international affairs.

As you look back over the long history of Soviet–American conflicts, the history of the Cold War and the arms race, do you now conclude that the Soviet Union bears some responsibility for this history and its negative consequences?

I would never argue that one side is guilty of everything and the other side is absolutely pure and innocent. That would be a gross over-simplification. But the United States is to blame for creating the arms race. It was the first to build all kinds of nuclear weapons, and it repeatedly rejected Soviet proposals to ban or abolish various weapons. The United States imposed the arms race on us. And it did so not just for military reasons but also to suffocate us economically, to keep us in a siege atmosphere and drain our resources. And why did the West spend so much money and so many resources trying to convince people that we are about to invade Western Europe and the United States? It's sheer nonsense—worse than nonsense since we have lived more than forty years with the fear that you would attack us. After all, we didn't start NATO. It was only four years later, in response, that we organized the Warsaw Pact.

Are you saying that the Soviet Union has never done anything to cause the United States to fear it?

Well, what, for example? Probably you mean Hungary and Czecho-slovakia, in 1956 and 1968. But what about the events that preceded those events?

Surely the origins of the modern-day Cold War are to be found in events following World War II. Did the Soviet Union do nothing at that time to give the United States reason to feel threatened?

It was Churchill's Iron Curtain speech at Fulton, Missouri, in 1946, that convinced us there was a real danger. And even earlier one of your generals, even the secretary of state, declared that the bombing of Hiroshima had been necessary to teach the Russians a lesson. That is when fear took hold of us, fear of the nuclear bomb, which we didn't have.

You seem to be saying that only one side, the United States, was responsible for the history of the Cold War and the arms race.

No, not entirely. The same political conditions in our country that gave rise to so many negative domestic processes probably also caused mistakes in our foreign policy. For example, we didn't have to react to the arms race you imposed on us in the way we did. Now we have rejected that build-up approach in favor of the concept of military sufficiency. And this is only the beginning. Sure we made mistakes, but remember that we were the first socialist country, and we have had to learn from our experiences. That we have learned from our mistakes is reflected in our new thinking about international affairs. I will tell you, for example, that I personally don't understand why we deployed the SS-20 missiles, in the 1970s, in Europe. I know there were some political reasons. Why were the French and British nuclear forces so close to our borders? And our military people say the deployment was just modernization. But for me it doesn't make sense. It wasn't beneficial.

As you know, an important debate about perestroika and Gorbachev's "new thinking" in foreign policy is underway in the United States. Some influential Americans argue that Gorbachev's policies represent an opportunity to create a new and better relationship between our two countries. Other influential Americans argue, however, that if perestroika is successful the Soviet Union will eventually emerge as a stronger country economically and militarily and thus as an even greater threat to the United States. What would you say to Americans who insist that perestroika is bad for the United States?

I would begin with the story about a girl who says to her friend, "Today is the first of January, so I've brought you a new calendar as a present." The friend replies: "What for? The old one I have is still good." This kind of backward thinking shocks me. All this talk about some threat to America's national interests is backward thinking. If every country based its foreign policy only on its concept of its national interests, what the devil kind of world would it be? Common human interests require compromise and mutual understanding.

Look, as you know, perestroika is a long-term policy to move the Soviet Union forward in economics, democracy, and morality. No domestic policy can be conducted in isolation from international affairs. We want better relations with the West, with all countries, based on cooperation, not conflicts and arms races. In this sense, foreign policy begins at home. At the same time, we understand that the entire planet has become exceedingly small. Mankind's history can be ended by the push of a button somewhere. An event becomes known to 5 billion people within hours. In our time, the concept of common human interests has become tangible. That is our new thinking. We have made our choice, and it is expressed in our recent policies toward the United States. Why should you fear it?

And why should the United States fear a well-developed Soviet

Union, particularly since we have proposed that together we abolish nuclear weapons? Moreover, perestroika is good for America because, if we prosper, we will fear you less. Today, we fear that you still might try to smash us by military means or try to strangle us economically.

You really fear this possibility?

Yes, we are afraid. And how could we not fear you, my dear friends? How many U.S. national security directives and doctrines have been drawn up to invade or bomb the Soviet Union? My own hometown of Yaroslavl was on a list of the first cities to be bombed. Such directives said that the next government here could do whatever it wanted with Communist Party activists. And after the war we went through in 1941–45, do you think this was a joke for us? Plans to dismember our country and create zones of occupation, specifying how many American troops would be sent in, how many bombs would be dropped and on which cities? Imagine if the Soviet Union had drawn up plans in 1947 to strike Philadelphia, New York, Chicago, San Francisco, Los Angeles, and I don't know what else. Oy-yoy-yoy! What a furor there would have been in America.

Surely you don't think that such documents, drafted years ago, were serious or characteristic of America?

No, but they changed America. When I studied at Columbia University, in New York, in 1959, students asked me questions that made my hair stand on end. Once I spent four days in Iowa living with a farmer's family, a very nice family. I have only gratitude and warm memories of that stay. But when the farmer's wife watched me playing with their five children, she expressed surprise that I liked children. I said, "Well, of course I love them. I have two of my own at home." "If you love children," she asked, "why do you have wives in common and communalized children in your country?" "Lord be with you! Who told you that?" "A priest," she said. And in downtown New York, in a little store, they felt my head to see if it was true that we Soviets have horns. That's the result of these anti-Soviet ideas. Of course, all this was a long time ago.

And how would all this be affected by perestroika?

If we were stronger and more prosperous, we would fear such things much less. We know that America is wealthier and most people live better there.

So where are we at today? There were five summit meetings between President Reagan and President Gorbachev, including one in Washington and one in Moscow. Our leaders signed the INF agreement to remove all intermediate range missiles from Europe. Many new talks are underway, including ones about major cuts in strategic and conventional weapons. Now there is the Bush administration in Washington. Are you optimistic about the future of U.S.–Soviet relations?

I am hopeful, even optimistic, but I am also a realist. I see many promising opportunities, but also dangers. First of all, there are many illusions in the West, especially in the United States. Some people, in your ruling circles, say that perestroika is a renunciation of socialism. It is not. Perestroika is the further development and strengthening of socialism. When this American illusion collapses, who knows how those people will react? They also say that our new approaches in foreign policy are an indication that we are retreating, giving in to resurgent American power. To interpret our actions in this way would be to make a serious, dangerous mistake.

We are calling for civilized relations between our two countries based on mutual security, intelligence, and common sense. There are signs of a positive response from the West and from the United States. But are your ruling circles ready to treat us as equals? They are trying to block the Soviet Union's admission to the General Agreement on Tariffs and Trade. Sometimes they flex their muscles. They send warships into our territorial waters. They continue to hold an annual "Captive Nations" week. We sign a new treaty, and then they produce a new load of rhetoric about what a devil the Soviet Union is. If the Soviet Union conducted itself in this way toward the United States, would you, Stephen Cohen and Katrina vanden Heuvel, feel that we were treating you as equals? You can't sign an agreement with a partner with one hand and smear him with dirt with the other. This kind of politics will sooner or later create contradictions. And so, I ask, is the United States ready for a serious, stable, constructive, equal relationship with the Soviet Union? I hope so, but I don't know. I want to be realistic.

And I don't say all this as propaganda. I am just pondering the realities of Soviet–American relations and trying to answer your question as a patriot of my country. Certainly, the meetings between President Reagan and President Gorbachev opened up many long-term prospects. The INF treaty, the first in the history of mankind to abolish an entire class of weapons, is a precedent whose significance cannot be overestimated. We may be approaching an intellectual breakthrough in matters related to international security.

But to be honest, and I put my hand on my heart, would these new possibilities have appeared had it not been for the new thinking and approaches of the Soviet leadership and our willingness not to react to petty stings and hurts? No, they would not have. And the proof is in the fact that so many influential Americans still say that we are just yielding to American power. I have the impression that the number of Americans who favor normal relations with the Soviet Union is growing, but I honestly don't know if your ruling circles are ready. We still see, for example, an old scenario. They took one step with the INF treaty, now they can't decide if they want to take another step toward nuclear disarmament or put more pressure on the Soviet Union.

What is the basic, underlying problem?

The whole problem is a lack of trust. We don't trust you, just as you don't trust us. Somehow this mistrust must be overcome. But trust isn't a philanthropic favor bestowed by one side on another. It's a mutual process. And if we don't negotiate as equals, nothing will come of it. We don't want to instruct anybody, but we don't want anyone to instruct us.

You know, you Americans are an amazing people. You're sort of simple and open—a little naive, a little pessimistic, a little sentimental, kind, somewhat egotistical. You're a good people. But most of you have this ever so tiny element of good-natured arrogance—the sense that you are the strongest and richest of all. I'd like to know why people in Washington think so stubbornly that all roads should lead to Washington, as they once led to Rome. The result of this attitude is that our talks don't always work out.

I do not mean that either side must abandon its own character or give up its beliefs and principles. But it cannot impose them forcibly on the other side. You can't consider yourself to be entirely right, while the other side is absolutely to blame for everything. We have to build stable relations in all areas on the basis of what unites us and what could unite us, not on what divides us. We have to reduce or eliminate common dangers, and we have to realize our special responsibility for the fate of the entire world. Progress in U.S.–Soviet relations is the key to avoiding the possibility of a nuclear apocalypse. That is what we mean by the new thinking. And it really is new.

As Americans, it is interesting to hear your description of the American character. Would we be the same if the Soviet Union did not exist?

You would be worse. We restrain you a little, bring you back ever so slightly to your senses and to the realities of life. But please understand, I am not a pessimist about our relations. I'm a realist. When I discuss the problems and obstacles, I do so with sincere regret. I would like to see a less mixed picture, but one has to go forward with his eyes open. Maybe I am also a little naive, but I think Americans are also pragmatists. When you understand that we are not going to attack you, and you say, well, we aren't going to attack the Soviet Union, there will be a different attitude. You'll say, I don't give a hang how you live or what you do in your country. And then these Cold War attitudes will diminish.

Anyway, I am convinced that in the end our two countries cannot escape a normal, working relationship. There's nowhere for us to escape to. Objective trends are leading us to it. And the sooner we acknowledge the need for that new relationship and achieve it, the less we will lose in the end. Both sides have weighty obligations in this respect. Both sides need new thinking and a perestroika in their foreign policies.

GEORGI SMIRNOV

Restructuring the "Citadel of Dogmatism"

THE CENTRAL COMMITTEE'S Institute of Marxism-Leninism has long
been known as the main "citadel of dogmatism"—guardian of Soviet ideological and historical orthodoxy and watchdog over the party's closed archives. In January 1987, Georgi Lukich Smirnov, until then Gorbachev's
personal aide for ideology, was appointed director of the institute, clearly
with the mission of dismantling dogmas going back to the Stalin era. A
philosopher by training, director of the Academy of Sciences Institute of
Philosophy from 1983 to 1985, and a candidate member of the Central
Committee since 1976, Smirnov worked for many years in the Central
Committee apparatus. Under his directorship, the Institute of Marxism-
Leninism has been dramatically transformed into an outpost of perestroika. It has become the scene of freewheeling debates and the source of
sharply revisionist articles about Soviet history and ideology, many of them
written by young people recruited by Smirnov and espousing ideas condemned as heresy only a few years ago. Despite the institute's staid granite
aura, Smirnov himself is a loquacious, earthy man with a folksy sense of
humor and outlook on life.

I'M ONE OF the very few men of my generation, those of us born around
1922–24, who survived World War II. I was born in 1922 in the Ok-
tyabrsky region, 180 kilometers south of Stalingrad [now Volgograd]. I
come from a Cossack peasant family. After World War I and the Revolution, my father became a tailor and eventually director of a children's
clothing factory. My mother was a worker. I graduated from high
school on the day before the German invasion, June 21, 1941. When I
woke up on the 22nd, after all the fun and dancing, the war had begun.
I've always had trouble with my eyes, so I wasn't in the army. But most
of my friends served, and few of them came back.

During the Nazi occupation, I worked in a plant and in the Komsomol [Young Communist League] underground. We were liberated on December 29, 1942. It remains the happiest day in my life. I still remember when I first heard those good old Russian curse words and someone calling, "Mother, mother," somewhere out in the night. I joined the party in 1943, after the Battle of Stalingrad, and became a party functionary. I worked as a secretary of a Komsomol district committee in the city of Kotelnikovo, not too far from Rostov, and then of a Komsomol regional committee. After the war, when I already had three children, I began my historical and philosophical studies. I graduated from the pedagogical institute in Stalingrad and from a party school in Saratov. Then I studied here in Moscow, in the Philosophy Department of the Academy of Social Sciences from 1953 to 1957, the years of the Khrushchev thaw.

In 1957 I was offered a job in the Central Committee apparatus, as a lecturer in the Department of Propaganda. You had to have my qualifications to hold the job, which was to give speeches around the country. It was a very interesting time, those years under Khrushchev, and I got to travel all over the country. I'm a rare case. I've worked at the Central Committee three different times, the first from 1957 to 1962.

Many people in this book say that the Twentieth Party Congress in 1956, where Khrushchev gave his so-called secret speech against Stalin's rule, was one of the most important events of their life.

We are all children of the Twentieth Party Congress. For those of us who were raised under Stalin and who were in the party, it had a powerful impact on our views. But even before the congress our attitudes toward Stalin varied. For example, a friend of mine, the second secretary of the Komsomol district committee where I had been first secretary, was sentenced to seven years in jail for telling critical jokes about Stalin. Stalin's authority was enormous by the end of the war, but we weren't a uniformly Stalinist generation. Some of us had been raised with critical views going back to the 1920s, to the old Bolsheviks, to literature that later disappeared. I don't want to exaggerate our anti-Stalinist mood at the time, but we sensed that Lenin's ideas and treatment of people had been different. By the time I joined the Komsomol in 1938, the worst mass repressions were ending. We accepted what we were taught in school. But I remember wondering how people like Trotsky and Bukharin could have been enemies of the people, as they were called, during the Revolution and Civil War. But life went on in its own way, the threat of war was already hanging over us, and we were already singing the song: "If tomorrow there's war/ And tomorrow we march,/ We'll be ready to march today."

The Stalin era was complex. But I felt after the Twentieth Congress, and I feel today, that for all his wartime achievements, Stalin did enormous harm to the idea of socialism, and we must feel great shame for the crimes committed under him.

In an article in Pravda, *back on March 13, 1987, criticizing measures taken by the Brezhnev leadership after Khrushchev's removal in 1964, you were one of the first officials to speak positively of him, at least implicitly, after twenty years. Now Khrushchev is being praised by many people, while Brezhnev is denounced, but you seem to have initiated this reconsideration.*

I've thought a lot about what happened in October 1964, and why. At that time, people felt the need to end Khrushchev's endless, erratic experiments, but they were also frightened by the process of democratization that he had begun in the party and state apparatus, albeit very unsystematically. The new leaders reversed certain democratic norms that had been put in the party rules, for example. They preferred stable, previously tested forms of centralized administration and the status quo in general. Eventually they froze the process of reform. Everybody now agrees with that, but, yes, my *Pravda* article caused quite a stir.

By the way, have a look at my article in the Central Committee journal *Kommunist*, back in November 1964, where I worked as an editor of the philosophy section from 1962 to 1965. The article discussed the need for more reforms—more mass participation in government, more commodity-market relations, more decentralized economic management. The chief editor thought the same way so my article passed easily through the censorship. Even now when I show the article to colleagues, they say those reforms are still necessary today. Those were the ideas of the Khrushchev era, they were in the air, and many people shared them. I was just a vehicle for the ideas. I'm a little embarrassed even mentioning the article to you.

After Khrushchev was removed, when did the situation change so that such reforms could no longer be carried out or even proposed?

The situation changed very gradually at first, not very noticeably. It was clear only when the 1965 economic reform was in effect killed within a year or a year and a half. Apparently, some of the leaders began to dislike the reform, even though our leading economists today, such as Leonid Abalkin and Abel Aganbegyan, say that it produced real achievements in the growth rate and national income.

And yet, despite the new situation, you returned to work in the Central Committee under Brezhnev.

Yes, but it wasn't like you think. In 1965 it still seemed that changes were possible. They were gathering a new staff at the Central Committee, and there was a lot of work to be done. I had an ability to write and speak, so they made me head of a lecturer group. Later I headed a group of consultants to the Department of Propaganda and then became assistant to the head of the department. I worked with Aleksandr Yakovlev. He was the first deputy chairman and I was the deputy chairman. After he was sent off to Canada as ambassador in 1973, I replaced him as first deputy chairman. But you know, I just wasn't happy there. During his first years as leader, Brezhnev had a lot of energy and a desire to improve things. Later he adapted to the existing situation and routines. For example, there was a Central Committee plenum that sharply criticized the economy, and a year later yet another, but nothing changed. By the third one, everyone was sick of it. Instead, there were lots of illusionary slogans.

In 1985, when Gorbachev became general secretary, you were appointed his personal adviser for ideology. When did you first meet him?

I first got to know Mikhail Sergeevich from afar. When he was first secretary of the Stavropol Party Committee and I was working in the Central Committee Department of Propaganda, we spoke many times on the telephone. But I met him in person only when he moved to Moscow to be a Central Committee secretary in 1978.

What does an adviser on ideology to the Soviet leader do?

I advised the general secretary on cultural and ideological affairs, all the things I had been involved with since 1953. I didn't handle all these questions. There's a Central Committee department and secretary for ideological matters.

Why should a Soviet leader need an ideological adviser? Presumably, he already knows Marxist-Leninist theory and ideology.

An adviser doesn't teach the leader the basics of Marxism. His job is to implement the leader's ideas and goals, to study materials, evaluate proposals, and present him with reports. It could be anything involving ideology—history, relations with the intelligentsia, with artistic unions, with individual writers who might come to see me for consultation or advice.

It was extremely interesting working with Mikhail Sergeevich. The situation had been very difficult toward the end of Brezhnev's life. Some sensible things had been written for Brezhnev, and his speeches weren't foolish. But nothing changed in policy or practice. When Gorbachev became general secretary, he was determined to reopen all policy questions. There was a mood of renewal and great enthusiasm at the Central Committee.

As director of the Institute of Marxism-Leninism, and as a specialist in this field, how would you define perestroika?

Both Marx and Lenin said the socialist revolution is not a single act but a long process that requires constant renewal. The revolution, which can only end with full-fledged socialism, rejects the prerevolutionary order but also that which becomes obsolete or deformed during the course of the revolution itself. In that sense, perestroika is the continuation of the revolution that began in October 1917. It is a radical discarding of things created under Stalin—of Stalin's concept of socialism and of the stagnation that developed under Brezhnev.

Let me give you an example of Stalin's concept of socialism. He said that in contrast to capitalism, under socialism people's needs must always exceed production. Such a so-called law would mean that socialism would never satisfy people's needs. We reject that concept. Or take Stalin's statement in the early 1930s that we lagged behind the West but we must catch up in ten or fifteen years or be crushed. That was a political statement, not a scientific one. Of course, we had to make a leap at that time or we wouldn't have been able to cope with Hitler's tanks. And the tanks we built needed mechanics. Therefore, however much you curse the collectivization of the peasantry in 1929–33, we trained millions of such mechanics, who came from the collective farms.

But I don't understand why repression was needed on such a massive scale during collectivization, or the physical extermination of all the former party oppositionists in the 1930s, long after they had ceased to be oppositionists. For me, that's an enigma. Recently I've been working on these questions so I now understand the terror better than I did a few years ago. But it is all so complicated and controversial. Take Rybakov's novel, *Children of the Arbat*. It contains some historical inaccuracies, but its portrayal of Stalin's psychology provides something of a key to those events and much food for thought. Now, of course, so many materials and details have been published on Stalin that any literate person interested in politics knows more about Stalin than Stalin knew about himself. It's said that victors are not judged. Well, in the Soviet Union they are now being judged, and how they are being judged!

Under your directorship, the Institute of Marxism-Leninism, which used to be so conservative, seems to have become the center of anti-Stalinism.

I wouldn't attribute such an important role to myself. The Communist Party has played a major role by steering discussion in this direction, and Gorbachev's speeches have been decisive. They stimulate, enrich, and provide new impetuses. Anyway, our institute doesn't have to be the center of anti-Stalinism. There are centers of anti-Stalinism in every institute. But we do important work, especially in the area of party history. We want to clean out all the Stalinist filth in our history.

As you review the Stalinist past, what is the most controversial subject—collectivization, the Great Terror of the 1930s, the war?

The terror is now the least controversial because Stalin's personal role in it has been revealed. Previously, people often said that Stalin didn't know what was happening, that he was lied to by the heads of the NKVD [political police], by Genrikh Yagoda, Nikolai Yezhov, and Lavrenti Beria, and so forth. But from everything that has now been published, it is obvious that from the beginning to the end, from the first arrests in the 1930s to the last arrests in the early 1950s, the personal initiative and directions came from Stalin. There's no escaping this conclusion.

If perestroika is about getting rid of Stalin's legacy, glasnost must be essential.

Yes, glasnost about the past and about the present. By the way, I once said, back at the Twenty-Fourth Party Congress in 1971, there's nothing cheaper than widespread information—I didn't use the word glasnost, but it's the same thing—and nothing we need more. Broad and systematic information about everything, about all the activities of administrative and government agencies, about decisions that have been made and have not been made, about decisions that have and have not been carried out, about why people are removed from their posts, about disasters.

We put ourselves in a ridiculous position. If an airplane crashed in the United States, we gave detailed information about it. If a plane crashed here, nothing. That wasn't in the interests of the Central Committee or the country. It was a victory for our domestic aviation agency, whose bosses didn't want anything bad said about their work. It was the same in all the bureaucracies. The minute a critical newspaper article appeared about some television program, the chairman of the State

Committee on Television and Radio would run to me at the Department of Propaganda to fuss and fume. I'd say to him, why are you all worked up? You're on the air with three different channels many hours each day. Is nothing foolish ever put on during that time? Newspaper people are just trying to help. He sort of understood, but he still didn't like the criticism. I remember another case of an uproar when a *Pravda* article portrayed the chairman of a small village Soviet as a drunkard. What bureaucratic protests!

Maybe this is an old Russian bureaucratic tradition?

Maybe it's Russian, maybe it's Asiatic. Here's the thing. Your country was never in conditions of historic encirclement, but for many years our country was. We were being threatened either by the Entente or by the Axis powers, by world capitalism, which didn't like the emergence of a mighty socialist state with its own messianic views, as you like to say. Meanwhile, our backward country had to make an economic and cultural leap forward. Three quarters of the population were illiterate. It cost us a lot to achieve this. And so there was all this vigilance on our part, the notion that our borders had to be locked up tight. That there had to be unity, that everything had to be held tight in one fist. That was the kind of psychology that existed here. Read Aleksandr Bek's novel *The New Appointment*. It's a kind of grotesque characterization, but very close to the truth. There really were such top Stalinist officials who didn't want to know anything other than their job and their goal. But what if there hadn't been people like that?

And so a certain psychology took shape under these conditions. That we had to do everything to strengthen the state and the people. We had to provide culture, and we did. We had to provide food, and we did. We had to clothe ourselves somehow or other, raise the next generation and give them an education—these children of workers and peasants, from whose ranks I personally came. We are everywhere. As the song says, "All of us came from the people. The family of labor's own children."

So it's not just a bureaucratic point of view. It's the psychology of a country that's always been on guard, that took an extremely defensive attitude, that had a very great need for unity. Even today, when Soviet tourists go abroad, they are constantly on alert against provocations.

Does that mean that everything had to be done exactly as it was done under Stalin? No. It was different under Lenin. A civil war went on in 1918–21, yet every year there was a party congress. Under Stalin, more and more time elapsed between congresses and Central Committee plenums, and eventually they virtually stopped altogether. Recently I told a meeting of propagandists, "Whoever fears democratization fears the people themselves." A person objected, "But the war forced us to put restrictions on democracy!" I answered, "The war ended in 1945." And so today we must develop democracy. We proceed from the assumption that we can allow ourselves today what we could not allow ourselves thirty years ago.

And yet, the Soviet Communist Party and the Soviet government have always claimed to have some kind of democracy—under Stalin, Khrushchev, and Brezhnev.

The fact remains that state and party democratic institutions did not work under Stalin's personality cult, the administrative-command system, or bureaucratism. In 1936 Stalin introduced a cunning constitution under which there appeared to be real elections. But it was the purest formality. Everybody was appointed. Even after Stalin, officials abused their positions. In full view of society, crooks operated on a scale that stuns us. That means we did not have the democracy we needed. That is why we have introduced elections, and multi-candidate elections, everywhere—in the factories, soviets, the party. Well, not everywhere. I am appointed, not elected. But maybe one day we'll also have an election for the directorship of the Central Committee's Institute of Marxism-Leninism.

The Nineteenth Party Conference adopted various political reforms that are supposed to lead to democratization, but some of your own intellectuals are worried about some of the provisions. For example, the decision that the party secretary at each level, from Gorbachev at the top to local party bosses, will also be head of the soviet at that level. Doesn't this provision conflict with another slogan of democratization, "All power to the soviets"?

We hope that the conference established democratic forms and guarantees that will be working reliably within a decade. As for the relationship between party committees and the soviets, this is a complicated matter and we have our own disagreements about it. On the one hand, it is normal that if a party comes to power the party's political leader heads the government. On the other hand, you might say that because we have only one party this isn't quite democratic. But here's the problem. We want the soviets to have real power, as the revolution and the constitution promised. In fact, however, it was the party that had the power, so everyone went to the party committee, not to the soviets, to have their problems dealt with. The party took on everything at all levels and started to choke from it all, like a drowning man whose lungs fill with water. That is Stalin's legacy, not Lenin's. Lenin wanted the party to be a political vanguard. In order to give social, economic, and political powers back to the soviets, we are making the party secretary head of the soviet. Otherwise, all these powers will remain with the party committee. Now the party will restrict itself to work with cadres, ideology, and so forth. Well, that is what we are hoping for, but life will tell.

Why does the Gorbachev leadership say that perestroika means "more socialism." The Soviet Union has already existed for more than seventy years, and it has claimed to have had socialism since the mid-1930s. Indeed, under Brezhnev, it was called "developed" or mature socialism.

Well, for one thing, we have an unfair distribution of material goods and a poor relationship between a person's work and what a person earns. I remember how Brezhnev once got concerned about the wages of the women who sweep the streets. So their wages were raised. But then people in the government slapped themselves on the head and said: "What have we done? We've raised the lowest levels of wages. Now engineers, doctors, and teachers are making about the same as a cleaning woman. What a mess. Why study to become an engineer if you can make almost the same amount as a street cleaner?" This is a violation of socialist principles. And is it really socialism to bureaucratize all forms of economic management? Not according to Lenin, who wanted local and individual initiative and who feared an administrative bureaucracy. Bureaucratization was just barely beginning, yet even then Lenin saw it as the worst enemy of Soviet socialism.

You might say that only private ownership can permit local initiative, but in the United States you have very large monopolies. Corporate managers are not usually the owners, and yet they are given plenty of leeway to work. So why can't our government give directors of state-owned enterprises more managerial rights—the right to control much larger sums, to hire and fire people. A director is so limited now that he can't even change the wage fund. That's not socialism. That's pure Russian foolishness.

You and others, including Gorbachev, have said perestroika became necessary because a "pre-crisis situation" existed in the Soviet Union. Was the situation really that bad?

Yes, it was. The rate of growth had fallen sharply, modern industrial technology was not being incorporated, and directors were bound and tied by the plan. There were also many social problems, including shortages and corruption. We built a lot of housing compared to the prewar level. We moved people out of barracks and cellars, so to say. But your "Voice of America" rightly criticized us for still having so many communal apartments. And what would have happened if we had continued to lag behind in all these areas? That kind of situation is fraught with economic, social, and political consequences, grave ones.

By the late 1970s, things became acutely worse. Meanwhile, there was a kind of political and practical feebleness on the part of the leadership that also was a result of insufficient democracy. It's not true that none of these problems were ever discussed. If you read our newspapers of that time attentively, you'll see there was criticism of this and that. Even Brezhnev criticized our economic performance. But no one saw any way out. The leadership lacked the intellectual capacity to make an evaluation, formulate solutions, and act.

Many Western observers believe that because so many serious problems have existed here for so long, Soviet citizens grew very cynical about Marxism-Leninism and socialism, especially in the 1970s. Not only ordinary people but also officials.

I remember a certain Stephen Cohen, an American Sovietologist, who wrote several years ago that the Soviet system should not be viewed as some kind of monolith where everything is the same color and everyone thinks alike. Many people did become cynical, but many did not. For example, there was the first secretary of the Stavropol party organization, Mikhail Sergeevich Gorbachev, a young party official with a university education, who could not help but think seriously about what was going on in our country. Read the confidential memorandum he wrote to the Central Committee, in May 1978, on the condition of agriculture. It was recently published for the first time. You will see what thoughts nested like birds in his head. And he wasn't the only one.

After all, who are the officials of the Central Committee and of the party? They are human beings who have seen an awful lot. Are they just bureaucrats? Didn't they also feel and suffer for their country? They knew and experienced more than many others, and as a result they developed a negative, critical attitude toward what existed. Soviet writers and journalists also held such views, as did many young people, who tend to be very critical-minded in general.

Was the cynicism about socialism that did exist one of the reasons behind the resurgence of orthodox religion and Russian nationalism?

There's a saying, "A holy place doesn't remain empty." Or as Lenin remarked when he was still young, ideology does not tolerate a vacuum. But don't exaggerate the attraction of religion for our young people. Go to the churches and see for yourself. Nationalism is a more complicated phenomenon. Perestroika is the self-criticism of socialism. And as this develops, it naturally arouses nationalist sentiments in various republics, such as Latvia, Estonia, and Lithuania, which were once independent. But at the root of these nationalist problems are incorrect political decisions made in the past.

Speaking of the Baltic republics, some of the manifestos and leaders of the peoples fronts that have emerged there call for considerable independence from Moscow and even, it seems, from the Soviet Union. Some of them are taking on characteristics of a political party. Does this worry you?

I don't think so. I think most of their members reject extreme positions and seek to carry out perestroika in a more coherent and thorough way. They don't want to babble, they want practical results. But we may have to talk about this again in the future, when we see how things develop.

Your idea that extreme tendencies generated in the republics by perestroika will not prevail seems to be a kind of political wager on the center.

I'm not a politician, so I'm not wagering anything. But why not count on the center, on the basic mass's desire to realize perestroika? These extreme currents in favor of separation are in opposition to democratic movements in the Baltic republics.

That's far from clear, but let's go back to the question of aggressive forms of Russian nationalism here at the center of the Soviet Union. We see it in the Pamyat Society and even in your official journals Nash sovremennik *[Our Contemporary] and* Molodaya gvardiya *[Young Guard].*

I'm not going to sit here and tell you that kind of Russian nationalism has no influence. That would be stupidity on my part. But if you take *Nash sovremennik*, its line isn't anti-Soviet. It just doesn't like people who seem to be scornful of the Russian past and Russian culture. More generally, though, perestroika is rallying those who really care about our country. Even people who left the country are now impressed by our reforms. They are inclined to say, "That's what we said, what we were for, before we left."

Now they are impressed. You see, as perestroika proceeds, Marxism-Leninism will renew itself and become more popular. It will prove that it is not a system of dogmas. Incidentally, we Communists are not the only ones who suffer from dogmatism. For all your so-called freedom of discussion and opinion, there is no less dogmatism in the West.

Maybe so, but with us it doesn't take the form of an official ideology.

Yes, but in your own special way you have one, too.

If perestroika depends so much on a struggle against dogmatism and on the renewal of Soviet ideology, your Institute of Marxism-Leninism must have a special role to play.

It must play a special role, and as I told you, first of all in reconsidering the history of the party. Above all we have to go back to the 1920s and 1930s and learn how and why the "braking mechanism," as we call it, took shape. We have to learn why Stalin was able to impose on the country his views of administration and the role of the party. That's why we attribute special importance to Gorbachev's statement about Stalin's terror: "We cannot forget or forgive what happened in 1937–38." We want to know why nothing came of the socialist alternatives discussed in the 1920s. You know as well as I do, Nikolai Bukharin is very relevant here. We have exonerated him of all the charges for which he was tried and executed in 1938, and now we are publishing and reexamining his writings of the 1920s, particularly those about NEP. That doesn't mean, of course, that we will rehabilitate anything like Trotskyism. Everyone understands, including you Sovietologists, that Trotskyism was different not only from Stalinism but also from Leninism.

No, that's not so clear. There are various Western opinions about Trotsky's ideas and role, but no serious person disputes that he was a major leader of your party and a very important historical figure. It is hard to understand why he, too, should not be rehabilitated.

I agree. It is necessary for us to show that Trotsky existed as a leader of the Revolution and as the person whom Lenin called "the most capable member of the Central Committee." But our historians must also show all the times Trotsky was mistaken and opposed Lenin.

You see, everything that happened has to be researched and thought about all over again. Even those of us of the older generation, most of the active officials today, know about these events only from Stalinist books. And the majority of scholars at other institutes had no personal experience in these complex, dramatic periods of our history. We will have to open up the archives, but that will take time. We will have to change the rules governing access to them. We will restore the truth. I am not afraid to use what sounds like a cliché to you: We will adopt a Leninist position toward all this. Lenin was never afraid to reject mistakes and untruths, even if he had to use his full authority against the Central Committee.

And yet, there are people, serious party intellectuals here in Moscow, who say that the Institute of Marxism-Leninism has always been a "citadel of dogmatism" and therefore cannot play a leading role in perestroika.

Oh, it was the historian Yuri Afanasyev who told you that, wasn't it? He said the same thing to us here, at a conference. Well, God be with him. The institute has a long history and has had a lot of problems, but I was given the job of restructuring it. Just wait and see.

When you were appointed director in January 1987, were the other members of the staff ready for a perestroika at the institute?

Of course not, but in two years we have brought in eighty new people and more than seventy have left. All the department heads now are new people. You should see our meetings. It's a pleasure to be there, listening to the slashing speeches and debates. Serious work is underway—a multivolume history of the Communist Party, a series of probing historical articles for the newspaper *Pravda*, a new full edition of Lenin's work. By the way, the subject index of the previous edition is repulsive. It didn't even reflect the nature of Lenin's thought.

Who are these eighty new people, where did they come from?

Most of them are of the new generation. The oldest were born in 1941. They came from Moscow institutes and party schools, but also from the provinces—from Latvia and the Ukraine, for example. It was a conscious decision on my part to find creative and courageous young people who could write well and think for themselves. I am happy with most of them, but not yet with the overall situation. Perestroika at the institute has to move more quickly and consistently.

You and Gorbachev have said that in the past, particularly under Stalin and Brezhnev, the official ideology became dogmatic. Now you say the official ideology is against dogmatism. Maybe there is something wrong with having an official ideology.

Your question should be put in a more sophisticated way. Every major doctrine—Christianity, Buddhism, Islam—develops dogmas. Lenin himself warned that there is creative Marxism and there is dogmatic Marxism. But we ourselves canonized and dogmatized Lenin, while ignoring his creativity. Now we are in an era of developing Marxism again. If I may say so, I wrote something quite good. By the way, I write my own things. You can see the callous on my finger. I wrote, "Not back to Lenin, but forward to Lenin." We went backward from Lenin. For example, Stalin made it a dogma that socialism had to be based primarily on state economic ownership, but Lenin said socialism was an association of independent cooperatives and their members. Now we are encouraging the creation of real, free cooperatives. Why did Stalin need this dogma that everything had to be statized? In order to run everything with an iron hand, to watch over everything as if it were in a fish bowl. That kind of economic system doesn't work. Things have to be loosened up so that Gosplan and a hundred Moscow ministries don't do all the thinking and managing. Let hundreds of thousands of managers think for themselves. Stalin also abandoned Lenin's concept of market relations and his call for a grass-roots democratic apparatus to keep an eye on bureaucratic agencies. Or take another example of how our ideology was dogmatized. Stalin was supposed to be a great authority on nationality questions. He declared that the Soviet Union's nationalities question had been solved. And yet it was obvious all along that there were problems. With so many different nationalities, how could there not have been? So now we are like fish out of water, floundering around. These are real problems. There's nothing unnatural or terrible about them. It's just that now we must use our intelligence to solve them. I could give you a stack of other examples.

In politics, where great reforms like perestroika encounter widespread dogmatism, there must be powerful opposition to reform.

A political struggle is underway here. Perestroika is a clash between different points of view. But there is no organized anti-perestroika opposition. Some people don't like the way perestroika is being conducted, for example, Boris Yeltsin [who was removed as Moscow party boss in 1987 and as a candidate Politburo member in 1988]. Or Yuri Afanasyev, who wrote in *Pravda* that he favors a more radical kind of perestroika, but he didn't say exactly what kind. He's keeping it a secret for now. I have nothing against Afanasyev, but many people are annoyed by his carping. And when he speaks out, there's no end in sight, as they say in the Don region, where I come from. But that's not anti-perestroika opposition. Or even take Nina Andreyeva, who published an anti-perestroika article in our *Sovetskaya Rossiya* newspaper back in March 1988. Later she told a Yugoslav newspaper that 5,000 people sent her letters of support. But letters aren't organized opposition. And Soviet television showed some delegates voting against Central Committee proposals at the Nineteenth Party Conference. But if a regional party secretary votes against a proposal, is that opposition—if twenty votes were cast against me at a party meeting? Anything can be called opposition, but it isn't serious.

Maybe not, but we have the impression that quite a few Soviet citizens are seriously opposed to democratization and glasnost on the grounds that these are dangerous reforms.

They are afraid we are losing our unity. They are used to having one person decide and everyone vote for it in unison. These are individual moods, psychology, not organized groups. Of course, the "braking mechanism" as a system still exists, so there are carriers of its viewpoints clustered in various organizations. They can slow down perestroika. But what really hinders us is backwardness and incompetence.

Let's talk about another aspect of dogmatism and democratization, one that relates directly to such an exalted official institution as the Institute of Marxism-Leninism. The Soviet Communist Party has a long tradition of what it calls the party line. In the past, that has usually meant one orthodox point of view or way of doing things. And the party line was imposed on all party members and even on society. You say, and it is evident in the Soviet press, that perestroika is a clash of views. Gorbachev even speaks of the need for "socialist pluralism." Does this mean there will no longer be a party line or what you call in Russian partiinost—partyness?

You are trying to get me to say that we need two or three political parties.

How many parties do you need?

We need one good party with a general line that is intelligent, not blockheaded. We now understand *partiinost* in a different way. It means a commitment to the interests of the working class and of socialism, but it should encompass various approaches and points of view. In the past, a party official was expected to act simply as a functionary of a higher party committee. We are renouncing this. We are giving party members a chance to conduct themselves in broader, more critically minded ways.

Your answer is very general. Take the example of Professor Georgi Smirnov, director of the Institute of Marxism-Leninism, and Professor

Yuri Afanasyev, director of the Moscow State Historical Archive Institute. Both of you are members of the Communist Party, but you disagree on fundamental issues. Are both of you functioning within the parameters of partiinost?

Yes, in general. Comrade Afanasyev hasn't renounced socialism. He just believes that Lenin did not have a developed concept of socialism, and I think that Lenin did. He sees Lenin somewhat differently from the way I see Lenin. It wouldn't be pleasant for me to be in the same party with someone who says the October 1917 Revolution was a mistake. Let him go to the Democratic Union [a group of dissidents who in 1988 announced the formation of a party of that name, many of whom reject the Communist Party takeover in 1917]. Of course, that is not Yuri Afanasyev's position. He does seem to think, however, that what exists in the Soviet Union today cannot be called socialism. I believe that we do have socialism—a socialism that was badly deformed and suffered great losses as a result of Stalin's rule, a socialism that is not yet fully built, a socialism that needs democracy and the release of economic initiative. But socialism is at the basis of what exists here.

In the Soviet context, your disagreement with Afanasyev is a serious one. Evidently he wants to persuade people that perestroika must be very radical, that Soviet socialism has yet to be created.

There is a group of Soviet political writers and scholars who argue that socialism doesn't exist in our country. Well, if we don't have it, then it does not exist in Hungary, Germany, Czechoslovakia, and so forth. Then there is no world socialism. And if this is so, why are you always building rockets against socialism?

You know, nowadays you can even find in our journals some articles rejecting Marxism and socialism on the grounds that their ideas were responsible for Stalin's crimes. But why should socialism be judged by Stalin's crimes and deformations of Marxism-Leninism? It is perestroika, not Stalinism, that reveals the true nature of socialism. That is what we mean when we say that perestroika means more socialism, that socialism is unthinkable without democracy, and that democracy is unthinkable without pluralism and glasnost.

Maybe the healthiest resolution of this dispute would be to conclude that the idea of socialism is simply the quest for a good society and let the quest always continue. That way the Soviet government would always try to improve its system and the lives of its citizens. Maybe we should say the same thing about capitalism.

It's a great idea, but you already have capitalism, no doubt about it. You even restructured capitalism in the 1930s, under Franklin Roosevelt. You carried out reforms that improved the lives of working people. Who knows what would have happened had you not done so.

It still isn't clear what kind of changes you foresee in the Communist Party as a result of perestroika and particularly democratization.

Gorbachev has put it well. We strive for unity, but we recognize that there is a multiplicity of ideas in society and in the party. We can't achieve anything without developing this multiplicity and a competition of minds and talents. This refers to technological inventions and to competition for leadership positions, and it applies inside the party as well. You know what it used to be like? If there were ten places on a party committee, God forbid there should have been an eleventh candidate. Someone would lose, maybe a veteran secretary. Guided by such pragmatic considerations, they always made sure there were the same number of candidates as there were posts to be filled. Today we are increasing the number of candidates.

If there is really going to be so much competition over ideas and elective offices inside the party, maybe you should repeal the 1921 resolution forbidding factions in the party.

That resolution was adopted in very different circumstances, when the party was exhausted from the Civil War and torn apart by discussions. Factions aren't a practical problem today. The question of the resolution hasn't even come up. Anyway, any resolution can be approached creatively. I advise you to concentrate on my statement about the present leadership's understanding of the need for competition inside the party.

Won't any real process of elections inside the party, and in the Soviet system generally, eventually collide with the vast hierarchical system of appointed officials known as the nomenklatura?

Even democratic systems have a mixture of appointment and election. In your country, factory directors are appointed by the company, aren't they? And you also have it in government, in the form of the civil service. It is hard to foresee exactly how all this will work out here. Some officials will be elected, judges, for example, and others will be appointed, as in the army.

But you are really asking me a different question. Western literature is full of misleading concepts about our nomenklatura as some kind of caste of lifelong privileges. Sure, nomenklatura officials have some rights, but also some obligations. And nowadays they're likely to end up beaten half to death in the pages of *Ogonyok*, *Moscow News*, *Izvestia*, and other newspapers. In fact, it takes a long time to become part of the nomenklatura, and a person can be dropped from it very easily. Even in the past, for many people it was limited to two, three, five, or ten years. You have to understand that the party controls political power first of all through cadres. But the nomenklatura isn't a closed caste or class. It's more complex. Of course it has certain bureaucratic interests. An economic minister, for example, wants to protect his ministry's interests and staff, no matter what, even to the detriment of the national interest.

At its highest and most powerful level, the nomenklatura has meant that the central party apparatus in Moscow appointed the most important party secretaries across the country. And under Brezhnev, those appointees held office virtually for life. Gorbachev seems to be proposing a system in which these party positions will be filled from below through elections.

As you see from the steps we have taken in 1988 and 1989, we have started down this road. Let's wait and see where it leads.

Earlier you said that perestroika means "forward to Lenin," but do you really believe that Lenin's ideas and practices, seventy years ago, are adequate for what Gorbachev means by democratization?

In many respects, we can and certainly will go further. We have to look closely at Lenin's concept of socialism, and this will take time. Meanwhile, we need to solve the problem of disarmament. That is more pressing. Once we have disarmament, we'll be able to argue about the problems of democracy.

You may have things backward. Many people in the West feel the need for weapons precisely because the Soviet Union is not democratic.

I understand that. But I believe that today disarmament must take priority over everything else. Otherwise, one of these days we'll be arguing about what is and what is not democratic in the other world.

Even if you are committed to democratizing the Soviet Union, are you certain that the country is ready? Debates about this in the Soviet press, about political culture, seem inconclusive.

It's an important discussion. The level of education and of general culture today is much higher than when Lenin was head of the government, so we have greater potential for developing democracy. But we still don't have a high enough political culture. Look at the way we conduct some of our discussions. For example, a person tries to give a scholar helpful criticism of his dissertation. The scholar may refuse to say hello to him the next day. Or he gets up and says, "This criticism of my dissertation is anti-Marxist and contrary to Leninism." We haven't learned to conduct fruitful debates. Or take glasnost. One factory director has a broad attitude toward glasnost. Having nothing to hide, he provides information. Another director, maybe working next door, won't accept any degree of glasnost. One director recently said, "Elections will take place only over my dead body." He didn't even want work brigade leaders elected by the workers. This reflects a low level of political culture. He's not even cultured enough to understand that it's in his interest to have brigade leaders who can rely on the support of the workers.

Will elections in the factory really be enough to win the support of workers for perestroika? A Moscow taxi driver told us that perestroika is just something for the intelligentsia, not for working people.

You ran into an intelligent man, and his view isn't completely wrong. Of course, taxi drivers are particularly independent people because of their special occupation. Like oldtime coachmen, they're only at the workplace when they pick up or turn in their cabs. But if we would go to a real workplace, say, a factory that makes automobiles or heavy machinery, we'd see great worker interest in the changes taking place there—in elections of their superiors, in their new wage system, in their control over social and cultural benefits. Wages will now depend on how enterprises and worker collectives produce as a unit, so workers can't be indifferent to what is going on. As someone has said about economic perestroika: "We want the workers to bust their humps two or three times harder, but some people still want us to foist directors on them from above. It won't work." That makes good sense. It's based on real relations between people and it's profoundly humane. What we now have to do is eliminate the shortages. People are sick of standing in lines and hunting and hunting for things. In the end, everyone has clothes and food, but so much effort is wasted on this. It's agonizing.

Gorbachev often says that perestroika must be made "irreversible." Does this mean there is a danger it may not last?

If there was no danger of reversion, there would be no need to say perestroika must be made irreversible. There are many dangers, hypothetically speaking. The economic reforms may not produce the results we need, for example. Or factors that brake and resist perestroika may keep people from becoming active and enterprising. The accumulated inertia may be too great. That is why we are worried and determined. You remember when Gorbachev was in Estonia, a big, solidly built worker came up to him and said, "Have you got the guts for all this, Mikhail Sergeevich? We're trying to carry out democratization here. Have you got the guts to see it through, Mikhail Sergeevich?" All of us want perestroika to go faster.

And what is the alternative if perestroika fails?

More stagnation. There is no alternative that could bring good results.

We asked Aleksandr Yakovlev the same question, and he said the only alternative is the death of socialism.

Perhaps he worded it a bit sharply, but I would give you approximately the same answer. Don't forget, though, if the United States and the Soviet Union don't find ways to coexist peacefully as capitalist and socialist systems, we shall all perish. That's why we developed our bold new thinking and overtures to the West.

Are you saying that in the past there were also dogmas in Soviet foreign policy?

Unquestionably, both dogmas and conservatism. I shouldn't be commenting on this, since I'm not a specialist in foreign policy. My colleagues in that field won't understand if I encroach on their area. But as a layman, I'll tell you this. Both sides got themselves into such a labyrinth of disarmament that no one could understand what they were talking about. They gathered in Geneva, or Vienna, or somewhere and seemed to be on an endless treadmill. Gorbachev's great achievement is having made this complex problem accessible and understandable, the property of an enormous international public. I'll tell you something else. If we don't set our ideological differences aside, we will never agree on very much. It doesn't mean we must stop arguing about our ideological views, but they must not prevent us from normalizing political relations.

Many people in the West believe the Soviet Union is to blame for bad relations because you are too ideological.

We are always being accused of being ideologically irreconcilable, dogmatic devils from hell. But now we are coming to you and saying, dear friends, let's resolve these ideological differences in peaceful, non-military ways.

Part of the problem is your cheap propaganda. Some American magazine complained a few years ago, for example, that Lenin wanted to take over Mexico. So I got a phone call. We checked all the archives. Lenin never said such a thing. As for ideology and our thinking, we have a right to change and we are changing, but so must you. You know, back in the 1930s we had great respect for Americans, and you embodied our idea of efficiency. Also during World War II, when we were allies.

That was long ago. Since the war ended we have insisted that you are to blame for our bad relations and you have insisted we are to blame. Maybe there was mutual responsibility.

I agree with that. I don't think we are little doves. Our international affairs people may tell me I'm wrong, but I think that when bilateral relations have reached such an extreme point, responsibility can't lie only on one side. This has to be studied. But it would be best to set aside the question of who was responsible or we'll have more endless disputes and irritations. Both sides have already said enough bad things. We remember Harry Truman saying, in 1941 when he was still a senator, that if Germany is winning the war against Russia, America ought to help Russia, and if Russia is winning, America ought to help Germany—so they will kill each other off. And you remember Khrushchev, who was impulsive, blurting out, "We will bury you." He didn't mean it literally. He was talking about our economic systems, but after thirty years he is still quoted endlessly in the West.

Now, for several years Gorbachev has been saying, Let's set all this aside. Let's do this together, let's do that together. But it doesn't seem to suit many people in the West. If he said something like Khrushchev did, they'd quote him on that forever. But Gorbachev would never say anything like that.

YURI AFANASYEV

"The Agony of the Stalinist System"

YURI NIKOLAYEVICH AFANASYEV *was virtually unknown to Western observers and even to many Soviet intellectuals before he burst on the scene in 1986 as an outspoken crusader for exposing the truth about the Soviet past and especially about the crimes of the Stalin era. Trained as a specialist in French history, he worked in the Komsomol organization and on the editorial board of the Central Committee journal Kommunist before being named rector of the Moscow State Historical Archive Institute in 1986. The institute soon became more than its name suggests—a public forum for lectures on once forbidden subjects and a haven for nonconformist students of history. Afanasyev's radical views and unvarnished statements have made him a special target of attacks by opponents of perestroika and glasnost, particularly by neo-Stalinists. For the same reasons, he is widely admired by young perestroika activists. In 1988, along with Andrei Sakharov, Yevgeny Yevtushenko, and other prominent reformers, Afanasyev was elected to the executive council of the Memorial Society, which has grown from a grass-roots movement to build a monument honoring the victims of Stalin's terror into a nationwide organization advocating radical de-Stalinization of the Soviet system. And in the national multi-candidate elections in 1989, he was elected to the new Congress of People's Deputies.*

I BELONG TO THE unlucky generation or what is usually called the generation of the 1960s. We lost twenty years of our creative potential in the period of stagnation between the fall of Khrushchev and the rise of Gorbachev. The intellectual and ideological stagnation of those years was worse than the economic stagnation. Now we have been given a second chance.

I was born in 1934 in Ulyanovsk, on the Volga River. My mother was a schoolteacher, my father a worker. He's still alive, living on his pension in Ulyanovsk. I confess that, like most of my contemporaries, I was raised a dogmatist. In the early 1950s, when I was studying history at Moscow State University, dogmatism was a kind of religious fanaticism. But I must also say that some of my elderly Russian history professors were wonderful. They were links to the old humanitarian tradition of the intelligentsia. Things were changing by the time I graduated in 1957. Yevgeny Yevtushenko and Andrei Voznesensky, the poets of my generation, were reading to large audiences of young people in institutes and museums around Moscow, and underground tapes of Bulat Okudzhava's songs were playing in every household. It wasn't until the mid-1960s that this thaw begun under Khrushchev came to an end.

In the late 1950s, I wanted to make history, not write it, so I went to Krasnoyarsk, in Siberia, where a hydroelectric power station was being built. I became a secretary of the Komsomol organization there, and later of the district committee. In 1961, while still working in Siberia, I joined the party. For a short time in the early 1960s I worked in the Komsomol Central Committee in Moscow, but in 1968 I started my postgraduate studies in history at the Academy of Social Sciences. I specialized in French history, particularly the history of the French Revolution. As a graduate student, I made several trips to France. I've spent a total of about three and a half years there. After I got my degree, I was appointed a deputy dean of the Komsomol's advanced school and then head of the section on foreign cultures at the Institute of World History, under the USSR Academy of Sciences. In 1980 I became editor of the history section of the Central Committee journal *Kommunist*. In 1986 I took on my present position as rector of the Moscow State Historical Archive Institute.

Since 1986 you have been the most consistently outspoken voice of historical glasnost—of truth about Soviet history. Many people here in Moscow say that you are one of the boldest of the bold, at least among party intellectuals, even recklessly so. And some of them wonder how and why you assumed this role, and who arranged for you to have this large institute as a platform. One explanation we've heard is that you have powerful patrons, even Aleksandr Yakovlev or Gorbachev, and that's the reason for your courage. Another explanation says that you are simply a brave man who has always believed what you now say and who has seized the opportunity to say it.

I'm not going to tell you which is true. It is important for people to speak out and take risks, and I am not alone in doing this. But I won't say that I have no patrons on the Central Committee. Let people think that I do, if it gives me more opportunities to speak the truth about our history. By the way, in some quarters, you can hear another explanation. They say I'm either a Jew or a Mason, or that I've been bought by the Jews.

Some historians insist that you are not qualified to lecture people about Soviet history because your specialty is French history.

My general specialization was French history, but I wrote my doctoral dissertation on the October 1917 Revolution. Moreover, when I think and speak about the history of the Soviet Union, especially about the Stalinist era, I do so as a person who is used to thinking historically and about history generally, not as a dogmatist who made a career writing about the subject.

Other people reproach you for having been a member of the editorial board of Kommunist *in the early 1980s, when it was a very conservative, even reactionary journal.*

When I worked at *Kommunist*, there were lively discussions and constant arguments among the editors. For example, I argued that we ought to publish radical anti-Stalinists like Yevgeny Ambartsumov and Anatoly Butenko, who are so outspoken on behalf of perestroika nowadays. But the overwhelming majority of people working at *Kommunist* at that time were opposed to those kind of views. More generally, though, perestroika has caused many of us to change. I, for example, spent almost twenty-five years puttering around in French history. But as a person I never forgot the elation and hope I felt at the time of the Twentieth Party Congress in 1956 or the great disappointment I felt when all the anti-Stalinist policies begun under Khrushchev collapsed. I'll never forget the creeping counterrevolution and surreptitious restoration of many Stalinist approaches that followed under Brezhnev. Maybe those of us who had that experience of the 1950s and 1960s have seized the present opportunity more actively than have others. I also think the fact that I studied Western historians made me understand just how badly the Soviet historical profession had declined. Of course, even during the 1970s some Soviet historians tried to eliminate the propagandist, rubber-stamp approach to history, but they were crushed organizationally.

Are you saying that you feel no personal responsibility for what happened during the Brezhnev years, even though you occupied official positions in the Komsomol organization and at Kommunist and thus had certain privileges?

I absolutely am not saying that. Along with the majority of the Russian intelligentsia, I was mired in shit during those years. Even those of us who did not personally persecute or harm anyone, and who sincerely wanted changes in the country, bear a heavy responsibility for having been silent. Unlike people like Andrei Sakharov, Aleksandr Solzhenitsyn, and Roy Medvedev, we did not openly or actively fight against what was happening in our country. Therefore, we—and I include myself—must repent for our responsibility.

Unlike you, many professional historians do not seem eager to seize the opportunities to reexamine the Soviet past. You have pointed out elsewhere that it has been the artistic intelligentsia, people like the poet Yevtushenko, the filmmaker Elem Klimov, and the playwright Mikhail Shatrov, who did the groundbreaking work of historical glasnost, not professional historians. Indeed, the sociologist Tatyana Zaslavskaya, whom we also interviewed for this book, in expressing her concern that Soviet men may lack the courage to carry out perestroika, cited historians as an example.

It is unpleasant to hear Zaslavskaya's charge, but it is a fair one. How many established historians have really spoken out since 1985? I can count them on my fingers. And there is so much that must be reexamined and rethought. Until recently, Soviet historians played the role of propaganda's errand boys. Dogmatism and falsification went hand in hand. All this goes back to the early 1930s, when the Stalinist regime grew more and more repressive and undemocratic. As a profession, history discredited itself, and even today, in its present state, it is not prepared to help the party or society find its way. That is why so much has been left to the cultural and artistic intelligentsia. I regret it, but the bitter truth is that history is the most conservative, dogmatic, and doctrinaire field. The party leadership has been calling for perestroika in the historical profession, but despite some changes for the better, historians themselves have been in no hurry to bring one about.

You do not seem to have many supporters among established historians. Does it worry you that there have been so many attacks against you?

I have plenty of opponents, particularly historians who write about the history of the party. No one who exposes stagnation in a profession will get a friendly reaction. Sure the attacks worry me, but they are also gratifying. And you should see the huge number of letters I receive every day—here at the institute and at publications for which I write. Most of them are filled with passionate expressions of support. They come from people I don't know, all kinds of people—military officers, intellectuals, philosophers, economists.

Of all the changes associated with perestroika, none has caused so much controversy as historical glasnost, and not only among intellectuals. Soviet newspapers publish passionate letters almost daily from ordinary readers crying out about historical events, on one side or the other, particularly about events of the Stalin era. Why is the past, and the writing of history, so important today?

As a result of all the lies and omissions of Stalinist historiography, many of which were maintained along with various half-truths during the Brezhnev years, no country and no people has had a history as falsified as ours. As a society we have been in a long, deep mythological dream. And now, as we awake from it and begin to tell the truth about ourselves, it strikes horror in the minds and hearts of many people. But it is absolutely necessary to tell the whole truth. We cannot ensure the success of perestroika without it.

A society cannot live or develop normally without knowing where it came from and what it is. All of the events of the past, all the old Bolsheviks falsely accused of being criminals and killed by Stalin, even the October Revolution itself, must find their true places and voices in our history. Otherwise we will not recognize ourselves when we look in the mirror. People must know about the alternatives of the past, which roads were taken and which were not, and why. After all, history isn't just an academic profession. It is part of our social and ecological psychology. I remember when they changed the names of many of our old cities, my father said, "Yuri, what are they doing? Soon we won't be able to find our way around." Psychologically, this is a serious matter. History is self-awareness and, thus, part of the present and the future. Perestroika seeks to change what now exists, but one of the problems is that we still lack sufficient historical knowledge and awareness to formulate effective policies. That is why historians face such a huge and important task.

In 1988 you set off yet another controversy with your opinions about what now exists, or does not exist, in the Soviet Union. So far as we know, since the mid-1930s no one in official publications has ever challenged the official axiom that socialism exists in your country.

Here too we have no need of half-truths. The usual idea that we have some kind of socialism today, at least some kind of deformed socialism, doesn't hold up to historical scrutiny or logic. We no longer have Stalinism in the top leadership, but we still live in the system Stalin created in the 1930s. If we really believe that socialism is a precious idea, we cannot take an on-the-one-hand and on-the-other-hand approach to that period, as so many people do. We can't say Stalin was both bad and good. We have to recognize the full extent of the so-called deformations he introduced into our life. They affected everything. Stalin repealed NEP, which Lenin saw as a way to socialism. Stalin transformed the Bolshevik Party into some kind of sect and created a huge bureaucratic state apparatus. In the course of collectivization, he enslaved the peasantry and destroyed it as a class. Stalin imposed a regime of discipline on the workers, suppressed the intelligentsia, created millions of prisoners under the control of the NKVD, and built a state on blood and terror. I do not accept this totalitarian course as inevitable, necessary, or socialist. It was counterrevolutionary and it affected the foundations of the Soviet system. We are not dealing with a deformed socialism but with an inhumane, regimented system whose foundations still have not been eradicated. Perestroika must uproot all vestiges of Stalinism from our life. Therefore, half-truths about the past will lead to half-measures today, which will lead to the collapse of our last chance to break out of this terrible situation.

Only conclusions based on the full historical truth can give conscious supporters of perestroika the strength and theoretical approaches to start again on the road to true, democratic socialism. Here I must protest the formula, widespread even among supporters of perestroika, that we can simply return to Lenin, repent, receive his blessings, and move onward. That is a foolish way of thinking, more of a religious idea than a political-historical one. We must return to the basic principles of Lenin's socialism—democracy, humanism, market economics, civil peace, and the rest. But Lenin didn't live long enough to develop a full conception of socialism. He changed his thinking in the early 1920s and had only begun to work out a new model, based on NEP, when he died in 1924. Nor could Lenin have foreseen, almost seventy years ago, all the problems of our time. Could Lenin have imagined, for example, that in 1989 we would still be rationing food and only just learning democracy? We must move forward with Lenin's help, but we will have to find our own solutions to our problems. And we still must work out a full conception of socialism. Here too perestroika means beginning the work of building socialism anew.

It is clear that Gorbachev himself, by insisting that perestroika is a real revolution, raised the question about the actual nature of the Soviet system today. But your answer is exceedingly radical and probably not very good politics. It shocks and outrages many people. It is doubtful that Gorbachev would or could agree with you.

Gorbachev is a politician, not a historian. I believe that we share the same goal. And he has said several times that perestroika is impossible without the full truth about the past. On the question of the nature of the existing Soviet system, however, we have different positions. But my interpretation is based on facts.

Would you agree that Gorbachev's perestroika, of the kind you describe, would not have been possible without the reforms begun by Khrushchev more than thirty years ago?

Yes, to some extent Khrushchev paved the way for the current reforms. At the Twentieth Party Congress he tried to tell the truth for the first time about Stalinism, about the terror and the crimes. As a result, the party and the people began the process of spiritual awakening. Khrushchev also undertook reforms to improve our economic system and the population's standard of living. But Khrushchev was part and parcel of the old system, a complex and equivocal figure. Today we cannot be content with his appraisal of the Stalin cult because he didn't try to analyze the political, economic, social, and spiritual processes that created it. He thought it was enough to get rid of Stalin by pagan methods. He threw Stalin's body out of the Lenin Mausoleum, but you can't eradicate Stalinism that way. I don't think Khrushchev understood the challenge he faced, so the system destroyed him. Still, his achievements are indisputable, and it is good that glasnost has extended to his leadership and that he is no longer a blank spot in our history.

How much historical glasnost has actually been achieved since 1985?

Quite a lot, and officially there are no longer any forbidden zones. Gorbachev is on record as saying that we cannot have too much truth. But there are still many problems and much to be done. I don't agree with the commonly asserted view that there were merely blank spots in our history-writing and we need only to fill them in. Stalinist historiography was one huge blank spot, so our entire history remains to be studied and written.

To do this, we must have access to the archives, which is still a major problem. Archives are needed to restore the nation's collective memory. Various official reports say that 60 percent or more of previously closed archives are now open, but gaining access is a very slow process. Moreover, there is no access to many really interesting archives such as those containing documents on the show trials of the 1930s, on the assassination of Kirov, on the 1939 Ribbentrop-Molotov Pact, on the Katyn massacre. We don't even know which documents and archives were preserved. After all, a regime that murdered millions of people certainly wouldn't have hesitated to destroy pieces of paper.

In many countries, limits are set on how long archives can remain closed and dates specified for when they will be declassified. But we still don't have a law that would guarantee democratic access to archives, though there is much vague discussion about passing one. You can't have democracy without information. Even I, the rector of the Moscow State Historical Archive Institute, am a victim, along with all other historians, of this lack of access. My professors and I teach our students democratic principles of archive access, but we can't shut our eyes to the real situation, and our students know what is going on. So we speak out against the restrictions.

Moreover, there is no real central control or regulation over archives. It's all completely arbitrary. The Ministry of Foreign Affairs, the Ministry of Defense, the Ministry of Internal Affairs, the KGB—all establish their own regulations and each requires different kinds of permission for access. Some republics even have recently adopted resolutions making their archives more inaccessible. And then there are the Communist Party archives, which are kept elsewhere.

But even if we had access to all the archives, glasnost would not automatically be complete. First of all, the result of all those years of censorship and dogmatism was not just taboo subjects but the exclusion of whole ways of thinking from our intellectual tradition. We developed in a state of intellectual isolation from the West, and we are still feeling the consequences of that experience. For example, our attitude toward non-Marxist scholarship is frequently that it is at best something half-baked, no more than a sack of facts that only we Marxists, possessing the philosopher's stone, can transform into genuine knowledge. We have to demolish this stereotype of Western thought. Similarly, we still have a one-dimensional way of looking at ourselves and the world, as expressed in the notion, "He who is not with us is against us."

Second, even though we have broken down aspects of Stalinist orthodoxy, much of its legacy remains deeply entrenched. For example, we have rehabilitated Bukharin and his ideas about NEP as socialist development in the 1920s. This struck a major blow against the Stalinist orthodoxy that there was no alternative to Stalin's policies at the end of the 1920s. NEP should not have been ended. By the way, I'm very glad that we have published Steve's book on Bukharin, but as he says in his foreword, now we have to write our own books about Bukharin. And even though we have begun to write about Trotsky without the criminal charges, the devil-image of Trotsky created by Stalin is still alive in people's minds. I don't mean that we must rehabilitate Trotskyism as a doctrine, but until we eliminate all these Stalinist images we cannot really explore our history. We haven't yet faced up to the fact, for example, that Stalin invaded and occupied Estonia, Latvia, and Lithuania in 1939–1940 or that he committed aggression against Finland in 1939.

And finally, as I said before, there is the problem of historians being willing to set out their own points of view, of taking positions different from that of the party and of the state.

Are you saying that some historians are still censoring themselves?

It is not just self-censorship. It's also fear, inertia, lack of resolve. It's habits bred by having led comfortable lives for too long.

If all Soviet historians did write based on their own perspectives, not those of the party or the state, there would be many different and conflicting points of view about the past.

Of course, absolutely.

Ever since the early 1930s there has always been a party line in history. You are suggesting that there should no longer be a party line, or perhaps there should be several lines in the Communist Party.

I can't imagine there being two lines in one party. Even if there are various schools of thought and points of view, it is possible to reach a consensus, to reach the truth, and thus to arrive at a party line based on real scholarship.

You seem to be trying to reconcile the principle of free historical research and opinion with the idea of a party line in history. One reason that terrible things happened to historians under Stalin—not only censorship but even imprisonment and execution—was the Stalinist desire to impose a party line. Moreover, why should historians agree about the complexities of the past? Isn't healthy historiography, as a Dutch historian once remarked, an eternal argument? Surely any kind of party line or what you call consensus about the past would have to be imposed and artificial.

It's true what you say about Stalin, but he had no use for history as scholarship. He needed a justification for his policies and repressions. But I don't see why a quest for truth can't lead to a party line based on scholarly research and facts. Why must historians reach conclusions that contradict the party line?

Either there is a fundamental difference between us or some confusion. Take a hypothetical example. Let's say that you publish a brilliant book on the history of the Soviet Union, including the history of the Communist Party. The party leadership and other relevant authorities agree that it is a wonderful book and it becomes the basic textbook in schools. What would be left to be done by other party historians? Merely write amplifications on your interpretations? Or could they attack your book on the grounds that it is fundamentally wrong about important events?

If they have the facts to prove that I am wrong, they must attack my book. The only principle of the party line must be facts, the truth. Different points of view are permissible, and we must learn to be tolerant of them. The purpose of scholarly dialogue is to establish the truth.

Your position still seems puzzling, if not flatly contradictory, but let's turn to the question of textbooks on Soviet and party history. History examinations in some school grades in 1988 had to be canceled, evidently because standard textbooks are now considered inadequate.

Some of our textbooks are not only useless but absolutely harmful. They present falsifications in the form of indisputable truths. Unless young people understand our history in its full dramatic context, they will lapse again into apathy and cynicism. Some people say we should not teach young people about all the tragedies and cruelties in our history, but they will learn about them anyway. And if we want to raise a generation that will try to improve our country, we must tell young people the truth about the past.

In one of your articles about the need for historical truth in the schools, you wrote: "Our country has paid a high price for the mistakes of the past." How does a historian calculate that price and convey it to students?

That is a very tough question and one that is still on the agenda. We will have to calculate the millions of people who were killed as a result of Stalin's policies, beginning with collectivization and including the country's unpreparedness for the German invasion in 1941. We will have to calculate the damage done to our economy by all these misdeeds. And we must take into account the very high price we and the world Communist movement have paid for the damage Stalin did to our reputation.

If the situation in the historical profession is as bleak as you describe it, where will new textbooks come from?

Various commissions and collectives are working on new textbooks, but I don't think much good will come of this soon. Our history is not suddenly going to be revealed to us in a superb textbook. In addition, I am opposed to having one main book about party history, some kind of catechism like the Stalinist *Short Course* or the *History of the CPSU* first published under Khrushchev. We need several textbooks on the same subject—five, ten, I don't know how many. We need a pluralism of textbooks and competition among them.

Your use of the word "pluralism" echoes a central aspect of Gorbachev's program for the democratization of the Soviet system. How do you understand his pledge to develop and tolerate what he calls socialist pluralism more generally?

People now recognize the reality of social pluralism in the Soviet Union—different groups and group interests. The need for economic pluralism—not just state enterprises but also individual and cooperative ones—has also been accepted, though not by everyone, of course. So why shouldn't there also be political and ideological pluralism in the Soviet Union? It is a perfectly normal part of political life.

In Western democracies, what you call normal pluralism involves a multiparty political system.

I know, but in our country we have not yet explored all the opportunities for allowing real socialist pluralism in a one-party system. It is possible that when democratization really unfolds, when social and economic pluralism have flourished, the one-party system probably will become inadequate. But for now there are immense possibilities for democratic changes within the existing system.

As the nominee of many young people and youth clubs, you were a delegate to the Nineteenth Party Conference in mid-1988. Were you satisfied with the results of the conference, which adopted Gorbachev's resolutions on democratization?

I'm pleased by the conference resolutions. The problem will be turning them into reality. I was one of the more than two hundred delegates who did not have an opportunity to speak at the conference. Had I spoken I would have supported Leonid Abalkin's objection that too many half-measures have been adopted in our economic reforms. I would have objected to the attacks on glasnost heard from some delegates at the conference, and on the unofficial groups that are playing such an important role in perestroika. I think the Communist Party must get used to being criticized from within its own ranks and from organizations outside its ranks. I would have also emphasized that we need before us a model of the socialism that we want to create. I don't know why no historians spoke at the conference.

Speaking of democratization, tell us about your remarkable victory in the March 26, 1989, elections to the Congress of People's Deputies. Many people in our book were elected deputies by social organizations, but you were one of the few chosen by direct popular vote. Why did you run in Noginsk, which is about fifty-three kilometers from Moscow and where your opponent was supported by the local party and administrative establishment? How did you manage to win so dramatically, with about 75 percent of the vote, despite the fact that local authorities and even the central party newspaper Pravda *openly opposed you?*

I decided to run in Noginsk for two reasons. Though I was nominated in several Moscow districts, I didn't want to run against other progressive candidates nominated in those same districts. We had to elect as many radical supporters of perestroika as possible. Second, Noginsk appealed to me because, though it has a scientific-intellectual community, many of its residents are workers and young people. If perestroika is to succeed, workers and young people, not just intellectuals, have to be deeply involved. I wanted to win the support of those people.

As for my victory, the local authorities and newspapers did strongly oppose me, though I must tell you that on the eve of the election one local paper refused to publish dirty material against me that had been sent anonymously from Moscow. The editor killed the whole issue of that day's newspaper rather than publish that stuff, though the paper was already printed. How did I win? During the alloted month, I campaigned every day and night, speaking to three or four meetings of 300 to 500 people a day. Usually I didn't get home until after midnight. I spoke to all kinds of people—workers, scientists, youth groups, housewives. You can't imagine the level of their interest. They asked so many questions about me as a person, my institute, my ideas about socialism, Soviet history. Voters were passionately interested in everything.

But I don't think that my electoral victory, or that of other radical reformers around the country, was just a personal victory. In voting for us, people were voting against this bureaucratic-administrative system. They were voting for radical perestroika. That was the real issue.

Now that you are a people's deputy and potentially a member of the Supreme Soviet, which according to Gorbachev's program is supposed to function as a real parliament, can you envisage the nature of this unprecedented Soviet national legislature?

Our quest for democracy is only beginning. The idea or principle exists, but not yet the concrete forms. We still have to find and develop those forms. Personally, I think we need even more radical reforms. The president should be elected by direct popular vote, not by the Congress of People's Deputies, as the legislation now provides. And important policy issues should be decided by popular referendums, which we do not yet have. As for the new Soviet parliament, the most important thing is that it function in a way that will break the party's monopoly on power, property, and people's souls. That means that members of parliament have to be thinking, independent, outspoken representatives of society who act and vote according to their conscience and the real everyday needs of our people. As I told the voters, the parliament must be a legal opposition to the party apparatus and state bureaucracies.

Is that kind of parliament possible in a one-party system?

I think so, though I'm not sure. In order to be a legal opposition and to break the party's monopoly, parliament will have to propose its own alternative ideas, policies, and laws. We'll see if this is possible. But you know, I'm certain that one day we will have a multiparty system in the Soviet Union. I don't know how or when that will happen, but in principle it would be a normal, positive development. Maybe it will begin with the Soviet Communist Party dividing into two parties—a radical one and a moderate one. Maybe there then will be a Green party and a peasant party. We'll see, but none of this will happen without a struggle.

We have asked all the people in this book about opposition to various reforms and to perestroika in general. We have gotten different answers. Some people say there is a great deal of opposition, others say there is very little. As a historian, how would you answer this question?

As you know, for me perestroika means the eradication of Stalinism. Therefore, I evaluate the progress of perestroika by the extent to which the Stalinist system is dying off. We are now witnessing the agony of the Stalinist administrative system. It has suffered a number of serious blows over the years—at the Twentieth Party Congress in 1956 and at the Nineteenth Party Conference, for example. But if it had really died we would be able to say that the process of perestroika was somewhere in the middle or even in its final stage. Clearly this is not the case. We are only at the beginning. The Stalinist system, including the party apparatus, is fighting back. It will try to obstruct, for example, the democratic political reforms adopted at the party conference. In addition, many other people who were educated during the Stalin era are still active in politics, administration, economics, education, and so forth. They can't change overnight and start thinking in new ways. If you view the opposition to perestroika in this broader social context, you see that the forces that oppose it are very diverse, though they do not necessarily form an organized opposition. Some of it is just old dogmatic ways of thinking and a general uneasiness about change. The most determined and frightening opposition comes from people who want to save their own skins—to protect their positions, privileges, and reputations.

One reason it is difficult to speak more precisely about opposition to perestroika is that such people will not state their views openly. I have in mind not only those who are truly against perestroika but also fatalistic people who believe it will inevitably be only another short-lived thaw followed by a winter. For example, I edited a very outspoken book of articles by some of our most outstanding intellectuals who believe that perestroika is a history-making opportunity which must be seized. It is called *There Is No Alternative* and it came out in June 1988, on the eve of the Nineteenth Party Conference. Incidentally, one of the authors is Andrei Sakharov, whose civic courage has proved that an individual's integrity can prevail over dogmatism and bureaucratic reprisals. I wanted to include in the book articles by anti-perestroika authors, but I did not even bother to invite them because I was sure they would not respond. They prefer to conceal their views or operate in the shadows.

Does it worry you that even today, after all the revelations, Stalin remains a positive figure and a symbol of Soviet socialism for so many Soviet citizens?

It is a widespread phenomenon. You might call it folk Stalinism. There are a lot of reasons for it. Because of the absence of democratic traditions in Russia, many people admire a strong-arm leader, a strong boss, and they associate Stalin with that kind of leadership. In addition, many people lived much of their lives under Stalin. When you take away Stalin and Stalinism, you deprive them of an essential part of their autobiographies. After all, many of these people laughed and loved under Stalin, married and had children. On the whole, it was a positive experience for them. They also believed that the socialism they were building would bring a radiant future. They believed it for years and decades, and they focused that belief on Stalin. If you take away Stalin, you take away everything—their happy memories, their beliefs, their hopes. Over the years, their consciousness was profoundly mutilated and deformed. They developed an irrational, even religious attitude toward Stalin. And this remains a serious problem even today. By the way, what is completely incomprehensible to me is the admiration for Stalin even on the part of some people who suffered under him. Historians who know something about social psychology ought to study this phenomenon.

That's one reason why the Memorial Society movement is so important. As you know, it began spontaneously in 1987 with young people around the country collecting signatures on a petition to build a national monument in Moscow to the millions of victims of Stalin's repression. By June 1988, when the Nineteenth Party Conference met, they had collected 54,000 signed petitions. They gave them to me and Elem Klimov, as conference delegates, to deliver to the presidium. I personally carried the huge bags of petitions to the conference hall. They were very heavy and it was very hot. There was a break in the proceedings, and all the delegates were milling around in the halls. I shouted, "Make way, make way! These are petitions to the presidium— petitions for a monument to Stalin's victims!" You can imagine the reaction. I took the bags right to the conference tribune. And as you know, Gorbachev endorsed the idea on the last day of the conference.

The Memorial Society has been very active ever since, organizing anti-Stalinist rallies, exhibits, and what we call meetings of conscience; uncovering evidence about the crimes of the past, including mass graves of people shot by the NKVD; and opening branches around the country. On January 28–29, 1989, it held a constituent conference in Moscow with more than 500 delegates. I was elected a cochairman of Memorial and head of its scholarly council. Our plans now call for building monuments to Stalin's victims all across the country, because the victims were everywhere. But we also want to build, particularly in Moscow, an entire complex that will house a museum, archive, and library detailing what happened in our country—a place with an ongoing program of activities devoted to those tragic years. A kind of shrine where the nation can repent and purify its conscience and soul.

Memorial doesn't pretend to have a monopoly on historical knowledge or understanding, but it wants the nation to come fully to grips with the terrible Stalinist past. We are proposing, for example, a public trial of Stalin and Stalinism. Not a prosecutorial trial that would name and convict all those who were guilty for the crimes, but a trial that would expose everything that happened and be a national act of conscience, repentance, and purification. Of course, Memorial isn't just a cultural movement. Because the Stalinist past is still such a large part of the present, it is also a political democratic movement surrounded by ferocious opposition. Its opponents include all those people who want to stop perestroika and all those who still cannot part with Stalin.

Perhaps something larger is involved here. We have the impression that many Soviet citizens prefer, even worship, a strong state. Isn't it possible that what you call folk Stalinism has less to do with Stalin personally than with his historical role as the symbol of a powerful Soviet state?

It is certainly possible. That may be why so many pictures of Stalin cropped up all over the place during Brezhnev's reign, when the state seemed to be decaying.

And yet, isn't perestroika itself a set of reforms that seeks to reduce the size and role of the Soviet state in relation to society? Reducing censorship, promoting democracy through elections from below, permitting nonstate forms of economic enterprise and market relations all seem to tend in that direction. Isn't de-Stalinization, as you define perestroika, a form of de-statization? Commenting on Lenin's famous book State and Revolution, *where he argued that socialist revolution would lead to the eventual abolition of the state, you once remarked, "We remembered the state and forgot about the revolution."*

That is exactly right. Over the years there has been a 90 percent statization of society. All the pores and living threads of society have been permeated and bound up by state bureaucracy, strictures, and prohibitions. Now the task is to reverse this long process by societizing the state and eliminating state domination.

But as a historian doesn't it worry you that perestroika may be in profound conflict with deeply ingrained popular Russian attitudes toward the state? Indeed, isn't state power over society perhaps the single most powerful tradition in Russian history, before and after the revolution? You recall the historian Klyuchevsky's famous remark about early eighteenth-century Russian history: "The state swelled up and the people grew lean." A pessimistic conclusion would be that perestroika is incompatible with Russia's traditions.

It is true that strong state power over a weak society is one of Russia's most powerful traditions. We historians need to study this question by tracing the evolution of civil society, particularly from the beginning of Stalin's rule to the present. We are only beginning to study this. I myself have recently caused yet another stir by relating the question to Marx's concept that the main goal of socialism is to end the alienation of people from power and property. I argued that from the late 1920s on, Soviet peasants and workers were alienated from property, while the state, which took control of that property, was alienated from society. As a result, the overwhelming majority of the people lost all sense of being in control of the country. They still lack that sense. Perestroika is a search for ways to end that alienation. You are right that we face colossal difficulties and complexities. But there is hope.

For a historian, the process of diminishing the Soviet state and overcoming what you call alienation may seem to be a necessity. But for Soviet politicians it must seem to be a process fraught with the hazards of instability.

Of course, particularly as it relates to the various nationalities of the Soviet Union, where the situation is sometimes explosive. But here too we must restore Leninist principles and regain what was lost under Stalin. Stalin established an extremely centralized state with very weak local governments. The Soviet Union is not made up of autonomous republics, as Lenin envisaged, but of provinces subordinate to the center. The USSR, the Union of Soviet Socialist Republics, must become a real federation of republics with equal rights. This applies as well to Eastern Europe, where there should be equal socialist countries with the same rights as the Soviet Union. In both cases, relations have to be based on real independence and sovereignty.

You have spoken of your own generation with great feeling. Can people your age really carry out perestroika, or must it be left for a younger generation to see it through?

You know, there is much talk here today about conflicts between different generations, but I see the problem differently. The main conflicts today are not between the older and the younger generations, between fathers and sons, but between some fathers and sons, on the one hand, and other fathers and sons, on the other. My generation, as I have said, is very active politically. Its main contribution to making perestroika irreversible is to help society rid itself of the negative legacy of the previous decades. In particular, we must help society become more polyphonic and more tolerant of diversity—of diverse views, diverse individuals, diverse economies. My generation must lead this country out of its long spiritual isolation and provide it with the harmony of different civilizations. In that respect, we must return to the diversity and complexities of the Soviet 1920s.

Is this country ready to tolerate such diversity?

Unfortunately, we don't have a scientific way to measure our current level of tolerance or, more generally, our political culture. But my impression is that there is great potential for democracy among the Soviet people. On the other hand, the country has had no chance to develop democratic traditions. It is ridiculous to say that democratic traditions were created under Stalin or Brezhnev. We have an enormous amount of work to do. And it will be extraordinarily difficult because totalitarian tendencies remain strong in our national consciousness, culture, and traditions.

Even now we can see that the process of perestroika is still very uneven. For example, economic results lag far behind political and intellectual ones. Pro-perestroika sentiments are much stronger in Moscow than in the provincial cities. There is more perestroika and glasnost in the media than in academic institutions. And in some fields there is still absolutely no perestroika at all.

And what will happen to the Soviet Union if perestroika fails or is overthrown?

The country will fall into another, longer period of drowsy stagnation, or it will come under the rule of the fist. Either way, there is no good alternative to perestroika. My hope is that we will continue to move forward toward socialist renewal. And I think we have a real chance.

If so, perhaps your generation is not so unlucky after all.

There is always an optimistic side to everything. We have a second chance. Some generations were even less lucky than we were.

TATYANA ZASLAVSKAYA

"Socialism with a Human Face"

THE PROFESSIONAL LIFE and political fortunes of Tatyana Ivanovna Zaslavskaya (born 1927) reflect the long odyssey of reform-minded intellectuals in the Soviet Communist Party. "In the past," she has said, "we were all
regarded as heretics. Today, we occupy the commanding heights." An
economist turned sociologist, Zaslavskaya left Moscow in 1963 to find
more freedom to research and write at a Siberian institute eventually
headed by the maverick economist Abel Aganbegyan. Sociology—with its
focus on social groups, conflicts, and change—was in official disfavor until
the Gorbachev period. During the long conservative Brezhnev era, the
Siberian institute was a haven for reform-minded social scientists. Its
monthly journal EKO, whose editorial board included Zaslavskaya, often
published articles forbidden in the central press. Zaslavskaya became more
widely known in the West in 1983, when a long reformist document she
wrote was leaked to foreign correspondents in Moscow. The "Zaslavskaya
Memorandum" caused a political scandal and led to the Aganbegyan institute being officially reprimanded. Two years later, Aganbegyan emerged as
Gorbachev's chief economic adviser. In 1987 Zaslavskaya was named president of the Soviet Sociological Association, and in 1988 she returned to
Moscow to head the newly formed Center for the Study of Public Opinion.
Her articles and interviews in leading newspapers, including Pravda and
Izvestia, are notable for their iconoclastic treatment of once taboo subjects
such as conflicting group interests, privilege, and injustices in the Soviet
system. Depending on how one interprets her remarks below, Zaslavskaya
is either an informal adviser to Gorbachev or an intellectual in whom he
has taken a special interest.

IF ABEL AGANBEGYAN hadn't invited me to work at his institute in
Siberia in 1963, I would not be who I am today. Probably I wouldn't

even be a sociologist. After graduating from the Economics Department at Moscow State University in 1950, I worked for more than twelve years at the Institute of Economics, under the Academy of Sciences, in Moscow. It was the best place for academic economics, and my life was all mapped out for me. After all, I came from an academic family. My grandfather was a physics professor and a dean of the faculty at Kiev University. Incidentally, I studied physics for several years. My father taught methodology at the Moscow Pedagogical Institute. And even my mother, who spent her life helping my father, raising two daughters, and earning money by typing, had studied philology at the university.

But at thirty-six, I was feeling restless and looking for something more exciting. Aganbegyan had been a successful young economist in Moscow, but he felt constrained by all the bureaucrats in the capital. So in 1961, when he was only twenty-nine, he managed to go to Novosibirsk, 3,000 kilometers from Moscow, to the now famous Institute of Economics and Industrial Organization, which was also under the Academy. He wanted to create a new school of Soviet political economy by gathering the best young scholars at his institute. Two of my friends had already gone there, and they kept writing to tell me how wonderful it was. Abel showed up with his invitation on January 25, 1963, and by February 9 I was at his institute in Siberia. The change gave me scope and freedom to work that I could not have had in Moscow. It freed my mind and my hands and led me to sociology.

But even then it wasn't easy. You know the tragic history of sociology in our country. It was persecuted for decades. Even today it still is in very poor shape. We don't have a single senior scholar who can say he or she was actually educated as a sociologist. I'm an economist by training, and the others are philosophers, legal scholars, or historians. There are only three sociology departments at Soviet universities—in Leningrad, Moscow, and Kiev—and they opened only in 1984.

All this is Stalin's legacy from the 1930s. Sociology is a mirror of society, but Stalin didn't want to see society, only himself. So despite the strong Marxist sociological tradition, going back to Marx himself, Stalin crushed the study of society. Collectivization was the turning point. In the 1960s I got to know some survivors who had done sociological research in the countryside in the early 1930s. They told me that when they returned from the villages they reported their findings on the horribly violent and destructive nature of collectivization to their institutes and party organizations. They demanded that higher party authorities be informed. Soon their institutes were closed, and henceforth all sociological conclusions were issued from above. For example, there was never any hard evidence for Stalin's dictum in the mid-1930s that Soviet society consisted of two friendly classes—workers and collective farmers—plus the intelligentsia. That scheme still prevails, but it never corresponded to all the real groups and strata that make up Soviet society, which is no less complex than capitalist societies.

Of course, the totalitarian nature and monstrous crimes of Stalin's regime did terrible things to the other social sciences as well—history, philosophy, economics, and the rest. Stalinism turned them into centers of ideological dogmatism with ideological overseers to persecute heretics. It put an iron curtain between our scholars and the outside world. The social sciences still suffer from that historical experience today. But at least the others continued to exist. Sociology was abolished. It became known as a "bourgeois pseudo-science," and even the word couldn't be used. It wasn't until after the Twentieth Party Congress that sociology slowly began to revive. By 1963 it was springing up in many places, like mushrooms after a rainfall, but still in the guise of economics, philosophy, or something else.

The situation was still so embryonic that when I began to move into sociology in the early 1960s I didn't even know it. My doctoral dissertation had been about income distribution, but I had always had an interest in agricultural life. Aganbegyan's institute had been asked by the Novosibirsk Regional Party Committee to study the problems of agricultural workers in the area. I was assigned to work on migration in the countryside. At first I wasn't fully aware that I was moving into a new field of study. Soon, however, a few sociologists sought me out and explained that I was one of them. In 1967 I became head of what was in effect the sociology section of Aganbegyan's institute. Twenty years later I became president of our national association of sociologists, and in 1988 I moved back to Moscow to become head of our new Center for the Study of Public Opinion.

There are reports in the Western press, and even here in Moscow, that in fact you also now play a more exalted role—that you are a member of Gorbachev's inner circle of advisers, along with Aganbegyan.

It's a myth. I am not a personal adviser to Mikhail Sergeevich, though we do have a very good relationship. He seems to read what I write very carefully. For example, when President Reagan visited Moscow in May 1988, he hosted a dinner party for Gorbachev at the home of the American ambassador. The American side made up the guest list and seated me close to Mikhail Sergeevich. We talked quite a bit that evening, and at one point he introduced me to an American senator by saying, "This is a very intelligent and daring woman. I like daring people." But no, I don't have any official party position. I'm just an ordinary party member. I've probably met Gorbachev no more than seven or eight times.

The first time was in 1982, while Brezhnev was still alive. Gorbachev was the national party secretary responsible for agriculture, and he was preparing a new food supply program. He invited six economists specializing in agriculture and me, a sociologist, to advise him. He wanted to know what we thought of his draft program. I wrote five or six pages arguing that the ideas were good but the plan was very weak on implementation, like a hand raised to deliver a blow that was not really going to be delivered. I said exactly what I thought at the meeting. I thought we were all allies. I think that meeting made him think I was daring or reckless, because at that time it was not customary to speak one's mind. Anyway, he responded very positively to my comments. In fact, he agreed with me and went on to say, "If only I could have written here everything I am thinking about." But of course he wasn't the number one man in the Politburo.

How did Gorbachev know about you at that time?

Possibly from his wife Raisa Maksimovna, who wrote her dissertation on the sociology of the village. Or possibly from one of the other members of the group that met with him, an agricultural economist and old friend of Gorbachev from Stavropol.

The story you tell about the 1982 meeting suggests that Gorbachev had something like perestroika in mind even then, well before he became general secretary.

Of course he did. I'm sure of it. You know about the confidential memorandum he wrote in May 1978 about the need to reform the economic system of agriculture. He sent it to the Central Committee when he was still secretary of the Stavropol Regional Party Committee. It was published for the first time in 1987, in the first volume of his articles and speeches. All the basic ideas of perestroika are laid out in that memorandum, or notes, as it is called. When I saw Gorbachev at the American ambassador's home, I told him, "It was very interesting to read the first volume of your works." He immediately responded, "So, you read the notes?" "That's exactly what I read." And then Gorbachev began telling the American senator, "When I became general secretary, I found out where the document was in the archives and what comments had been written on it. Now it has been published."

So, of course, Gorbachev, had all these ideas back then, even earlier than 1978. People who knew him when he was a student at Moscow State University from 1950 to 1955 also say this. They say that even then he was preparing himself for serious political activity, that he already stood out, and that he already understood a lot. He worked in the library from morning to night, and he studied things that puzzled people. For example, books published in the NEP 1920s and all sorts of things.

Of course, I don't know whether in 1982 Gorbachev understood the need for the kind of radical political and economic perestroika we are calling for today. At my meeting with him in 1982 we only discussed a perestroika of the economic system. If he had such political ideas then, he probably hid them. And it is possible that his ideas and plans have gotten more radical since 1985, as the work has gone on. I'm certain that they have.

By the way, if the political situation was still so antireformist in 1982 that even Gorbachev, a Politburo member, could not propose the kind of reform that was actually on his mind, how did he become leader only three years later?

It was not a random, accidental development. There was an enormous historic need for such a leader, and history produced him. Of course, it could have taken another ten or fifteen years. What if Viktor Grishin [a senior member of the Politburo who was removed in 1986] had become general secretary in 1985? It's horrible to contemplate how bad things would have been.

You too wrote a famous document calling for a kind of perestroika before 1985, what became known in 1983 as the Zaslavskaya Memorandum. But before we talk about that incident, was there anything else in your life that prefigured or shaped the radical reformer you later became?

Like most people, I suppose, I was always a person of contradictory impulses. I was only ten during the Stalinist repressions of 1937–38, so I don't feel any guilt or personal responsibility for what happened then. But by the time I entered the university in 1946 I was already experiencing a sense of inner struggle. During the first two years, I happily and greedily gulped down everything, but in 1948–49 the Stalinist repression against so-called cosmopolitans imbued the department with suspiciousness. And I was a little rebellious intellectually. In three years of studying physics, my professors had instilled in me a mode of hard scientific thinking. You had to have evidence, and things are supposed to be logical. So when I moved to the Economics Department I asked a lot of questions, which was taken as a violation of decent behavior. We were taught, for example, that Comrade Stalin was Lenin's best disciple. But if I saw that Lenin had made statement A and Stalin statement B, I would ask how B followed from A. Such behavior created the opinion in the department that I was somehow an alien element and untrustworthy. So my last two years at the university were difficult for me. And when I graduated I couldn't get a recommendation for graduate school, even though people with lower grades were given recommendations.

I also remember that I wept and felt terrible when Stalin died in 1953. I think almost everybody did. Like many young people, I felt that I had to join the party to make up for the loss of Stalin. Or something like that. I applied for membership in the spring of 1953 and became a member in 1954. And yet I joined with terribly contradictory feelings. It was impossible not to see some of the terrible things that had been going on. The Twentieth Party Congress was a great joy to me, but I can't say that it recreated me. I was already thirty, and by thirty a person is who she is. Under the circumstances, my generation did all that it could. We weren't saints, but we led honest lives. Our misfortune and tragedy was that our hands were tied and our mouths were gagged.

I'll give you an example that happened later. In 1957 a colleague at the Institute of Economics and I were asked to compare labor productivity in the United States and the Soviet Union. We researched for two years and wrote a hundred-page report. There was enormous interest in the subject, so about a hundred copies were sent to various institutes in Moscow, and a date was set for a discussion of the report. It was September 29, 1959, or 1960. I remember the day because it's my wedding anniversary. At nine that morning my colleague and I got urgent calls that the director of our institute wanted to see us immediately. When we arrived he met us downstairs, his face as white as a sheet. All morning his driver had been retrieving copies of the report from everybody who had received one. All the copies were locked in the institute's safe and classified, including even our personal copies. It turned out that Khrushchev had just announced that American productivity was three times greater than Soviet productivity, while our findings showed that it was more like four or five times greater.

A commission investigated our work for several months. It included no real scholars, only some people who wanted to wipe us from the face of the earth and others who did not. In the end, the commission voted three to two that our methodology had been scientifically correct. If it had voted against us, we would have been fired. We weren't, but our report never saw the light of day. Two years of our work disappeared, and we were supposed to thank them for not having fired us.

That incident may have been kept within the confines of your institute, but the 1983 Novosibirsk document you wrote on the need for economic reform, and for which you were also reprimanded, gained international attention when someone leaked it to Western correspondents in Moscow. Looking back, that memorandum reads like one of the first calls for perestroika. Indeed, virtually all of its arguments have been repeated in the Soviet press since 1985. You must be proud of what you wrote in 1983, even though it caused you some grief.

Yes, I am proud of it. And yes, there was a scandal and a party reprimand, even though the whole thing started peacefully. By 1982 it was already clear to many scholars that our economy had basically run aground. Economists gave their explanations—the Soviet Union had the wrong technology, citizens had too much leisure time, etc. But several of us at Aganbegyan's institute were firmly convinced that the reasons were social in origin, so we began a study of what we called the social mechanism underlying our system. We wanted to look at economic processes as social processes—at different classes and groups, their interactions, their status, and their conflicting interests. All this was new to us at the time, so it took months to develop our basic theoretical propositions and approaches. But then we thought, before starting down a completely new research road, we should discuss our ideas with a larger scholarly audience. So at the end of 1982 we sent ten copies of the proposal to various institutes in Moscow and scheduled a seminar for April 1983 in Novosibirsk. Somehow word got around, and we were swamped with requests to attend. As it turned out, scholars from seventeen Soviet cities came to Novosibirsk.

I delivered the opening report, which set out our research ideas as well as the need for basic economic reforms in light of our social theories. My report generated enormous interest and even seemed to inspire a lot of people. They got the idea, I guess, that these kinds of ideas and proposals could now be made. Well, you know what happened next. The call came from the regional party leadership. It charged us with lax security over official documents—my report—and officially reprimanded us. Two years later, there would have been no reprimand.

It is hard to believe that all this was so innocent. Your group must have sensed in 1982, even before Brezhnev died, that the time was ripe for bolder thinking and change.

Yes, it was clear that things could not go on as they had and that the time had come for new thinking.

Your experiences before 1985 seem to support our own view that many Western observers have greatly exaggerated the homogeneous nature of the Soviet Communist Party over the years. We take the view that even during the conservative years after Khrushchev's overthrow a kind of community of party reformers existed at various levels of the Soviet system, including in many scholarly institutes across the country. And though this community of reformers was not as organized as a political party, for example, its members knew of each other, exchanged ideas, and waited throughout the 1970s for a party leadership that would be receptive to their ideas.

I think that is an accurate image. But it was a very long wait. In the 1970s Aganbegyan had a favorite toast: "We will outlive them." And if such people had not worked on all our country's problems for all those years, no political leadership could have started perestroika. People had to do the groundwork first.

After four years of Gorbachev's policies, do you, as a sociologist, have an understanding of the process of perestroika that differs in any fundamental way from what we usually read in the Soviet press?

Everyone understands that we began these revolutionary reforms because we had reached an economic dead end and we had to find a road to real progress. The country had entered a crisis. It was lagging behind the world economically, technologically, and scientifically, and mass dissatisfaction was growing more acute. So everyone also understands that restructuring the economy is our most pressing task. But I remain convinced that the primary reasons for the need for perestroika were not the sluggish economy and rate of technological development but an underlying mass alienation of working people from significant social goals and values. This social alienation is rooted in the economic system formed in the 1930s, which made state property, run by a vast bureaucratic apparatus, the dominant form of ownership. By the 1980s, 15–18 million functionaries administered this statist system, from Moscow to the thousands of enterprises. For fifty years it was said that this was public property and belonged to everyone, but no way was ever found to make workers feel they were the co-owners and masters of the factories, farms, and enterprises. They felt themselves to be cogs in a gigantic machine.

Maybe this system was necessary in the 1930s, when the country was so terribly backward. The majority of the working class came from the countryside. Workers were uneducated, knew only their narrow slice of life, and had nothing. I don't know. Personally, I think the Stalinist 1930s were our Thermidor, when the socialist revolution was thwarted and Stalin carried out an anti-Leninist *coup d'état*. The claim that socialism was being built camouflaged the emergence of some other kind of system, maybe some kind of Asiatic despotism. Now we have to squeeze Stalinism out of ourselves drop by drop.

I do know that this system no longer works because people have changed enormously in the last fifty years. Now they are educated and well informed. They have a much higher standard of living, apartments, free medicine, free education, and they don't have to work hard to get it. The bureaucratic-command system can no longer direct and control them. Man is resilient—you push and he pushes back. The bottom is no longer willing to work efficiently, and the top can no longer force it to do so.

Therefore, if we want people to be creative, productive, and efficient, we have to change the whole system of social relations. That is why I say perestroika must be a social revolution. It must bring about a fundamental redistribution of power, rights, freedoms, wealth, and control of property among the various strata and groups that make up the Soviet Union. It must democratize social relations. That is also why perestroika cannot be carried out only from above. It requires broad participation and activism on the part of the masses. I would even say that perestroika must be a second socialist revolution in the Soviet Union. This will shock some people, but it is not so strange. The revolutionary transition from feudalism to bourgeois capitalism went through several stages over many decades. What I want for my country is real not fictional socialism, where people can be happy as creators, not just as consumers, and where they will be able to pursue all of their talents. Where people will feel like human beings and not feel constantly oppressed.

In particular, we have to open up new social-economic roads for millions of people that will allow them to identify with the means of production—to feel they are the owners and masters of property and that their income depends on how it is used. To do this, we must have economic pluralism—not just state ownership but also cooperative and individual ownership. And there must be real competition among these forms. Personally, I think that the cooperative movement has the greatest potential. Groups of people of various sizes, maybe 10 people or fewer in a small cooperative, or as many as 600 or 700 in a large cooperative farm, who will share control over the means of production and have full economic responsibility for what they produce.

But officially the Soviet Union has always had cooperatives. Ever since the 1930s the collective farms, for example, have been said to be a cooperative form of production.

In reality they lost their cooperative character and became state-run enterprises. Many specialists on agricultural economics protested the turning of collective farms into quasi-state farms, but they were overruled by the false dogma that under socialism state property is a higher form. If we hadn't statized the collective farms decades ago, we would not have food shortages today and be importing food; we would be exporting it. The only exceptions are farms that somehow escaped the deadly influence of state intervention. In Lithuania, for example, they just ignored orders to enlarge the collective farms, which in effect would have turned them into state farms. As a result, they have relatively small farms with 200–300 people. And when Khrushchev told them to shut down private farming, they also ignored him. That's why Lithuania has the most productive agriculture in the Soviet Union.

For farmers, perestroika means returning to Lenin's concept of real cooperatives. We have to destatize the collective farms by freeing them from incompetent state tutelage. In general, the most important thing about cooperatives is that people join them voluntarily and run them democratically, deciding what they want to buy and sell without anyone telling them what to do. We need these kinds of cooperatives throughout the country and the economy, in the countryside and in the cities, where the shops are empty. There are enormous opportunities for such cooperatives in consumer goods and services. And for private middlemen, who will play a big role as a free market for all these goods and services develops. That is why we have passed new laws removing the bans on cooperative and individual enterprise. The thing to do is to begin. Then people will take the initiative, and nothing can stop them.

Maybe so, but throughout 1988 and 1989 the Soviet press has reported a great many obstacles to both cooperative and private enterprises.

The situation is developing in different ways around the country. Partly it is a matter of different social and economic traditions. In Armenia and the Baltic states, free enterprise is developing very quickly, but not in the Russian Republic because so many people have lost the tradition.

It's not just the people, of course. Even though the laws are supposed to be the same everywhere, their application varies greatly depending on the attitude of local party authorities toward cooperatives, individual enterprises, and the market. In Novosibirsk, for example, it is incredibly difficult to get permission to open a shop. The authorities find any excuse they need to turn down applications. In other regions, the political climate is more favorable.

Clearly you prefer cooperative forms of economic enterprise over ones that are private or individual. It is surprising, for example, that you say little about the future role of private family farming, especially in light of the new law allowing peasants to lease land for as long as fifty years.

A third of collective farm produce already comes from the household plots of collective farmers. So it's not that I think private farming is unimportant but that it will produce only a small percent of the gross national product. Nonetheless, this small percent is and will continue to be very significant because it will be in areas where the state performs particularly badly—in the production of meat, fruit, vegetables, milk, butter, cheese, and eggs, for example.

You foresee a mixed Soviet economy composed of three kinds of production and services: state, cooperative, and private. Can you tell us roughly what their respective percentages could or should be as perestroika unfolds?

A social scientist should not make predictions, but I would guess that eventually the state sector would encompass about 40 percent of the economy. That would include heavy industry, the defense industries, and transportation—what was called the "commanding heights" during NEP. In agriculture I see no real role for the state. About 70 percent would be made up of genuine cooperative farms, about 20 percent would be people working both on cooperative farms and their own small plots, and about 10 percent would work only as private farmers. It is harder to foresee the situation in urban consumer goods and services because we have so little experience with cooperatives or private enterprises in the cities. They are just getting underway.

You assume that if people's income is directly linked to their labor, either through ownership of property or a new wage system in state enterprises, they will work more and better in order to increase their incomes. But since there are so few consumer goods, why should people want more money? You have said yourself that their meager incomes bring them all they need to live comfortably. Should the Soviet Union import large quantities of consumer goods, as some of your economists are proposing?

A country like ours cannot depend on imports. We aren't Hungary. We have to manufacture our own products. That is why we are trying to create a positive atmosphere for those branches of the economy that produce directly for consumers. If we do it properly, we can satisfy the market for food very quickly. Light industry and services will take more time to develop. But public morality and confidence are very important here. General public morale had collapsed before perestroika, partly because of widespread corruption and the fact that the ruling elite was taking a disproportionate part of the public wealth. People knew what was going on and decided they should take their own portions. That's why there was so much petty thievery and embezzlement of state property.

Now I am worried about public reaction to cooperative and private enterprises, some of which will make a great deal of money. We are ready to support and defend the rights of such people against local authorities, but we want them to realize their profits by meeting market demand through honest, efficient means. Unfortunately, some of them are engaged in shadowy or criminal operations, using stolen materials, avoiding taxes, and worse. I'm afraid that the cooperative and private enterprise movement might slip on its own banana peel. They already have enough enemies, especially among local party authorities. All those authorities need to do is to find a few cases of corruption and they'll say, "We told you so. You see what you are supporting and where it is leading." That's what I am afraid of.

This problem relates to one of the major themes of your own writings about perestroika as a quest for social justice in the Soviet Union.

There are so many system-wide social injustices that we must eliminate. Some of them are economic, but I prefer to speak of social justice because it includes political rights. Unless these injustices are eradicated, we won't be able to create socialism with a human face—a humanized, democratic society. The principle of social justice is the first principle of socialism.

It may seem obvious, for example, when Gorbachev says that the law must be the same for everyone. But there has been a colossal, just colossal, corruption of our whole legal apparatus—so many very unjust legal decisions and sentences. And this has had a terrible influence on the way people work and live. They have lost faith in the justness of the whole system. When people believe that evil triumphs, they just give up.

Or take another basic principle of socialism: to each according to his needs, from each according to his abilities. But social injustices prevent many of our people from working in accord with their real abilities. For example, people born in the countryside have many fewer opportunities to develop their innate abilities. City children have far greater access to child care, high quality schools, and cultural life. A survey at Novosibirsk University showed that only 3 percent of the students came from rural areas. Rural students take the entrance exams, but they can't pass them. And when students do graduate from higher educational institutions, who actually gets which jobs? Are decisions really made on the basis of their abilities? An enormous social mechanism of family connections, social ties, string-pulling, obedience, and conformity is at work here. Theoretically, people with ability and talent rise. In practice, those who are gray and mediocre rise more easily and swiftly. Even then, people aren't able to work to their full creative ability because their hands and feet are tied by bureaucratic instructions and prohibitions. To say nothing of our very skewed wage and salary system, which is strictly regulated by a state committee. Engineers, doctors, teachers, and others are badly underpaid. Service industries pay far less than manufacturing. I could mention many more examples of injustices.

And yet, the perestroika advocated by you and by most reform economists is certain to lead to other kinds of social injustices. The economic reforms you propose are a kind of wager on the most able and entrepreneurial peasants, workers, students, managers, scientists. Is this social justice?

I know that the economic reforms will produce some new injustices. We are not going to be able to exercise strict control over private enterprise. Some people will amass great fortunes, sometimes through sneakiness and machinations. Some people will have to be laid off and find new jobs. This is an organic social price we will have to pay, but existing injustices are so much greater.

Moreover, why shouldn't people who are more able live better than those who are not? The people who live best today are not those who do the best work. Is that just? Anyway, you can't escape the fact that people are born with different levels of ability. I mean, if someone is born a mongoloid, what can you do about it?

That's an extreme example. The point is that if under what you call perestroika the most enterprising and able people are to live best, the difference in how capitalism and socialism reward their citizens seems to vanish.

I don't agree. If the labor of some people yields more results for society, let them earn more. That is fair and just in socialist terms. Moreover, under capitalism some workers are paid based on the quality of their work, but much of the profit, the results of their labor, goes to the factory owners. Here, the profits will be distributed among the workers.

Let's pursue this. As you know, the economist Nikolai Shmelyov, who is also in this book, has formulated what he calls a new law: Whatever is economically efficient is moral; whatever is inefficient is immoral. Is that compatible with your thinking?

I can't agree with Shmelyov's position. It strays from socialist values, and it is too extreme or absolute. By the logic of his law, the most economically effective thing to do would be to shoot the elderly because they eat but do not produce. The question can't be posed that way. The principles of economic efficiency, morality, and socialism are distinguishable, and they may come into conflict with each other. The task is to find ways to reconcile them.

It remains to be seen whether or not the Soviet Union can reconcile these principles, indeed whether they are even reconcilable. One thing is clear, however. The changes you and evidently Gorbachev himself are proposing—perestroika as a "social revolution"—are so fundamental that they would profoundly affect the longstanding social contract in the Soviet Union, the explicit or implicit relationship between state and society. And that, of course, could affect the political stability of the Soviet system. For years, you have had, for example, a kind of cradle-to-grave welfare state, which guaranteed citizens all sorts of free or cheap benefits if they complied with the rules of the game. Now, you say these guarantees are part of the problem because they have deprived people of incentives to be productive. You are telling people that there will be less guarantees in economic and social life and they must take more risks. But if you affect people's psychology in those ways, they may decide to take more political risks as well. They may stop being so obedient and deferential to the state in other areas.

Yes, that is possible and maybe inescapable. As I see it, people will develop the habit of taking their fate into their own hands, first of all in economic life. They will turn into different kinds of people, confident and energetic in their work. And that will have positive political consequences. It is hard to imagine such energetic, economically independent people voting for just anyone. It will contribute to the general process of democratization by enhancing the importance of opinion from below, as people overcome their political alienation. If you have a passive citizenry, with 99.9 percent of the people voting for the same person, as we had in the past, you have the stability of a cemetery. If you want real life, you have to have conflicting interests and democracy. Without democratization, you can't have perestroika.

According to Gorbachev, Aleksandr Yakovlev, and other Soviet leaders, you can't have democracy without glasnost. You have complained that there was no glasnost in the realm of sociology and that there are still important zones forbidden to sociological research. At the same time, you have insisted that the leadership needs such research in order to have a strategy for perestroika and to know the social consequences of its policies. What does all this say about the progress of glasnost in your own field since 1985?

In the past, no sensitive social issue was open to research, from crime to our sexual lives. Well, occasionally some serious research was done, but it wasn't published. And anything thought to compromise our society in the eyes of the West was forbidden. We have made some progress since 1985, but there still is not full glasnost. Socioeconomic studies are underway, and information is being published. Much more is being written about crime and other forms of corruption. Igor Kon's book on the sociology of sex has appeared. We are surveying public and group opinion and publishing some of the results. Things get more difficult when we approach the political system, the life of the elite, and that sort of thing. There are no bans. It is just generally understood that these people would not answer our questions. Indeed, the whole concept of the sociology of power is poorly developed in the Soviet Union. Once I used the phrase "distribution of power" and the editor asked me what it meant. We've lost so much understanding over the decades. Even certain things written by Marx and Lenin could not be published.

Can you foresee a time when there will be no forbidden zones or a great many fewer?

I want to believe so, but it won't happen without a struggle. There are some positive signs. The Central Committee resolution on enhancing the role of sociology, which was published in June 1988, rehabilitated sociology as a full-fledged and essential science. It also encouraged a range of sociological studies and said that official statistics should be made available to us. And of course, the establishment of this Center for the Study of Public Opinion, which I head, is a step in the right direction.

Personally, I hope the center can play the role of mediator or organizer for a dialogue between the government and the people. We want to give governing bodies truthful information about what is going on and what people think in this enormous country. As things stand, ruling bodies get information through the bureaucracy, which distorts it. In this respect, we would also be defending the interests of the people by communicating those interests to the government.

The problem is that people were made so passive by what happened under Stalin and Brezhnev that there is essentially no public opinion on many vitally important questions. Under the old system, nobody cared what the people thought. I don't mean that public opinion doesn't exist but that it isn't expressed, except by the intelligentsia. Broad masses of people didn't have enough information to think about things. Our hope is that glasnost and public discussion of ideas and policies will compel more and more people to think, take a position, become active, and therefore support perestroika. In a country where the rulers have long lost the habit of any sort of dialogue with the population, where they have viewed the population as simply an object to be manipulated, this kind of public opinion is very important.

Without such a dialogue, democratization won't work. A certain model of democratization was behind the political reforms adopted by the Nineteenth Party Conference, and particularly the resolution "All power to the soviets." Symbolically, this resolution is very good, though it won't be realized without a big struggle. But if it is to have a chance, if one day we are to have a more decentralized political system in which the soviets are real parliaments with much more power and the Communist Party has control only over its own members, public opinion will have to be a very important element. No matter how wonderful a deputy to the soviet might be, he or she will have to know the real interests and opinions of the people.

As you know, we are beginning to have elections on a broader scale, including elections of economic managers. One of the first public opinion polls we did here at the center asked people at a number of enterprises what they thought about electing managers. It turned out that there are diametrically opposed views about this. Where elections were really democratic, people strongly favored them. Where they were not really democratic, people dismissed them as a game. This is, of course, part of the conflict between democratization and the entrenched nomenklatura system of appointed officials.

That brings us to a question we have asked other people and to which we have gotten various answers. As a sociologist who presumably studies

these matters, tell us about the nature and extent of opposition to pere-
stroika.

Earlier you asked me if my view of perestroika differed from what is usually written in the Soviet press. I emphasized the need for a social revolution. That is also why I do not share the view that perestroika is somehow in the interest of all groups and everybody in the Soviet Union. It affects the vital interests of millions of people, of virtually everybody in the country. The interests of those people vary widely. Therefore, perestroika conflicts with the interests of some groups and many people. That is why I do not agree with the statement Gorbachev sometimes makes that there are no opponents of perestroika. Though it may not be organized, opposition grows out of the vested interests of various groups in our society.

This is a large and complex question that cannot be discussed fully here. I tried to examine it in a long article published in the book *There Is No Alternative*, edited by Yuri Afanasyev. I took the position that there are eleven groups, from workers and peasants to various kinds of execu-tives, administrators, and political leaders, whose interests and atti-tudes will determine the fate of perestroika. I went on to argue that in these groups one finds a wide range of attitudes toward perestroika, including those of ideological supporters, social supporters, allies, quasi-supporters, onlookers, conservative opponents, and reactionary opponents. In my opinion, the essential and most intense struggle is expressed in the polarization between radical democratic-minded seg-ments of society and conservative-reactionary segments.

The Western media sometimes give the impression that there is virtu-ally no popular support for Gorbachev's perestroika because it is asking ordinary people to change their basic outlook, make sacrifices, and work harder, but without giving them any immediate rewards. That, it seems, is not your view.

Of course not. It is very one-dimensional. There are different strata and groups among workers and peasants. Some of them feel threatened by perestroika, but some of them believe or sense that it is in their interest and support it. By the way, it is not true, as is sometimes thought, that all bureaucrats and managers are against the reforms. I know many of them personally, and some of them are passionate sup-porters. More generally, here too we have different strata and groups whose attitudes toward perestroika vary greatly. Nor is it true that the entire intelligentsia supports perestroika. A great many of its members do, of course, but many others profited from and bear responsibility for the years of stagnation. The point is that Soviet society is very complex. There are many different groups and attitudes at all levels, so one can find supporters and opponents at all those levels, as well as people who are neutral.

Do you have any polls that can give us some sense of how Soviet public opinion breaks down nationwide into supporters and opponents of perestroika?

No, not yet. One 1987 poll suggested that optimism about perestroika was waning among working people, but given the slow economic results, that is not surprising. There is much discontent with the status quo, but nobody should be surprised that there is also a lot of conservatism. The Soviet Union has been through a history of transformations that made people tired or frightened of them. Even Khrushchev, who basically played a very positive role in history, wore people out with his changes. But even if we did conduct a national survey, the question as you formulate it would yield no meaningful results. First of all, every person today has his or her own perception of what perestroika means. So you would have to ask more concrete questions, such as, What do you think of making state enterprises self-financing? or What do you think about elections at the workplace? Second, it is very difficult for anyone to respond, "I am against perestroika." Not even a diehard conservative bureaucrat or reactionary would give that response. It is like a questionnaire in the 1960s that asked, If it was necessary for the country, would you give up your life for the motherland? Ninety-eight percent replied that they would. Later we used this as an example of questions that should not be asked. Who is going to say, "No I would not give up my life, even if it were necessary for the motherland"? A question asking if you are for or against perestroika would be similar.

Perhaps, but you seem to have a clearer sense of political attitudes in the high levels of the Soviet political system, among ranking state bureaucrats and in the party apparatus, for example.

What you are asking relates to a terribly controversial question. Marxism taught that there would be no exploiting class under socialism because there would be no private ownership of the large-scale means of production. And yet, our nomenklatura of bureaucrats and apparatchiks has acquired some of the characteristics that Lenin attributed to such a class. He emphasized the class's control over the means of production, access to a disproportionate part of the social wealth, and economic exploitation of the population. From what we now know about how our system functioned under Stalin and Brezhnev, it is possible to say that a layer or strata of the nomenklatura indirectly exploits the basic mass of the population. Even if it hasn't yet been able to transform itself into a class, it has moved in this direction. I say this conditionally and only about a layer of the nomenklatura. We need serious economic and sociological research on this question.

I do know that perestroika conflicts with the interests of a sizable part of the administrative bureaucracy, which is full of groups whose interests and attitudes are very conservative. One reason that perestroika is proceeding with such great difficulty is that officials of most of the state ministries are trying to strangle the economic reforms. They are finding ways to use the reforms, which are supposed to free enterprises from ministerial control, to tighten their hold on the enterprises. And don't forget the outright reactionaries in the state bureaucracy and party apparatus. Some of them are mafiosi types with ties to organized crime on a grand scale, as we have seen in Uzbekistan. If they had the chance they'd shoot Gorbachev and perestroika five times over.

It is not clear whether you are speaking of the state economic ministries or of the party's political apparatus.

Both. The party apparatus had enormous influence over almost everything in the past. Perestroika means it will have to give up much of that influence and devote itself to fewer but more complex problems in the area of ideology, spiritual leadership, and training new cadres. Unfortunately, the majority of senior officials of the party apparatus are still conservative, probably like Yegor Ligachev. Some of them are willing to accept aspects of perestroika, but others are just plain reactionary. Even the quasi-supporters of perestroika in the apparatus are dangerous. They pay lip service to the reforms, but they are determined to nullify the most radical ones. They are seeking ways to undermine, for example, the democratization reforms adopted at the Nineteenth Party Conference.

This applies also to people in ruling political positions throughout the system, who sit on the Central Committee and other governing bodies. Gorbachev, his aides, and some other political leaders do have the historic vision, will, and courage to see perestroika through to the end. But many political leaders do not. They were formed by past practices, they remain profoundly authoritarian, they lack the ability to govern the country in new democratic ways, and they have done things in the past that cannot be forgotten. The whole party apparatus must be greatly reduced, rejuvenated, and radicalized. And this is true also of the ruling group of political leaders.

If your account is accurate, it is very hard to conclude that there is no organized opposition to Gorbachev's leadership. Maybe there was no organized opposition to Khrushchev in 1963, but the bureaucracy hated him, and by 1964 that hatred found expression in the Politburo, which overthrew him. As a sociologist who studies bureaucratic groups and political elites, don't you think it follows that Gorbachev has put himself at political risk by attacking the bureaucracy so strongly?

You don't have to be a sociologist to see it. Everybody talks about it in the Soviet Union. I've heard people say in various circles, "What risks he is taking! It is so dangerous!" You even see old women in church praying for Gorbachev's health. So many people have put their hopes on him, they are very worried about his health, political and otherwise. When Gorbachev says there is no organized opposition to perestroika, I think it is a political statement to reassure people. Maybe it is also an attempt to persuade opponents to become supporters. I think Gorbachev understands that there is political opposition. But politicians don't have to always say what they are thinking. That's what makes them politicians.

Other people, including some of your economist friends, argue that perestroika is going badly or too slowly partly because Gorbachev has adopted too many half-measures. Do you think his leadership is as radical as it should be?

There is a reason Gorbachev says that politics is the art of the possible. If he had been any more radical—and it is hard to imagine how he could have been much more radical—it's unlikely that he would still be general secretary. It really is an art to steer a ship through all the problems we have. And it is absolutely impossible without compromise. I'm not a politician, but it makes no sense to take on too much. Moreover, economic reform is more difficult than political reform. Economic reform requires so many things that we lack—economic reserves, consumer goods, food supplies. You don't need a 100 billion rubles to redistribute political power. And don't forget that perestroika is being compromised in politics and in economics. Opponents are putting the brakes on radical reforms.

From what you say, perestroika faces enormous opposition and obstacles. Of course, you foresaw all this back in your 1983 Novosibirsk memorandum, where you warned that any reform leadership would need a well thought out strategy to overcome opposition and resistance. Does Gorbachev have such a strategy?

I can't be certain. I can't get inside his head. But I think he does. He has to get rid of the people at high and middle echelons who are braking perestroika and replace them with radical reformers. He has to bypass these echelons and activate the great mass of people. That is what he is trying to do by traveling around the country, meeting with people, and through his television appearances. But the overall strategy must rest on closer ties, or an alliance, between supporters of perestroika at the top and at the bottom. This can be achieved only through the reforms we've already discussed—glasnost, destroying dogmas in popular consciousness, rule of law, reducing the bureaucracy, democratizing the election system, decentralizing and pluralizing the economy, and generally eliminating bans on society.

For the leadership to have a direct dialogue or alliance with all of its supporters at different levels around the country, I personally think we need a new national political organization—a People's Front, or a People's Alliance, for Perestroika. Tens of thousands of informal organizations, movements, clubs, and federations have mushroomed all around the country. They are positive signs of mass activism in favor of perestroika, but they are being strangled by local authorities. Everywhere they try to do something, even here in Moscow, somehow it turns out to be forbidden, even though their slogans are the same as Gorbachev's. A national front or alliance, led by truly committed perestroishchiks like Yuri Afanasyev, Mikhail Ulyanov, the economist Gavril Popov, and others, would enable all these individual and group supporters of perestroika to unite. The organization could accept public contributions, establish branches around the country, monitor adherence to law and the implementation of reforms, publish its own newspapers and journals, and have its own time on television. It would be an important step toward abolishing the bureaucratic system and democratizing the country.

Yevtushenko has proposed something similar. He's not a member of the Communist Party, so he calls his idea a "party of nonparty members." Under the political reforms passed at the Communist Party conference and the new electoral laws, such an organization no doubt would also want to nominate candidates for the soviets. Aren't you proposing what in effect would be a new political party?

No, this would not be a party. You know, when people talk about a multiparty system in the Soviet Union, I think—well, the Communist

Party is headed by Gorbachev today, so who would be in the other party? People like Sharaf Rashidov, the late party boss of Uzbekistan who presided over all the mafia corruption there? The Communist Party is already frightfully heterogeneous. It includes Gorbachev, people like Ligachev, and the Uzbek bosses. I don't deny that it is terribly bureaucratized, that it has a huge apparatus extending down to city committees and district committees. No other party could compete with it. No, what we must do is cleanse this party. I know it is a very difficult, complicated political problem, but the national front I am proposing will help. It will include party members, but it will also support Gorbachev's call for nonparty members to be elected to leading positions in our society.

What if it turns out that the Soviet Communist Party is not actually the party of Gorbachev but the party of the conservatives or even the reactionaries?

The Central Committee itself has proposed the creation of a mechanism inside the party that will allow the airing and resolution of such problems. I admit all this will take time, but a new generation is emerging and the troops of perestroika are forming to do battle.

Almost everyone has told us that perestroika will take many years and that its fate depends on the role and attitudes of various Soviet generations, though no one has been very precise on exactly which generations.

Generations are shaped by their specific historical experiences. My observations suggest that the fate of perestroika depends most on two age groups: my generation—people who are no younger than about fifty-five to sixty; and much younger people who are not older than about thirty-five to thirty-eight. My generation had a chance to spread its wings from the mid-1950s to about 1968, when our wings were clipped. So we are very active today. People who are now in their thirties have also had an adult whiff of freedom since Brezhnev died in 1982. They are becoming active. It is bad when a generation is deprived of any freedom by the time it has reached about thirty, which is what happened to people between Gorbachev's generation and younger people today. They reached that age in the 1970s, during the years of stagnation and corruption. Now in their forties, they are lost to society. They have few socialist values—they are pessimistic, skeptical, and socially passive. But the younger people, not just those in their thirties but those who are twenty-five, they are really wonderful. I knew many of them in Novosibirsk, and I work with them here in Moscow. They have had a four-year gulp of freedom, so they will not be passive if there is a reactionary effort to reverse perestroika. They will fight.

As you think about this problem, do you see a special role for women in perestroika? On several occasions you have complained that your male colleagues in the social sciences are too often passive and lacking in civic courage. And as we watch the unusually prominent role played by Gorbachev's wife, Raisa Maksimovna, in Soviet public life, we get the impression that he and she are consciously encouraging Soviet women to be much more active participants in public affairs than they were in the past.

I have personally heard Gorbachev say that he hopes women will play an important role in perestroika, but I do not see a special role for them. It is certainly true that women drink less and are more stable than men. It is also true that women are generally under-utilized in our society, even though 94 percent of them are in the workforce. Few of them rise to the top in their professions. In the Academy of Sciences, for example, it is rare to find women serving as section or department heads at institutes. Nor have I yet to see women playing an active role in perestroika. At the many meetings I've attended, it's always men, men, men.

But it is not only the system that holds a woman back, it's also life itself the moment she starts a family. Take my own case. I have two daughters, which made things very difficult. But I would have been a very unhappy person without a family and children. There was a time when life was hard. I had to write my dissertation, and the four of us were living in a cramped communal apartment. Even together, our salaries, mine and my husband's, were meager. Constantly I was taking one daughter to kindergarten and the other to the doctor. It was only because I was irresistably drawn to scholarship that I was able to do so much. So it is not surprising that many Soviet women would like to leave the workforce if their husband's salary were large enough. And this may not be a bad thing. We have a generation of children who have been raised without mothers, who were all out working—an abandoned generation. These children have a lot of problems, including a sharp drop in morality among them. No one can replace a mother.

I also think that women are different from men. We find all the extremes in men, vivid expressions of good and evil. Men are more diverse in their talents and inclinations to innovate and organize life. Women incline toward a golden mean. They are more stable and conservative because they are the bearers of life.

But whether we are talking about men or women, perestroika has to give people faith in its goals and the freedom to be active and creative. Otherwise there will be no social revolution in our country. Working people are watching and waiting to see if the changes are really going to affect their lives. They've grown accustomed to a discrepancy between words and deeds. The greatest danger is that we will disappoint them again and lose their support. That is why the party and the bureaucracy must give them room to become active. When you untie a person who has been tied up for a long time, he can't run. His legs are cramped and he can barely stand. But if you really untie a person and give him a chance to stand, his legs may be wobbly at first, but he will walk and then he will run. If you don't untie him, he will never even walk.

Maybe that is what your conservative officials really fear—that if Soviet citizens are unbound, they will run very fast and in extreme directions. The policies of perestroika have already unleashed kinds of unrest and turbulence that many ordinary citizens also seem to find objectionable.

Some people think these developments are dangerous. Many officials don't want to give citizens their rights because they know that when you give a man his rights he straightens up and after that it is very hard to put him down on all fours again. Bureaucrats are masters only so long as slaves are willing to remain slaves. So they don't like it when people begin to rise up and exercise their rights, state their interests, and even demand the removal of certain party secretaries, as they have been doing in some places.

In general, the apparatus is scared of all forms of conflict—it's afraid of protests, of strikes, of everything. But we cannot rule out the possibility of even more acute political, social, and nationality conflicts as perestroika goes on. They are growing not only in the Baltic republics and the Transcaucasus but also in a number of large Russian cities. Some of them, alas, have taken extreme forms—hunger strikes and even people setting themselves on fire. These things reflect the country's low level of political culture and lack of democratic traditions. That is why the Soviet Union faces a choice: either carry through the radical reforms we have begun in all social relations or return to the repressive methods that produced this situation. Meanwhile, as perestroika goes on, the party and the state have to find ways to maintain a balance between constitutional procedures and social order, on the one hand, and the growth of democratic mass activism, on the other.

Your comment that the Soviet Union now faces a choice suggests that you disagree also with Gorbachev's frequent assertion that there is no alternative to perestroika.

The country could take one of three roads: a revolutionary democratic road, a kind of conservative liberalizing road, or a reactionary road back to Stalinism. Maybe I am too much of an optimist, but I don't think the road back to Stalin is really possible. The Soviet people have changed too much. So the real choice is which kind of perestroika will we have. A perestroika based on radical democratization or one based on a moderate liberalization of the existing bureaucratic system—a somewhat unclenched fist that could be clenched into a fist at any moment. If we take the democratic road, I believe that you will see a miraculous transformation of the Soviet Union into a truly modern, dynamic country. If we take the road of conservative liberalization favored by so many officials, the nation will fall irreversibly behind the modern capitalist countries. Eventually it will have to be fenced off again from the world and its democratic forces crushed by repression.

NIKOLAI SHMELYOV

"The Rebirth of Common Sense"

NIKOLAI PETROVICH SHMELYOV *is a vivid example of people brought into the limelight by the politics of perestroika and the possibilities of glasnost. A scholarly economist who had worked for almost thirty years in the relative obscurity of Academy of Sciences institutes, he bolted to the forefront of glasnost in 1987 with two publications: a bold article entitled "Advances and Debts" (Novyi mir, June 1987) calling for full-scale market reforms; and a powerful novella entitled* Pashkov's House *(Znamya, March 1987). The article radicalized public discussion of economic perestroika and stirred wide controversy, including some comments by Gorbachev, while the novella established Shmelyov as a major Soviet writer. Since then, his "publicistic" writings on the economy—as Soviet intellectuals call their contributions to the press—have continued to gain him many admirers and critics, while a flow of novels and short stories contribute to his growing literary reputation. Two aspects of Shmelyov's autobiography also are of interest. Like several other people in this book, he once worked in the Central Committee apparatus under Aleksandr Yakovlev. And until 1962 he was a member of the Khrushchev family by marriage.*

BEFORE 1985 I was personally frustrated and deeply pessimistic. For 30 years I had studied the international economy, while my own country remained isolated from it. And for 20 years, 2 or 3 hours a day, 365 days a year, I had written novels and short stories, for the drawer, as we used to say. I almost never tried to publish them. Toward the end of the Brezhnev era I had the hopeless feeling that the Soviet Union had reached a dead end and that our great experiment to build socialism had failed. My hopes rose briefly in 1982–84, when Yuri Andropov was general secretary, but then came Konstantin Chernenko and more pessimism. Chernenko may not have been a bad person, but he was hopeless as a political leader. Gorbachev and perestroika have restored my optimism and I am personally indebted to glasnost. My country is changing its economic policies radically and my novellas and stories are being published in many Soviet journals.

Since my fiction began to appear in 1987, people sometimes ask me how a scholar who had published more than twenty books on economics could also write works of prose. Actually, the same theme appears in all of my writings: For our society to have a social and economic future, it must return to common sense and human decency. Only those factors, not grandiose and complicated theories, make it possible to harmonize the needs of society and those of the individual.

My two occupations were the result of autobiographical circumstances. Like many intellectuals of my generation, I am a child of the Khrushchev years. I was born in Moscow in 1936. I entered Moscow State University in 1953, the year Stalin died, and I joined the Communist Party in 1962, while Khrushchev's anti-Stalinist policies were still underway. I began writing fiction when I was a student, but I already sensed that I would not be able to make a living at it. For example, in 1961 one of my short stories was published in the literary journal *Moskva*, but the editors changed its meaning by giving it a happy ending. After that I rarely tried to get my work published. When I did try, everyone praised it but no one wanted it. My theme, the struggle of the individual to cope with life, injustice, and society, was too controversial.

While I was still at the university, I decided to pursue my humanitarian interests as a scholar. I chose economics by a process of elimination. This was the year of Stalin's death, so you could hardly say there was any law to be studied. Philosophy had been frozen. History hardly existed. And I wanted to write literature, not study it. Our economics has been a large-scale human drama and it was a good choice for me. I was able to study with outstanding older economists who had miraculously survived, and this being the Khrushchev era, common sense was reviving. People were beginning to remember that economics isn't a system of caprice but a science with its own objective laws.

After I finished my education, I worked for three years at the Institute of Economics, which deals exclusively with our domestic economy, and then for seven years at the Institute on the Economics of the World Socialist System (IEMSS), which studies other socialist countries. In 1968 I left academic life to work at the Central Committee's Department of Propaganda, where I worked under Aleksandr Yakovlev, who was deputy head. Being a scholar by nature, I stayed there only a little over two years and went back to IEMSS. Twelve years later I again felt the need for a change. You Americans can understand that; you seem to change your place of residence every five years. So in 1982, when Georgi Arbatov asked me to join his Institute on the USA and Canada, I accepted with pleasure. I head the department that studies the role of the United States in the world economy. Actually, my colleagues and I spend a lot of time studying the Soviet Union as well, especially today, when we are being asked for recommendations on Soviet cooperation with the United States.

Arbatov is well known to Americans because he frequently visits the United States and often represents the Soviet point of view on television and in other forums. As a result, many Americans think of him as being an official Soviet spokesman. They would be surprised to learn that he had people like you at his institute. But it seems that even before Gorbachev became general secretary, Arbatov had brought a number of nonconformist scholars to his institute, including some who had been in trouble elsewhere and needed a haven.

It is a misperception or exaggeration to think that Arbatov's institute just did propaganda for the Soviet government. He had his own ideas and he recruited many like-minded people. I had some personal problems myself at other institutes—no scandals, just personal problems. Arbatov, who is an economist by training, understood the need for change, and not just in our foreign relations. And you know the old Russian saying, "It is better to lose with a clever person than to win with a fool."

Several of the other people in this book also worked in the Central Committee apparatus about the time you did—Aleksandr Yakovlev, Smirnov, Arbatov, Aleksandr Bovin, Fyodor Burlatsky. Is this just a coincidence?

Maybe not. Quite a few of today's most prominent perestroishchiks worked at the Central Committee during those years. It was a good education, like a little university, and I didn't regret it. You had a chance to understand things in a much broader context and to see from inside how policy is actually made. You have to understand that for people like us to work in the Central Committee apparatus just meant being assistants to the big politicians. We could study issues and make recommendations, but they made the decisions.

In the United States it is sometimes said that you can judge a political leader by the people around him.

We say that too, but when all is said and done, those people are just assistants.

Many American observers assume that anyone who works in the apparatus of the Soviet Central Committee must be a careerist or orthodox apparatchik, so to speak.

That's an uninformed opinion. People are people wherever they may be or work. I have a theory that any ten people gathered in one place for some purpose are a microcosm of the world. Among them will be a genius, a madman, a superworker, a fool, an informer, and so forth. The Central Committee apparatus is no different in this respect, though the staff's professional and educational caliber may be somewhat higher than it is at other institutions.

Also like other people in our book, you think of yourself as being a product of the Khrushchev era. Presumably, you are referring to the Twentieth Party Congress.

The Twentieth Congress was a turning point in the history of our country, a moment when the people at the top confessed that there had been something not only wrong but truly tragic in our recent history.

But I also knew Khrushchev personally and I liked him a lot. As you may know, I was his son-in-law for five years. Or more exactly, I was married to his granddaughter. He adopted her when she was very young because her father, Khrushchev's son, was killed in the war and her mother was arrested in 1943. Even Khrushchev could not protect her. She spent ten years in a Stalinist concentration camp. So my wife met her real mother only when she returned from the camp in the 1950s. By the way, please note that she and I divorced in 1962, not after Khrushchev was ousted. It was an American-style divorce, not a political divorce.

Khrushchev was a very interesting man. He was sincere in his reforms and efforts to improve people's lives. Of course, he could be a bit of a bully, but he had a lot of common sense, human understanding, and even humor. Unfortunately, he was only semi-educated and not sufficiently skillful as a politician. I'm sure that if he had been more skillful he could have avoided his political fate. Nonetheless, he achieved a lot. His speech at the Twentieth Party Congress gave us hope that the Stalinist system would be changed in politics and in economics. The process of economic rethinking and reform began under Khrushchev. Even his limited and improvised economic reforms were important, especially in agriculture, where he tried to free our peasants from their administrative bonds. Of course, he was very erratic. But even the more ambitious attempt at economic reform legislated in 1965, after his departure, owed everything to what had been written during the Khrushchev thaw. And so do many of the ideas of perestroika.

Why did that earlier attempt at economic reform fail?

Our leaders didn't understand how badly we needed economic reform or what kind of reforms were really required. Many entrenched conservative interests were opposed to any changes. The country wasn't ready to swallow so many new ideas. And then the political crisis in Czechoslovakia in 1968 [when Soviet military forces deposed the reform communist leadership of Aleksandr Dubcek and ended the Prague Spring] badly hurt economic reformers in my country.

As someone who knew Khrushchev so well, you must have a special reaction to the positive things now being written about him in the Soviet press. He is being rediscovered.

I am happy generally that we are beginning to speak honestly and fairly about important figures in our history. It is part of the process of cleansing ourselves of the tragedies and sins of the Stalin era. Because I was personally close to Khrushchev, it gives me great personal satisfaction that they are no longer hypocritical about him, that people here are starting to speak well of him. He was a contradictory man and he made many mistakes. But history will forget Khrushchev's mistakes because they were minor in comparison with the truly great things he did. He was the leader who first called Stalin a criminal, exposed the horror of the terror, and freed millions of people from the labor camps. That will sustain his reputation for centuries.

How did a person like you, with your reformist views and commitment to personal decency, manage to work professionally during the long period from the fall of Khrushchev to the rise of Gorbachev? Others like you seem to have had different fates during what are now called the years of stagnation. Some made major compromises, some became dissidents, some just fell silent, others drank.

As I said, the main theme of my fiction, and I suppose it is a little autobiographical, is the importance of struggle on the part of a single, lonely individual. I have an almost fanatical belief that no system can break a person's spirit if he struggles. A system can kill him, but not break him internally. I believe that this is the most honest form of struggle. When an organization or a collective undertakes a struggle, it is not the same, not as honest or pure. If anyone takes the time to read the more than twenty books and dozens of articles I wrote on economics during those years, they will find that I found ways to express myself honestly.

It is true that the Brezhnev years were lost years for many of our people. But people in the West are mistaken in thinking that life in the Soviet Union was so suppressed during the two decades before Gorbachev that nobody with good brains, a strong spirit, and a good conscience could exist. It's just not true. It was very hard for such people to publish articles, poems, or novels, but some people managed to do so. In very reserved and disguised ways, you could express almost everything, if you were skillful enough. There may have been peace and quiet in the press, but some intellectuals and even ordinary people found useful ways to say what had to be said. Even a few leaders raised the real questions that faced the country in their speeches and memorandums. We must give credit to all these people who carried on forms of honest struggle before the beginning of perestroika.

What was the main reason that perestroika finally began?

We faced an economic crisis that threatened the system's stability. The growth rate had fallen to zero, maybe even below zero. We were lagging behind in modern technology, and living standards were declining. But don't think the crisis would have affected the military sector of our economy. Historical experience shows that the Soviet Union has always had enough to keep that sector strong. So this wasn't the main reason behind perestroika, as so many Americans think.

What was the cause of the crisis?

It's our entire economic system, what Professor Gavril Popov has called the Administrative System and what I call Administrative Socialism. It is the system built by Stalin in the 1930s, based on state ownership of virtually everything and on bureaucratic directives. It is the system that perestroika must replace with one based on various forms of ownership, the market, and self-financing.

There have been two economic models of socialism in our history. One was Lenin's model of socialism, NEP, which he created in the early 1920s and which Stalin intentionally crushed at the end of the 1920s. And then there was Stalin's model of the 1930s, whose legacy is still with us. As an economist, I would say that perestroika is a return to Lenin's model of the 1920s, but by adapting it to today's economic conditions. The economic principles of NEP are the principles of perestroika—a mixed economy, planning as guidelines rather than directives, and a free market. As you know as well as anyone, Steve, that is why the rehabilitation of Nikolai Bukharin is so important for our economic reforms today. We have rehabilitated the Bolshevik leader who was the last one to defend NEP and Lenin's real economic ideas publicly. It is an important blow against Stalinism as an economic model.

People here sometimes doubt there was really such a great difference between Lenin's economic model and Stalin's. They were absolute opposites. I'll tell you the difference. Lenin's NEP was a system in which a sheep's wool was shorn a little bit for the benefit of the state, but the sheep was allowed to live, develop, and grow more wool. In that system everyone was content—the state and the sheep, that is, the economy. Under the Stalinist system, the sheep was simply slaughtered for its wool, or its skin was ripped off on the notion that it might grow back.

And yet, many Soviet and Western specialists argue that the Soviet Union's greatest economic achievements came in the Stalinist 1930s. Moreover, they insist that Stalin's economic policies were necessary in order to modernize backward Russia and prepare the country for war, which came in 1941.

Oy, that's all legend and myth. The seven or eight years of NEP, from 1921 to 1928, were the golden economic era in Soviet history. The facts are that the average rate of industrial growth during that period was 18 percent a year—the highest industrial growth rate in our entire history. Using real as opposed to concocted figures, the annual industrial growth rate of the 1930s did not exceed 5–7 percent. In other words, we would have industrialized faster if we had stayed with NEP. As for agriculture and collectivization, Stalin simply created modern feudalism in the countryside. His policies destroyed half the livestock and killed God knows how many peasants—maybe 9–10 million, maybe more. Nineteenth-century Russia exported about twice as much grain as the Soviet Union did in the 1930s. And for half as many exports Stalin nearly killed the country. We could have gotten as much, probably more, simply by taxing private peasant farming. So you see, if we had stayed with Lenin's model, we would have had a stronger industry and a stronger agriculture when war came in 1941. There was absolutely no need for Stalin's policies. None.

By the way, this also shows that people are wrong when they say Soviet socialism never had an effective economic system. We had one that was productive and viable in the 1920s, until Stalinism tragically destroyed it. It's a historical example of how a departure from common sense leads to immorality. That's why we are confident in saying that perestroika must be a rebirth of the common-sense principles of NEP.

Among Soviet economists, you may be the most enthusiastic and outspoken advocate of the role of an unfettered market. That alone has been enough to make your recent articles on economic reform highly controversial. Everybody seems to be talking about them, even Gorbachev.

Common sense tells us that there has never been and never will be an efficient economy without a real market. Too many people here still are against the market or think of it as something localized and marginal. We have to decide between the fist and the free market. I think of the market as something that must be a full-scale and regular part of the Soviet economy. It is where the components of a new Soviet economic system—state enterprises, cooperative enterprises, and private enterprises—must make their economic calculations and their contributions, and where they must compete. If cooperative and private enterprises are allowed to flourish and compete in the marketplace, they will saturate the market with consumer goods and services, all the things we so desperately need.

What would this new economic system look like? What would be the relative size of its components or different sectors?

What I call planned market socialism, or economically accountable socialism, which I hope we can achieve sometime in the 1990s, should be something like this. Ideally, no more than 20–25 percent of production will remain under direct state planning. The other 75 percent will be regulated by market forces. We have to go further in the direction of market reform than even Hungary has done; only about 30 percent of the Hungarian economy is regulated by market forces. I'm in favor of limiting direct state planning to defense industries, energy, strategic metals, and computers, leaving the rest to the market. Of course there will be a large state-owned sector, but most of its enterprises will have to function within the market, be self-financing, and perhaps even issue stocks and bonds to raise capital. State-owned enterprises will be accompanied by a powerful cooperative sector in manufacturing, services, transportation, research, and other areas. And there will be small family enterprises in the cities and in the countryside. With the exceptions I have mentioned, old-style direct planning, which now controls 80–100 percent of the economy, depending on the area, has to be abolished.

These reforms are particularly urgent in the countryside. The crisis in agriculture is the price we are paying for more than five decades of abandoning common sense and depriving people of any reason to be productive. We are at a turning point. Without a rebirth of common sense, the countryside may be doomed forever. Essentially, direct state planning should be completely abolished in agriculture, mandatory deliveries ended, and state and party bureaucratic agencies stripped of their economic functions. We must immediately put an end to administrative tyranny in the countryside. All forms of agriculture, whether state-owned, cooperative, or private, should be fully self-financing. And we should return to the situation that prevailed under NEP, when the state's relations with agriculture were governed by a regular process of taxation.

I am not calling for any one form of agricultural production. In a country as large and diverse as ours, what might be efficient and appropriate in one place might not be in another. In some places, state and collective farms, and even large agricultural-industrial combines, are viable. But in other places they are not. They produce only under state pressure and very inefficiently. In the central black-earth region of Russia, for example, many of them are clearly worthless and the land should be turned over to real cooperatives or to families on a long-term lease as soon as possible. Many officials are afraid that, if administrative control over agriculture ends, output will fall sharply. But we have plenty of experiments to show that real cooperatives and family farming have the potential to make up for and even exceed any imaginable decline.

If the situation in the countryside is so dire, why didn't Gorbachev begin his economic reforms in agriculture, as the Chinese did when they undertook their own perestroika in the late 1970s, rather than in industry? Had he done so, and had the reforms been as successful as you think they can be, there would be fewer food shortages and more popular support for perestroika today.

I think there were two reasons. It is less risky to make changes in industry because it is not so painful if production declines for a while during the transition. The risks in agriculture are much greater because if total output falls even for only a year or so, it is very painful. In addition, to begin radical reforms in the countryside, Gorbachev would have needed the full support of the entire party structure, and I doubt that he had it. Major economic reforms aren't possible unless the party gives up its economic functions. Here too it is easier in industry, where the party has fewer functions than it does in agriculture. In the countryside, the power and influence of every district party secretary is based on his economic authority, which makes him 100 percent master of the district. If he gives up that authority, he may still be master, but not a 100 percent one.

Incidentally, in 1986, at the Twenty-Seventh Party Congress, Gorbachev announced that state and collective farms could market freely about 30 percent of their produce, as they saw fit. Well, that reform was never implemented. There is an enormous administrative-bureaucratic pyramid in the countryside that exists solely for the purpose of extracting obligatory deliveries. There may be 3 million of these rural administrators. They are stifling reform because it would topple their pyramid. They're blocking the transition to family leasing and market relations. They ought to be punished and an example made of them.

But whether we are speaking of agriculture or industry, the whole problem is peeling all the layers of state bureaucratic administration off the economy. The state has an important role to play in the economy, but it should play it through economic means such as prices, interest rates, and taxes, not by using its fists and commands. If you look closely at the existing administrative system, with all its bureaucratic layers, you'll see that the top layers are completely irresponsible economically, whatever incentives exist have nothing to do with the actual productivity of enterprises or workers, and nobody knows what anything is worth or costs because of the administered system of distorted prices. Many industrial enterprises and state and collective farms are operating at a loss. All this is completely contrary to common sense and to a system of economically accountable socialism.

But when we talk about dismantling the administrative system, do you know what many of our economic officials say? They say it will cause economic anarchy and the growth rate will fall. Except in some areas of consumer goods and service, it would be healthy if our growth rate fell. The main problem isn't quantity but quality and marketing. The Soviet Union isn't a backward country in production. We produce more shoes than any country in the world, but they aren't any good and nobody wants them. We produce twice as much steel as does the United States and just as many machine tools. We produce many more farm tractors and combines than you do, but we buy grain from you. Even in agriculture, the most pressing problem is not producing more but using what we actually produce: 20 percent of the grain and well over 50 percent of the fruit and potatoes never reach any consumer. We lose more food than we import. Again, layers of bureaucracy and administrative tyranny are responsible for this mess. They prevent producers from caring about the quality of what they produce and from marketing it properly. There's no transportation and so much waste.

Your analysis of the problem is clear enough, but your solution seems to put the cart before the horse. Like most Soviet reform economists, you assume that if people are allowed to work freely and market the fruits of their labor, they will do so energetically and well in order to earn money to buy consumer goods. But as everyone knows, and as you emphasize, consumer goods are in terribly short supply all across the Soviet Union and those that do exist are of very poor quality. Nobody wants them—or at least nobody will work hard to get them. Given this dearth of consumer goods, where are the incentives for people to want to earn more rubles? There's so little to buy with them.

You are right, we must flood the market with consumer goods. A solution to the food shortages is within our grasp. If the radical reforms in agriculture are allowed to proceed, cooperative and private farmers will supply the market with surpluses rather quickly. As for other kinds of consumer goods, well, I am in the minority here. The Soviet Union is a large country, with ample gold and other reserves and with a relatively small foreign debt. While we are in the process of manufacturing more and better consumer goods of our own, we should borrow billions of foreign currency to import consumer goods for our market.

That proposal will outrage a lot of Soviet officials. It's easy to imagine the political-ideological howling: "Shmelyov wants to sell our independence to the West!"

What does political independence have to do with it? Everyone in the world borrows with one hand and pays back with the other. The United States has quite a large foreign debt, doesn't it? I'm telling you as a specialist, there is as much money in world markets as you want, so long as lenders believe you are a reliable borrower. Say what you will about the Soviet Union, but it has always paid back what it has borrowed. As for independence, let me cite a saying going around in international financial circles. If you owe someone 5 dollars and can't pay it back, you are in the hands of your creditor. But if you owe 5 billion dollars, then the creditor is fully in your hands. The Soviet Union guarantees the return of the money it borrows and the interest it owes on it. This is a normal commercial procedure. It would be better to engage in this kind of borrowing with a convertible ruble, and I hope we will have one, along with a fully open economy, reasonably soon. But we can borrow now in order to import consumer goods.

There is another reason why we should do this. We are suffering terribly from inflation Soviet-style. The deficit in the Soviet budget is about 100 billion rubles, but official prices are fixed so they cannot rise. Therefore, people chase after whatever meager goods exist. The result is even worse goods shortages on the official market and soaring prices on the black market. Importing consumer goods would at least ease this situation. In 1989 the government increased its imports of manufactured consumer goods by about $500 million, but it is far from enough.

All of your criticisms and proposals seem to relate in one way or another to what people are calling Shmelyov's Law. Since it has aroused a good deal of controversy, we should allow you to explain it.

It is very simple. Everything that is economically inefficient is immoral and everything that is economically efficient is moral.

The formulation seems a little cold or heartless.

Obviously it can't be followed in an absolute way. It is an appeal for the rebirth of common sense, in particular, that economic results ought to exceed economic costs. All the economic theories and schemes invented in offices have ended up violating economic laws and life itself. For years it was thought that these violations of common sense were working, but it turned out that life had gone its own way. I think you can prove, as I am trying to do in my prose and in my economic writings, that inefficiency is evil and efficiency is good. What was behind the mindless plundering of all of our natural resources for so many years? An economically inefficient system of calculating costs. What was behind the collapse of labor productivity and the rise of drunkenness that now threatens the nation? Economically inefficient constraints on enterprises, wages, cooperatives, and private undertakings. And what is behind our epidemic of bureaucratic corruption, bribe-taking, theft, hidden privileges, and the rest? Economically inefficient practices that have produced universal shortages. To say nothing of the inefficient political practices that cost our culture so dearly by driving many writers into emigration—Aleksandr Galich, Viktor Nekrasov, Joseph Brodsky, Naum Korzhavin, and others. I think my common-sense law has to guide perestroika and be introduced into all spheres of public life.

But surely this law, even the way you have qualified it, is in conflict with some basic ideas of socialism, which you say yourself is the goal of perestroika.

What do you mean by socialism? An ideal or the way our life has really been in the past? If you are talking about the past, well, it was a very, very far cry from the ideals of socialism. If you are talking about the real ideals of socialism, I don't see a fundamental conflict, only the problem of finding the optimal combination of economic efficiency and social justice. I'm sure that such an optimum exists and that we will find a way to give people some social security but also incentives to work. We are not the only country to face this problem. Look at your welfare state. Maybe this is banal, and I feel uncomfortable saying it to you, but I've seen more miserable people in New York and Los Angeles than I have seen here. I don't mean this as criticism of your system, only that you too have problems in sorting out ideals and realities.

Your answer is a little evasive. The Soviet Union may not have had real socialism in the past, but there are traditionally socialist ideas, in the Soviet Union and in the West, which your emphasis on the priority of economic efficiency would seem to violate. We aren't socialists, so reconciling your economic ideas with socialism isn't our problem. It's your problem. And insofar as Gorbachev's perestroika adopts any of your ideas, while also claiming to create a more virtuous Soviet socialism, it is perestroika's problem. Maybe you can clarify some of this for us by commenting on a few of your specific proposals. You have proposed, for example, some kind of Soviet stock market. Surely a stock market symbolizes many things that socialists have always objected to about capitalism.

I don't see anything objectionable in the idea from an ideological or socialist point of view. It would be efficient and advantageous for the Soviet economy because of all the unused savings lying around and because there is so little to buy. There are long waiting lists of people ready to pay cash for cars and apartments, which are very expensive, for example. Some of it is in savings accounts, but Soviet banks pay such a low interest rate that people keep God knows how many rubles in a trunk or under the mattress. This money needs to be put to use, and enterprises need capital. Why shouldn't the state issue bonds at a good rate, and why shouldn't cooperative enterprises issue shares? Workers and managers could become shareholders in their own enterprises, which might sharply increase their efficiency, and shares could be sold to the public. It would give people a choice in how to invest their money. What's so terrible about this? It is already being practiced in China, and it is being tested in Yugoslavia and Hungary. Certainly it is better than letting huge sums remain idle. It would allow state and cooperative enterprises, in industry and in agriculture, to raise tens of billions of rubles.

It's interesting that you emphasize cooperatives but omit private enterprises from this argument, even though they are now legal in the Soviet

Union, at least within limits. Are you assuming that private businesses are inefficient? Or is this a case where ideological, socialist considerations collide with Shmelyov's Law?

I admit this is a problem, not so much with small family businesses but if there were to be large private firms that hired labor and started issuing stock. Not only are official bureaucrats and ideologists against this, but the man on the street wouldn't accept it either. Purely in terms of economic efficiency, yes, we ought to have such a private sector, as there was under NEP. But we have to take into account people's psychology, which is the legacy of the last sixty years. For them, a private enterprise hiring a lot of labor would mean exploitation and they might burn it down. Some of our economists think we should allow private firms to hire ten to twenty workers, but I personally don't know where to set the limit. A thousand people working for one person is clearly immoral. When a skilled professional hires three students, I don't see a moral problem. But I don't know what people are prepared to accept.

All right, you admit that Shmelyov's Law has to be qualified by important political factors. Let's take one more specific example. You have often said, and every serious economic reformer agrees, that real reform and efficiency in the Soviet economy are impossible without fundamental changes in retail prices. And yet, here we are in 1989 and there is still no price reform.

This is a crucial problem and the most difficult, painful one politically. It is not just prices but the approximately 90 billion rubles the population receives each year in state subsidies of goods and services. Under the existing system, hundreds of thousands of prices are being set by the central authorities. The result is an economic madhouse. Some items are priced wildly above their cost of production, others wildly below. There's no rational economic relationship between cost and price. In order to have meaningful reforms and real efficiency, as well as a convertible ruble and an internationalized economy, price setting must be turned over to the market. The state can and should set only a few hundred prices. This has to be done; there's no alternative.

But we must not rush into it. People are profoundly opposed to raising the prices of many everyday goods and services that they are accustomed to getting very cheaply because they are subsidized by the state—bread, meat, a whole range of other consumer items, apartments, municipal services, medical care. The problem is under intense discussion in our press and in the leadership, but our officials are also afraid of the social and political consequences of price reform. It's the same with unemployment and retraining people when state enterprises are allowed to go bankrupt, which to some extent is also unavoidable if economic perestroika is carried out. But the prospect of higher retail prices is particularly frightening. What happened in Poland may not be a good analogy, but our officials think about it. And they remember the public protests that led to violence in Novocherkassk in 1962, when prices were increased while wages were reduced. If price reform is implemented clumsily or surreptitiously, there could be major social tensions.

The only solution is to go over to market prices and an abolition of state subsidies slowly, stage by stage, as more consumer goods come onto the market and while informing the population honestly and fully about each stage of the process. All of the lost subsidies must be passed on to people in the form of higher wages, salaries, pensions, and reductions in the prices of goods that now cost too much. But no matter how or when it is done, many prices will rise and the majority of the population won't like it. This is a real danger for perestroika. The people might conclude that all the economic reforms add up to nothing more than higher prices. That is why we have to wait until people understand the situation, have had a chance to earn more money, and more goods are on the market, which will help hold down some prices. Above all, we have to safeguard people's real incomes and standard of living. Meanwhile, it is critical that we implement the radical economic reforms and new laws that have already been adopted. Many of them are going badly, as I already told you.

Are they going badly because they were poorly conceived or because there is so much opposition to them?

There is enormous resistance and opposition. The main resistance is the monstrous inertia of the sixty-year-old system, which over the years has shaped the thinking and habits of the people as well. But there is also the powerful opposition of entrenched interests, which is at work openly or secretly at all layers of the administrative bureaucracy. I've already told you how local officials are blocking reforms in the countryside. The same is happening at the center and in the cities. We passed a law giving state enterprises significant independence from the ministries and the right to be self-managing and self-financing. The state ministries are finding ways to circumvent if not suffocate the law. We passed a law giving people the right to form free market cooperatives. The Ministry of Finance nearly destroyed it by imposing excessive taxes on cooperative earnings. We have all these economic ministries in Moscow, scores of them, and probably one would be sufficient. But hundreds of thousands of people work in the ministries, with power, good jobs, and good incomes. So we talk about reducing the ministries, but we haven't got around to what is necessary—abolishing them. It is a real struggle and it is underway throughout the country. All these levels of state, party, trade union, and farm administrators have something to lose. It is not their fault. They are not evil people. There are many decent and intelligent people in the bureaucracy. It's the administrative system that forces them to act the way they do. It is no accident that Gorbachev has used the word "struggle" so often. The question is who will prevail: Gorbachev and the forces of perestroika, or the administrative system and the forces of opposition and inertia? We may not know for years.

As an economist who was elected a people's deputy in 1989, do you think Gorbachev's democratization program helps or hinders economic reform? Some Western economists have argued, for example, that the political reforms may undermine economic reform by creating additional disorder, by further antagonizing or threatening powerful officials, and by introducing workplace elections that might impede efficiency.

For me, the democratization program is very important in three respects, just from an economic perspective. Glasnost is crucial because without full information about our problems and a full discussion of their nature, we can't solve them. Second, the Communist Party has to give up its economic role and for me this is an important part of democratization. Politics belongs to the party, but economic decision making has to be turned over to factories, farms, cooperatives. And if democratization really does penetrate the party and state apparatus at local levels, this would weaken considerably their power to resist perestroika. Finally, personally I like the idea of electing managers of state and other enterprises, though it is still in the experimental stage. I like it in human terms.

Have you forgotten Shmelyov's Law? For the sake of efficiency, presumably you want the most qualified professional people as managers. Why assume that workers would prefer or elect such people? Maybe they would choose cronies or people who seemed to promise less demanding work.

It is possible that electing managers will prove to be inefficient and we will have to give up the idea. But there is another form of workplace democracy that is interesting. A worker's council, call it what you want, that would meet once a year to evaluate the manager's performance. He would give a report and the council would decide if he should stay on or not, and though the manager may be appointed, no one could override the council's decision. Whatever the case, some kind of economic democracy is important because it is a way of awakening the nation, getting people interested and active. We have embarked on a bloodless revolution from above, but it cannot succeed without the mass participation of people below. That's why the multi-candidate campaigns and elections for the Congress of People's Deputies, in 1989, were so important. In them we saw the political awakening of the people, the renewal of society, the beginning of a real political life in our country. Without this, perestroika will fail.

You began our conversation by recalling how pessimistic you were before perestroika. Having observed all the obstacles that perestroika faces, has your outlook changed significantly?

When I think about the future, I am optimistic because my faith has been restored. The return to common sense is well under way. I am certain that my nineteen-year-old daughter and her generation will not face the kind of problems that have tormented us for so many years. Her generation will have its own problems, but not such difficult ones. It may be that a truly free Soviet generation is only now beginning kindergarten or isn't yet born. It is for them that we and our perestroika are preparing the way.

As an economist and as someone who visits the United States occasionally, you probably know that some Americans worry that perestroika will succeed in creating a much stronger Soviet Union, one with the economic potential to build even better weapons and be an even greater adversary of the United States in world affairs.

I'm not a specialist in international politics. You should ask Arbatov about this. Moreover, Gorbachev's disarmament proposals speak for themselves. The Soviet Union wants to become part of the world market, to establish healthy international trade, to join international financial organizations. It would be stupid of the United States to oppose our membership. Americans should understand that if perestroika continues, our main goals and efforts for the next one hundred years will be here in the Soviet Union, not outside the country. For the next one hundred years. I'm sure of it.

From left to right: Yegor Ligachev, Aleksandr Yakovlev, and Mikhail Gorbachev presiding at the Nineteenth Party Conference in June–July 1988. *Tass photo*

Aleksandr Yakovlev in his office at the Central Committee.

Georgi Smirnov in his office at the Institute of Marxism-Leninism.

Tatyana Zaslavskaya during a recess at the Nineteenth Party Conference, June 1988. *Anatoly Morkovkin, Tass photo*

Yuri Afanasyev *(standing)* and Yevgeny Yevtushenko at the constituent conference of the anti-Stalinist Memorial Society, January 1989. *Yuri Abramochkin, Novosti photo*

Nikolai Shmelyov *(left)* and Yuri Karyakin at the Academy of Sciences elections to the Congress of Peoples Deputies, 1989. *Boris Kaufman, Moscow News photo*

Yevgeny Velikhov at a press conference. *Boris Kavashkin photo*

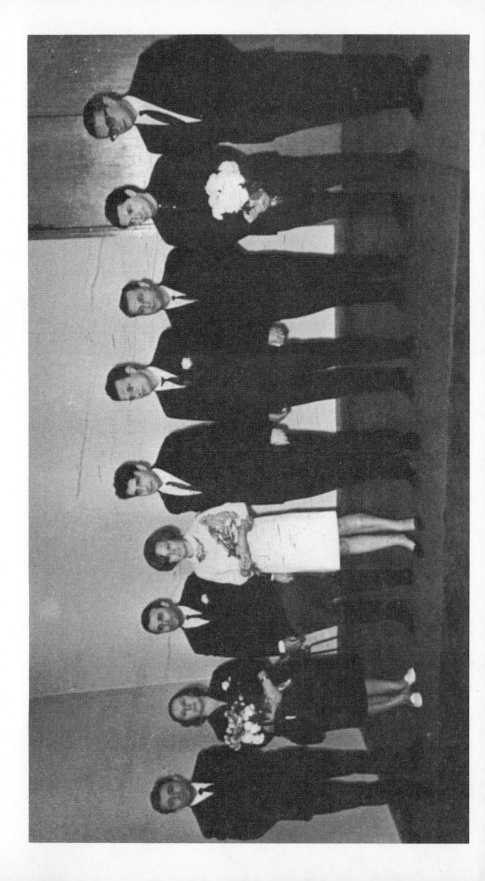

Yegor Yakovlev, *(far right)* at Karpinsky's wedding in 1967.

Len Karpinsky, 1989.

Yegor Yakovlev, 1989. *Moscow News photo*

Fyodor Burlatsky in his office at *Literaturnaya gazeta. Yuri Rybchinsky, Novosti photo*

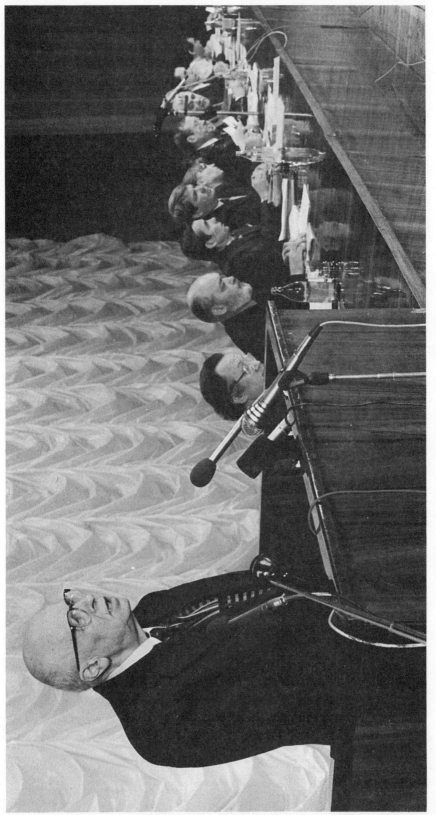

Constituent conference of the Memorial Society, January 1989.
Above, from left to right: Andrei Sakharov (*standing*), Ales Adamovich, Yuri Karyakin, Lev Ponomarov, Yuri Afanasyev, unidentified woman, Yevgeny Yevtushenko.
Below: Yevtushenko with conference delegates. *Yuri Abramochkin, Novosti photos*

Aleksandr Bovin in his office at *Izvestia*, 1988.

Elem Klimov *(right)* and Boris Yeltsin arriving at the Nineteenth Party Conference, June 1988. *Novosti photo*

Mikhail Ulyanov during a theatrical reading. *Novosti photo*

Ulyanov exchanging remarks with Gorbachev during his speech to the Nineteenth Party Conference, June 1988.

Yegor Yakovlev speaking at the Congress of Peoples Deputies, May 1989. *Boris Kaufman, Moscow News photo*

Yevgeny Velikhov *(below left)* and Yevgeny Yevtushenko *(below right)* voting at the Congress of Peoples Deputies, May 1989. *Boris Kaufman, Moscow News photos*

Above: Georgi Arbatov *(right)* with Roald Sagdeyev during a recess at the Congress of Peoples Deputies, May 1989. *Left:* Tatyana Zaslavskaya at the Congress. *Boris Kaufman, Moscow News photos*

Yuri Afanasyev addressing the Congress of Peoples Deputies, May 1989. *Boris Kaufman, Moscow News photo*

YEVGENY VELIKHOV

"Chernobyl Remains on Our Mind"

YEVGENY PAVLOVICH VELIKHOV (born 1935) is probably the most influential scientist in the Soviet Union, certainly of his generation. A physicist by training and a vice president of the powerful Academy of Sciences
since 1977, he was appointed director of the famous Kurchatov Institute of
Atomic Energy in 1988. Velikhov is also a prominent public figure—a full
member of the Central Committee and an adviser to Gorbachev who often
accompanies the Soviet leader on trips abroad. Velikhov is best known
outside the Soviet Union for his daring leadership of the effort to cope with
the Chernobyl nuclear disaster in 1986. He is also a cofounder of the
International Foundation for the Survival and Development of Humanity,
an ambitious organization created in 1988 with offices in Moscow, Washington, and Stockholm, and a governing board that includes Andrei Sakharov, Tatyana Zaslavskaya, and several Western public figures.

GORBACHEV PREFERS independent-minded advisers, and I've been
that way ever since childhood. I think because I have always been
interested in science. I became interested in physics when I was in the
sixth grade, and by the time I was in the seventh grade, when I was
twelve, I had already read a calculus course and a set of books on the
theory of relativity. When you start studying science that early, you
become independent from adults. Many of my teachers were afraid of
me because I knew more than they did. That quality stayed with me
when I entered Moscow State University to study physics in 1953, not
long after Stalin died. I was part of a group of university students who
organized a Komsomol meeting in 1953 to protest the very bad situation in the physics faculty. It was full of stupid teachers who sabotaged
any student initiative and denounced the ideas of Albert Einstein and

Niels Bohr. The meeting adopted a collective letter to the Politburo demanding that real scientists be added to the faculty. A special Politburo commission investigated our complaints and supported us. As a result, sweeping changes took place in the administration of the physics faculty. Of course, things could have ended badly for me had it not been for the new political atmosphere after Stalin's death. It was the beginning of the first period of glasnost, or what we then called the thaw.

One more thing. For many people of my generation, Khrushchev's attack on Stalin at the Twentieth Party Congress was a great revelation and a shock. It wasn't for me. I already knew many things about Stalin, even details, from my family. Even as a child I had heard critical things about Stalin from my mother, who was an artist—she died just before World War II—and from my father, an engineer, who died in 1952. But I learned most of the truth about Stalin from my grandmother. So while many of my contemporaries had to undergo a loss of faith in Stalin in the mid-1950s, I had always had a negative attitude toward him.

When I graduated from the university in 1958, I joined the Institute of Atomic Energy, in Moscow, headed by Igor Kurchatov, where a large group was doing thermonuclear research. It was a very important moment in my life. I was lucky to work in the section led by the famous theoretical physicist Mikhail Leontovich. The atmosphere was wonderful. Plasma physics was just emerging, and we felt that we had very few rivals anywhere in the world. I was only twenty-four years old. I was attracted to practical science and began to work in the field of magnetic hydrodynamics. We made several mistakes in this field, but I eventually stumbled upon an idea that has had very good results in this area over the years. Beginning in 1966, I also taught physics at Moscow State University.

In 1968 the physicist Lev Artsimovich, who then was a major figure in the Academy of Sciences, appointed me head of a commission to look into the whole question of thermonuclear synthesis. My commission wrote a report recommending that the Soviet Union move actively in this field and stating that it was possible to build the Tokamak reactor. We were right. The reactor was the prototype for the development of cheap, environmentally safe nuclear energy, and for joint international projects, so I am proud of that report.

I joined the Communist Party in 1971, and in 1974 I was elected a full member of the Academy of Sciences. In 1977 I was elected a vice president of the Academy. I think I was the youngest vice president. That was Artsimovich's doing. He promoted a whole group of young scientists, including me and Roald Sagdeyev, who until recently was director of the Institute for Space Research. By the way, many people of my generation were held back too long under Brezhnev, especially in other fields like biology. The older generation didn't want to make way. We shouldn't repeat this mistake. Perestroika cannot be successful if we rely only on my generation, which is so active today. We also need the thirty year olds, because thirty, not sixty, is the creative age. I'm a little frightened by the generational chauvinism of my contemporaries. We must not be disrespectful toward younger people, particularly in science. After you are forty, you have to face the fact that young kids know science better than you do.

Anyway, when I became an Academy vice president, my foremost responsibility was for cybernetics and computer technology, which were in very bad shape. Soviet backwardness in computers even today dates from a wrong decision made in 1962, under Khrushchev. In many areas, Khrushchev had healthy instincts, but he was poorly educated and badly advised in other areas, particularly the sciences. Until 1962 our computer technology had been developing very well. We were about at the American level. But we made our last good computer in 1962. Then a decision was adopted to remove all applied sciences from the Academy. Research and development were separated. Academy institutes lost their independence in these matters, which were turned over to state ministries and various industries. Cybernetics was still considered a pseudo-science. When I took over responsibility for this field in the late 1970s, I knew little about it, but I knew enough to know that the situation was catastrophic. After Andropov became general secretary in late 1982 I spoke with him several times about the situation, and he favored taking radical action. He didn't live long enough to see things through, but in 1983 a department of computer technology was established at the Academy. Now it is a powerful department with its own institutes and centers. We hope to have more than a million personal computers in the schools before 1992–93.

You speak of your scientific life but not of your involvement in Soviet politics. After all, in February 1986 you were made a candidate member of the Central Committee of the Communist Party and in April 1989 a full member, which on paper at least is a very important political position.

My political life began because when I became a vice president of the Academy I had more experience working with Americans than any other leading member of the Academy, except Georgi Arbatov. Remember, that was the late 1970s, when our contacts with the United States had declined sharply. Those that remained were primarily in the area of science, where there were various U.S.–Soviet committees on nuclear safety, arms control, and so forth. I played a leading role on the

Soviet side in those undertakings. Then in December 1981 the Pope sent an envoy to discuss the nuclear threat with Reagan, Brezhnev, and Thatcher. Brezhnev, whom I met once, decided the Soviet Union should participate in the Papal Academy's conference on this matter. I was sent to Rome.

By the way, at the Rome meeting I met several important and interesting Western scientists. The American Victor Weisskopf made a great impression on me by his commitment to abolishing nuclear weapons. It's one thing when preachers say this must be done, but Weisskopf had worked on the Manhattan Project and lived through all of atomic history. He and I worked together on a declaration, signed by more than thirty academies of sciences, adopted in Rome in September 1982. If you read it you'll see some of the ideas we now call the new thinking—the need for a nuclear-free world, the impossibility of nuclear superiority or of a defense against nuclear weapons. I won't say that the declaration influenced Gorbachev, but I know that he read it and reached his own conclusions. Compare that 1982 document with what Gorbachev said about nuclear weapons in 1986.

Did you know Gorbachev when both of you were students at Moscow State University in the 1950s?

No, he's older than me. I was just starting in the physics department when he was in his last year studying law. But I knew Gorbachev well before he became general secretary, as did several other scientists. I first met him in 1978, when he was national party secretary for agriculture. He was interested in the possibility of using computers in agriculture. In fact, he was the first such person to show real interest when I demonstrated some of our original personal computers at the Academy in 1981. He asked what was new about all this and when I explained, he immediately understood the revolutionary implications. Gorbachev has always been very interested in science in general.

Can we conclude that you were an adviser to Gorbachev even before he became general secretary?

He asked me for advice on certain matters, and we discussed various complicated issues having to do with national security and strategic weapons. He was interested in these questions even during the Brezhnev period.

What is it like to advise Gorbachev?

It is very easy to talk to him if you really have something to say. It is not easy if you have nothing to say. He demands that advisers be properly prepared so that there are results. In my case, the subjects are usually nuclear issues, strategic weapons, and computers. As a rule, our meetings are long, serious, thoughtful conversations that last an hour to an hour and a half. Gorbachev doesn't like brief, formal, protocol-like meetings. He cares about substance, and you are in trouble if you have no substance. Gorbachev talks during the meetings, but he also listens attentively. He is a good listener. That's a rare quality. It is easier to talk than to listen. Gorbachev is never formal or intimidating with me and other advisers, but he is businesslike. He wants to solve problems. He is very unusual if you compare him with Brezhnev or Chernenko. Many people had great hopes for Andropov, but I don't know how it would have turned out had he lived. I'm not sure what vision Andropov had of the future. Gorbachev has a vision of the future, and he is a person who can change the course of events.

As someone who knew Gorbachev before 1985, what was your reaction when he became general secretary? What did you expect?

It was one of the happiest days of my life. You see, I had understood ever since my school years that the existing system had to be changed, that it couldn't go on. But that is not the same as seeing how necessity can become possibility. I saw the possibility when Gorbachev became general secretary. I don't think that any of us individually—myself, Zaslavskaya, Fyodor Burlatsky, or others—had a full conception of the reforms that were needed. It is not as though we came to Gorbachev with our concepts and he just started implementing them. But many people did play an important role in working out perestroika—people who work closely with him now, such as Aleksandr Yakovlev. I got to know Yakovlev when he returned from Canada in 1983 and became director of the Institute of World Economics and International Relations. He made a strong impression on me. He's the kind of person who writes his own speeches. We developed a close relationship under Gorbachev, when the reforms were being worked out. I always knew Gorbachev would move in the right direction, but I wasn't sure how decisively and quickly he would act on what he was being told. Certainly, he listened. But I think perestroika was also his own vision—his own ideas and thinking.

For you the nuclear disaster at Chernobyl, in April 1986, must have been one of the first and most traumatic personal episodes of the Gorbachev period, since you took charge of coping with the emergency.

I spent a month in Chernobyl after the accident, and I saw what it was like to live in the midst of radioactivity. Previously I had understood what it meant only in an abstract way. Before the Chernobyl explosion, many important specialists and political figures believed that a nuclear reactor could not explode. Now they know the truth. That is why it is wrong to believe that there cannot be accidents involving nuclear weapons. And there will be an accident if we don't start eliminating them very soon. Gorbachev agrees. He doesn't believe in the infallibility of nuclear weapons, and Chernobyl strengthened his feelings about them. After Chernobyl he extended the Soviet moratorium on nuclear testing, and he thought you would have enough sense to follow this example. But you didn't.

During the Chernobyl disaster, you took some incredible personal risks. You flew repeatedly over the plant in a helicopter while the reactor was still open and belching radioactive material and flames. You even climbed the side wall of the reactor to survey the damage.

I wasn't the only one and it had to be done. Everything was unprecedented. We had no experience with that amount of radiation and those kinds of circumstances. We didn't know at first exactly what was going on. I couldn't send someone else to have a look. I'm not a general. We had to know what to do next—where all the fuel had gone, the amount of damage, if the entire reactor had been destroyed. At first I flew over in the helicopter, hanging above the reactor, while checking the levels of radiation. But we had to get closer to learn what we needed to know. It wouldn't have been moral to send someone else if I hadn't gone myself.

A deeply concerned Soviet official told us recently that the Chernobyl accident proved that the Soviet Union must allow independent organizations to emerge to monitor the state-owned nuclear power industry. That the Soviet state cannot be trusted to monitor itself.

I don't agree. The fact that your nuclear energy industry is largely in private hands and ours is in state hands doesn't mean a thing. Your organizations that are supposed to monitor the industry don't tell the public everything. You need Ralph Nader and his team to get at the whole story. The problem on both sides isn't ownership but safety. We have the same problems, and they are handled equally badly on both sides. What is needed are qualified, responsible people who know what they are doing. If the people at Chernobyl and at Three Mile Island had simply put their hands in their pockets and done nothing, nothing so bad would have happened. Instead, they made a mass of mistakes, unthinkable mistakes. You must have competent people. There's no way to make things foolproof for fools. I'm not saying there's no role here for independent social organizations to express their concerns about nuclear power and the environment. People should have a right to organize and protest. But once an organization exists, it tends to express its own interests, not those of society in general. We have a ministry here that is supposed to protect our resources and the like. It has an enormous budget and an enormous number of employees. Generally speaking, it is in love with ruining the earth rather than protecting it. That ministry is more harmful than a nuclear reactor.

But it is true that Chernobyl was a terrible disaster and that another disaster like it would be a catastrophe for perestroika and for people's trust in the state. That is why the party leadership is taking great care. We build nuclear plants too fast. Now we've revamped the whole system of management and control. It will slow our energy development by five years, but we had to do it for safety. Chernobyl remains on our mind. It highlights one aspect of what we are striving for with perestroika. Nobody wants to live any longer under the kind of socialism—it isn't really socialism—that we have. We want to live normally. I don't mean just from a material point of view, but so that people can use their abilities in full. So that people don't have to speak with a forked tongue, saying one thing in private and another in public. People want a normal life. I don't think we have any fanatics left. Well, maybe a few hidden in the corners. But above all people want a safe future for their children.

Other people in this book have told us that perestroika arose because of grave economic or social problems, even a kind of social-economic crisis, in the Soviet Union. Was there the same kind of crisis, or "precrisis," as Gorbachev calls it, in science and technology?

Soviet technology was lagging seriously behind the most developed nations, but the picture in science and technology was mixed. In my own field, for example, I never had the sense we were lagging behind. In thermonuclear synthesis and in the area of magnetic hydrodynamics, we were ahead of our American colleagues. Except for my experience with cybernetics, there wasn't much political interference—or hair in my soup, as the Russian saying goes. And while other areas of Soviet life did suffer badly from a lack of freedom, there has always been somewhat more in the sciences. We always had more communication and stronger ties with the outside world, more freedom of discussion and of opinion. Otherwise we would have had no science.

But more generally we lagged behind because the system created by Stalin, and the way industrialization was carried out under him, created bureaucratic forms of management and government that stifled initiative and adaptation. A cumbersome bureaucratic system reacts badly to the need for innovation and change and cannot utilize what we produce. We produce more steel and energy resources that you do, for example, but we can't compete with you. So many things are irrational here. The Japanese produce a camera that costs a thousand dollars and weighs half a kilo. We produce products that cost three roubles for half a kilo. And as I said, for all practical purposes we don't have personal computers. The five-year plan calls for producing a million computers, but a million is a drop in the bucket. We need computers in all areas—in schools, agriculture, science, technology, in offices, for everything.

The Stalinist system may have worked decades ago, under different circumstances, but now the planning system seems to plan backwardness in advance. It tries to plan so far in advance that it leaves no room for quick changes and innovations. Given the speed of the scientific technological revolution, that is a disaster. Nor does the system give talented, creative people enough freedom. Such people should be given resources and bonuses. In practice, they aren't, while people who waste resources get too much. That is why we have to introduce experimentation and competition throughout scientific life. What we have had in science essentially is a feudal system where powerful directors have run their fiefdoms as they saw fit. Now we must diversify scientific life, creating new ways of obtaining and utilizing resources, new opportunities for talented people, and new forms of competition.

Basically, we have to think of science and knowledge as precious commodities and create a domestic market for them. It's a way to reunite research and development. In the past you could receive money for research you had done on a contract basis, but you could not sell knowledge or the product of your knowledge. It was even considered illegal if a scientific institute sold its work as a commodity to a factory. We are changing that. A decision has been made that applied science can be marketed as a commodity. It can be sold as many times to as many different factories as there is a demand for it. Take computer software. We have almost as many computer programmers as you have in the United States, but we lag far behind you because they have been unable to work to their full potential. Now they can sell their software to buyers in the marketplace. Of course all this requires new laws and new attitudes. It won't happen overnight.

We are making other changes as well. We are creating a system of grants, based on competition, for promising scientific projects. Whoever has a good idea, whether a senior or a junior person at an institute, can apply. And we are setting up temporary laboratories for younger scientists who have no institute affiliation. This can't be done overnight either, but it must be done. I think eventually we should think of all applied science as commodities subject to market competition and contracts. It is the only way to break down the feudalism in science.

Most of the people we have spoken with have said that perestroika was long overdue, perhaps by decades. A few of them are worried that it may have come too late to revitalize critical areas of Soviet life, particularly economic life. Some of your remarks suggest that the Academy of Sciences, which is a very large and powerful realm within the Soviet system, has been part of the problem in science. You seem to be proposing, for example, various ways to circumvent the Academy's control over science and technology. Can the Academy itself be reformed?

The Academy has had an interesting history. It has always been proud of its democratic internal procedures. It has a tradition of multi-candidate, secret ballot elections for academicians and corresponding members. Even during the worst years, when the Stalinist charlatan Trofim Lysenko was an overlord of science and did so much harm, and despite the repression of scientists and then the stagnation under Brezhnev, the Academy was able to defend real science in many ways. But the general situation also affected the Academy. Membership was made available to officially favored people who had no real scientific credentials. Bureaucratism, inertia, favoritism, and the like spread through its structure. Directors headed institutes for an eternity. The director and his staff often lost all interest in real scientific work. There was no outside audit of institute budgets. Again, a form of feudalism prevailed.

Take glasnost, for example. Formally, we always had glasnost in science. Except for military and commercial secrets, there was no formal censorship. We had problems getting enough Western scientific journals because we didn't have enough foreign currency to pay for them, not because of censors, though occasionally they would rip out a page or two. But many scientific administrators had an interest in exercising a monopoly over certain kinds of information and knowledge. In your system, people seek to monopolize capital. In our system you can't get capital, so people usurped chunks of governmental power by creating monopolies in various areas of science. There was no way to challenge their authority. We had and still have a ton of formal mechanisms that are supposed to do this. We have more elections than any other country in the world, but they are usually formalities.

In the United States you have a real mechanism for peer review of scientists. Every year, thousands of American scientists help evaluate proposals for government grants. We need a system like that here, so that real scientists can review and evaluate the work of other scientists. Of course I know that your system isn't perfect. You too have forms of lobbying and favoritism, as when Edward Teller sold President Reagan on the idea of Star Wars. It reminds me of Lysenkoism. Lysenko persuaded our leaders that it was possible to alter plant organisms, which is impossible, and nobody cared what science had to say. Reagan was persuaded that it is possible to create a shield that cannot be penetrated by nuclear missiles, which is also impossible.

You are giving us a very mixed picture of the Academy of Sciences. You say that it had more democracy and glasnost than other Soviet institutions, but that the situation in science was very bad. Does the Academy need the kind of radical reforms Gorbachev is calling for in other areas? Does it need, for example, democratization?

Of course it needs democratization in the sense of real elections, competition, and the other things I have mentioned, though there are different points of view about this. Some people think the entire Academy of Sciences should be disbanded and restructured. Certainly science must be depoliticized. There cannot be, for example, a party line in science, only objective truth. The party should only set national priorities; scientists aren't always wise enough to do this. But you also have to understand that a kind of conservatism is needed in science. There are no miracles in science, no miracles to helping society advance. Not every new idea should be greeted with equally open arms. So while we now are having real elections to scientific positions—to high Academy positions and at the institutes—it is important that real scientists be elected. That is why we've made a compromise. The entire Academy elects a scientific council, which evaluates several candidates for the head of an Academy section or institute. The Academy then approves the slate of candidates, and the section or institute elects its head.

Perhaps the most dramatic political episode involving the Academy of Sciences in recent years was the banishment of one of its most illustrious members, Andrei Sakharov, to Gorky in 1980, because of his dissident views, and the decision by Gorbachev in 1986 to allow Sakharov to return to Moscow.

Though we did not have a lot of scientific contact at that time, I knew Sakharov before he was exiled to Gorky. The decision to exile him was horrible and stupid, and I did everything I could to bring about his return. So I was very happy when Gorbachev made the decision. I don't agree with Sakharov about everything, but he is one of the few members of the Academy who has really thought long and deeply about the question of disarmament. Now he and I work together as members of the board of a new international organization called the International Foundation for the Survival and Development of Humanity. In that connection we traveled together to the United States in November 1988.

Sakharov plays an important and positive role in the Soviet Union today because he can express an independent point of view. I wouldn't say that my own point of view is dependent on others, but I am constrained by my work with the Ministry of Foreign Affairs and the Ministry of Defense. And of course I am in a position where I discuss these issues with Gorbachev. Before perestroika I spoke out rather freely in interviews that I gave. Have a look at them. But I understand the need for compromise in government and politics. And I understand why politicians have to do things a little differently. In this respect, Sakharov can be more critical of official policy because he does not participate in government activities. His point of view is not only useful, it is necessary for us. As I said, I wasn't surprised by the decision to allow him to return to Moscow. I expected it. Indeed, I discussed it with others and I helped prepare for his return. I knew that Gorbachev would bring him back. The only question was when.

Sakharov was never expelled from the Academy, even during his exile, but a number of prominent academicians and other scientists signed letters calling for his expulsion. Some of them, we are told, resented Gorbachev's decision to free Sakharov and even to honor him in some ways for his dissent since the late 1960s. This is a case of how perestroika threatens not only powerful elites and groups but many eminent individuals who may now have to account, publicly or privately, for their past behavior. From your perspective, how great is the opposition to perestroika?

There is a Russian saying that goes roughly as follows: I need not fear my enemies because the most they can do is attack me. I need not fear my friends because the most they can do is betray me. But I have much to fear from people who are indifferent. And that is the greatest force against perestroika—indifference and passivity. It is very sad. You see, we can't realize perestroika by using the methods of the past, by imposing or forcing it on people from above. Gorbachev's main idea is to create a social movement for perestroika, a movement of people whose consciousness has been raised and who have become active. But there are so many people who just sit there—not just in science but in society at large—and say cynically, "Perestroika is Gorbachev's affair. Let him handle it and we'll see what comes of it." Not that there aren't powerful people who are unhappy with the reforms. The ministerial apparatus is being cut by half. People are being fired. But they aren't going to unite into an opposition party. No, what I really fear is indifference and passivity. People who actually think they live better when they work less.

You may be talking about the majority of Soviet citizens. Can a minority, even one in power, carry out changes as radical and far-reaching as perestroika?

No, the majority has to have an interest in it. The minority somehow has to find a way to bring them to life. That is what Gorbachev is looking for. Here's the problem. On the one hand, the majority doesn't like the way we now live, but on the other hand, it isn't ready for much change. Perestroika involves risks, and Soviet people have gotten used to avoiding or minimizing risks. They prefer the course of minimal risk. The only hope is gradually to get them to see the necessity of perestroika, risks and all.

How will you get people to recognize this necessity?

One important way is through economic reforms making enterprises self-financing. Until now, you got your salary simply by coming to work. As a rule, workers and directors of enterprises that functioned badly got the same wages as people at enterprises that worked well. Now all that is going to change. If you do not work well, you will not receive as much. People will start to see that they can benefit directly from perestroika. When one factory shows a profit and another doesn't, it will affect them directly. Some people may prefer to work less and earn less, but we will start selecting directors on the basis of their business abilities.

The same thing is happening in the state ministries. They are being cut in half and deprived of their control over economic enterprises. Ministry officials who are able and energetic—who have self-respect and care about their reputations—will remain and be committed to the idea of perestroika. In the past, ministers held their jobs for too long. Now, if they aren't qualified or committed to perestroika, they won't get a second term.

Isn't there another more diffuse but important source of opposition that objects to perestroika precisely because it calls for the modernization of the Soviet Union? The old Russian tradition that saw modernization, or

Westernization, as a betrayal of Russia's true destiny and that has its modern-day expression in reactionary movements such as the Pamyat Society?

This tradition exists, but perestroika can overcome it. The Pamyat Society, for example, has some popularity because of past official policies that ignored Russian monuments and arts and destroyed churches. Perestroika is encouraging other independent groups that want to restore these cultural treasures. Such groups will make the Pamyat Society superfluous, just as glasnost is making Western Kremlinologists superfluous.

Indeed, when Gorbachev says we must make perestroika irreversible, he means that we must never return to the kind of despotism that Pamyat is really clamoring for. To prevent this kind of reversion, we have to end the secrecy that fed despotism, hid the real state of affairs, and monopolized information as a source of power. Of course, we have to maintain some level of secrecy because of our conflicts with the West, but as those conflicts diminish, so will secrecy. Less secrecy, more elections, and more power to the soviets are what we need. I am hoping, for example, that our political reforms will end the ceremonial role of the Supreme Soviet and turn it into a real parliament. As the chairman of its standing committee on energy sciences, I can tell you that I have tried to make changes, but until now it has been difficult.

We really don't have a choice. You've been to the Soviet Union many times. You know what it was like before, where our society was headed. If perestroika fails, I can't even imagine what would happen. Or I don't want to. You say Aleksandr Yakovlev told you that it would mean the end of socialism. Maybe it would mean the end of both socialism and capitalism.

Assuming that both Soviet socialism and Western capitalism continue to exist, we would like to hear your views on U.S.–Soviet relations. As you pointed out, you have had a lot of experience in this area. Indeed, when the Central Committee was reorganized in the fall of 1988 you were made a member of its international commission, headed by Aleksander Yakovlev. And in the West, as well as in Moscow, you are widely regarded as an important representative of Gorbachev's "new thinking" about international affairs—as one of the leading new thinkers, so to speak. Virtually all of the ideas that you and Gorbachev call new thinking are directed against Cold War dogmas on both sides, which suggests that the Gorbachev leadership is offering the United States an end to the decades-long Cold War. If so, does it matter which side was responsible for the Cold War over the years?

Americans who know me know that I am a fair-minded man, but I cannot accept the proposition that both sides were equally to blame for the Cold War. That isn't fair and doesn't correspond to historical facts. We bear some responsibility, of course. Otherwise, we would not be rethinking many of our own dogmas. But just consider some of the things America did. You tried to impose your own values on our society, while you didn't yourself always live by those values. Your media dehumanized our society. We didn't do this to you. We wrote many negative things about America, but Soviet people knew how to read our newspapers between the lines. Moreover, everybody here knew about America's attractive face, about your high technological level, etc. There was no devil image of the United States in the Soviet Union.

For a long time we have been ready to improve relations despite the differences between our systems. That hasn't been true of you. Many Americans actually believed that my country was some kind of satanic empire. And then there was the notion that we sought superiority or domination in Europe. By the way, former President Jimmy Carter doesn't believe this. I spoke with him several times about it. He doesn't believe we have any military advantage that would allow us to fight and win a conventional war in Europe. Now we are substantially reducing our troops in Eastern and Central Europe, but we never had the desire or ability to take over Western Europe. And yet, the United States kept saying that we did. So I don't accept the theory that we are equally to blame for the Cold War.

You acknowledge, however, that the Soviet Union was partly to blame. Would your government's unwillingness to allow free Jewish emigration be an example? After all, this sort of Soviet policy caused hostility toward your country even among Americans who otherwise would have been proponents of detente and cooperation, including many American scientists.

The policy was unwise, and now we are correcting it. But if you want to talk about emigration, why not put it in general terms—why always, or mainly, in terms of Jews? Shouldn't everyone have the right to leave the Soviet Union? And here another problem arises, one that Gorbachev called the brain drain. He was referring, I think, to a tradition or social contract that derives from the nature of our system, which provides people with free education and professional training. You do not have this. Take my case. I received all of my education and all of my degrees free. I had no college debts. Now my family lives well and I have the opportunity to travel around the world. Therefore, I feel that I have an obligation to repay my society, to give something back. Maybe other Soviet citizens don't always share my feelings, but they should. You don't have this kind of social contract, so your feelings about emigration are different.

The solution is to carry out changes in the Soviet Union so that everyone—Jews, Russians, everyone—can work and live well. So that musicians and scientists can pursue their professions freely. Of course, it will be a long time before we have a material life in Russia as good as it is in the West. But the main thing is that when people are harassed and not allowed to work they naturally want to leave.

A number of American experts on Soviet military preparedness also point to what they take to be your civil defense system as a sign of Soviet hostile intentions.

That's nonsense. What good was civil defense at Chernobyl, where we had to mobilize the entire country to clean up a relatively small nuclear mess? It is absolutely crazy to think that any kind of civil defense would have any significance in a nuclear war. Civil defense cannot work and we do not have it. That is what I tell our military people. I don't even have it at home.

Other Americans pose the question in a more exalted or intellectual way. They argue that the Cold War and the arms race have been a major driving force behind scientific-technological development in modern times and that, if the Cold War were to end, scientific progress would slacken.

Speaking about Chernobyl, one of our top atomic energy officials explained that science demands sacrifices. Someone justly responded, "Who needs science that demands such sacrifices from people?" That is right. Who needs the kind of progress that threatens to destroy our children? There are means other than the arms race to promote scientific progress. Do such people think that without war or an arms race everyone will fall asleep? Look at the Japanese. Without war or an arms race they put their money into civilian technology and beat both of us. Anyway, healthy forms of competition—economic, moral, spiritual— are enough to spur progress.

And what do you say to Americans who protest that the new face of Soviet foreign policy is merely a lure to obtain Western technology?

No country can live only by importing technology but no country can progress without importing technology. The question is what you produce and what you import. Not even America can survive without using foreign technology—Japanese technology, for example. The point is that fast technological progress occurs because there is international integration and cooperation. If the Soviet Union relied only on its own technology, we would continue to lag behind. But we also must produce more technology of our own and we can do that, though it will take time. I showed our school computer to a vice president of one of your computer companies. At first he winced, but after he examined it more closely and met the two Soviet scientists who had designed it, he said that if he had those two people he could defeat IBM.

As for so-called technology transfer, let me tell you a story. Back in the late 1970s an energetic American physicist, Robert Hirsch, and I worked together on a project involving thermonuclear synthesis. I had problems getting support and he had his own problems. Our cooperation had to survive professional American anti-Sovietism and all of [former national security adviser] Zbigniew Brzezinski's sanctions. Even some of your scientists tried to stop the project on the grounds that dangerous technology transfers to the Soviet Union would occur. So I had a talk with President Carter's science adviser and said, Write down all the technological devices that worry you and, if you insist, our side will furnish them for the project. All of them are produced in the socialist camp. Although international cooperation is the best way for both sides, we can build a thermonuclear reactor by ourselves. So where is the real problem of technology transfer? It's a myth.

Maybe you're right, but some influential Americans are worried that perestroika generally is not in the interest of the United States. They argue that if the reforms are successful, the Soviet Union will be stronger and thus more capable of defeating or threatening the United States in some way.

If we wanted to threaten America, the cheapest way would be to build more nuclear weapons. Nuclear weapons do not require a strong economy, only a certain level of scientific and technological development, which we have. They are cheap and they are so powerful that a technological advantage on one side or the other is of no military significance. But we are not building up our nuclear arsenal. We are building down and we are asking you to join us in abolishing nuclear weapons. The reason is that Gorbachev believes there will be a terrible catastrophe if we don't get rid of them. This is even more important than our economic problems, though of course we want to rid ourselves of the burden of military expenditures. If the Cold War and arms race continue indefinitely, it will make perestroika very difficult, limiting our economic capabilities, preventing our participation in the international economy, slowing down our development, and keeping our standard of living low.

Well, as the Americans we are referring to would say, why would that be bad for the United States?

People like that seem to think they're going to wake up one morning and the Soviet Union will have disappeared from the face of the earth. That isn't going to happen. There are only two possibilities for the United States. It can face a Soviet Union with very difficult internal problems and therefore a country that is very defensive toward the outside world. Today, to be defensive means to have a great many nuclear weapons, which threaten all of us. Or there can be, as a result of perestroika, a reformed Soviet Union—a stable and reasonably prosperous Soviet Union. That is the Soviet Union the United States needs.

What do you mean by a stable Soviet Union?

A Soviet Union where there is more glasnost and democracy, where control over people is reduced, where the role of the army and the KGB is diminished. A stable Soviet Union would be good for America because it would not be defensive or dangerous. But a Soviet Union full of problems and tensions would have to be held together at home by force and would always be your enemy.

It is stupid to believe, as too many people do, that everything bad for us is good for you. What is good for you is a Soviet Union with only a minimal need for military power and no need for nuclear weapons that could kill all of us—and our children. That is the very first thing to think about. Not to do so is suicidal.

Those Americans who want to continue the Cold War are actually proposing to dig their own graves—and ours. The Cold War will undermine our glasnost and democratization. Don't they understand what the consequences of that would be? Those Americans denounced the Soviet Union before perestroika and they denounce us today. But they have to make a choice: Do they want a safe world or not? They don't even see America's real problem, which is not a military one but the growing economic strength of Japan and Western Europe. Those countries are a greater threat to the United States than a reformed Soviet Union would be.

FYODOR BURLATSKY

"Democratization Is a Long March"

FYODOR MIKHAILOVICH BURLATSKY personifies many Communist Party reformers who have been waiting for perestroika all their adult lives. A longtime anti-Stalinist, he has been advocating radical reforms in the Soviet system for thirty-five years—sometimes as an aide to Soviet leaders, sometimes as an out-of-favor scholar and journalist. A speechwriter for Khrushchev and chief adviser to Andropov in the early 1960s, Burlatsky soon ran afoul of the Brezhnev leadership. For fifteen years he wandered from research institute to institute, from one political run-in to another, publishing books and articles that were heavily censored but also full of Aesopian or double meanings. During those years without glasnost, he managed to cofound and become vice president of the Soviet Political Science Association, another profession long in official disfavor. In 1983, following Andropov's election as general secretary, Burlatsky was made a regular columnist on international affairs for the influential weekly newspaper Literaturnaya gazeta. Since 1985, his columns and other writings have treated many once-taboo subjects in Soviet history and politics. Several of his candid "political dialogues" have been dramatized on Soviet television and his play about the 1962 Cuban missile crisis, which he observed firsthand as an aide to Khrushchev, opened in Moscow in 1986. Burlatsky's writings on political reform, or "democratization," have been particularly important as the struggle over this dimension of perestroika has unfolded. Though no longer affiliated with the Central Committee apparatus, he is again politically active. He was a member of the delegation accompanying Gorbachev abroad on three of the Soviet leader's summit meetings with President Reagan. In 1987 Burlatsky was named head of the new Soviet Public Commission for International Cooperation on Humanitarian Problems and Human Rights. As he says below, he wants to turn the human rights commission into a "legal opposition to the bureaucracy." And in March 1989 he was elected to the newly created Congress of Peo-

ple's Deputies, which is supposed to be a step toward the real parliamentary system that he favors.

———

I'VE BEEN STRUGGLING against Stalinism and for the democratization of my country for more than thirty-five years, ever since 1953. There have been ups and downs in my life—times when I worked closely with Soviet leaders and times when I had to resign or I lost my job. Perestroika is a fight that may involve more setbacks—for example, my nomination to be a delegate to the Nineteenth Party Conference was blocked—but I don't have time to worry about that. I'm already sixty-one years old.

The most active reformers of my generation are children of the Twentieth Party Congress, but I was an anti-Stalinist before that. My first anti-Stalinist attitudes came from my parents, particularly from my mother. They were members of the original Bolshevik movement, and they fought in the Civil War of 1918–21. My mother, who completed two years at a musical conservatory before the Revolution, was proud that Lenin's wife called her one of the first nightingales of the Bolshevik Revolution. When I was born in 1927, in Kiev, my parents named me Fyodor in honor of Friedrich Engels, and my mother raised me on songs of the revolution. In 1961 I wrote a line from one of those songs into Khrushchev's speech to the Twenty-Second Party Congress; he liked it very much.

My mother remained devoted to the Revolution, and she never believed the false charges Stalin brought against all the old Bolsheviks in the 1930s. My parents survived Stalin's terror, probably because they had left party work by the late 1920s. My mother became a doctor and my father went to work in a Soviet financial institution. But I was the only member of my family to survive World War II unscathed. My father joined the labor army when he was almost sixty, got tuberculosis, and died. My mother also got tuberculosis and my sister died at age eleven.

When I graduated from high school in 1945 I wanted to be a pilot. But the war was ending and the aviation school didn't need me, so I entered law school in Tashkent. I graduated in two years instead of four, and in 1950 I went to Moscow for graduate study at the Institute of State and Law. I began studying what many years later we were finally allowed to call political science. I got my degree in only one year. Having joined the Communist Party as a candidate member in 1948, I became a full member in 1952, before Stalin's death.

I also got a private education during my graduate studies in Moscow. I was living with an old Communist, a friend of my family, who had been a leader of a revolutionary soviet as far back as 1905. He too had quit politics and managed to survive Stalin's terror. An old man who taught English for a living, he had in his tiny apartment a secret library of totally forbidden Soviet books and old party documents— Lenin's testament against Stalin, writings by Bukharin, Grigori Zinoviev, Lev Kamenev, and other old Bolsheviks, stenographic records of early party congresses—things no longer available anywhere. In 1950, while doing graduate work in the day, I'd sit by candlelight at night and read the real history of the party. It was clear to me that Stalin's version was a monstrous lie from beginning to end. I suppose it was dangerous. A neighbor could have denounced me and the old man. And it wasn't as though I kept my views to myself. Sometimes I blabbed them to my friends. But that is why my political convictions did not change as a result of the Twentieth Congress. I was already a confirmed anti-Stalinist. By the way, I didn't include one reference to Stalin in my dissertation, even though that was always done in those days, no matter what the subject.

In 1953 I was about to start an academic career when chance—or biology, shall we say—drew me into politics. Stalin died. A new era was already beginning, and they were looking for new people. The journal of the Central Committee, *Kommunist*, offered me a job. From 1953 to 1960 I was deputy head of its international section. During those years I sometimes edited articles for the journal written by Yuri Andropov, who headed the Central Committee's department for relations with other socialist and Communist parties. In 1960 he asked me to come to work in his department as a consultant. To tell you the truth, I had real misgivings. I've never liked a regular office job, and I felt no urge to work in the party apparatus. But when Andropov assured me that my job would be to write theoretical articles, I accepted the position. Then he asked me to create a group of consultants under him, so I brought in a number of people who now are very prominent—Georgi Shakhnazarov, who's a personal aide to Gorbachev; Gennadi Gerasimov, who's the spokesman of the Foreign Ministry; Oleg Bogomolov, who is director of the Institute on the Economics of the World Socialist System; Georgi Arbatov and Aleksandr Bovin, who also are taking part in your book; and others. It was a very unusual group of young party intellectuals, perhaps the first ever in the Central Committee.

Though we didn't plan it that way, it turned out that most of the people in this book have known each other since the 1950s, when they were young

*and just beginning their careers. This seems to be true of many of the
radical reformers whom perestroika has brought to the fore. Indeed, a
writer in a Soviet newspaper recently referred to your generation of intellectuals as the "vanguard of perestroika."*

Yes, in one way or another we've worked together or stayed in close
contact since the 1950s. In fact, some of us who worked together in the
Central Committee in the early 1960s, under Khrushchev, developed
some of the first anti-Stalinist ideas. I even set out some of these ideas as
early as mid-1953, in an editorial I coauthored for *Kommunist* called
"The Role of the Masses in History." I criticized bureaucratism, the
cult of the leader's personality, and corruption, and I raised the issue of
developing democracy in the Soviet Union.

In the early 1960s my group in the Central Committee apparatus
drafted some of the main reformist documents of that period, and during the eighteen months prior to the Twenty-Second Party Congress, in
1961, I was part of a group writing the new party program. For example, I was one of the people who formulated the idea that we should
have a "state of all the people" instead of a "dictatorship of the proletar-
iat," as it had been characterized until then. I remember how one leader
was outraged that we wanted to drop the concept of dictatorship, which
he claimed was the essence of Leninism. But we won. I also prepared a
memorandum on democratizing the party and particularly on the need
to limit the tenure of party officials. This provision has been adopted
under Gorbachev, but it originated under Khrushchev. My original
draft stipulated that members of the top leadership could remain in
office no more than two terms. But Khrushchev couldn't get it through
the Politburo, or Presidium, as it was then called. The younger members were vehemently opposed.

When Brezhnev became general secretary in 1964, many things
began to change. By early 1965 you could see that they were breaking
with the Twentieth Party Congress and taking a new approach to Stalin's role in our history. You could even see it in international affairs.
They began to change our approach to Yugoslavia and China and to
express sharper attitudes toward the West. Very soon I started getting
orders to write speeches contrary to what I had been writing. I was
young and emotional, so I quit. I think it was the only case since the
1920s of anyone actually resigning from the Central Committee apparatus. I loved Andropov and I told him frankly why I was leaving—that I
was no good for the new policies. He was angry at me, but I left anyway.

Pravda hired me to be a political observer, or what you call a political columnist. It is a very special journalistic position in our system—I think I was the first—and even now there aren't many. That gave me a chance to continue to publicize my views, but my position at *Pravda* lasted only from 1965 to 1967, before they shot me in the back, as Vladimir Vysotsky [the late Soviet bard, poet, and actor] used to say. The last straw was the article I wrote about censorship in the theater with Len Karpinsky, but the real reason was a series of articles I wrote about Spain, in which I criticized authoritarian regimes and analyzed the possibilities of democratization after Franco. Everybody understood they were really about the Soviet Union. Then I published a short book on Spain—somewhat milder—and wrote three long articles criticizing the rule of Mao Tse-tung. The articles on China were sent to the Central Committee, where they caused a lot of irritation. They refused to publish them. But I'm a stubborn man; I published them in a book about Mao years later.

After I lost my position at *Pravda* I went into academic life. I had got my Ph.D. in 1964, while I was working at the Central Committee, and I joined the Institute of World Economics and International Relations. Within a year I was involved in another doomed undertaking. Along with Aleksandr Rumyantsev, who was a vice president of the Academy of Sciences, I tried to create an institute of sociological studies. Rumyantsev soon came into conflict with the Central Committee overseer of social sciences under Brezhnev, Sergei Trapeznikov. Trapeznikov, who had neo-Stalinist views, really hated me because I had once called him a little mutt with a limp. But the main problem was that many social scientists, particularly the philosophers, were opposed to a sociological institute. In 1972, after a long polemical discussion in the press, Rumyantsev lost his post and I resigned again.

Over the next few years I worked at other academic institutions. From 1972 to 1975 I was head of a section at the Institute for State and Law, where I tried without success to form a department of political sociology. Then I became head of the philosophy department at the Institute of Social Science and in 1976 vice president of the newly formed Soviet Political Science Association. I kept writing. Finally, in 1983, after Andropov became general secretary, I was given back my position as political observer, this time at *Literaturnaya gazeta*, where we now sit.

It is clear how you clung to your reformist ideas during the Brezhnev era, but what did other people with your radical views do?

The most honest and persistent reformers did what they could. They found areas of work where they could continue to promote their ideas. In my case, my book about Mao was really about Stalin and Stalinism and my book on Machiavelli was relevant to our political system and situation. I also wrote about political science, trying to develop the concept of political culture and its relation to democratization, and about international relations. And I wasn't the only one. I knew dozens of such people here in Moscow alone—people who tried to keep alive the ideas of the Twentieth Party Congress.

Other people who were reformers in the Soviet establishment in the 1960s chose or were forced to resort to other kinds of activities during the Brezhnev years. Some, like Sakharov and Roy Medvedev, became dissidents, and your old friend Len Karpinsky was turned into a half-dissident, as he explains in his conversation with us. How would you evaluate the contribution of former dissidents, some of whom are now playing officially accepted roles under Gorbachev, to preparing the way for perestroika?

I'll give you my own sincere opinion. In every political system, there is the problem of how to influence the actual political process. Real ideological or policy influence on the process is exercised by people who do not put themselves outside the political system. In the United States, when the Republican Party is in power, the Democratic Party tries to achieve its objectives through legal means, within the framework of the system. The same is true of the Conservative and Labor parties in England. Dissident forces rarely have had a serious influence on the political process in any country—only where there is a revolutionary situation and they are planning a revolution or coup based on their ideas.

Our dissidents never had a direct or serious influence on the political process. Individuals like Sakharov and Aleksandr Solzhenitsyn had a large impact on public opinion but not on political practice because they were rejected by the political system. Conservative and reactionary forces even used them to roll back and narrow permitted political and ideological boundaries. Some dissidents did play constructive roles— for example, Roy Medvedev and his brother Zhores [who has lived in London since 1973]. They wrote in a spirit that left some ground under their feet here. Many dissident books published abroad were useful. They were read here, and people thought about their ideas. But none of this had any direct influence on political practice or the leadership's thinking. On the contrary, when one of us expressed a similar opinion, or any view that reactionary and conservative forces didn't like, they immediately said, "So, you're drifting toward the dissidents, are you?" Or, "Ah, you're repeating the words of Roy Medvedev." And that made it harder for us.

No, I don't think you can say that our dissidents prepared the way for perestroika. Perestroika was prepared by people within the system who continued to speak out for revolutionary structural reforms. First and foremost, Khrushchev had a great and lasting influence, but there was a whole galaxy of Soviet editors and writers—Aleksandr Tvardovsky, Vladimir Dudintsev, Vasily Grossman, and many others. These were people who did not allow themselves to be pushed outside the political system, who did not retreat into dissidence. But maybe I praise these people who stayed in the party and in the system because I was one of them—one of those who clung to what others called the delusion of thinking that we could change things from inside.

There seem to be many different kinds of political people in the Soviet Communist Party, even among party intellectuals. A famous quip is attributed to the late Soviet writer Ilya Ehrenburg, who reportedly remarked back in the 1960s, "The problem with a one-party system is that anybody can get into the party, even fascists."

I'd put it differently. There are people of different political outlooks in every political party. In Western political parties you have people on the left and on the right. It's the same here, except all of them are in one party. That makes it harder and riskier to express dissenting views. I've studied the political histories of other countries, and I know that honest and talented people everywhere face the same choice that we face: either be a conformist or endanger your career or political position. That's how it's always been, from the ancient world of politics to modern one-party and multiparty systems. It boils down to personal choice. No matter what the nature of the system, one-party or multiparty, individuals go on thinking with their own heads, whether they are progressives or reactionaries.

Are you saying that the progressive wing of the Soviet Communist Party came to power with Gorbachev?

No doubt about it. But this meant, first and foremost, Gorbachev himself and his circle of close associates. It will take time for the progressive wing to come to power throughout the party and at all levels of society. This process is underway, but it is a struggle, and it will take many years.

You have known and even worked with most of the Soviet leaders of the post-Stalin era. You've had an unusual vantage point. Say a few words about the political qualities of the leaders you have personally known or observed.

I accompanied Khrushchev on trips abroad six times as his speech-writer, including the last trip he made—to Czechoslovakia. He was a very vivid and unusual politician. Unfortunately, he lacked a real education and a high level of political culture. He also liked to talk too much. A tradition began under Khrushchev that seemed to equate a leader's authority with the number of public words he uttered. But Khrushchev was politically brave, sometimes desperately so. He was the only political leader at the time brave enough to give that speech against Stalin at the Twentieth Party Congress in 1956. It was one of the rare instances in history when a political leader risked his personal position, even his life, for the sake of what was right. Khrushchev knew that the overwhelming majority of delegates to the congress would be against his disclosures about Stalin's terror—I would guess 80–90 percent of them. And it was no accident that he gave the speech only after the congress had elected the Central Committee. Otherwise he might not have been reelected general secretary, or first secretary, as the post was then called.

There's no doubt that Khrushchev achieved a lot. His policies fore-shadowed perestroika. He began the process of de-Stalinization, which we are now renewing in a deeper way. He established some guarantees against a return to a regime based on personal dictatorship and mass repressions. He initiated the process of reform in the Stalinist economic system. He began the process of detente or peaceful coexistence with the West and of limiting the arms race. And his role in the compromise that ended the Cuban missile crisis in 1962 was tremendous. Both he and President John F. Kennedy exhibited great leadership qualities. Both were ready to do anything to avoid a nuclear confrontation.

But Khrushchev also had two important weaknesses. We used to call him the man in worn-out slippers because his poor judgment of people allowed him to keep too many time-servers and sycophants around him. He didn't rely enough on real supporters of his reforms. Instead, he surrounded himself with men like Nikolai Podgorny [a Politburo member who became Soviet president after Khrushchev's overthrow]—people who licked his boots and were prepared to agree with anything he said or did.

Khrushchev was so confident of himself that he had no use for independent-minded people. His other weakness was that he lacked a well thought out concept of reform or any clear strategy of how to achieve his reforms. In particular, unlike Gorbachev, he tried to carry out reforms only from above, without mass participation. Our group, headed by Andropov, had some influence on Khrushchev, but there were other groups in the Central Committee apparatus with opposing and stronger influence, particularly in domestic policy. In general, Khrushchev was too erratic and too emotional, traits that are weaknesses in a leader. I heard him speak privately several times of his intense hatred of Stalinism, but he had been part of Stalinism—he bore some personal responsibility—and that accounts for some of his limitations and contradictions. Most important, though, neither the party nor society was ready for major reforms.

Brezhnev, on the other hand, was a typical product not only of our system but of yours. He blew with the wind, and he was conservative by nature. He had no real expertise on domestic or foreign policy, and he admitted that he knew little about theoretical issues. But he was very flexible, and he understood very well the psychology of power. Unlike Khrushchev, Brezhnev never spoke first at leadership meetings; usually he spoke last. He would see what others had to say and shape his remarks accordingly. If the group had misgivings or was divided, he would just put off a decision. He was a sort of Soviet Tory, but without the high cultural level of British Tories.

Brezhnev was a leader only in the sense that he made himself acceptable to the political elite. When he came to power his motto was "stability," and that kept him in power for the next twenty years. He promised the elite and the country that everything would somehow be okay and that everyone in the elite would hold on to their posts. He changed things as little as possible. The result was greater problems, stagnation, corruption—all the crises glasnost has revealed.

As for Andropov, he was the most vivid political personality I ever knew personally, at least before Gorbachev. He had an enormous passion for politics, and he worked from morning to night, even on weekends, despite chronically high blood pressure. Andropov had an extraordinarily sharp, imaginative mind, and he was exceptionally well read, especially in political philosophy. He was a very decisive man, but also one who was flexible, who knew how to adapt to circumstances. Sometimes I find it hard to reconcile his decisiveness with his flexibility.

There is confusion in the West as to whether or not Andropov, during all his years in high political positions, was a reformer in the true sense of the word. There seems to be strong evidence that he was, including the steps he took during his brief period as general secretary in 1982–84, but there are also his fifteen years as head of the KGB, from 1967 to 1982, which witnessed the sharp crackdown on Soviet dissidents and even on many ordinary nonconformists.

Andropov was absolutely a reform-minded person. He was a man of the Twentieth Party Congress. I remember the first speech he gave after

Khrushchev was removed. He said, "Now we shall move more firmly and consistently along the road charted by the Twentieth Congress." It turned out that he was wrong. But that was his hope. Even back in the mid-1960s Andropov expressed in his speeches and articles reformist ideas about modernizing the economy and changing the way the party and state functioned. He understood the need for major reforms as well as his group of young advisers, which I headed. But unlike us he knew even then how hard it would be to carry out such reforms. When he finally became general secretary in 1982 it was too late. His health failed him. Even so, look at how much he began in that short time.

As for Andropov becoming head of the KGB in 1967, I'll tell you what really happened. He was forced to leave his post as a Central Committee secretary and go to the KGB. Under Khrushchev, Andropov was being groomed to become the successor to Mikhail Suslov [a senior and very powerful member of the Politburo and Secretariat under Khrushchev and Brezhnev]. The first thing Suslov did after Khrushchev's ouster was to demand that Brezhnev remove Andropov as a Central Committee secretary by sending him to the KGB. Suslov thought this would make it impossible for Andropov ever to return to leadership politics because after Stalin's death there was no precedent for a KGB chief becoming a Central Committee secretary. Suslov wanted to end Andropov's political career. But Brezhnev was a man of grand compromises. He agreed to Suslov's demand but at the same time promoted Andropov to candidate membership on the Politburo. Eventually, after Suslov's death in 1982, that made it possible for Andropov to return. It was always his dream while he was at the KGB. I remember when he left the Central Committee in 1967, he gathered his associates and pledged, "I will return to the Central Committee."

There seems to be some confusion in the Western media about your relationship with Gorbachev. Some newspapers describe you as a personal assistant or adviser to Gorbachev.

I'm not an assistant or adviser to Gorbachev and I got to know him personally only after he became general secretary. Generally speaking, only people who actually work at the Central Committee are advisers in this sense. By the way, it seems that Gorbachev writes his own speeches. Apart from Andropov, I think he is the first Soviet leader to do so since Lenin. I don't mean that Gorbachev writes all the little formal hello-goodbye speeches, but the major serious ones. Materials are gathered and prepared for him by his personal assistants or other people who work in the Central Committee apparatus, but he writes the speech or report, as they are usually called. Sometimes people outside the Central

Committee apparatus are asked to contribute ideas or material on various topics. For example, I have been asked to send thoughts on democratization and human rights. I don't send suggestions directly to Gorbachev because the protocol is to go through the apparatus. That's what those people are there for. But I can and have sent them proposals to pass on to Gorbachev—for example, that there be an amnesty for all prisoners of conscience and that foreign newspapers be sold openly in our cities.

Having traveled with Gorbachev to his summit meetings with President Reagan in Geneva, Reykjavik, and Washington—mainly in my capacity as a writer on international affairs—I've gotten to know him. He has praised a number of things that I have written, including, by the way, my big article on Khrushchev that appeared in *Literaturnaya gazeta* on February 24, 1988.

Incidentally, do you think that the fact that Gorbachev studied law as a student has anything to do with his emphasis on the need for what he calls "a state based on the rule of law" as a central aspect of political reform?

I'm sure that his legal education plays a significant role in his political thinking and in his conception of how our political system ought to function. More generally, I'd say that Gorbachev is the first Soviet leader since Lenin who really understands these things and knows what he is doing. The others sort of felt things out and guessed at the consequences. Certainly, Gorbachev has an unusual education for a Soviet leader. But the idea of a state based on the rule of law is not connected solely with this or with Gorbachev. It is a central goal of perestroika because of the epoch of mass lawlessness under Stalin and the gigantic gulf between our written laws, which were not all that bad, and actual practices under Brezhnev—the corruption, bureaucratic abuses of power, violations of human rights, all that. The understanding of a need for the rule of law is a reaction to those experiences, as is perestroika in general.

As someone who has thought about and struggled for reforms in the Soviet system for so many years, how would you explain the essence or essential purpose of perestroika?

To create a model of socialism that people really need and want. The existing Stalinist model—call it state socialism or barracks socialism—fits neither of those requirements. People don't want to live that way any longer. We need economic and political reforms that will enable Soviet society to achieve the highest possible living standards, to reach the technological level of the most advanced industrialized countries, to express moral values and people's abilities, and to have democratic mechanisms through which public opinion can shape major decisions and individuals will be free. Essentially, this means that the Soviet state must give up much of its power and many of its functions to society and its organizations. Instead of a state-run economy, this means a self-managed economy based on market relations and competition among state, cooperative, and private enterprises. Instead of bureaucratic dictates, this means democratic political procedures based on mass participation and competitive elections. That is why I call perestroika a transition from state socialism to civil socialist society—to a more efficient, democratic, and humane model of socialism.

As you know, this new model of socialism has antecedents in our history, particularly in Lenin's NEP of the 1920s. Our history has witnessed a struggle between these two models or tendencies—Lenin's NEP, which relied on market relations and competition in cultural life, and Stalin's state model, which operated on the basis of commands. Khrushchev tried to revive some aspects of Lenin's model, but under Brezhnev, even though there was no personal dictatorship or mass repressions, the state grew even larger than it had been under Stalin. Under Stalin there were thirty-five state ministries and under Brezhnev more than a hundred.

Perestroika, or our transition to a real Leninist socialism, now is possible for at least two reasons. Many of our leaders and people have stopped denying that contradictions and crises can exist in a socialist country, and not only in the Soviet Union. The magnitude of our problems, what Gorbachev calls stagnation, is clear. Our standard of living and technological development lag behind not only Western countries but even Eastern European ones. We have shortages of everything, from food and razors to personal computers. Bureaucratization and corruption are pervasive, and in some places we even have mafias. And the decline in morale and the loss of socialist values among our young people is serious. These are the objective preconditions for perestroika. On another level, people have changed and are ready to live differently. All of their abilities and demands are greater—economic, cultural, informational, and psychological. They are ready for the new model of socialism.

Your general conception of perestroika is clear enough, but be more specific about the political features of what you call the new model of Soviet socialism. Everyone we have spoken with says that democratization is an essential part of perestroika, but exactly what this means remains unclear. Over the years, you have written a great deal about the need for political reforms, both as a political scientist and as an advocate. When you speak of the need for democratization, what specifically do you have in mind?

Perestroika means a fundamental redistribution of power in the Soviet system. As I said, we must emancipate or rid society of state control. The state will continue to play its leading role, of course, but it will have to be subordinated to society. First and foremost, this must take place in economic life, but that naturally has far-reaching political implications. Our economic and political reforms cannot be separated.

As for specific political reforms, we must accept the basic principle of a division of executive, legislative, and judicial powers—the need for separation and sharing of power. For us, this would be a major change. We need a presidential way of electing the country's leader. The general secretary of the Communist Party should be elected by a party congress and then submit himself to direct election as president by all citizens in secret ballot. He and all other elected officials should be limited to two five-year terms in office. This presidential reform must be accompanied by reforms that will transform the Supreme Soviet from a ceremonial institution into a working Soviet parliament of deputies chosen in multi-candidate elections. Unlike in the past, the Supreme Soviet, which now will be elected by a larger assembly, the Congress of People's Deputies, ought to be in session more or less full time. A country of nearly 285 million people can afford to pay the salaries of a few hundred elected representatives. Deputies must have time to articulate the diverse opinions that exist in our country, prepare legislation, and control the executive branch. The third branch, the judiciary, also requires major reforms. Judges and courts must be made independent of party and state bodies. Defendants should have the help of a defense attorney immediately. Jury trials should be introduced for major offenses. Punishment for most crimes should be made less harsh. Capital punishment should be abolished, as it was under Lenin in the 1920s. And we should have laws guaranteeing and protecting glasnost and the freedom of opinion, speech, organization, and orderly demonstrations.

The Nineteenth Party Conference mandated most of these political reforms, though it decided that the president should be elected by the Congress of People's Deputies rather than directly by all the people. The national elections to the Congress, which were held from March to May 1989, were an important step toward real democratization. The campaign and elections were generally successful. They allayed many doubts that the new, multi-candidate electoral system would actually work, and many supporters of perestroika, including me, were elected deputies. But the experience also showed that we have to think more about the electoral process and probably revise it in some respects. The procedures for nominating and electing deputies from various social organizations showed, for example, that the entrenched leaderships of these organizations sometimes had too much influence over the process. Two popular figures in the Academy of Sciences, Sakharov and Sagdeyev, were not even nominated during the first stage of the process. We will need more political reforms, more laws, and considerably more practice before socialism and democracy are fully combined. But the party conference and the 1989 elections laid a good foundation.

And if all these political reforms work out, will Soviet democracy eventually resemble American democracy?

They will have some things in common, such as mass media that reflect public opinion, elections, and other forms of mass participation. But what you Americans don't seem to understand is that there are various kinds of democracy. Democracy isn't just a constitutional or legal system but a form of politics that rests upon a nation's historical traditions and political culture. Therefore, it is naive to think that there should be only one kind of democracy everywhere in the world. It is also naive to expect the Soviet Union, which inherited antidemocratic traditions from tsarist Russia, to develop in the way the United States did. We have had centuries of patriarchal, authoritarian culture in Russia, which had no liberal tradition. Stalin's personality cult was not merely imposed from above. It also grew from below.

Another important difference is that we want democracy in economic life, so that the economy is not controlled by an elite. We want workers to control state-owned enterprises and to have economic power, something that does not exist in America. But I don't think we will achieve economic democracy in the next decade or so because of the diseases of bureaucratization and centralization, which plague both of our systems.

Another difference is that we will preserve the one-party system. Our problem is to find some combination of traditional and nontraditional ways to develop democracy within our one-party system. Glasnost and freedom of expression are traditional ways, and we are using them. But we also have to develop new ways, such as redistributing power and functions between the party and other institutions—state ministries, local soviets, labor collectives. Elections are a crucial part of this process, but we have to find an electoral system that produces talented and honest officials. That will depend on how well and fast our political culture develops. What's the point of electing corrupt leaders?

Above all, there is the problem of elections inside the Communist Party. In our political system, intraparty democracy is the decisive factor if there is to be democracy elsewhere in the system. All political changes in the history of the Soviet Union have begun inside the party. Everything has always started with the election of a new party leader and a new leadership, and the rise of a new generation of leaders.

If everything depends on democratic elections inside the Soviet Communist Party, the prognosis for the democratization of the Soviet Union doesn't seem very promising. There doesn't seem to be much real voting in the party.

It has been more widespread in the party than in any other organization. Look at the contested elections of the last three general secretaries—Andropov, Chernenko, and Gorbachev.

Wait a minute. Are you saying that the choice of a leader by a handful of men on the Politburo, at the very top of the political system, was some kind of democracy? Maybe it's oligarchy, but it is hardly democracy.

It also happens below, in rank-and-file party organizations. I would call it the beginning of democratization.

A handful of Politburo members have chosen a general secretary before, and it didn't lead to democratization in the party or the country. Anyway, are you saying that Gorbachev was elected general secretary in a democratic way?

Yes. He was first elected by a majority of the Politburo members and by the Central Committee.

You mean there was a minority against Gorbachev in 1985?

I wasn't there, but I'm sure there was a majority and a minority. And I'm sure that there continue to be majority and minority opinions because the issues connected with perestroika are so large, complex, and contentious. This principle of majority and minority should spread to all levels of the party in the form of multi-candidate elections for party leadership positions. There should even be election campaigns inside the party by the various candidates. That is the way it was under Lenin, beginning in rank-and-file organizations, then at local party conferences, and so on.

You and other advocates of democratization inside the party talk about such elections, but how would they actually work? How would rival candidates be nominated, for example? In Western democracies, this function is performed by the multiparty system. Say, for example, that one of us— Katrina or Steve—was a member of a local party organization here in Moscow. Say the higher party committee with jurisdiction over our organization had been run by a group of inept or corrupt officials for many years and one of us wanted to be elected to that party committee or even to the first secretaryship of the committee.

You would first have to persuade your own local organization to send you as a delegate to the relevant party conference. Then you would have the right to address the conference. If you are brave, you could make a speech criticizing the party committee. There are examples of that happening today around the country. In the past, party conferences sometimes voted against candidates selected by the committee itself—a kind of vote of no confidence—and higher party authorities tried to prevent this from happening. But if they continue to do so today, there will be a very serious struggle.

But even today, if we wanted to be nominated, to stage such a mini-rebellion in a Moscow party organization, wouldn't we need the support of some higher authority, perhaps even in the Central Committee apparatus? A benefactor, so to speak?

That would be useful, of course, but it is useful in every system. After all, George Bush got the nomination in 1988 partly because he had the support of President Reagan. The formation of a political elite is a complicated process in any system. Often there are both authoritarian and democratic elements.

But to return to the Soviet system, there is an example that addresses your question. Elem Klimov's election as first secretary of the Filmmakers Union, in 1986, was a mini-revolution. When you interview him, ask him about it. The point is that when party organizations, institutes, unions, and other bodies begin deciding which candidate they want to elect, real elections will become the norm. But there will always be a struggle between democratic and bureaucratic procedures.

You are avoiding the question about standing for election inside the Communist Party. To be successful, without the support of a party apparatus, wouldn't we have to organize like-minded party members?

Why beat around the bush? Say it outright. You are asking me about the permissibility of factions inside the party, which have been banned since 1921.

And for which, over the years, party members have been denounced, expelled, and, under Stalin, even shot.

If there is to be democratization inside the party, it will have to become a standard, normal process for a candidate to ask for help and support in his campaign. For there to be real competition among people, ideas, and programs, people will have to join together around this or that position. As for Lenin's 1921 resolution banning factions in the party, he said at the time that it was a temporary measure, though it is still on the books. But that was a long time ago, and I don't think we should debate keeping it or abolishing it. We should just find a model that allows us to choose among candidates for party offices.

By the way, a very important step toward democratizing the party was taken in March 1989, when the Central Committee published the results of its voting for its own candidates for the Congress of People's Deputies. For the first time in sixty years, Central Committee voting was made public. Previously, such disagreements in the leadership were kept secret. Even though all of the Central Committee's one hundred candidates were elected, when people read in the newspapers that twelve people at the plenum voted against Gorbachev, seventy-eight against Ligachev, fifty-nine against Aleksandr Yakovlev, and so forth, they understood that pluralism of opinion and policy disagreements in the leadership are a normal fact of life, or should be. I hope it puts an end to the old idea that the leadership has to be completely united.

Yes, but it is hard to imagine any kind of real democracy without accepting the legitimacy of organized opposition. If the Soviet political system, even after perestroika, still has only one political party and that party still will not permit organized factions within its ranks, how can there be any effective kind of opposition?

Other organizations can play that role. Take, for example, the Soviet Public Commission for International Cooperation on Humanitarian Problems and Human Rights, which was established at the end of 1987 with me as its chairman. This is an independent human rights commission composed of well-known Soviet writers, artists, journalists, and scholars—representatives of the progressive intelligentsia. Its purpose is to develop legal protection for individual freedoms and to strengthen the independence of the Soviet judiciary. I have written about these problems for many years, and now, as head of the commission, I have a chance to fight for these causes. My personal hope is to use the commission as a lever for radical democratization and to see the commission become a legal opposition to the bureaucracy. I think that is a real possibility because it is part of what Gorbachev calls socialist pluralism. The public must have ways to express opinions that are different from and critical of the views of party and state bureaucracies, so that the leadership can choose between them. When I speak of the human rights commission as a legal opposition, I mean above all in the area of human rights.

Given all the disputes over human rights between the United States and the Soviet Union, you should be specific about which rights you have in mind.

In the past, our concept of human rights was limited mainly to social and economic rights—education, housing, jobs, and the like. But my commission is primarily interested in civil or political rights, because these have been our most acute problems, particularly during the Stalin years, when such rights were violated in monstrous and tragic ways. The commission is concentrating on the freedom of speech, conscience, opinion, organization, assembly, travel, emigration—those kinds of liberties. That is why we are so active in the area of legal reform and are even drafting proposed laws. We proposed, for example, a new section on human rights in the Soviet constitution and deleting from the criminal code some articles that were used to persecute people politically. In 1988 we asked the Supreme Soviet to grant amnesty to all people convicted for their religious beliefs. The Soviet Union has to be a free country where everyone can pray to his or her own god. In fact, religion has to play a role in our return to elementary moral values. There have been so many crimes and so much corruption in our history, nobody knows what the foundation of morality is anymore. I personally think that religious and Marxist morality have much in common, or can have. We also intend to investigate conditions in prisons and corrective labor camps, and we are already lobbying for trial by jury, less harsh sentences, and abolition of the death penalty.

You know, of course, that according to polls in your own press, a substantial majority of the Soviet people is in favor of capital punishment.

Many people don't think things through. They think biblically—an eye for an eye, a tooth for a tooth. But if we are going to break radically with our criminal past and restore our political conscience, it is very important to renounce the death penalty. Too much blood has already been spilled in Russia. And even if you limit capital punishment to a few crimes, tomorrow you can pass new laws applying it to other crimes. We have to renounce it on principle.

The larger problem is that people have problems finding justice in our judicial and bureaucratic system. The human rights commission has already received thousands of complaints from Soviet citizens who have been mistreated in some way. Complaints range from petty bureaucratic abuses to denials of exit visas and mistreatment of people in prisons, camps, and psychiatric hospitals. People crawl around from one level of the bureaucracy to the next, beating their heads against closed doors, and they can't get justice. The commission is trying to help them, but all the members of the commission are volunteers and we have no paid staff. We are trying to deal with every case by appealing directly to the Supreme Soviet and the procurator's office. In one out of ten cases we get results.

The only real solution is a complete revamping of our judicial system. By comparison with Western countries, we have very few courts. Judges receive low salaries and are dependent on local authorities and local party organizations. There is too much of what has been called "telephone justice." Defense attorneys are able to intervene only when proceedings are already far along. We are still far from establishing the judiciary as an independent third branch of government.

In this area of reform, the Gorbachev leadership has put forward and attached great importance to the principle, "Everything that is not forbidden by law is permitted."

Because the opposite principle has prevailed in practice. Under the authoritarian bureaucratic system, people got used to thinking that if something wasn't expressly allowed by law, they could not do it. For example, if there was no special decree saying that you could build your own dacha, it meant that local authorities would not allow you to build one. If people are to be active and free, we have to stop this kind of thinking and behavior. But the new principle is hard to put into practice because of people's attitudes and because of all the bureaucratic prohibitions. The problem is that nobody pays very much attention to the actual law. We have to raise people's legal consciousness, but we also need laws clearly spelling out people's rights. The human rights commission, for example, is trying to get a law passed defining the rights of the many informal political organizations that have sprung up as a result of perestroika. Everything is unclear. Do such organizations have to register, and if so, in what way? Are all kinds of such organizations permitted, including anti-Semitic ones like the Pamyat Society? The Gorbachev leadership wants to assist the democratic informal organizations as a transition from state socialism to a socialism governed by society, but we will need a law to help them develop. Otherwise, local authorities will try to destroy them.

You seem to be deeply worried about opposition to political reforms on the part of local authorities.

It is not just the political reforms or local authorities. Conservative forces are grasping any opportunity and pretext to slow down all of the radical reforms. They are trying to take advantage of the discrepancy between glasnost and economic shortages. They use any means at hand to thwart the growth of cooperative and family economic undertakings in the cities and in the countryside. They use ideological dogmas to frighten backward elements of the population about perestroika. These conservative forces—our native Tories—are the enemies of radical perestroika. They have stepped up their opposition because they know that if perestroika continues to develop, it will become irreversible.

Stay for a moment with the question about political reforms. Isn't democratization in effect an assault on the whole nomenklatura system of appointing officials from above? Therefore, isn't opposition bound to be very large-scale and powerful—perhaps too much so to be overcome?

Certainly the system of elections will clash with the system of appointments from above. And certainly a large part of the nomenklatura wants to retain its power and privileges. But there is a struggle underway in the nomenklatura class between democratic and bureaucratic forces. After all, the reform ideas themselves emerged from segments of this nomenklatura class, under Khrushchev and Gorbachev. Even our present ideas about democratization came from above. So there is a struggle between these two trends. The Gorbachev leadership must try to guide this process, and the masses should strive to democratize it. It is true that opposition to democratization is strong within the nomenklatura, particularly in the managerial ranks. But there are also forces in the nomenklatura that want to change the balance of power and thus will support democratization. For example, in lower party organizations there are younger, more capable people who want to replace the old guard, and they see democratization as a way to do so.

Part of the conflict in the nomenklatura is a struggle between two kinds of perestroika—between the radical structural reforms advocated by Gorbachev and a more traditional conception of reform that involves merely reorganization and appointing new people. Everyone sees the problems and the need for change. There are no blind people here. But many officials want to adopt the traditional solution, which I call the organizational accordion—decrease this and expand that. This outlook is widespread among many functionaries, even intelligent ones. They are ready for an economic and cultural perestroika, but not for democratization and widespread glasnost, which they insist are destabilizing the political system. That is why Gorbachev keeps insisting on the need for revolutionary reforms.

Where are the neo-Stalinists in all this? During our dozen or so trips to Moscow since 1985, we have gotten the impression that they are growing increasingly strong or at least clamorous.

Yes, but those people verge on open opposition to the whole idea of perestroika. There are two reasons why neo-Stalinist moods are widespread. One is that many people still want simplistic answers to all of our problems. For Stalin or against Stalin. So naturally, given the complexity of our problems, a sizable number of people are for Stalin. As for the other reason, a very intelligent man told me many years ago, "Never raise the question of Stalin. It will split the party and the people down the middle." I don't agree with him that the question should not be raised, but he's right that it is the most controversial issue in our history. Stalin's name is linked to thirty years in the lives of many people— to events that shaped several generations. And there were so many different events during those years. So if you ask people what they think about Stalin's mass repressions, a large majority may be against them. But if you ask about Stalin's leadership in World War II, a large majority may be in favor of it. Again, don't forget our authoritarian-patriarchical traditions and the fact that Stalinism came from above and from below.

That raises the very large question of whether or not Soviet political culture has really changed fundamentally—whether or not it now is high enough to support the kind of democratization you are advocating. You have written about the importance of this factor over the years, but you don't seem to think that the Soviet Union has already achieved a democratic political culture. You still emphasize the weight of Russia's statist and authoritarian traditions. Recently you even wrote, "We must create a new political culture." But you know that political cultures can't be produced according to some plan or timetable; they are the product of hundreds of years of history. If so, how can you imagine or hope that the Soviet Union is ready for any kind of democracy, or for what you call self-managed socialism instead of state socialism?

We are faced with a paradox. We must democratize power in order to democratize society, but in order to democratize power we need a democratic society. You are right that democratization is a long march, but I think that the Soviet leadership and the Soviet people have already traveled a long way toward it. It was very important, for example, that the Nineteenth Party Conference identified human rights as a main criterion of democratization. This is the beginning of the end of our antiliberal tradition. But there is still a long way to go. It will take decades. But as we implement the political reforms and begin to accumulate real experience with democracy, we will learn democracy and our political culture will rise significantly. In that sense, we are ready.

I don't deny the huge problems that remain. Even though Soviet society is ridding itself of Stalinism and stagnation, those decades of experience have left deep scars. Look at the lack of tolerance, even among educated political people. Too many of them don't know how to live with an opponent. They want to deprive him of the right to speak, destroy him, or put him in a concentration camp. Tolerance of pluralism, the ability to understand another person's interests and viewpoints, are true signs of a democratic culture. And look at the intense national feelings and hatreds that are erupting around the country. All these problems were created by the authoritarian past, including Stalin's genocide of entire nationalities, and yet they erupt just as perestroika holds out the possibility of democratic solutions. We are paying the price for decades of graveyard silence.

Nothing seems to test the tolerance of Soviet citizens as much as glasnost. Apparently, many people are sincerely outraged that Soviet newspapers, magazines, and television are openly discussing so many formerly taboo subjects, from prostitution, homosexuality, drug addiction, and AIDS to Stalin's terror and the persecution of nonconformists in the 1970s. As a journalist, in your articles in Literaturnaya gazeta and elsewhere, you have done as much as any writer, perhaps more, to expand the boundaries of glasnost in several different areas, including contemporary Soviet politics, history, and international affairs. It seems fitting to end our conversation by getting your views on the present state of glasnost and its future.

Perestroika began with glasnost, and it cannot exist without it. Glasnost is giving birth to independent public opinion in the Soviet Union, which is a prerequisite of democratization. We have achieved quite a lot in this area since 1985. Many taboos and zones previously closed to criticism have disappeared, though some important ones remain. The media are beginning to play their proper role in promoting openness and information. And a significant pluralism of opinions is emerging.

What we need now are laws that will institutionalize glasnost by guaranteeing and protecting it. Again, it is a problem of our political culture. Glasnost has aroused all sorts of conservative passions that can be reduced to a simple impulse: If two people are arguing, one must strangle the other—then everything will be okay. So there are people who want to strangle the press because of glasnost. We need a law guaranteeing freedom of the press. Several drafts of such a law have been written, but none of them has satisfied enough people. A real struggle is going on over this issue. Some people even are trying to draft a law that will severely limit the press.

Presumably you favor a situation where glasnost and the press are unlimited.

To tell you the truth, I am worried that we may already have more glasnost than society can stand. There is already a great imbalance between what glasnost is promising and actual political and economic changes. When a worker is free to criticize his manager, for example, but nothing changes in his economic situation, I worry that will be a source of additional social tension. Faster economic changes would eliminate this imbalance, but meanwhile there is a danger that glasnost could go too far.

What do you mean "too far"? As a writer who has criticized abuses of power and policies of the past, wouldn't you like to have enough glasnost so that the press would be free to criticize the Politburo or the top leadership today?

I know this may seem contradictory, but I don't think our glasnost will go that far. I don't even think that would be a good idea. For one thing, glasnost could then be used as an instrument of political struggle at the highest levels and for the wrong purposes. But mainly we are back to the problem of our political culture. We still lack the kind of traditions that would enable such criticism of our leaders to be constructive and positive. Ideally, yes, it would be good to have glasnost like that. But we must live and carry out perestroika in the conditions that we have inherited from the past. We are overcoming those traditions, but they aren't dead yet. And you know the old saying: The dead always seize the living by the throat.

YEGOR YAKOVLEV

"Flagship of Glasnost"

GLASNOST HAS MEANT, *above all, a substantial reduction of censorship—
of "forbidden zones" and "blank spots"—in the Soviet press. Though
forms of censorship still exist, the importance of this liberalizing development should not be underestimated. In a one-party system without a free
parliament, meaningful public discourse and debate—not to mention effective public opinion—are impossible without significant freedom of the
media. Since 1985, the Soviet press has been freed to cover much of what it
previously ignored or denied, from crimes of the Stalin era and present-day
abuses of power to poverty, excessive privilege, prostitution, and organized
crime in the Soviet Union. At the same time, the media have been filled
with so many conflicting opinions about so many subjects it is unlikely
anyone will ever again imagine that the Soviet system or its people are
somehow "monolithic." Soviet public opinion, which now has emerged
above ground, has long been as diverse and fractious as that in any other
country, perhaps even more so. Two Soviet publications are widely regarded as being "flagships of glasnost"—the glossy weekly magazine
Ogonyok (edited by Vitaly Korotich) and the weekly tabloid newspaper
Moscow News, edited since August 1986 by Yegor Vladimirovich Yakovlev. Before Yakovlev took charge, the newspaper was best known as a
handout for tourists in Soviet hotels and airports. Three years later, despite
its relatively small Russian-language edition of 350,000 copies—it is also
published in eight foreign languages, including English—and stiff glasnost
competition from other newspapers, Moscow News remains indispensable
reading for Soviet citizens who care about public affairs. Its regular con-
tributors are a galaxy of the boldest advocates of radical reform and include
many of the people in this book. Guessing which remaining taboo the
newspaper will violate next has become something of a popular pastime in
Moscow. Not surprisingly, the limited number of Russian copies of Moscow News are sold on the black market at extraordinary prices, while its
editor Yakovlev is openly despised, along with Korotich, by the enemies of
perestroika. Yakovlev says this reaction is "normal," an ambiguous remark*

from a journalist who has been fired during his long career more times than he can easily remember. Western readers should not think, however, that Yegor Yakovlev has anything less than a fully Soviet political pedigree. He is a devout party member, the author of dozens of works about Lenin, and the son of an old Bolshevik political police official.

WHY HAVE I BEEN FIRED or had to resign so often? I suppose it is because I've always been a noisemaker by nature. I've never cared much about material things. I always wanted to defend what I believed, not what I had. Probably that is why I like Oscar Wilde's remark that recalcitrant people make progress possible.

I've been a journalist all my professional life. I started out back in the 1950s on a newspaper published by GUM, Moscow's biggest department store, for its employees. In 1956 I wrote an article exposing GUM's party secretary as a scoundrel. I took it to *Moskovskaya pravda*, which gave me my first real job.

Before being appointed chief editor of *Moscow News*, I had worked for more than thirty years as a writer or editor at many leading newspapers, and I lost my job at most of them. I was fired, for example, as deputy editor of *Leninskoe znamya*—I think it was in 1959—and at the same time as secretary of the regional Komsomol organization. In 1966 I had to resign as deputy editor of *Sovetskaya Rossiya*. Oh yes, and once I was dismissed from *Komsomolskaya pravda*. In 1967 I was founding editor of the magazine for journalists, *Zhurnalist*. I had Ernst Neizvestny [a nonconformist artist who now lives in New York] do a cover and some graphics. I was fired in 1972. Then I went off to Prague to work at a Marxist international journal. In 1975 I returned to Moscow to be a feature writer at *Izvestia*. When Andropov became general secretary in 1982, they asked me to be editor of *Izvestia*'s department of Communist education, but after Chernenko came in, I quit and went back to Prague as *Izvestia*'s correspondent. I could see the same thing starting all over again.

In August 1985, a few months after Gorbachev became general secretary, I got a call from Valentin Falin, who was then head of the Novosti Press Agency, which publishes *Moscow News*. He offered me this job. He said it was very important to turn *Moscow News* into a special newspaper in the spirit of glasnost—that it should publish articles other Soviet newspapers weren't publishing. I thought about it for a long time. My wife Ira and I were happy in Prague, and I wanted to work on my books and screenplays. But of course I couldn't remain abroad with perestroika unfolding in the Soviet Union. So I accepted Falin's offer, though Ira and I had real misgivings. We figured I'd end up with my bare ass on the sidewalk again.

If so, I'll go back to my writing. I didn't start out to be a journalist. As a child, I wrote short stories. And after I graduated in the early 1950s from the Moscow State Historical Archive Institute, where Yuri Afanasyev now is rector, I really wanted to be a playwright. Newspapers have killed the writer in me—they made me think about facts and reality and took away my imagination—though I've written about twenty books and more than thirty screenplays.

You are especially well known for your books, articles, screenplays, and television scripts about Lenin. Why did he become such an important life-long subject for you?

My main subject is not just Lenin but the Revolution, probably because my father was a revolutionary. I wrote a book about him called *I'm Walking Alongside You*. It came out in 1965, just as the anti-Stalinism of the Khrushchev period was about to collapse. They didn't let the second edition come out in 1966 because it was critical of Stalin.

My father was head of the Odessa Cheka [as the Bolshevik secret or political police was originally known] right after the Communist Party came to power, then deputy chairman of the Ukrainian Cheka, and later deputy people's commissar for foreign affairs of the Ukraine. Then he became a Soviet economic official. In 1935 my father decided that he wanted to return to the Cheka. He had held a high rank when he left, the equivalent of an army general, and he had known Feliks Dzerzhinsky [the founder of the Cheka who died in 1926] well. See that portrait of Dzerzhinsky? It hangs in my apartment because he gave it to my father. But when my father spoke with his friends at the Cheka, they told him not to return—that methods were changing. He was lucky. He died of cancer in 1937. Not a single one of his Cheka friends survived Stalin's terror.

Some people must find it odd that you are both a fervent anti-Stalinist and a son who still loves and admires his Cheka father.

My father wasn't a Stalinist. Moreover, every person has his own intellectual development and convictions. I was born in 1930, and my generation had few doubts about Stalin when we were growing up. We believed in the promises of the Revolution and didn't understand the terrible things that were happening. When I was in school in Moscow, and even in the Komsomol organization, we didn't see the big gap between words and deeds. Or when I did, I'd fall back on the old Russian proverb, "When you cut wood, the chips fly." It was the Twentieth Party Congress that set me on a new course and determined my intellectual development. Not just anti-Stalinism but the deepening of my ideological commitment to the Revolution and to Leninism. After the Twentieth Congress, I made a distinction between Lenin and Stalin, and I am still clarifying that distinction. Even today, some people defend Stalin, despite all the tortures and bloody massacres that took place. They use these utterly immoral on-the-one-hand and on-the-other-hand formulas. It's like saying, well, yes, the murderer killed ten people, but he wrote an excellent article about it.

But as I said, people think differently. My mother was an interesting case. She came from a gentry family, and her parents, my grandparents, took part in the 1905 revolution. As a result, her father was exiled, and in exile he abandoned my grandmother. My grandmother then married an English businessman named Pullman, who was working in Russia. They moved to London, along with my mother, who was fourteen, in February 1917. My mother met my father when he visited London as a Soviet official in about 1927. She returned to Russia, pregnant with me, in 1930. My mother, who worked as a translator, died in 1972. By then, she was my sharpest ideological opponent. Despite the fact that all of my father's friends had been shot, mother continued to believe in Stalin. I guess all of us have to hold on to some kind of conformity. For all my noisemaking, I have traces of conformism in me.

Even so, you edit one of the least conformist newspapers in the Soviet Union, possibly the most nonconformist one. If what you say about people needing some kind of conformity is true, maybe yours takes the form of a devotion to Lenin. Moscow News has published most of the radical perestroishchiks, including their divergent views on the relevance of Lenin today. What is your own position in this discussion?

I don't agree with those who say we must merely go back to Lenin. I know we have to go beyond Lenin. But I am not ready to criticize Lenin, for two reasons. First, I don't think I am wise enough. And second, Stalin never gave Leninism a chance. He perverted it before Lenin's policies could be proved right or wrong. But I do think Lenin had one weakness, if it can be called that. He assumed that in taking power in a backward country like Russia, whose culture was not ready for socialism, the party's leaders would always use that power wisely and kindly to prepare the country for socialism. That turned out not to be the case. In history, you can't depend on kindly intelligence.

That is a big reason why we need glasnost, public opinion, and democratization, including inside the party. The party has to stop playing its monopolistic role and share power with the soviets. The anonymous power of the party apparatus has to end, and the power of the party rank and file must be increased. The rank and file mistrusts party bureaucrats. And of course we need the legal foundations of democracy. Gorbachev can't just give us democratic institutions as a gift, like sausages from Moscow. All of us have to participate. For example, there are some regional party secretaries who are against democratization. We need party secretaries who aren't afraid to stand in democratic elections, who will be elected democratically, and who therefore won't fear democratic soviets either. So when I say perestroika must go beyond Lenin, I mean that this kind of democratization now is possible because the country has changed so much since he was alive.

In that connection, what was your reaction to the 1989 elections to the Congress of People's Deputies—the first multi-candidate elections in many decades, in which you were a successful candidate?

It was our biggest leap forward to democracy in the Soviet Union. Much was unclear when the political reforms and electoral laws were legislated in 1988, but the elections showed us what democracy is and can be. The television and newspaper debates, campaigns, rallies, and public interest were unprecedented. I never imagined that so many people would care so passionately and sincerely about who was elected. And so many profound issues were discussed—even the nature of political power in our system and the question of a multiparty system. The elections were a great expansion of political glasnost.

I must tell you that when Gorbachev announced the 1989 elections back in mid-1988, at the party conference, I was dubious that we could move toward a democratic process so quickly. But the elections demonstrated Gorbachev's greatness as a political leader. He argued that democratization was needed for perestroika and could not be delayed. He was right.

Let's talk about the role of Moscow News *in perestroika, particularly in glasnost, and your role as its editor. In 1987 an advertisement for the newspaper read "Moscow News—The Flagship of Perestroika." Is that your conception of the paper's role?*

No, if I had seen it in advance, I would have cut it out. It's too immodest and it isn't accurate. Compared to the really influential, big newspapers like *Pravda, Izvestia,* and *Sovetskaya kultura,* with print runs in the millions, *Moscow News* is merely light cavalry. Though our total printing, including all the foreign language editions, is 1.2 million, our Russian-language edition for Soviet readers is only 350,000. Of course, it could be much more—in the millions—if they would allow it. But the influence of *Moscow News* isn't a tenth of that of *Pravda* or *Izvestia*. A half a line there is more important than a whole story in *Moscow News*. They can get ministers fired, for example. By the way, you know our current joke: What do a minister and a butterfly have in common? Both can be killed by a newspaper.

You may be feeding us some false modesty. Surely you are pleased by the newspaper's great success among Soviet readers. Muscovites run around every week trying to get a copy of the latest issue, and single copies are selling for exorbitant prices on the black market and in the provinces— even just to be read and returned.

Maybe I've gotten old. I don't get pleasure from that kind of fame anymore, though I do like one anecdote that has been circulating for a while. A man finishes reading the newspaper and immediately calls his friend. "Volodya, have you read the latest issue of *Moscow News?*" "No, what's in there?" "It's not something we can talk about on the phone. I'll be right over."

I did set myself two goals when I took over the paper in 1986. The first was to take what was essentially a newspaper for tourists and give it a real political identity. For example, I wanted to report stories that other papers weren't reporting. Old habits were hard to break here. Once there was a fire at the Zagorsk seminary. When one of my reporters called to get the details, a priest refused to answer any questions unless we assured him that the story had been cleared by the Central Committee. Imagine, a priest!

My second goal, since *Moscow News* is also for foreign readers, was bridge building. I wanted to break down our stereotypes about the outside world and the outside world's stereotypes about the Soviet Union. I didn't want to turn *Moscow News* into a Western newspaper but into a Soviet newspaper that writes honestly and critically about Soviet affairs. When I took over, I told my staff to write for the paper as they talk at home. One of our officials recently objected that there aren't enough positive stories in *Moscow News*. I had a talk with him, and it turned out that positive stories mean articles about happy milkmaids. Of course, we've published some lousy things. But a newspaper is defined not by its worst but by its best materials, and we have also published some very good things. By that I mean articles that do not try to conceal our problems.

More generally, I'll tell you what I think about on Tuesday evenings, when the paper has left the editorial offices and gone to the printer. I like to think that each new issue is like an oar rowing us farther and farther from the joyless past we are leaving behind—from the old regime that lost society's trust. That is one reason why historical themes have been so prominent in *Moscow News*. We have to look back at that shore to remind ourselves how far we must go and to be sure we aren't standing still.

Putting modesty aside, how do you explain the very considerable popular and critical success of Moscow News *under your editorship? Many well-informed Muscovites have told us that while they read as many Soviet newspapers as possible,* Moscow News *is one of the two or three papers they feel they must read.*

A large part of our success is due to the staff I have built since I took over. There's still a mix of old and new people, but I fired a lot of people, about sixty, and hired that many new ones. Then there is the constant stream of outside authors who bring their articles to be published by *Moscow News*. You've been at the offices, you've seen them. Many of these people work at other newspapers and journals or in other professions, but some of them don't have regular jobs. You have been talking with quite a few of them—the actor Ulyanov, whose talent and civic courage I greatly admire; Klimov, who was in recently to talk about his work on a film about Stalin; Afanasyev, who has stirred up so much controversy about history; and Karpinsky—you know his complicated biography. And many others. A lot of these people are my old Moscow friends, but for all of them *Moscow News* is a place where they can write about what is most sacred to them.

What is your own role in all this? Give us a sense of your typical workday as the editor.

I get up around 6 A.M., and my suffering begins. I want terribly to go to the swimming pool, but if I do I won't finish reading all the manuscripts I have to take with me to the office at 9 A.M. Unfortunately, the manuscripts usually win out over the pool. I perform my only household duty—I fix tea for Ira and serve it to her in bed. Then I read the manuscripts and get angry with my staff for giving them to me in such bad shape. By the time I get to the office, I am exploding. Staff people know they better not be late, and we start right in on the manuscripts. Meanwhile, the flow of outside authors begins. I spend much of the day dealing with them, getting their ideas, explaining why I can't publish this or that, calming them down. Sometimes I spend the whole day with visitors to the office, which is why I must read manuscripts at home.

You see, we have two kinds of editorial arrangements in the Soviet Union. If you look at *Pravda* or *Izvestia*, you'll see printed at the bottom of each issue simply "The Editorial Board." That means that the paper is signed when it goes to press not by the chief editor but by the board. In those cases, the editor must defer to the editorial board when there are disagreements. But other newspapers, including *Moscow News*, are signed personally by the chief editor. This means the editorial board is an advisory body and the chief editor, Yegor Yakovlev, is responsible for making the decisions.

I meet with my editorial board and the staff every Wednesday to evaluate the issue that has just come out and decide the contents of the next issue. I'm a despot by nature, but the other members of the editorial board speak their minds. We argue, fight, and sometimes they scream at me. But I take the responsibility.

And at what point does censorship come into play and determine what you cannot publish?

There is a representative of the formal censorship office, Glavlit, at *Moscow News*. His name is Misha, and his office is near mine. I pointed him out to you the other day. He reads the contents of the upcoming issue. He's not very bright, but he's a sweet and mild-mannered fellow—just a regular guy. All he can do is object that something might disclose military or state secrets. Or to something pornographic, but we don't have any of that in *Moscow News*. He or his own superior can say to me, "Aren't you worried about this article for this or that reason?" Sometimes they are right and occasionally I correct something, but they can't forbid me to publish something. I can say, "Thanks for your opinion, but I'll make the decision."

You have to remember that glasnost has eliminated more and more zones that were once forbidden to newspapers. And *Moscow News* has sometimes been the first to enter those zones. You remember back in June 1987 when I ran a photograph of the small airplane that the German boy, Mathias Rust, landed on Red Square? Everybody said I'd never be able to print it, but I did. And have a look at Gavril Popov's article in the March 20, 1988, issue. He invaded a different kind of forbidden zone. He pointed out that while Yagoda and Beria [Stalin's secret police chiefs] had been bloody scoundrels, they had not been spies, as was alleged when they were executed. Popov argued that if we are serious about restoring historical truth, we have to overturn those false convictions as well, though we can condemn Yagoda and Beria for their real crimes.

We have come a long way in openness and honesty in these few years. We've even come a long way since April 1987, when at the very last moment they yanked from *Moscow News* a letter by two Soviet writers who had been expelled from the Writers Union under Brezhnev—they've since been readmitted. We had to run around looking for something to put in its place, and we couldn't get the paper out on time. The phone was ringing off the hook. People wanted to know what had happened, but we couldn't tell them. Now *Moscow News* just wouldn't give in to that kind of pressure.

In some ways we are ahead of you in glasnost. I remember when I was in London not so long ago, talking with one of the bosses of the BBC, and he said perestroika at the BBC was going slower than perestroika in the Soviet Union. Being an editor, I immediately said, "Write an article about it for *Moscow News*." He replied, "What are you talking about? Do you think we have the same level of glasnost that you have?"

Of course, there are still problems, and the glasnost mechanism has broken down a few times, as when the Chernobyl nuclear disaster happened. Or when Joseph Brodsky [the exiled Soviet poet] won the Nobel Prize in 1987. That was a great event worth reporting, but we couldn't announce it right away. And then there is the kind of logic that insists, for example, that full reporting of the demonstrations and violence caused by the controversy over Nagorno-Karabakh, in Armenia, would inflame the situation there. I don't agree with this view, but it exists in some ruling circles. So there are still some high-level forbidden zones, but fewer and fewer deep ones.

Please understand that I speak only of my own situation. I don't know about the situation of Viktor Afanasyev at *Pravda* or Ivan Laptev at *Izvestia*. They have their own problems. I had terrific difficulties when I first took over *Moscow News* and we began asserting ourselves, but now they've gotten used to us and more or less leave me alone.

That doesn't square with reports in the Western press, most of them originating from Moscow, that you are under constant fire. Vitaly Koro-

tich, editor of the equally bold magazine Ogonyok, *remarked that being a glasnost editor means making a lot of enemies. Should we assume that all your enemies have forgiven you?*

I have my enemies, and a lot of complaints about me and *Moscow News* are sent to the Central Committee. A lot of these people think everything new that is published is automatically bad. But not all of them are dogmatic. One can talk with them. Some of them are worried that the Russian-language edition of *Moscow News* is having a negative impact on Soviet readers.

Falin left Novosti in the fall of 1988 to be head of the Central Committee's International Department, but presumably he protected you when he was your immediate superior. As a candidate member of the Central Committee—he was made a full member in April 1989—presumably he had considerable influence. It is reported that Falin told a Western correspondent, "I gave Yegor Yakovlev freedom, but he gives me little sleep." What was your working relationship with Falin? For example, did you clear controversial articles with him before publishing them?

For God's sake, it's probably ridiculous to tell you this. Here I am, a fifty-nine-year-old man, but Valentin Falin is still my favorite person. I respect him enormously, and it was infinitely interesting to work with him when he was head of Novosti. Of course, I went to him for advice on many matters. And in all my life, I've never had a more intelligent and educated man to consult with. As *Moscow News* asserted itself, there were many difficult moments, and when we made a mistake, Falin would tell me so to save me from more serious problems. He also took some of the fire on himself. Sometimes he asked to read particularly troublesome materials, but usually it was I who went to him about prospective articles, particularly those having to do with international affairs. After all, I'm not a specialist on international affairs and he is. Georgi Arbatov also helped us in this area. When things get bad for us, Arbatov can help us a lot as a full member of the Central Committee who frequently is in touch with Gorbachev. But as a rule, Falin never asked to read things. He read what I brought him to read.

But you know, even over at Novosti there are different points of view. Once I had to give a report on *Moscow News* to Novosti's editorial board. Some of the members praised me, but some of them sharply criticized me. There are wise men and fools everywhere. Those who criticized me, in my opinion, were fools. But as you see, I'm still around.

In our current circumstances, bold newspapers are like an oven filling with gas. The gas builds up, and if there is one spark the oven can explode. After the explosion, the air clears until the gas begins to build up again. That's why I am very nervous when everything is going well and is quiet at *Moscow News*. When things are bad, I know the explosion is coming. But when it is quiet, I don't know when the next wave of trouble is going to begin.

In addition to periodic calls for your resignation, there were reports that on one or more occasions you threatened to resign. In September 1987, for example, there was a rumor that things were so bad you offered your resignation to Gorbachev personally.

That's not exactly what happened. There was a moment, in the fall of 1987, when I did write a letter to Gorbachev. He was vacationing in the south, and I was having some serious personal doubts about whether or not I should continue as editor. *Moscow News* was getting support and respect, but also very harsh criticism about our group of writers, our subjects, our alleged isolation from the people. So I addressed Gorbachev by letter, saying that if I have become a problem or if I am no longer useful in the post of editor, I am ready to leave this job and work elsewhere for the party and for perestroika. I got an oral reply, by telephone, saying that if we all were to resign, who would carry on with perestroika? That's all.

I don't think I could actually resign. Sometimes I come home at night, I'm tired, I'm sick of the complaints, I think about free time to work on my book, and Ira says, Leave the newspaper. I say, How can I leave? I brought so many people with me to *Moscow News*. I came at Falin's request, and he has supported me in everything. If I quit, it would be like spitting on all these people, a circle of people I'm tied to.

As a matter of fact, I hold a grudge against Boris Yeltsin for resigning as secretary of the Moscow party organization in 1987. I didn't know Yeltsin personally—he was from Sverdlovsk, not Moscow—but I sympathized with many of his views and much that he did as Moscow party secretary. And he sympathized with *Moscow News*. My complaint against him is that he had a key position in the party, he was on the frontier of perestroika, but when he disagreed with some things and came under fire, he resigned. Nobody took his post away from him. It's not like in the past, when there was nothing to do except resign. Yeltsin should have fought to the end. I don't like some things today, but I'll struggle so long as glasnost continues and I have any influence.

In that connection, how does your election to the Congress of People's Deputies, in 1989, affect your position as an editor in the struggle for glasnost?

Well, let's say that being a member of parliament strengthens my position against the opponents of glasnost in the corridors of the apparatus.

Incidentally, you were elected a deputy from the Filmmakers Union, not the Journalists Union. We understand that you have written many films, but could you have been elected in the Journalists Union, where most of the progressive candidates were defeated?

I don't know, but certainly the Filmmakers Union is much more radical in its commitment to perestroika and glasnost. The Journalists Union is still dominated by utterly untalented people from the provinces.

It is clear that glasnost is Gorbachev's own policy and that his political fortunes are closely linked to it, but why does he meet so often with a group of representatives from the Soviet media? That is unusual for a Soviet leader, but it has become a regular event for Gorbachev. Is this his way of trying to establish the boundaries of glasnost and keep the media from going too far?

I don't think so. I am often at those meetings and I can tell you there is a real give and take of opinions. It is natural for Gorbachev to want to meet with editors and direct their attention to what he thinks are the most important aspects of perestroika at a given time. He begins by explaining what he thinks is the most important subject, his own views about it, but he doesn't impose any limitations on the discussion.

Is it normal for the top leader of a political system to direct the media, even in this way?

I think it is very important when the leader tells us frankly what he thinks about what is going on.

Maybe you think that way because this particular leader, Gorbachev, is a radical reformer and you share his views. But what if it were a different leader with different views?

Then I wouldn't be at the meeting. Someone else would be in my place. At every one of his meetings with the editors, Gorbachev emphasizes the importance of glasnost. Glasnost has opened up tremendous possibilities for the media, and I am trying to exploit those possibilities.

Are most Soviet editors seizing the possibilities of glasnost in the same way?

Many of them are practicing glasnost badly. Partly this is because as a profession we journalists lack experience. In some ways, we are more professional than our American counterparts. By the way, that's one reason why I am signing contracts with Western publishers to increase *Moscow News'* circulation abroad. I want to put to rest the legend that your journalists are the real professionals and we are some kind of ignoramuses. But in some ways we aren't fully professional. We still have a hard time, for example, presenting opposing views. For instance, I would like to publish a real discussion about our history between the anti-Stalinist Yuri Afanasyev and someone of directly opposing views. But I can't organize a genuine discussion, partly because the other side won't speak out candidly and partly because of my own inadequacies as an editor.

If some other Soviet editors fail to take advantage of glasnost, maybe it simply means that you, and the other editors who do, are braver. Anyway, that is what many Muscovites think.

It's more complicated than that. It is not enough just to be courageous. You have to be brave in a professional way. A real editor has to walk along the edge of the abyss if his newspaper is to play a useful, positive role, but he must protect his paper by not going over the edge of the abyss. That is hard to do. Every day you have to grope for the political openings and possibilities. It is very hard to walk along the edge of this abyss.

What it means is that good editors will make good newspapers and bad editors will make bad ones. And the bad newspapers will be punished by their readers. Newspapers and magazines that have embraced glasnost have soaring subscriptions. But look at the newspaper *Trud*. Once it had the largest circulation and was gaining subscribers regularly. Then it started losing readers because it wasn't dealing with urgent, topical issues. Glasnost ought to be the golden age for Soviet newspapers, as it is for our journals.

Looking back over four years of perestroika and your own almost three years as a glasnost-maker, how have your own views and expectations changed?

When perestroika first began, many of us were euphoric, almost intoxicated by the freedom glasnost promised us. It seemed that nothing could stand in the way of democratization. But now we've come to realize that there is huge resistance and that we will have to work long and hard for perestroika. I like the way Korotich put it recently. "Yegor," he said, "we used to keep trying to find out what's going on, what the situation was. We overlooked the fact that we ourselves are creating the situation." That's the point. We used to wait for a situation or a directive. We don't do that anymore. For example, when *Pravda* published an article by conservative historians attacking Mikhail Shatrov's anti-Stalinist play *Onward, Onward, Onward*, we didn't wait to see what it meant—we just published a defense of Shatrov. In other words, we know that perestroika is a struggle between ideological outlooks and principles and we are ready to fight.

But we have to fight democratically, which is another thing we are learning. I remember when I was at one of Gorbachev's meetings with editors and he said, "We are all on the same side of the barricades," and "We are all in the same boat." It was a sweet thought, but I couldn't accept it in my soul. I didn't want to be in the same boat with our reactionary writers like Anatoly Sofronov, for example. But then I thought about it and I realized Gorbachev was right. It's an important part of his new thinking. In effect he was saying that we have to overcome our legacy of putting opponents on the other side of a barricade and fighting them to the death. We progressive journalists must win the struggle for glasnost and perestroika, but not by destroying other newspapers and magazines. We have to learn to coexist with them. That's why I didn't get hysterical, unlike many of my friends, when *Sovetskaya Rossiya* published that anti-perestroika article by Nina Andreyeva back in March 1988. People think that way, so let them speak out. It's normal. If we try to put them in camps, Stalinism will win again. By the way, Americans aren't very good at this kind of tolerance when they write about us.

I also remember one of Gorbachev's meetings with editors where one editor, who is also a member of the Central Committee, began criticizing a provincial party secretary for having spoken out at a Central Committee meeting against glasnost. Gorbachev interrupted him, "But think how good it is that the man said what he thinks. And how much worse it would have been had he not spoken and just quietly kept his opposition inside himself."

You see, when we say we are learning democracy, it doesn't just mean we are learning to vote. It means we are learning that democracy is a two-way street that requires a two-way psychology—the ability to tolerate opposing views. We even have to learn to coexist with the Pamyat Society, which I detest. A few years ago I would not have objected if those people had been sent to Siberia to hold their meetings. Now I understand that if the Pamyat Society is sent to Siberia, eventually I'll be on my way there, too. Not everybody thinks this way. There is a group that wants to impose order by punishing people who say something wrong. People on both sides of our debates still want to prove that their opponent has dirty underwear. The problem is, we just aren't used to normal debate. God grant us the wisdom to learn to act democratically, in the spirit of the Nineteenth Party Conference, though I can't say I have great faith that it will happen. The chains of the past still weigh very heavily on us.

Many people here seem to think it won't happen if something isn't done very soon about the economic shortages. They worry that the working class will turn against perestroika, will turn to more despotic forces in high circles, out of a growing conviction that perestroika has brought ordinary people nothing—that glasnost and democratization have nothing to do with them.

I know this view, but I don't share it. I am certain that Soviet workers value democracy over goods. I know many workers and I knew some during the Brezhnev era who were more radical than the whole intelligentsia put together. It is true that there still are terrible shortages, but you wouldn't believe how glasnost has changed the way workers think. Public opinion has been created. In the old days the authorities could pull anything on workers. They used to increase the number of workdays on the grounds that that was what people wanted. Just try to deceive or lie to a worker today. He'll just tell you to fuck off.

Not long ago a group of us met with workers at a factory. We are broadening *Moscow News'* coverage of everyday life. We have to give people a platform to say what they really want and think. I was amazed by how much the workers knew about every issue of *Moscow News* and how many opinions they had about the stories we had run. And just the other day my wife was in a taxi and the driver started complaining that he couldn't get the latest issue of *Moscow News*. When he learned who she was, he wouldn't let her pay the fare. The notion that perestroika matters only to the intelligentsia is absolutely wrong. The thinking of workers is a hundred times more important.

I'll tell you something else. The bosses are incredibly afraid of the workers. I saw a famous director of the Volga Auto Works talking to workers on strike. His hands were shaking. Management's horror and fear of dealing with workers is absolutely incredible. I don't mean there will be a Solidarity movement here. There won't. Management just has no experience in dealing with any kind of organized resistance by workers.

It is hard to tell if you are optimistic or pessimistic about the future of perestroika.

It isn't realistic to think that my generation, whose representatives appear so often in *Moscow News*, can build the kind of society we want. Much of the work will fall to our children. They will have to find their own path, but I hope they learn the lessons of our life. We should have gotten around to perestroika much sooner. We began only when we already were fathers and even grandfathers.

Perestroika will take a long time. In a country like Russia, there are no shortcuts. There may be setbacks—both hopes and tears. Personally, I'll fight on, for the sake of my hopes and convictions. The ideals of perestroika are as great as those of the October Revolution. If I get fired again, I'll go back to writing. I might even be happier. What would be harder for me would be to be expelled from the party. I am absolutely not ready to give up my party card. But even if we don't live another day, my generation is lucky to have the second chance perestroika is giving us. Even if perestroika were to be stopped by the dogmatic forces that oppose it, and I'm not talking here about the Pamyat Society.

And if it were to be stopped by those forces, what would you do?

Try to overthrow them and start again. They can't win. They have nothing positive to offer the country.

ALEKSANDR BOVIN

"Semi-Glasnost"

ALEKSANDR YEVGENEVICH BOVIN *has long been one of the most popular journalists in the Soviet Union. Since the 1970s his iconoclastic columns in the government newspaper Izvestia, with a circulation in 1989 of more than 10 million copies, have won him an enormous readership, while his frequent appearances on television talk shows have made his caustic manner, rotund figure, and walrus-like mustache familiar to millions of viewers. Another self-described "child of the Twentieth Party Congress," longtime party reformer, and equally longtime bête noire of party conservatives, Bovin's Izvestia office seems designed to provoke unsympathetic visitors. It is adorned with a framed picture of his one-time mentor Yuri Andropov, a large caricature of himself as Don Quixote, and a life-size poster of a nude woman. But Bovin's purpose is intensely serious. A specialist in international affairs, his writings have done much to expand the parameters of glasnost in that highly sensitive area of policy. He has also lent his bold and influential voice to the struggle for radical reforms inside the Soviet Union. Though known to most people as a columnist, Bovin began his career as a judge and later worked for a decade in the Central Committee apparatus, along with several other people in these pages.*

IF I HADN'T worked in the Central Committee apparatus for almost ten years, I wouldn't be the journalist I am today. It was the best school of my life—dealing with large political issues, arguing with my colleagues, working with politicians, reading all kinds of scholarly and Western literature. But I didn't start out to be what you call an apparatchik or a journalist. My first occupation was as a judge.

When I entered the university in Rostov at the age of eighteen, in 1948, for some reason I wanted to be a diplomat. They told me that to become a diplomat one had to study history or philosophy. I decided to become a lawyer instead. Like so many young Soviet men, I joined the Communist Party through the Komsomol, in 1951. After I graduated from law school in 1953, I was elected a people's judge in a district of

Krasnodar province. I think I was the youngest judge in the Soviet Union.

I handled all kinds of criminal and civil cases. Even though this was the Stalin era and the situation was different elsewhere, especially in political cases, I wasn't answerable to any higher authorities. I was in a small remote place, and I dealt with ordinary matters—petty crooks, murder, civil complaints, and the like. I was very young and idealistic and I tried to be a good judge. I did my best to be sure that, when I handed down a sentence, everybody would understand that it was just. If I had to resolve a dispute, I tried to work it out so that the loser would see that he had lost in accordance with the law.

But I couldn't take it for long. No happy people come before a judge. You go before a judge when somebody has deceived you, let you down, or hit you. So a judge sees the world only through dark glasses and if he stays in office too long, it inevitably affects his psychology. In the middle of my second term I decided to find another profession. In 1956 I enrolled in the philosophy department of Moscow State University. It was a very interesting time, not long after the Twentieth Party Congress, and we had many heated discussions and meetings.

When I finished my graduate study I intended to work in a party organization in the Urals, but in 1959 I was offered a job in the philosophy department of the journal *Kommunist*. For a young person it was interesting and important work. I stayed at *Kommunist* until 1963, when Fyodor Burlatsky asked me to join his group of advisers working for Andropov at the Central Committee. My job was to propose solutions to certain problems and present reports on them to the leadership.

Andropov was the first major political figure in my life—a kind of mentor. You see his picture on the shelf here in my office. Andropov was a born politician—he had politics in his blood—but he was also an undogmatic, knowledgeable intellectual. We'd spend hours arguing about some problem, he with his coat off and his shirtsleeves rolled up. It was a particularly interesting and complicated period for our department because the conflict with China was beginning. That took up half of our time. When Burlatsky left the Central Committee, Georgi Arbatov replaced him as chief of the advisory group. And when Arbatov left to become director of the Institute on the USA and Canada, in 1967, I replaced him as head of the group. There were interesting people in that group. Most of them are playing leading roles today in perestroika.

Many Americans would find some of this baffling—for example, that the Central Committee apparatus housed a batch of critical-minded young intellectuals.

My condolences to Americans who judge what they do not know. I wish they could have heard our heated arguments. There were five of us in the advisory group, and there were five points of view on every question. That's natural in any society. Then we unloaded our disagreements on our bosses. They arrived at one point of view, of course, but that's the job of people who must make decisions. You and I can argue endlessly, but decision makers have to decide. Of course, I wouldn't say all their decisions were good ones.

It is also hard to reconcile your portrayal of Andropov with the man who became head of the KGB under Brezhnev. Can you explain how this happened?

I think so. After Stalin the party leadership apparently wanted a head of the KGB who had clean hands and a good brain, someone they trusted. That was Andropov.

Burlatsky told us that your entire group at the Central Committee in the 1960s was strongly anti-Stalinist, including Andropov.

We were all children of the Twentieth Party Congress. Not Andropov, of course, he was older, but the congress was just as important for him. As for me, after the congress, I looked at the world with different eyes. I began to think differently—in an antidogmatic and democratic spirit. I began to understand that socialism is impossible without democracy.

Before the congress, my attitude toward Stalin had varied. I was raised wholly in the Stalin era and under the influence of his ideas. My father was a military officer and my mother a housewife. Though I was born in Leningrad, in 1930, we lived in the Soviet Far East for eleven years. My father wasn't touched by the terror, which hit the military so hard in the late 1930s, but our neighbors and other people in his garrison were arrested. I didn't feel it then, but later I understood that Stalin's most terrible legacy was the fear he implanted in people—in bosses, in every Communist, in every person. People were terrorized, and we still haven't overcome that legacy.

Of course, I was a child and understood none of this, but something happened in 1951 that shook me. You need three recommendations from members in good standing in order to join the party. I asked a fellow student in Rostov to give me one of the recommendations. He was about eight years older than me; he had served at the front during the war. After he wrote the recommendation, he asked to talk privately with me. I remember it as though it happened this morning. We sat on a bench on the bank of the Don River while he told me things about

Stalin's cult and terror very similar to what Khrushchev told the Twentieth Congress five years later. He explained that despite these things he still believed in the party's ideals, but he felt he had to be honest with me. I'm a rational not an emotional person, so I understood what he was saying. The basic principles of socialism and communism exist regardless of who is at the helm of the party. I joined the party because I wanted to realize those principles. After all these years, after all we have been through, I think I made the right decision.

Those principles were the hope of my generation in our young adulthood, in the years between the Twentieth Congress and the mid-1960s. You asked the other day why I have Yevgeny Yevtushenko's portrait hanging in my apartment. He is my favorite poet. More than anyone else, it was Yevtushenko who expressed in his poetry all of our dreams, hopes, and suffering. There are different opinions about his poetry, and later maybe he wrote some weaker things. But nobody can be great all the time. For me, he still is poet number one, and he's still playing an important role today.

My generation has produced so many remarkable people. Of course, Yevtushenko is well known in America. But take Mikhail Ulyanov, whom you are going to interview. He is such a great and popular actor. Having played Marshal Georgi Zhukov [who headed the Soviet armed forces in World War II] and Lenin so often, he is part of our folk culture. He also has a classical, Shakespearean side—his Richard III is absolutely stunning. Not long ago I was walking down a street in the United States with Ulyanov and I thought, Americans don't know who this is. They should have screamed and rejoiced at the sight of him. He exudes such dignity and empathy. He wants to make the theater a force for political culture and democratization. I'm glad he's now the head of the theatrical union and presiding over the reforms in the theater.

Like you, Yevtushenko, and Ulyanov, most of the people in our book began their political and creative lives under Khrushchev. When you began working in the Central Committee, he still was the Soviet leader. Did Khrushchev influence your own thinking in any way other than by his speech at the Twentieth Congress?

Khrushchev's greatness was that he dared to take the first step of de-Stalinization, but his legacy was one of half-measures and impulsive policies. He and his generation were limited by the fact that they had been raised to power by Stalin. In addition, Khrushchev was surrounded by people who were not as radical as he was—people who held different views. He was almost always engaged in a battle. So he would take a step forward and then retreat. Had he published his speech to the Twentieth Congress, for example, his influence on our lives would have been greater. It has finally been published here, thirty-three years later. Winston Churchill put it well when he said that it is impossible to leap across an abyss in two jumps. Khrushchev was a transitional figure. He did much to break with Stalinism, but his half-measures and impulsiveness contributed to the reaction and stagnation that followed him.

And yet you stayed at the Central Committee until 1972. If the work was so interesting, why did you leave to become a journalist?

Sometimes the Communist Party feels that an individual ought to have a new assignment somewhere else. In my case, it was suggested to me that I ought to go to *Izvestia* as a political writer.

It sounds like you were fired or banished from the Central Committee.

Well, that's life. I've got friends and I've got enemies. I'd be an unhappy person without enemies. If a person has no enemies, he is doing something wrong. Anyway, I make more money at *Izvestia* and I enjoy my work. I've been here seventeen years, and I still like to write my regular commentaries, particularly now under glasnost.

One thing about my journalism that really grieves me is my inability to help all the people who write to me. I get a huge amount of letters. Look at this stack, just from the last two months. All of them are cries for help—complaints about a lack of justice, legality, housing—from people who have been deprived or humiliated. Here's one, for example, from a man who was wrongly convicted. And here's another from two old Jewish people who aren't being allowed to join their children abroad, even though the daughter has cancer. I'm powerless to help all of these people. There are too many of them. I do what I can. In some instances, I call a minister or a prosecutor. I try at least to answer all the letters. I express my sympathy, try to explain the situation, and advise them to be patient. But we Communists have been telling people to be patient for several generations. It's almost immoral to continue to do so.

You see, I'm not like an American columnist who just writes. I go to the people. I speak at factories, collective farms, institutes. I need to interact with people. They are my audience. After I talk with them, it is easier to write because I know what they need and want. I sit among them for two or three hours and say, "Comrades, please ask me about whatever you want." And we talk about everything. This is very important for me.

Why do people with grievances write to you for help? You are a journalist, not an official.

Our system has developed a cold layer of bureaucrats who make all these decisions affecting people's lives. People try to get around this damn bureaucracy, but they can't. So they read me in *Izvestia* or see me on television. As a journalist, I try to use my creativity to arouse warm feelings in people, so maybe they think I am a kind person. One of my themes is the difference between good and evil, so maybe they think I will help them find an apartment. I wish I could help all of them, but there's no way other than to be patient and give perestroika a chance to produce results. That's why we must not lapse into half-measures, as we are doing in some areas.

Is glasnost any consolation for people who are deprived in these concrete ways? Everybody we have spoken with agrees that there is a pervasive shortage of consumer goods and services, but there is some dispute about whether ordinary consumers care about glasnost or consider it to be a luxury for the intelligentsia.

It is primitive to make such sharp distinctions between the intelligentsia and the people. People who do so aren't so far in their thinking from those authorities who would divide Soviet society into an elite with the right to know everything and an amorphous mass which must be rationed information. Sure, Elem Klimov uses glasnost to make good films and I use it to make good television programs. But taxi driver Vasya and cleaning woman Masha also want to see good films and enjoy good television. That is why glasnost isn't a process that affects only the intelligentsia. People in the street praise it highly because they too need glasnost in their life. Everyone needs good schools, medical clinics, housing, and other things, and we will get them if we implement the economic and social reforms. But these reforms are unthinkable without glasnost. People understand this relationship, though some of them better than others. I agree that the intelligentsia fights more energetically for glasnost, but that is its profession. But if workers ignore Klimov's films, he will have no one to make them for.

Some people don't understand what perestroika is really about. We are trying to create a new kind of socialism. The old kind has reached a dead end. At the risk of being accused of plagiarism, I will say that we want socialism with a human face—a society in which everyone feels himself to be a full citizen and master of his destiny. A system in which the people no longer thank the Communist Party and the state for what they have, but the party and the state thank the people. Perestroika may be the greatest undertaking in the Soviet Union since 1917.

The most important element of perestroika is democratization. Without it we won't be able to solve our economic or social problems. But there can't be democracy without glasnost, because it is through glasnost that people will be transformed into real citizens who control the economic and social processes in the country. Democratization is above all a change in our psychology. The essence of democracy is when people feel that important matters depend on them and they are the masters of the economy, the party, the country. You can have a hundred candidates in every election for every position, but you will have no democracy unless people have this psychology.

That's both a very abstract and narrow conception of what is needed for democracy. Most political thinkers, from Rousseau, Mill, and Locke to Marx and Lenin had more specific ideas about democracy, including the need for certain institutions and procedures. For you, it seems to come down to Pavlov or Freud, or perhaps what other people call political culture.

All of us need some Pavlov and some Freud. You can't escape psychology. It's up here in the brain. But you're right, I'm talking about political culture, though the notion is too hazy. Some people attribute Stalinism to the legacy of tsarist psychology. I don't find this very persuasive, though I admit that after having destroyed Stalin's personality cult Khrushchev tried to create a little one of his own. And then there was a third kind of cult under Brezhnev. But I think most of this old leader-oriented psychology is being overcome.

Are you saying that democratization in the Soviet Union requires a transformation of psychology but not new political institutions?

We don't need any significant new institutions. What we need is a change of the political regime within our existing institutions, and this is a matter of political traditions, habits, and behavior. We have to force existing institutions to operate democratically. After all, within the same set of political institutions there can be a democratic or an antidemocratic regime. Of course, we need partial changes—different ways of electing people, for example. But the overall structure is okay.

Many people think the Soviet Union needs a second political party.

I don't think so. As we say, this train left the station a long time ago and it is too late to change course. We should not retreat to a multiparty system, though we must have pluralism in the one-party system.

Are you sure that you believe in democracy in the fullest sense of the word and that what Gorbachev calls perestroika is real democratization?

Absolutely. You know the old adage, every nation has the government it deserves. In my opinion, this adage is true only if a nation has democracy. Perestroika is giving us a historic chance for democracy. How we use it will show what we deserve. That is why glasnost is so dear to my heart.

On the basis of your experiences as a journalist, how much glasnost is there? Four years after glasnost began, how have the Soviet media used this chance?

Compared to the situation in 1985, glasnost today is remarkable. But compared with what is needed, it is still semi-glasnost. Bureaucratic agencies continue to ration out information to journalists. Control over the media and the number of forbidden zones have been greatly reduced and there is much more information, but some areas and events remain off limits to the press. Look, for example, at our failure to report fully on the demonstrations and violence in Georgia in April 1989.

In a moment we want to ask you about reporting and commenting on international affairs, which is your own specialization, but first give us some other domestic examples of what is still off limits.

The situation is changing rapidly as glasnost expands, so what I mention today may no longer be off limits tomorrow. At the moment, we can criticize politicians, decision making, and abuses of power, but only up to the level of minister. It is still difficult to criticize the Central Committee or the Politburo. The KGB and its affairs remain largely a closed area, as does much of the military. The military has been very slow in giving the media information on various subjects, including its expenditures and the size of its forces. Here too the problem is partly psychological. We suffer from a mania for secrecy that is incompatible with a civilized nation and is suffocating us. Ironically, we conceal information not so much from foreigners who wish us ill but from our own people. Many of our so-called secrets can be found in open publications in the West. I also get a lot of letters complaining that we shouldn't write about our problems because we already know about them and now the Americans will find out and laugh at us. I understand this attitude because I too find it unpleasant to read about our corruption, crimes, and shortages. But we shouldn't worry about what you Americans think. We should worry about whether or not we really want perestroika. If we do, we have to go through the purifying fire of glasnost, and we can't allow anybody to put it out.

It's clear that you are proud of what Soviet journalists have achieved since 1985 but also disappointed that there still is what you call semi-glasnost. Does the fault lie solely with bureaucrats or are journalists also to blame?

As a rule, journalists are free to write whatever they want today. Unfortunately, some of them haven't shaken off old habits. Some of them still practice self-censorship.

Or perhaps they aren't supported by their editors. According to Yegor Yakovlev, glasnost has given editors great discretion as to what they publish.

Some editors help more than others, and others interfere more than they help. But don't make too big a distinction between journalists and editors. They are people of the same breed. They graduate from the same school. Today a person is a journalist, tomorrow he is an editor, and vice versa. The point is that journalists and editors can decide how high they want to fly today. Some of them feel safe at one height, others at another.

Yegor Yakovlev said that when he took over Moscow News *he told his staff to write the way they talk at home.*

That's very good advice. When I worked at *Kommunist* the editor-in-chief once told me that he couldn't publish one of my articles because it was too much like something I'd say at home or privately to my colleagues.

Is Yakovlev a good editor?

Yes, I like him and I subscribe to *Moscow News*. By the way, he's an interesting person. He had a lot of trouble in the past, moved around a lot. And he has always studied Lenin, not in the spirit of our anniversaries or other celebrations but in search of what is deep and complex in Lenin. As for *Moscow News*, I read it with pleasure, but my reaction is not that of its general readers. For them, it is providing real glasnost—about drugs, prostitution, and many other things. But I already knew about all this. We journalists didn't write about it, but we knew about it.

A number of people have told us that glasnost exists primarily in Moscow and perhaps a few other large cities, but that the situation in the provinces is quite different.

It's hard for me to say because I rarely visit the provinces, but no doubt the situation is significantly worse there. Provincial journalists are more dependent on a group of officials than are journalists in the center. The editor of a regional newspaper, for example, may feel that he is bound by the authority of the regional party secretary. If so, he'll have less freedom than does an editor of a big newspaper in Moscow.

But you have to understand, nothing I've said means that journalists cannot and should not fight to publish what they want. Perestroika is a fight, and in any fight you hit and you get hit back. Some journalists are being illegally fired or otherwise punished, more often in the provinces than in Moscow. If journalists want glasnost, they have to fight for it. Nobody is going to give it to them like a sausage sandwich. They have to climb into the ring. And when you get in the ring, you have to expect to take some blows.

Will the proposed press law help journalists?

I've seen several drafts and none of them satisfied me. The higher the draft goes in the apparatus, the worse it gets. Some of my colleagues think we shouldn't be in favor of a law like that because any draft will only hurt journalists by limiting rather than expanding their rights. I disagree. I think we need a good law protecting the press, and I think one can be drafted.

Let's go back to your own journalism and specifically your special field of international affairs. Are you now free to write about and say whatever you want?

I can't, not yet, but you have to understand the special problem here. We ought to have full glasnost in our coverage of Soviet foreign policy and world affairs, but we still are limited by concerns of the Soviet Foreign Ministry and the government. We can criticize what happened before 1985—the deployment of the SS-20 missiles in Europe and the invasion of Afghanistan, for example—but I can't disagree with what Foreign Minister Eduard Shevarnadze said today, yesterday, or last year. And the reason is the old habit, yours and ours, of associating everything that appears in Soviet newspapers with the Kremlin. We don't have a tradition of journalists expressing their own personal views on foreign affairs. So if I write something sharp or critical or new, foreign governments and observers say it is the opinion of the Kremlin. Similarly, I can't write critically about things I don't like in Eastern Europe or elsewhere in the world Communist movement. Leaders of those countries and parties immediately complain to Moscow. Or they say the Soviet Union is interfering in their affairs. It's also why it is not easy for me to write my opinion of Khomeini or Muammar Khadafi.

We have to establish a tradition that enables journalists to speak only for themselves and express what is clearly their own personal opinions, so that nobody will identify them with the Soviet Foreign Ministry or the Kremlin. Everybody agrees that this is sensible, that we should do it, and we have made some progress. But there still are problems. It is a matter of perceptions and reactions abroad. I am trying to make it clear in my articles that they represent my own personal opinion and should be read as such, but complaints still come from foreign governments and from Soviet ambassadors abroad. When I was in Japan, for example, I said in an interview that the Soviet Union, the United States, China, and Japan should acknowledge that there are two Koreas and grant diplomatic recognition to both of them, and the two Koreas should recognize each other. Well, they got upset in North Korea and protested to Moscow. Same old thing. Except that in the past I would have gotten an angry call from our Foreign Ministry. This time I didn't hear from them. Maybe they are coming to accept it as normal.

There's another, much worse example. When Ayatollah Khomeini sentenced Salman Rushdie to death for his novel *The Satanic Verses*, in February 1989, the Soviet government, unlike many others, did not publicly protest. It feared that a protest would jeopardize the government's diplomatic relations with Iran. Though I wrote a protest in *Moscow News*, most of our journalists were silent. I was ashamed that Moscow was silent. Politics prevailed over morals. And glasnost again came only in dribbles.

That previous act of glasnost on your part took place in Japan. Could you make the same argument about Korea in Izvestia?

It would still be difficult, I'm afraid.

Are you equally limited in what you can write about Soviet–American relations?

Actually, there is more running room in this area. In fact, I'd say the Soviet government is more optimistic about improving Soviet–American relations than I am. I see problems ahead, though I wish it were not so.

You once said, perhaps on television, "I repent for how Soviet journalists have described America." What did you have in mind?

Unfortunately, the logic of the U.S.–Soviet confrontation over the years led Soviet journalists to portray America as being worse than it actually is. Until a few years ago, Soviet television showed only negative images of America—as a country of only the extremely rich and the extremely poor, a country of racial problems, narcotics, and crime, an aggressive, arrogant country. There is much to criticize in the United States, but much that is positive as well. I'm hoping that as our relations improve, our more balanced coverage will continue and Soviet readers and viewers will have a multicolored image of America.

Incidentally, I have the impression that Soviet journalists may be psychologically better prepared to depict America objectively than American journalists are prepared to depict the Soviet Union objectively. Maybe I'm wrong, but there are so many negative stereotypes of us in your media, textbooks, and popular culture—they are like sediment in the minds of Americans.

What is the worst or most offensive stereotype you have encountered in the United States?

That the Soviet Union is a barbarian country ready to invade you and kill your women and children.

In a pluralistic culture like ours, it is easy to find all sorts of examples, including the ones you mention and ones you haven't mentioned. But take us back to Soviet journalism by telling us your hopes for Soviet coverage of international affairs in the future.

As younger people who regard glasnost as normal enter the profession, I think we will have more diverse, intelligent, and interesting journalists. There will be fewer blank spots and off-limit zones as well as commentaries that need not coincide with those of the Soviet government. It would speed this process, I think, if Western newspapers were sold freely in the Soviet Union and if Soviet television were to broadcast Western programs.

But if journalists write their own opinions, what will happen to the party's control over the press—to the idea of a party line, which was enforced for so many years?

Like me, the majority of Soviet journalists belong to the party. When I express my own point of view, it doesn't mean that I am going against the party. We can have a thousand points of view and quarrel about them. Why should this affect the party line? I can't imagine a journalist in *Izvestia* proposing to build capitalism in the Soviet Union. But otherwise there is plenty of room for very different viewpoints on all sorts of issues.

You mean there no longer will be party directives, only general princi-ples?

Yes, but when the party has taken a decision, party members are supposed to accept and support it. Even so, the boundaries of what we call socialist pluralism are very broad. Who can even say where they are? Party member Nina Andreyeva publishes an article in 1988 oppos-ing perestroika on the grounds that it is endangering real Soviet social-ism. Later, party member Yuri Afanasyev publishes an article calling for radical perestroika on the grounds that socialism doesn't exist in the Soviet Union. Personally, I think Afanasyev made his point in a primi-tive way but that *Pravda's* reply to him was even more primitive. If I had to choose between these two primitive positions, I'd be closer to Afanasyev. I know that all this is imprecise, but we are in the process of searching for new standards of journalism, and we lack the experience that could guide us. The simplest formula is in the Soviet constitution, which provides for freedom of speech in the interests of socialism. But this formula isn't working. We need to find something new.

To what extent is the search for something new, for the kind of glasnost you want, hindered by opposition to glasnost?

Self-interest dictates life. Glasnost and perestroika generally threaten a lot of interests. You can't expect man to leap out of his skin or society out of its history. Ministers and government officials don't like glasnost because it allows people to curse them. Factory directors don't like it because workers can criticize them. Provincial authorities say glasnost is too negative—that the masses need positive examples. Ideological opponents of perestroika charge that the economic reforms are a return to capitalism and that multi-candidate elections are sub-verting the political system. Pragmatic opponents are worried about protecting their high-level positions and privileges. Old habits play a big role in all this. The apparatus doesn't want to give up its old way of running things, and people are having a hard time learning not to be afraid of their bosses. The result is half-measures and all sorts of linger-ing administrative prohibitions, even though we now say that what isn't prohibited by law is permitted.

Have your own contributions to glasnost brought you into conflicts with the bosses?

As I said, you can't get in the ring and expect not to take a few blows, but nothing serious has happened to me. They threw me off television for a while after I complained about closed zones back in 1987 at the Congress of Journalists. I don't know exactly what happened. People tell me that Comrade Ligachev [who oversaw television at that time] called the television offices and told them to keep me off. That's life; nothing stands still. I took a few counteractions of my own. Anyway, I'm back on television, though recently they cut part of what I said about Afghanistan from the program "International Panorama." I took a counteraction. I got the original text published in a Soviet newspaper.

Has your editor at Izvestia *reprimanded you for anything you have written?*

He has never reprimanded me, though occasionally we have a discussion. He might read my typescript, call me, and say, Sasha, I think this or that phrase ought to be omitted. I'll think about it—maybe I'll omit it, maybe I won't. We reach an agreement. Of course, editors everywhere like to have their own way. Not long ago, for example, I had an article about the danger of war and arms control. I quoted George Kennan as saying that resolving regional conflicts could wait because they paled in significance compared to the danger of nuclear war. The chief editor called me up and said we should remove Kennan's part about letting regional problems wait because they too require speedy solutions. I thought about it and cut that phrase.

You can't compare this kind of thing with what happened before glasnost. I didn't have a lot of difficulties then, but there were occasions when they yanked my articles. I had a terrible time once with a series of three articles about Poland, one of them on religion. I had problems getting it cleared both with our Central Committee and the Polish Central Committee, which finally refused to approve it. After that happened a few times, I just stopped writing about socialist countries.

Izvestia *has more than 10 million subscribers and you are one of the most popular and widely read Soviet journalists. In the letters you receive, do most of your readers support you?*

Most of them do, but I also get letters saying I should be hanged. After I wrote a positive article about the television spacebridge program featuring Phil Donahue and Vladimir Pozner, some people wrote, "You should be shot as a defender of American imperialism." Old habits.

You are also known as a leading proponent of Gorbachev's "new thinking" in Soviet foreign policy and indeed as one of the foreign policy special-

*ists who contributed to it. Could this new foreign policy continue if glas-
nost were to be shut down?*

I don't think so, because self-criticism is an essential part of the new
thinking. How can you understand the need for new directions if you
don't know what you are leaving behind? That's why we have to discuss
openly our previous foreign policies. Here too there is a need for a
change in psychology. After World War II we based our entire ideology
and outlook on the psychology of a dangerous encirclement. That is
why our behavior was sometimes bad and why we followed you in the
arms race. We made a lot of mistakes. We need glasnost to rid ourselves
of this psychology. Moreover, a fundamental element of the new thinking is that more weapons means less security. Because we can destroy
each other, it means that the key to Soviet security lies in Washington
and the key to American security lies in Moscow. We can't just build
weapons. We have to think about each other's security. But it is hard to
pursue that kind of new thinking without a change of psychology.

We also need glasnost in order to change the whole relationship
between Soviet public opinion and Soviet foreign policy. For decades,
the people have had no control over the foreign policy apparatus or
policy making. The public found out about decisions after they had
been made. Public opinion has to be brought into the discussion of
foreign policy, which is limited to a narrow circle of people. We can't do
that without glasnost.

*What is the main way in which the new thinking has actually changed
Soviet foreign policy?*

We are out of Afghanistan—after so much loss of lives and expenditures, we recognized that every country must decide its own destiny.
And we have accepted many of your proposals for reducing nuclear
weapons. You proposed no intermediate-range missiles in Europe, we
accepted. You wanted on-site verification of nuclear weapons facilities,
we said, okay. You proposed a 50 percent cut in strategic weapons—
when Secretary of State Cyrus Vance proposed this back in 1977, we
rejected it—and we have said, okay. These are examples of real changes
in Soviet foreign policy.

*If you have been accepting our old proposals, maybe the United States
had new thinking before you did.*

That's funny but not correct. Your government is rejecting some of
our acceptances of its proposals. That's the problem with bluffing, as
your government was doing in the past. And it is hard for us to pursue

the new thinking here when your government seems to want to continue its military buildup. Our military comes in and says, "Give us money. Look what they are doing in America." It's hard to persuade military people to think differently when they are responsible for the nation's security.

You said earlier that you are less optimistic than your own government about the future of U.S.–Soviet relations. Are you pessimistic?

Absolutely not, only realistic. President Reagan and President Gorbachev created a solid foundation for much better and safer relations. I hope President Bush will join Gorbachev in building on that foundation. But I am worried about a deep-rooted American psychology. You seem to have so many doubts and second thoughts and double standards.

I'll tell you a funny story that illustrates the difference between the Soviet Union and the United States. A drunk Russian is stumbling around looking for his apartment. He rings the wrong doorbell, the door opens, and a man says, "Go away. I live here, not you." The drunk stumbles around a bit and ends up at the same door. Again the man says, "I told you, comrade, you don't live here." The drunk makes a tipsy circle and rings the same door bell a third time. Again the man says, "This is my apartment, not yours." Whereupon the drunk shouts, "This guy lives everywhere and I live nowhere!" According to the American psychology, the United States lives everywhere and the Soviet Union lives nowhere. Americans think nothing of saying, We are going to build an airfield on Easter Island. Imagine their response if we decided to build one on Easter Island! The Americans say they can do whatever they want in El Salvador and Nicaragua, but the Soviet Union better stay out of the Third World. These are your own old habits and psychology. You are a great nation, but no more than that. Let's have the same rules for both of us, then we will have very good relations.

Now some circles in the United States seem to be worried by perestroika. They say we resorted to reform because we are weak and perestroika will make us strong. Poor America. Why should you be frightened of perestroika? We aren't undertaking it because we are weak but because it represents our socialist principles. And if it does make us stronger, why should this threaten you? We want to cooperate with you, not present you with ultimatums. We are going to restore good relations—not an alliance but good relations—with China. Indeed, I would rank this as our number one foreign policy priority of 1989. But this too probably will upset poor America. Why should it?

We respect your interests and you should respect ours. We will try to solve our problems at home, and you should try to solve yours. You can have your beliefs, we will have ours. We don't have to stumble over each other's heels in Africa or anywhere else. Let's go to Mars together instead.

No, I'm not pessimistic about U.S.–Soviet relations, just a little worried. We may be at the beginning of the end of the Cold War, thank God. If we both behave responsibly and with restraint, we may achieve a breakthrough in world politics. The new talks between NATO and the Warsaw Pact on reducing conventional forces in Europe are especially important. The primary danger of another arms race is in the area of conventional weapons—the Pentagon is eager to gain an advantage in "smart" weaponry. We must find a way to head it off. That is one of my hopes for the future, along with shorter lines in front of Soviet shops.

And are you optimistic about the future of perestroika in the Soviet Union, about the prospect for shorter lines?

When Gorbachev and his team introduced perestroika, they knew that the number of both its supporters and opponents would grow as the reforms were introduced. I'm certain that the majority of party members and nonmembers now support perestroika. But I'm also certain that confidence in perestroika will evaporate if reasonable amounts of consumer goods and services aren't made available in the next few years.

The danger is that all of us, even the supporters of perestroika, might not do enough to implement the reforms. The time for colorful words and slogans is past. The time for difficult, invisible, even boring deeds has come. Perestroika can't be achieved by words or by decisions of the Central Committee alone. All of us, each Soviet citizen, must now turn these decisions into realities. Unfortunately, too many people prefer the verbal aspect of perestroika. They dream, grumble, tell jokes, and rely too much on Gorbachev to do everything. They are still waiting for miracles.

ELEM KLIMOV

"Learning Democracy": The Filmmakers' Rebellion

AS WAS THE CASE WITH Khrushchev's reforms thirty years earlier, Gorbachev's perestroika faces powerful resistance and even opposition from the vast state bureaucracies that administer much of Soviet life from Moscow to the localities. Glasnost has developed much more rapidly than economic reform partly because bureaucratic control over cultural affairs was weaker than it was over the economy and Gorbachev had many eager supporters among the creative intelligentsia. The filmmakers' democratic rebellion in May 1986 was an important turning point in the history of glasnost. At the Filmmakers Union Congress, a movement led by Elem Germanovich Klimov outvoted and ousted the old leadership, thereby seizing control of the union from the State Committee for Cinematography, in effect a state ministry. The new leadership, with Klimov as first secretary, proceeded to establish several pathbreaking precedents by forming a "conflicts commission" to review and release banned films, declaring war on cultural censorship, and striving for an independent system of filmmaking that would be a model of democratization and market-oriented economic reform. Until Klimov emerged as a leading perestroishchik in 1986, he had been an admired but largely proscribed filmmaker. At the time he was elected head of the union, for example, the official two-volume encyclopedia of Soviet cinema included no entry on him or his work. Even though his first feature-length film, Welcome, or No Unauthorized Persons Admitted, won two prizes in Cannes in 1963, most of his subsequent films, including the now famous and widely acclaimed Agony and Come and See, were not released for general distribution until 1985. In 1987 Klimov was elected an honorary member of the American Academy of Motion Picture Arts and Sciences and of the British Cinematography Institute. As a pioneer of perestroika, Klimov's union has lent its support to various unofficial move-

ments in the Soviet Union, including democratic youth clubs and the anti-Stalinist Memorial Society.

Some people were suprised that I was willing to be a candidate for head of the Filmmakers Union at its congress in May 1986. They knew I wanted to work on my own films, that I am an artist not a bureaucrat, that I lost years of creativity fighting the bureaucracy and censorship. A film I made in 1965, a satire about the Soviet system, wasn't released until twenty years later. *Agony*, my film about the end of the tsarist family, the Romanovs, lay on the shelf for ten years. It was released in the spring of 1985. And it took me eight years to make and release *Come and See*, a film about Nazi massacres in Belorussia and how hard it is to remain human in wartime. The authorities said the scenario, written by me and Ales Adamovich, was antipatriotic and "abstract humanism." Now we are embracing those human values. After I was elected, an arrangement was worked out so I could be on leave part of the time. One of my associates, Andrei Smirnov, became acting head of the union in mid-1988. But I am ultimately responsible until my five-year term expires.

So it was a sacrifice when I took the job. As you may have heard, when a group of writers tried to overthrow the conservative leadership of their union later in 1986, they called a prominent author and urged him to run for the position of first secretary. He hung up on them, disconnected his phone, and refused to leave his apartment until it was all over. But unless bold, honest, and talented people take over leadership at all levels of our system, from the Communist Party and creative unions to local soviets and factories, we will never end the dictatorship of mediocrity and liberate ourselves from its chains. If those of us in a position to seize the opportunity don't do so, how can we set an example for others and particularly for the next generation, which is our hope for perestroika?

I can't say that I always held these views. I matured slowly. Even after high school, my only real obsession was basketball. I was good at it. Of course, traces of my childhood are in my films, such as *Come and See*. I was born in Stalingrad, in 1933, and spent my adolescence playing in the city's postwar rubble. Stalingrad had been completely leveled, as if it had been hit by a nuclear bomb. It was a wasteland laced with explosives. Some kids playing there were blown up. Except for my father, a Stalingrad party secretary who stayed to defend the city, my family and I had been evacuated during the fighting to a village in the Urals. The remains of the tsarist family, the Romanovs, were buried in a nearby forest. It seems ironic that I later made a film about this.

My father was a very respected and kind man who gave much of his life to people. He wanted to be an architect, but the times made him a party official. When we were evacuated to the Urals and left him behind in Stalingrad, his hair was black. When we returned, it was white. In 1951 my father was assigned to work in the party's Control Committee, so the family moved to Moscow. He worked there until he died in 1986. He never had time to retire. He just worked hard and finally had a stroke.

There were traumatic episodes in my father's life. After the Twentieth Party Congress, as an official of the Control Committee, he was deeply involved in the process of rehabilitating victims of Stalinism. He had to read many of their dossiers. It was a great spiritual shock for him. I remember him coming home after work and locking himself in our dining room. He would turn off the light and stare into the darkness. Then he would go to bed. A short time later he began planting flowers. He became one of Moscow's best-known flower growers.

As we know, the kind of victims' dossiers your father had to read probably contained terrible accounts of torture, forced confessions, executions, and fates in the Gulag. Did his experience with victims have an impact on your own thinking?

He never spoke to me much about his work, certainly not in any detail. He didn't feel he had the right. I had to fill in many things for myself and find my own way.

I had graduated from high school with honors, which allowed me to enter any higher educational institution without taking entrance examinations. I didn't feel any special calling, but aviation was all the rage at the time, so when we moved to Moscow I entered the Moscow Aviation Institute. I got involved in student satirical revues, which were very fashionable. At the institute we had our own group of authors, directors, actors, and stage designers and our shows became well known around town. It was my first contact with cultural life. Soon a friend and I began freelancing in radio, variety shows, and the theater, staging skits, plays, and concerts. By 1956 I had lost interest in being an aviation engineer and decided to enter the State Institute of Cinematography. But my father wouldn't let me drop out until I got the aviation degree. "I don't understand what a person can do with a filmmaker's degree," he said. So I graduated from the aviation institute and worked for a year as a helicopter designer before I entered the film institute in 1957.

Because I was still a little immature, the Twentieth Party Congress in 1956 didn't have an enormous impact on me right away. It was the subsequent atmosphere created by the congress and by the Twenty-Second Party Congress in 1961 [where Khrushchev publicly attacked Stalin's reign] that really influenced me. I joined the party in 1962, in the spirit of those congresses. My generation of film directors—we are a rather small group—emerged in the early and mid-1960s, in that little historical niche between the artistic renaissance generated by Khrushchev's thaw and the onset of the Brezhnev era. It was a remarkable time. New theaters such as the Sovremennik [Contemporary] and the Taganka were born and the Soviet film industry was starting to move forward again. A few of us managed to make our first or second film in that short-lived period. Then the bosses and philistines took over and things got terrible, especially for filmmakers.

You have a very radical reputation in Moscow, even among ardent supporters of perestroika. One writer described you with admiration as a "maximalist." Why are you perceived in this way?

Probably for several reasons. My colleagues and I were the first artists to expand glasnost by defying state bureaucrats at Goskino [the State Committee for Cinematography], throwing out the old corrupt union leaders headed by Lev Kulidzhanov and Sergei Bondarchuk, and establishing an independent system for artists. And partly because I'm known to be against any kind of half-measures, compromises, or tactical retreats in the struggle for glasnost and democracy.

In my opinion, perestroika is impossible without a real moral cleansing and a public condemnation of those responsible for what happened in the past. I mean during the Stalin era and in the 1970s. The things done under Stalin happened in the presence of adults who could have done something to prevent them. They could have intervened, objected, fought. Many people don't want to admit that there was that possibility. They refuse to repent. Same thing in the 1970s. The bureaucrats didn't execute people, but they executed good films and killed talent. And not only on someone's orders, but because they took pleasure in doing it.

We can't forgive the old union leadership. They could have fought for us, defended our interests, but they didn't lift a finger. They were content being an appendage of Goskino and its chairman Filipp Ermash. Those people who sinned not only don't want to admit it, they still want to teach us how to live. People like that repel me. We should publicly name those who were responsible for the stagnation of the Brezhnev years, but when I tried to do it in an article the editor struck out the names. It would be a good lesson for the future, and I'm not talking only about the film industry.

Do you think this way because you have a special conception of perestroika or glasnost?

Foreigners—Americans, Scandinavians, the French—have a hard time understanding what is going on in the Soviet Union. They ask if glasnost is for real, where its limits are, will it last long? These are questions asked by people who already have glasnost and take it for granted. As though you get it when you need it, like a shower. But for us, glasnost is the very oxygen of change, of perestroika, and it is a struggle every step of the way. We are fighting for a system in which every person has the right and the means to express himself. The previous Soviet generation had to live in an atmosphere that suppressed ideas. People had to live double lives, repressing their own talents. Many of them lived and died without ever having the chance to realize their potential and fulfill themselves.

I also have a messianic conception of perestroika and glasnost. Film is a popular art form that can have a tremendous impact on society. I think it can help restore morality and justice, not only in the Soviet Union. The world is moving toward a precipice of moral and spiritual emptiness. Mass culture and the mass media are guilty. Nations today are so interconnected by the mass media and by computers that if we can carry out perestroika in the Soviet Union, it can improve the moral and spiritual atmosphere around the world. Films can make a big contribution, but of course we have a lot to do here first.

Some of your colleagues have said that the stagnation in the Soviet film industry prior to 1985 accurately reflected the broader stagnation in the Soviet system. Tell us something more specific about the situation in filmmaking before you took over.

If you look at it in economic terms, most of the films made lost money and most of the thirty-nine studios should have gone bankrupt. Attendance had declined sharply, but officials just concocted a supposed average number of viewers, or norm, to justify the production of films. An average film costs 400,000–500,000 rubles to shoot, and it is very expensive to make copies, but actual revenue wasn't really counted in kopeks or rubles. Most of the films never should have been made or shown.

Surely some films made money to cover losses on other films, or some of the losses.

There were a few popular, commercially successful films. The two record-breakers were one called *Pirates of the Twentieth Century*. The other was *Moscow Doesn't Believe in Tears*. Hollywood gave it an Academy Award for best foreign film in 1981. They were made for mass audiences, real commercial films. But they didn't offset the losses. To keep the studios from going broke, foreign films were imported, like the French film *Angelique* and the American *Some Like It Hot*. They made good money and subsidized our bad films.

If Moscow Doesn't Believe in Tears was just a commercial film, why did it win an Academy Award?

My friend Viktor Dyomin, the film critic, thinks it was because it resembled an old Hollywood movie. It's a kind of fantasy. The woman is always cheerful in the face of adversity. She struggles and becomes director of the plant. She finds a lover who is an engineer. She raises a child without a husband. Then she finds a husband. It's like an American Cinderella story except this Soviet Cinderella doesn't marry a millionaire, though we have a few of those around. She marries our movie version of the ideal Soviet man and the dream of all Soviet women—an intelligent mechanic.

Apart from the few exceptions, why didn't Soviet films attract an audience? People seemed to be desperate for any kind of popular entertainment, especially in the 1970s.

The films were gray, which means worse than ordinary. They were mediocre, dull, drab, badly directed, badly acted, with banal themes. They got worse and more numerous year by year. They had nothing to recommend them.

Were they the equivalent of what writers called "secretary literature"— works published by or for the people who were then secretaries of the various writers unions?

Exactly, but there were some differences that reflect the difference between the Writers Union Congress and Filmmakers Union Congress in 1986. For writers, the word is everything. For filmmakers, the script is only words, just the beginning. To make a film, they have to stick together and work together. So at their congress, writers delivered some nice speeches and went home. At our congress, we had fewer beautiful words, but we acted together and changed things.

But if filmmakers know how to work together, what kept talented people from making good, bold films in the 1970s? After all, some writers did publish important literature during those years.

Good films were made during those years. When we established what we called the conflicts commission in 1986 to examine and release some thirty films that had been banned or otherwise shelved, there were very good ones among them. Just have a look at Aleksei German's *Roadchecks* and *My Friend, Ivan Lapshin*. The whole system discriminated against such films. Goskino bureaucrats had many ways to kill films they didn't like and show ones that pleased them. They could simply ban a scenario. Or they could censor a script. There was a whole staircase of censorship—at the studio, in the union, at Goskino. If they didn't like a phrase or a whole scene, they'd cut it out.

There were generally accepted rules of the game. Films were supposed to picture an orderly, blissful Soviet life and a triumphant history. The authorities wanted jubilee movies. When a film got made that defied these rules, they found ways to deal with it. For example, German's *My Friend, Ivan Lapshin*, about the Stalinist 1930s, wasn't banned outright. The authorities told German, your film isn't acceptable in its present form. You slander the country's history, you lie about the real situation in the 1930s, the film's too pessimistic, too sad. Lighten it up, put in some optimism. They told him to study sunny, happy films about the 1930s, where people laugh and sing. The problem was that German had shown the truth about everyday life on the eve of the terror—the crowded communal apartments, the shabbiness, people who could be as cruel as children and as blind about what awaited them. He violated all the official clichés about the period.

Goskino tried actually to destroy only two films. One was *Commissar*, a sympathetic portrayal of a Jewish family during the Russian Civil War, by Aleksandr Askoldov. It was only by a lucky accident that a copy of the film survived. The other one was *The Onset of An Unknown Age*, a film directed by Andrei Smirnov and Larissa Shepitko, my wife, who died in a car accident in 1979. The film was based on two stories, one by Andrei Platonov, the other by Yuri Olesha. The film was prohibited and the celluloid washed away with water before Shepitko could complete it. We got a copy because a cameraman paid a worker a few rubles to steal it for him.

These are only a few examples of the fate of films before 1985. When we began to examine those that had lain on the shelf for so many years, there were many wonderful surprises. Had these films been released when they were made, the state of our art would be very different today. It's not just that we lost so many interesting films, so many moral perspectives. Behind each of those banned films was a wrecked career or worse—so much injustice. Filmmakers were forced to betray themselves by adapting to the situation, or let their work be buried, or not work at all.

But Goskino was only one bureaucracy. Why didn't filmmakers appeal to higher political authorities?

They did, and some pictures were released because of those appeals. German's second film, *Twenty Days Without War*, was saved by the famous writer Konstantin Simonov [a much honored author and editor who died in 1979]. Simonov appealed several times to the Central Committee, showed them the film, and persuaded them.

The only way to appeal was to approach someone on the Central Committee?

Yes. I think it was the same way in tsarist Russia, when artists had to get help from someone high up and it didn't have to be someone connected with cultural life. Here's an example from the 1970s. A film director was part of a delegation to Canada and by chance he met a member of the Central Committee at the Soviet embassy in Canada. When the director got back to Moscow, everybody said, "Now he has a place to go and plead his case." Then other filmmakers began to ask him to plead for their projects as well. So the director would send a letter to his Central Committee contact. But the letters would just be forwarded to Goskino. And Goskino or the union leadership would summon the director and say, "Stop complaining." Usually, that was the end of it.

All this resentment seems to have come to a head at the Filmmakers Union Congress in 1986. Some people here in Moscow say it resulted in the first major act of perestroika in cultural life, even the first act of democratization in the Soviet Union.

I agree. It was a historic event, though some people prefer to call it hysteric.

Since it was such an important event, it would be good to learn exactly how the rebellion you led against Goskino and the old union leadership came about. We have heard two explanations. One claims it was a rebellion

from below—by you and other members of the union. The other explana-
tion says that you got the signal to act from Gorbachev or from his allies on
the Politburo and Central Committee, such as Aleksandr Yakovlev.

There is truth in both explanations. At the time I sensed that the
two currents, below and above, were converging. In the depths of the
film industry there was widespread unrest and a desire for changes. On
the other hand, don't forget that our congress was held after Gorbachev's speech to the Twenty-Seventh Party Congress in February 1986,
which built upon the speech he had made to the Central Committee
back in April 1985. After those two events, everyone in the union realized that we were right and Goskino was wrong. The party congress
gave new momentum to the mood for change in the country, for different approaches to problems and a new system of elections. The party
congress coincided with impulses already underway in the Filmmakers
Union.

I think our congress would have taken the course it did even without the party congress because our anger and desire for change were
ripe. So many filmmakers and studio workers were sick of being shack-
led. After all, even after the party congress some of the other creative
unions didn't do much. The Composers Union Congress, for example,
was very peaceful and quiet. At the Writers Union Congress, people
talked a lot and expressed a strong desire to change the situation, but
they ended up mainly with private disagreements and settling personal
scores. Nothing radical happened.

Are you telling us that nobody at the Central Committee told you to
undertake the rebellion in the Filmmakers Union?

Nobody. As a matter of fact, there were a number of prominent
political figures as honorary guests at the precongress meeting where
the rebellion began when we elected delegates. Some of the politicians
had assumed that things would remain the same. And the congress
itself was like a children's game. We were just learning democracy,
lurching to the left and the right. The deposed first secretary of the
union even delivered a speech as a honored guest, as did several other
union officials who hadn't been reelected.

I think we would have thrown out the old union leadership even if
there hadn't been new leadership in the Central Committee. But you
know, it wasn't hard. We really didn't have to do much. When the
rebellion began, the old union leadership could have fought back by
showing Tengiz Abuladze's *Repentance* [a film about the Stalinist ter-

ror made in 1984 and which became a new milestone of glasnost when it was released in 1986] on the opening day of the congress. They could have said, this is our banner. They could have brought a few new people into the leadership, criticized Goskino a bit. Had they done that, our congress would have had a mixed outcome, like the Writers Union Congress. I'm not sure I would have been elected first secretary. But the old leaders were so frightened that all they could think to do was run to the Central Committee for consultation. They discovered they had lost their support at the top. They had been abandoned. They were like blind kittens facing their fate.

In other words, the rebellion began below, but at a critical moment it had the blessing of forces in the Central Committee?

That's right. Everybody knew there was a crisis in the film industry except the officials at Goskino. I'm confident that with every passing day it gets harder to return to the way things were.

Even allowing for the initiatives from below that you have described, is the struggle for creative freedom still closely tied to Gorbachev's fate as leader of the Soviet Union?

Yes, very closely.

And are you confident that Gorbachev shares your radical perspectives on the nature of perestroika?

I think so. He knows we have to create a democratic system in which we all live in accordance with laws, even the leadership. Gorbachev shares our radical ideas, but of course he is an experienced politician who knows that the car can't immediately accelerate to 100 miles an hour. It has to build up speed and pick up passengers along the way. And we can't rely on Gorbachev to do everything by himself. That's why when people ask me on whom the fate of perestroika depends, I say on all of us—on me and on them.

What have you actually achieved since you and your people took over the union?

We are not engaged in superficial reform in the film industry. We are creating a new model of filmmaking based on the principles of perestroika—glasnost, decentralization, democratization, and self-financing. Goskino will continue to coordinate the film industry, but it will no longer exercise petty tutelage over the studios. This is a transition from the administrative model to a self-managing one. Filmmakers will decide themselves which films to make. Studios will have creative and financial independence. Of course this means they will no longer be subsidized, that they will have to cover their costs with the revenues they earn from their films. It also means that a studio can go bankrupt, but all of them have an equal chance. There's no other way if talent is to win the war against mediocrity.

Isn't there a basic contradiction in your thinking? You began by emphasizing the need for talented, even messianic films. But if studios must exist on their own earnings, won't they have to make films that entertain and attract millions of moviegoers rather than message-oriented films that seek to enlighten people? Won't the process of commercialization itself lead to a new kind of mediocrity, by your own standards?

We know this is a danger. We are very worried that the new model of filmmaking will commercialize the Soviet cinema and we are trying to find ways to prevent it. For example, we have set up a fund to help young directors who want to make highly intellectual films that may not attract large audiences. One percent of all revenues will go to this fund, about 3 million rubles a year. We also want to create a special studio for experimental films. It too would be subsidized. And we must do what is done in America—conduct studies of what moviegoers want. My close associate Dyomin says jokingly that we will have to give films showy titles and hope that reviewers say the director has "bourgeois tastes." Our readers know how to read between the lines. They'll know it means the film has violence and sex, and they'll run off to see it.

We know very little about our audiences. Sociologists can help us learn about the film market, distribution, and what people really think is topical. In the past, allegedly topical themes were just invented at Goskino. But the larger problem is that people's taste has been spoiled by all the bad cheap movies made here in the past and imported from abroad.

That seems a little elitist on your part. But even if it is true, where's the hope that the exalted films you want made will find an audience?

It's a fact unfortunately that people are inclined toward bad mass culture. And it is not only the authorities who are responsible. Many filmmakers produced bad films that helped lower the viewer's level. As a result, many people go to moviehouses just to relax and enjoy—to stop thinking. We have to enlighten them and make them want to think.

Have many good films already come out under the new system?

Not yet, at least not feature films. The fruits of our reforms won't be clear until sometime late in 1989, when we expect a big leap in quality. Up to now, most of the best films, the ones that have won prizes, were made earlier, shelved, and released after 1985.

What is going to happen to people in the film industry who can't adapt to the new system? Tengiz Abuladze has remarked that in the past most Soviet directors just made films for the authorities.

They will have to leave the cinema. They have no right to make films. They will have to find other work. We need good taxi drivers, for example.

That's why perestroika is a drama. It involves the fates of many, many people who are against it for many different reasons. Perestroika threatens their habits, status, and security. You can see it in the film industry. Studios now are allowed to hire and make contracts with whomever they like, but in the past they could sign agreements only with people permanently assigned to the studio. No freelancers were permitted. As a result, the studios filled with trash. Now those people realize they won't automatically be given work anymore. Some of these people have honorary titles and posts. They are accustomed to certain forms of respect and a guaranteed salary. They have families. Suddenly it looks like life is going to pieces. And this isn't happening just in the film industry. Even the state and party apparatuses are being cut back. Many people won't have the positions they had before, and they don't know how to do anything else. That's why the struggle for perestroika is so serious.

No one doubts that it is serious, but a few people around Moscow think that when all is said and done, perestroika will turn out to be little more than the replacement of one group of privileged officials by another. Maybe such people are habitual cynics, but that sometimes has been the outcome of reform movements in history—in the Soviet Union and elsewhere. Take your union, for example. Creative unions have claimed to represent and fight for artists in the Soviet Union for more than fifty years. Union leaderships have come and gone, but the problem of artistic freedom remains. What is to prevent the new union leadership under Klimov from becoming another group of bureaucrats with its own special interests and privileges?

I agree that's a danger. Man is weak. Human psychology is such that even good new people in official chairs can be corrupted by privilege and flattery. That is why democratization is so important. All Soviet officials should have to stand for reelection every five years and not be allowed to serve more than two terms in office. That includes union officials. In the old system, they served from here to eternity. And if they perform poorly during their terms, union members should call for new elections. I think the Soviet people are ready for this kind of democracy. They have been waiting for it. Not all people, of course, but many of them.

As for Klimov, I wouldn't agree for the life of me to another term as first secretary of the union. Let the new generation take my place. Let new people come to power. I have films to make, one about Stalin—an urgent subject—and one based on Mikhail Bulgakov's novel *Master and Margarita*. As for privileges, I stand in line like everybody else. This is one first secretary who has turned down the privileges offered to him. People sometimes forget that the intelligentsia also stands in line. I have no special shops. Klimov stands in line.

We also have heard some complaints that you and your colleagues in the film industry are spending too much time abroad developing ties with Western filmmakers instead of working at home.

These international ties are very important. The Soviet film industry has wonderful talent and themes, but much of our equipment, including the film itself, is primitive. We need to buy Western equipment, but to do that we must earn foreign currency. But even more important than currency, we need full-scale cultural cooperation with the West for spiritual reasons. Our philosophical and historical traditions—the best of them—have much to offer mankind and at the same time Western traditions can enrich us in the era of perestroika. As Gorbachev made clear during his summit meetings with Reagan, including the one in Washington in December 1987, we aren't going to reject any opportunities for mutual understanding and cooperation with different nations.

But there is another dimension to the question about what has actually changed or will change. Your main complaint against the old regime is that it denied talented artists freedom. Have you now ended censorship?

You have to understand that generally we didn't have conflicts with the formal censorship, which made sure that no military or state secrets, no pornography, and no incitement to violence appeared in films. Our conflicts were with the censorship exercised by the self-proclaimed watchdogs at Goskino, who took it upon themselves to speak in the name of the people, to judge what was and was not needed. They were the ones who interfered in everything, from screenplays and an actor's performance to finished films. The new leadership of the Filmmakers

Union is trying to establish a common understanding with the new leadership of Goskino so that we can cooperate in ways that give filmmakers the freedom they need. I am fairly confident about this, though the Russian branch of Goskino remains quite conservative. They are worried, for example, about the new documentary films, which are very sharp and honest. We have to squeeze those films out of them. They still want to ration glasnost from above.

As a party member, are you really free to wage this campaign for artistic freedom? Aren't you bound in some ways by whatever may be the prevailing party line?

It depends on how you understand the party line. I am against any dogmatic understanding of the party line, but I adhere to the major principles of communism. How can one object to ideas about a healthy society and moral harmony? Unfortunately, those ideals haven't been fulfilled. That's why if you are a real Communist, you are an active supporter of glasnost and democratization.

It's still not clear how artistic freedom is fully compatible with any kind of party line, dogmatic or otherwise.

Studios will have the right to choose their own scripts and make a film without showing it to the authorities. Anyway, why would anybody brought up in this society make a film that conflicted with the ideals of the society?

But who is to decide what conflicts or does not conflict with society's ideals? In the United States, for example, filmmakers raised in America sometimes make films that other Americans think are anti-American.

Yes, you have a critical-minded movement in your film industry, and there is no reason why we should not have one here. Then viewers and the mass media can argue about those films. But they won't be antiparty films.

You know the American film Apocalypse Now, *which was very critical of the American War in Vietnam. Could there be a similar Soviet film about the Soviet war in Afghanistan?*

Yes, if the war greatly offended a filmmaker's conscience and if he made a convincing film. I would defend his right to make such a film. It would be my responsibility.

When I say perestroika is a fight for freedom, I always add, "and responsibility." A person who is free to act must be responsible for his actions. To tell you the truth, this is a new sensation for us and many of us aren't ready for it. Many people are afraid to take responsibility. They even try to avoid it. They say, we must improve things, but let's do it in a way that I won't be responsible for the process. They are accustomed to having someone else take responsibility. It used to be very convenient, for example, for our magazine and newspaper editors to turn down bold new pieces by blaming censorship. An editor would say to an author, "I like it very much. You're a genius. But nothing can be done. They won't allow it." Editors can't do that anymore because they are responsible and have to decide. Some of them don't like it.

Are artists themselves—writers and filmmakers—ready to take advantage of the new freedom?

Now you have touched a sore point. Perestroika also involves a drama of personal conscience. Too many creative people still are being guided by what we call the inner censor or inner editor. Even I still feel him inside me—a cautious little man sitting behind a small desk somewhere on the right side of my brain saying, "You better not do this. Don't take that step." It's torture. There should be in each of us a moral censor telling us to do the right thing. Instead, there's still this little inner censor implanted there by years of terror and fear.

But if a man like Klimov, whom people say was brave even before 1985, isn't completely free of this inner censor, what can be expected from less bold artists or ones who have less standing?

How do we liberate people from these chains? I'm certain that many people of my generation, even honest and talented ones, won't be able to get rid of the chains. Our hope is the next generation, which will grow up in the atmosphere we are creating. They will be bold. That's why all the people who want to make changes, all the people who don't want the next generation to have to live the way we lived, must make radical changes now. There may not be another chance.

Is that radical outlook, for which you seem to be well known, the reason why the young people who formed the Memorial Society turned to you when they needed help?

Of course, but not only my outlook—also that of the Filmmakers Union. They came to me in early 1988 when they were collecting signatures for a monument to Stalin's victims. They asked me to speak at their rallies, and I did so along with people like Yuri Afanasyev, Yevtushenko, Sakharov, and the writer Yuri Karyakin. Later, Afanasyev and

I arranged to have their petitions delivered to the Nineteenth Party Conference. In addition, the Filmmakers Union gave Memorial other kinds of support—office space, halls for its meetings, money, and so forth. Other unions also played an important role—the architects, artists, and theater workers. But the Writers Union came in only later, when it was embarrassed by having not participated earlier. The Memorial Society became a formal nationwide organization in January 1989, but it still has many opponents and problems. Even now, many local authorities refuse to recognize its legal status.

Does your own boldness derive from optimism or from desperation over the future of perestroika?

I know all the problems. I know that we have to produce goods, apartments, sausage. The transition period will be terribly complicated. The next two or three years will be very dramatic. It is easy to be skeptical and pessimistic, but if we are, we won't achieve anything. On the other hand, we shouldn't be optimistic idiots. Anyone who knows the history of our country and our temptation to resort to repressive measures can't be too optimistic. On balance, though, I am optimistic. I think our history has turned a new page, that new historical circumstances favor perestroika, and that the majority of party members are ready for it. Personally, I am very encouraged by the Gorbachev leadership, whose policies reflect new trends in the party elite. And I think they are supported by Russia's best people, who are ready to start a new life.

But maybe this is simply my character. If I climb a ten-meter tower, I always have to dive from it. I never climb back down, even though I once broke my spine diving. Some of my colleagues in the union leadership are a little more cautious. Sometimes they say we shouldn't hurry, that we should take this or that into account, that we shouldn't hurt the feelings of this person or that person. But for me, once I've climbed to the top, it's natural to dive.

Are you sure there is water in the pool below?

For now, there is water in the pool. A lot of it.

MIKHAIL ULYANOV

"The Preaching Theater"

IN MANY RESPECTS, the rebellion among theater professionals, which began in October 1986, was a sequel to what had happened earlier in the Filmmakers Union. A group led by the actor Mikhail Aleksandrovich Ulyanov, the director Oleg Efremov, the playwright Mikhail Shatrov, and other prominent theater people sprang a coup by democratic ballot. They disbanded the old, compliant All Russian Theater Society and formed a Russian Theater Workers Union headed by Ulyanov. Once again, the underlying issues were cultural freedom from state bureaucratic control and censorship. The difference was the important role played earlier in 1985–86 by several Moscow theaters, whose boldly outspoken plays contributed to glasnost by creating an atmosphere of "parliamentary discussion" in the nation's capital. Long before Ulyanov was elected head of the union, he had been a towering figure of Soviet cultural life for many years—the country's best-known and probably most beloved actor due partly to his many film and stage roles as Lenin and as Marshal Georgi Zhukov, the conqueror of the Nazi invaders. Ulyanov's fabled versatility has been displayed in roles ranging from Shakespeare's Richard III to Tevye in Fiddler on the Roof. In 1987 he became director of Moscow's prestigious Vakhtangov Theater. As Ulyanov explains below, great Russian actors often play public roles outside the theater. Indeed, a 1987 article about him in Moscow News was entitled, with an oblique reference to the career of Ronald Reagan, "An Actor Who Could Have Been a President." Having joined the Communist Party in 1951, Ulyanov is now a member of its Central Auditing Commission and of the Central Committee Commission on Ideology. In March 1989 he was elected by the party Central Committee to be one of its one hundred deputies to the new Congress of People's Deputies. As was clear from our conversation with him, Ulyanov has a kind of raging passion for perestroika and a hatred of Stalinism.

I'M AN ACTOR, not a politician. There have been a lot of politics in my life, but politics rooted in the profession and vision of the theater. I only have one program, and it is based on the difference between good and evil.

Let me put it like this. An actor's profession may seem to be very simple—learn the script, paste on a mustache, come out on stage. But as with any creative work, acting requires a perspective, a point of view. No artist can create just in general, as they say, without a perspective on life and on the world around him. As Aleksandr Bovin argues, there isn't even such a thing as an independent press—one not subject to influences. He believes that our press knows it is dependent, while the American press considers itself to be independent, even though it is dependent on outside influences in different ways. As an artist I am dependent on the times in which I live. That doesn't mean I'm subservient or a lackey. I'm not and I've never been. A lackey simply says, "I listen and I obey." I, on the other hand, have tried to select roles that enable me to awaken people's own feelings of self-worth and dignity. Probably that's what attracted me to the theater in the first place.

I was born in 1927 in Tara, a small town in the far corner of Siberia. My father was an ordinary peasant who became chairman of a village collective farm. There was no theater around, and my family had no interest in the theater. But like every little boy, I loved the movies. There was one movie house in our town and I saw every film that came there. Now and then a repertory company visited our town in the summer and I would go to see it. As fate would have it, a small Ukrainian theater was evacuated to Tara during the war and one of its members, a marvelous man, started a theater class for the local boys and girls. I went to his class, and that led to my becoming an actor. In 1945 I went to study acting in Omsk, but within a year I had a thirst for more knowledge and a desire to go to Moscow. In 1946 I was accepted by the Shchukin Theater School. I have lived in Moscow ever since.

After I graduated in 1952 I was accepted as a member of the Vakhtangov Theater's repertory company, where I now am the artistic director. Since 1952 I've also appeared in a lot of films. I used to do maybe two films a year, but nowadays I work mainly in the theater. And of course as chairman of the board of the Theater Workers Union of the Russian Republic.

Of all the films I made, *The Chairman* had the greatest political and civic reverberations. I've played Marshal Zhukov too many times over the last twenty years so I am always associated with him, but *The Chairman* still is my most famous film. It was released in 1964, right at the juncture between the Khrushchev and Brezhnev periods. The film had a strong point of view. It told the truth about our lives, just as we are doing today. It was about the chairman of a village collective farm that had been destroyed by the cruelties and inhumanity of World War II and the difficulties he faced in trying to raise the farm from the ruins. *The Chairman* aroused widespread argument. I still remember the long lines of people waiting for tickets and the heated debates about the film. Some people said it slandered our system and our history. Other people were inspired by the film to join the Communist Party.

Fortunately, the film wasn't shelved. I even received a Lenin Prize for it. Unfortunately, soon after the film appeared, the Brezhnev leadership began to embellish our history, as though it were afraid of the people and of the problems that lay ahead. Some good films with a strong point of view were made during the Brezhnev era, but most of them were shelved.

It seems that like so many people of your generation, you identify yourself with the anti-Stalinism of the Khrushchev years.

Even though I joined the Communist Party in 1951, I have long considered the Stalin years to have been a plague upon our country. I was too young to remember the terror of the 1930s. And because we lived in remote Siberia, my family was not touched by it. But I remember the postwar repressions when I was living in Moscow—the insane attacks on so-called cosmopolitanism, the attacks on the composer Dmitri Shostakovich and the writers Anna Akhmatova and Mikhail Zoshchenko. Stalin was a horrible person. And yet even today our country remains deeply divided between people who believe he brought us terrible misfortune and those who think that without Stalin we would not have been ready for the war. I belong to the first group. Stalin's inhumane methods were completely unnecessary. His campaigns against the kulaks [peasants who were alleged to be prosperous or hostile to the Soviet government] and enemies of the people were just invented. Of all the misfortunes Stalin brought to the country, the worst was the fear he planted in so many souls. He made people permanently frightened—frightened of being arrested. Any kind of terror in the soul is terrible, but it is fatal when it is caused by state terrorism. Stalinism was the greatest tragedy in our history.

That is why the Twentieth Party Congress was the turning point in our life—at least prior to the Twenty-Seventh Congress thirty years later. The Twentieth Congress broke Stalinism's back. And no matter how many mistakes Khrushchev may have made later, he performed a great and invaluable service to our country by daring to smash the Stalin cult. I say this even though Khrushchev later created his own little cult and Brezhnev hung medals all over himself. Compared to the horrors of the Stalin cult, those cults were poor theater. After Khrushchev's speech at the Twentieth Congress, no one could believe in cults like that. That is how eventually we arrived at the Twenty-Seventh Party Congress.

I don't mean that the struggle is over. Stalin ruled the country for thirty years, and during that time a huge bureaucratic machine was created. Even though it treated people like cogs, people attributed anything good that was achieved first to Stalin and then to this machine. They never had a chance to get used to real Leninism—to democracy and glasnost. Lenin died too soon. I was at Stalin's funeral, and I remember how people identified their lives with him.

The machine outlived Stalin. Khrushchev tried to break its power, but the struggle continues today. The nomenklatura doesn't want to give up its power anywhere—in the economy, the arts, politics. Some people even defend this machine by saying there has been no order in the country since Stalin died. They forget that wasn't order but the whip. Real order is a society of free citizens with rights no one can violate. That's what perestroika is about. It's a choice between *apparat* tyranny and people's power. Many people are fiercely opposed to perestroika and some of them even try to sabotage it, but Stalinism can no longer prevail. Since 1985 the forces of freedom, democracy, and glasnost have been unleashed.

Maybe so, but why did thirty years pass between the Twentieth Party Congress and the beginning of perestroika? What happened in the 1960s that led to the 1970s, or the era of what Gorbachev calls stagnation?

If we had begun perestroika right after the Twentieth Congress in 1956, the country would be very different today. Instead, the authorities continued to think of people as cogs, and too many people fell silent. We lost thirty years. There were no mass repressions, no blood, but there also was no oxygen. They didn't let anyone breathe, though to be fair to Krushchev, he tried to find ways to do so. Even today we remain silent about some things. We have named a lot of our problems, and we name people who are no longer in power. But there still are people working at the top who remain unnamed. We haven't gotten used to attacking those people, but just wait. We'll get used to it because you can't solve problems without identifying the underlying structures that produce those problems and the people who defend those structures.

Does that mean Soviet newspapers should have the right to criticize the Politburo and perhaps Gorbachev himself?

Why would we criticize Gorbachev? He is the leader of perestroika, and we need him if we are to change the system. As for the Politburo, I will not take it upon myself to judge. In the short term we probably will not go that far. We are moving in that direction, attacking ministers, but I don't know about the Politburo. If we begin to attack that, there won't be anything to hold on to.

Speaking of ministers, an article about you in Moscow News, *entitled "An Actor Who Could Be a President," reported that in the past many officials disliked you because it was impossible to control you. What was the article referring to?*

Let me put it more generally. Even before perestroika there were people, especially among the intelligentsia, who were not silent or subservient. I could name many of them. The singer-actor Vladimir Vysotsky, writers like Yuri Nagibin and Vasily Shukshin, the poet Yevtushenko, the filmmakers whose films were mutilated or banned. Such people found ways to remain faithful to the Twentieth Party Congress, some more successfully than others. They knew that eventually things would change. But unfortunately a great many people served the authorities profitably during the Brezhnev years. Now they shout eagerly in favor of perestroika, but they are not to be trusted. Believe only those people who have always held to one position. Personally, I have always had one position. It is simple, perhaps even primitive: I love my motherland very much and I want the best conditions for her. What helps my country, I support. What does not help my country, I do not support. That's all. I have no other platform or point of view.

Let's talk about your platform in the context of what has happened in the theater since 1985. Along with a number of other well-known actors, directors, and playwrights, you staged a kind of coup against the Ministry of Culture in the fall of 1986 by transforming a meeting of the old Russian Theater Society into a constituent congress for a real union. From what we have read and heard, the rebellion grew out of a situation in the theater similar to what had prevailed in the film industry.

An entire apparatus of officials sat on the creative head of the theater. We had to deal with hundreds of these officials. They wouldn't let us breathe. We needed their approval before we could accept a play for production. And even after a play had been accepted, it had to be "improved" from the official point of view. Sometimes plays were improved so much they bore little or no resemblance to what the playwright or director had conceived. Ministry officials also decided almost everything else, including salaries in the theater and the price of tickets.

We have gotten rid of that system in favor of a decentralized one. You see, we created our union for several reasons. To help theater workers—to get them good pensions, build retirement homes, and that sort of thing. And to be a full partner in making decisions about the theater itself. The Ministry of Culture still exists, but we are on an equal footing with it. It can no longer decide important issues without our participation. The most important thing is that theaters now can decide their own repertories and stage any plays they want. They also have extensive economic powers. They can vary salaries and the price of tickets. Not everything goes smoothly of course. When we adopted our charter giving the union equal rights with the Ministry of Culture, some ministry officials were very unhappy. They still aren't reconciled to the new situation. We have to struggle. The ministry has the money to influence the general situation in the theater, but we have public opinion behind us. Moreover, the artistic councils and directors of theaters now are being elected by people who work in the individual theaters, rather than being appointed. It's a revolutionary development.

How did this revolution in the theater begin?

It was rather simple. They decided above and we implemented it. At the Twenty-Seventh Party Congress in February 1986, the party said let there be glasnost and democratization and the artistic intelligentsia took it from there. The filmmakers were the first. That was the first time a union leadership had been elected democratically and not appointed from above. Then at our congress we elected a slate of candidates different from the one composed of party regulars. That's how I was elected.

There are reports that Gorbachev himself played some role in the events leading up to your rebellion.

In his speech to the Twenty-Seventh Party Congress, he criticized official attitudes toward the arts and emphasized the importance of cultural life. He particularly loves the theater, you know. Then in December 1986, two days before the opening of our founding congress, Gorbachev came to speak with people who were organizing the union about his favorite topics—glasnost and democratization as the oxygen of perestroika. He asked a lot of questions, and we spoke frankly about our past problems. It was clear that he sympathized with us.

It will be hard for Americans to understand why a busy national leader should bother taking a political interest in the theater. Indeed, why did the theater play such an exceptional political role during the early months of glasnost in 1985–86? As much if not more than any other public forum, it was the source of many new political ideas and much controversy. One of your playwrights even said that during those months, "The theater was our parliament."

I can understand why Americans might have a hard time understanding this. When I was in the United States not long ago I saw twelve of your plays, ranging from *A Chorus Line* to a Sam Shepard play. The technical quality of American productions is fantastic, but the plays made a profoundly strange impression on me. Strange because while your theater is content to try to understand why man is not well, our theater tries to help him become better.

This is our tradition. More than a hundred years ago, Aleksandr Herzen [the Russian liberal socialist thinker] pointed out that when there is no free political tribune in Russia, the theater takes on this role. It provides the stage for topical public discourse. In tsarist Russia, the theater was often a kind of second university, where the most substantive social and human questions were raised. So we have a tradition of what you might call the preaching theater. Our actors, directors, and playwrights want to stand for something and preach. Like your theater, we have our successes and failures. But unlike most Western theater, which pulls away from life, we want to explore it and sort it out.

That's why some of the plays of 1985–86 were so important beyond the theater. Aleksandr Buravsky's *Speak . . .* tried to raise public consciousness and get people to say what they really thought. Aleksandr Misharin's *The Silver Wedding Anniversary* exposed official corruption. Mikhail Shatrov's *Dictatorship of Conscience* and *The Brest Peace*, in which I played Lenin, explored very painful historical and political subjects. At some point, of course, glasnost overtook these plays, as newspapers, radio, and television became the main political tribune. Some of those plays, perhaps most of them, are already dated, and there's no point just repeating what they had to say. Why call a thief a thief after everybody already knows he is a thief? Now the challenge is to produce plays that dig deeper, that analyze the heart of our problems, that seek the sources of corruption. We haven't produced those kinds of plays yet. It will take time.

Why are you so confident that the creation of another union is going to lead to that kind of theater in the Soviet Union? Other artists unions have existed here for many years without achieving much for their members or their professions.

In the past, union leaders were afraid of offending anyone. That's why they never threatened anyone and never protected anybody. But the creative intelligentsia now feels the need for real unions that will defend and represent their interests. It doesn't matter that we still call these organizations unions. The substance matters, not the title. Look at *Moscow News* and *Ogonyok*. A few years ago, nobody read them.

The content of the theater will be different because we will have a competitive democratic system. From now on, for example, actors will have only a one- or two-year contract, for a season, and then they will have to face a competition judged by a theater's artistic council, which itself is elected. All this is very painful. We have socialist problems that you don't face. In the Soviet Union, everyone has a right to work. There are eighty to ninety actors in every theater. We don't need all of them, but what are we going to do with them? Firing them violates our principles, but we can't run a charity. We haven't solved the problem yet, though competition is part of the solution. In the past, an actor could spend his life at one theater. Now some of them will have to leave.

To be honest with you, there still isn't full democracy in this respect. Older, well-established actors like me—actors, say, with the title of People's Artist—are exempt from the competition. I think we have to go farther. To improve the theater in a real way, we have to start with the head, not with the tail. You can't have democracy over here and plutocracy over there.

On the other hand, I will have to be reelected as chairman of the Theater Workers Union when my five-year term is up. It didn't used to be this way in union leaderships. The authorities appointed a person to the job, and if he conducted himself properly and quietly, if he voiced no objections, he could stay for twenty-five years. At most I can be elected for one more term. The guy before me sat here for twenty-eight years. The first secretary of the Composers Union has sat in his chair for forty years. This boondoggle is ending. And because the turnover began from below, I think the process is unstoppable. People at the top will no longer support me if people below no longer want me.

I even think that the model of democratization in our union has implications for society. The theater is a drop in an ocean, but if in that drop there are solutions for solving larger problems, why can't they be enlarged? If you look at our union charter and the way we drafted it, it's a kind of model of democratization. We worked on it for months with the help of lawyers, economists, and other experts. The draft was published in a newspaper, and a long public discussion followed. The draft has many provisions needed by society at large. Elections, secret balloting, rights for people to say whatever they want, limits on officials' tenure in office and on their right to make decisions.

Many things have been written on paper in the Soviet Union over the years that were never acted out in real life.

Sure, we don't live in a vacuum. Our union procedures would not have worked under Brezhnev. It wouldn't even have been possible to adopt them. And I agree that the legacy of the past still weighs heavily. Some theater people are frightened by this freedom. They aren't used to it. In the past a director could say, "I'm not permitted to do that," or if the production was bad he could blame it on somebody upstairs. Now you can't hide behind the official line. If you screw up, it's your own fault and responsibility.

Here's the root of so much opposition to perestroika in general. People are essentially conservative and perestroika is asking them to change their psychology. There are a huge number of people who only know how to fulfill orders blindly, without thinking. Now we demand that people be truly useful—that talent, ability, and competitiveness be the norms. That frightens many of our people. You Americans are used to it because you live in a system where competition is a constant race. You live with monstrous tension.

But people here have gotten used to not racing anywhere. They are used to decent salaries, nice offices, and taking responsibility. People used to wink away the loss of millions of rubles. "Oh yeah, we shouldn't have built this here. We should have built it over there. Who's responsible? Oh yeah, the state." Now it will be their fault. That's why they don't want perestroika. They're not fools. Those kind of people understand that our system is wondrously convenient for laze-abouts, time-servers, and careerists. For years our system cultivated those kinds of people, while a person who thought or acted independently had a very hard time—in the arts, in economics, in science, anywhere. We can't support do-nothings any longer at the expense of those who work.

The only way out of this is democracy and competition. I remember our first experience with democracy in 1986, when we were electing people to run the union. We could nominate twenty people from Moscow, and we presented a list of proposed candidates. You should have heard the screams and hysterics. People were accustomed to lists coming down from above and being composed on the basis of quotas. They started shouting, where's this group, where's that group? Why so few women, why that woman, not this one? It kept on and I had to preside over this thing. Finally I said, Comrades, we can only send twenty people, and you've already listed ninety, but if that is what you want, okay, let's vote. And you know what happened? The twenty we had originally nominated were elected. Everybody calmed down. But if I had tried to impose the twenty it would have gone badly. And now these principles are spreading throughout society, even to the party. It's normal.

Was it normal that 47 of the 641 people voting for deputies to the Congress of People's Deputies at the Central Committee meeting in March 1989 voted against your candidacy?

The important thing is that the Central Committee made public its voting for the first time that anyone can remember. The Communist Party set this example to show the people that it is serious about democratizing the Soviet system. It was an important step toward democracy and glasnost inside the party. After all, if it can acknowledge that twelve people in high party positions voted against Gorbachev, the leader of the country and of perestroika, it can publicize many other things.

As for the forty-seven votes against me, I was a bit surprised. I'm not a politician like Aleksandr Yakovlev or Yegor Ligachev. They received even more negative votes. Of course, I'm not happy that forty-seven people voted against me, but nor am I upset. It was a natural reaction to my strong stands in favor of perestroika and glasnost. Given the struggle underway among different viewpoints in high echelons, how could it have been otherwise?

It sounds exciting, especially the way you tell it, but where is the outer limit of all this freedom and democratization? It is unfolding in a one-party system in which the Communist Party has long insisted on some kind of partiinost, or partyness, in the arts. You are yourself a substantial party figure, a member of the Central Committee's Ideological Commission and of the party's Central Auditing Commission, which enables you occasionally to attend and even speak at Central Committee meetings. Should we assume that partiinost in the arts is now a thing of the past, superseded by the freedoms of democratization?

Why should it be a thing of the past? Our system and society haven't changed. Whether you like it or not, the party remains the leading force and the motor of our society. Society supports the party's ideas and decisions. If the people follow the party, it would be ridiculous for cultural figures to go in some other direction. So whether you like it or not, *partiinost* hasn't left our art and it's not about to either.

It is not a question of whether we like it or not, but of understanding your outlook. Let's say two plays about Stalin, to take a subject you raised earlier with some passion, are running in Moscow at the same time. One play indicts Stalin for the plague of terror he brought upon the country. The other play praises Stalin for bringing order to the country. Indeed, this conflict already exists in Soviet literature and in the press, so it is likely to show up in the theater as well. Which play represents partiinost? *Which theater is following the party line?*

Why not both of them, since ferocious arguments are going on about Stalin?

You mean even in the top party leadership?

Yes, they probably have the same arguments up there.

And what if tomorrow the Politburo or the Central Committee decides that Stalin had been a virtuous leader and says so in a resolution? Will Soviet theaters then put on only pro-Stalin plays, as was once the case?

That isn't going to happen. You must understand something simple. Gorbachev and the Politburo—or rather his majority on the Politburo—want people to discuss all these questions. Eventually we may have to arrive at one point of view, come to a decision, as a result of these discussions, arguments, and confrontations. That point of view will constitute a kind of party law, which will have to be obeyed. If our arguments about Stalin help us consolidate our strength, then we have to argue about Stalin. If the arguments begin to rock our society, to generate factions and endless fights among ourselves, then it wouldn't be democracy. We want every question—political, economic, moral— to be discussed in full, but then we must adopt a position. This doesn't mean that I must change my personal point of view—about Stalin, for example—but it means that I must subordinate my personal viewpoint to the party's point of view. A family will fall apart if the wife and the husband always argue about their opinions.

On the one hand, you are right. Assuming that there are fair rules of the game, all democracies require defeated viewpoints to abide by the outcome. On the other hand, democratic principles also prize constant argument and minority points of view.

I agree, so long as I listen to the majority and my argument doesn't harm anyone. But the problem of Stalin, which we are discussing, is so huge and so horrible that it won't end for five, maybe ten years. Anyway, the principle of glasnost allows for a pluralism of opinion about such questions.

From your perspective, how much glasnost is there?

It depends where you look. I go to the provinces more than most people do. The situation is more difficult there. Newspaper editors, for example, need protection from provincial party authorities. There are many different authorities here in Moscow. If I can't get something resolved with one of them, I go to another. But in the provinces there is only one master—the regional party secretary. If you can't work things out with him, there's no one else to turn to. His word is law. This is a case where Stalinism has penetrated very deeply. Eventually we are going to have to get at this structure, too. It would help if editors were elected instead of being dependent on provincial party authorities.

But there is a lot of glasnost in the center and in the theater. Formal censorship still exists for military secrets and pornography, but we never had many problems with it. That's dogshit. What kind of secrets are there in a play? Our problems were with the Ministry of Culture, and I still have to struggle all the time with those officials. But we get our way. There's plenty of glasnost in the theater. Take any political theme you want. There's another kind of glasnost, too. It seems like all Russia has risen up on her hind legs to protest. The union gets hundreds of letters demanding that this or that director be removed because he wasn't elected.

Yes, but as you said earlier, glasnost was unleashed from above. Presumably one day people at the top could decide to put an end to it.

Theoretically, you are right. They can close it down and open it up. In fact, I wrote an article comparing glasnost with sluice gates that are now open. Bovin didn't like this expression because it implies the gates could be closed again. But given the changes that have occurred in people, glasnost cannot be stopped. To the same degree that Stalin beat the fear of repression into the souls of people, Gorbachev has released the desire for freedom and democracy in people's souls.

When you say "the people," do you mean the majority of Soviet citizens or the rather small layer of society that you have been calling the creative intelligentsia?

I mean the people—the masses. It's easy to handle the intelligentsia but not the people. Once the people have begun to speak, it is very difficult to stop them. Now it would require a counterrevolution that would shake the entire country. Nobody would be able to hold on to their positions. Our entire history from the Twentieth Party Congress to the Twenty-Seventh Party Congress—Khrushchev, Brezhnev, Gorbachev—has changed people's souls in such a way that everything is possible except one thing—turning back the clock. It is already impossible psychologically and economically to turn back the clock. The country would fall apart.

How do you know the state of people's souls and what people are thinking? So far, under glasnost, it has been the intelligentsia and politicians who have done most of the public talking.

How do I know? People write to me. Every week I receive a huge number of letters from all over the country—from Omsk, Tomsk, Vladivostok, Sakhalin. I could never answer all the letters. People write to me about everything and with all kinds of questions and requests. "What is love?" "What shall I do?" "Help me get an apartment." "Help me with money." "My child is sick." "What did Stalin do to our country?" "My daughter wants to be an actress." I know what people are thinking from these letters.

Why do so many people write to you about things that have nothing directly to do with the theater?

They write to me personally because as an actor I have preached a certain point of view and taken certain positions. People have come to think of me as a person who can solve all problems. I can solve some of them, but of course many I can't. I can't decide what is love or cure a child, though I can arrange for a hospital to take that child. You see, acting is a mystical profession. Few people actually know me as a person. They know me through the roles I've played. The problem is that while I've played Marshal Zhukov very often, I don't have any of his troops to order around.

People also write letters for other reasons. They write to a lot of people for help because we have this massive, indifferent bureaucracy and they need a human response. Americans don't write letters like that probably because they don't believe letters can solve their problems. It may also have to do with the extreme contrasts between the rich and the poor in America. It is a Russian tradition to write to actors. People know we don't make much money. But who's going to write for help to Jack Nicholson or Marlon Brando? Your actors are more like pin-up figures. Ours are considered civic figures. Your actors make enormous sums of money, buy islands, and rarely give a damn about this dog's world. I go home at night after running around all day and people are still calling me for help.

It also has to do with the special connection between our theater, our intelligentsia, and the people. It is different from yours. In America these groups are cut off from each other. The layer on top tries to figure out what people below want to buy today—*A Chorus Line* or a Sam Shepard play. Then they decide what to produce. Here the intelligentsia does not write poems for the sake of poems or stage performances for the sake of the performance. They do it for the people. To ignite or excite in the people one or another feeling. That is the tradition of our intelligentsia.

The whole intelligentsia?

Of course not, only a part of it. Another part of it exists only to hold on to its dachas and comfortable positions in life. We don't have a homogeneous intelligentsia. Look at the people you've chosen for your book. You're not going around talking with reactionary writers like Georgi Markov, Pyotr Proskurin, or Anatoly Sofronov. You're talking with those of us who are fighting for perestroika.

We would like to interview opponents of perestroika among the intelligentsia and political class, but they aren't very talkative or candid, at least not in public. But let's go back to your generalizations about the Soviet people. Not all supporters of perestroika are as confident as you that the people are ready for such radical reforms. You have spoken yourself about citizens' pervasive conservatism. And a number of Soviet scholars have openly worried about the low level of Soviet political culture. They seem to suggest that people here might not yet be ready for democratization.

Who says the people aren't ready? Are you saying that your people are ready for politics and our people aren't? Don't judge our system by your standards. Your system has things I don't understand, and we have things you don't understand. I remember when I was in Germany performing a play called *The City at Dawn*. It's about how young people built the industrial city of Komsomolsk in the 1930s out there in the swamp, in the harshest conditions. The country desperately needed that city and its factories. There was no money and little equipment, but a force of young people built it—heroically. The Germans were puzzled by the play. They couldn't understand why roads weren't laid before the city was built. When I explained there was no time or money for roads, they still didn't understand.

Soviet people haven't read a lot, but I think they are more ready for politics than your people are. Not long ago I was in Italy during one of its so-called political crises. Another government fell. Italian people paid no attention, and when I asked them why not they said, "The politicians are doing their thing and we are doing ours." The people I asked were more interested in how much they sold that day or how many people were eating in their restaurants. What goes on in their government doesn't affect them.

Here it is the other way around. Everything that happens at the top is quickly reflected at the bottom. This may seem paradoxical, but the rift between what goes on above and what goes on below is greater in your system than it is in ours. Sure, you have democracy and all that, but you know that the next president, whether it is Bush or someone else, isn't going to make a catastrophic difference. But for us it might be a catastrophic difference—the difference between a Stalin and a Gorbachev. In this sense, we are better educated politically than the Italians and the Americans.

So who says our people aren't ready politically? It's true that they have been subservient for a long time. But they don't want to be mere subordinates or mute cogs any longer. They want to be loyal partners in things they believe in. That's what perestroika is about. Events in our history have taken so much out of the people—the tragedy of Stalinism, the Twentieth Party Congress, which destroyed faith in Stalin, the cynicism and corruption of the Brezhnev years. We need a new faith—not in somebody but in something. The faith is perestroika—democracy and glasnost. People want to believe in it, and they do believe in it. But they are tired of lies, promises, and of bureaucrats dominating their lives. That's why we must devote ourselves to making sure that perestroika turns out the way it was conceived.

I don't mean that my generation can finish the job. The task is too large and complex. Too many people of my generation have the wrong brains and psychology, and you can't change that with legislation or orders. The older generation will have to die off. But before we do, we must lay the foundations of the new house for people now in their thirties. As in any society, there are drug addicts and other sorts of trash among them, but the majority of them are excellent people— really knowledgeable and critical-minded. If we lay the foundation of perestroika now, they will build on it. If we don't do that, I'm afraid people will never believe in anything again. It is now or never.

YEVGENY YEVTUSHENKO

"A Time for Summing Up"

YEVGENY ALEKSANDROVICH YEVTUSHENKO (born 1933) scarcely needs
any introduction. The most popular poet of the Khrushchev era, he remains an extraordinary celebrity in the Soviet Union and probably the
best-known and most widely translated living poet in the world. Opinions
vary about Yevtushenko's poetry and political life over the years, but for
many Soviet citizens he is still the daring "poet-tribune" of anti-Stalinist
reform whose earlier poems—among them, "Winter Station," "Stalin's
Heirs," and "Babyi Yar"—exemplified the thaw of the 1950s and early
1960s. Looking back, those years were the first chapter in the history of
post-Stalin glasnost. Though never persecuted, Yevtushenko denies that he
capitulated to the conservative dictates of the Brezhnev regime. And there
is ample evidence that he was heavily censored and frequently embattled
behind the scenes on behalf of victimized writers, despite the fact that he
(alone among the people interviewed for this book) is not a member of the
Communist Party. In 1968 he sent a personal telegram to Brezhnev pro-
testing the Soviet invasion of Czechoslovakia and associating himself with
Aleksandr Solzhenitsyn, who already was under fire. Whatever the full
story, since 1985 Yevtushenko has reemerged as a poet, essayist, and activist in the vanguard of perestroika. Indeed, his long narrative poem "Fuku,"
published in September 1985, and his speech at the Russian Writers Union
three months later, were milestones in the development of Gorbachev's
glasnost. In May 1989, running against eight other candidates in Kharkov,
Yevtushenko was elected to the new Congress of People's Deputies with
more than 70 percent of the vote.

I AM A POETICIAN, not a politician. I don't like prisons, borders, armies, missiles, or any policies connected with repression. I've never
glorified those kinds of things in my poems. I've always fought them.
I've fought to make my country better and freer, and to help people.
I've written poems against Stalin and Stalinism, against anti-Semitism,

against bureaucracy and bureaucrats. I really hate bureaucrats. Secretly, inside of me, I kill them or splash ink in their face. It's been my hobby since childhood.

Probably that's why I never joined the Communist Party, even though all my roots are revolutionary and I am a convinced socialist. Since childhood I've hated careerists who hide behind and use the party card. I used to ask my mother why my father wasn't a member of the party. Later he told me that he respected people who were in the party during the Revolution, the Civil War, and World War II, but too many careerists joined after that. But I believe in socialism. I remember an argument I had many years ago with Vasily Aksyonov [a very popular Soviet writer in the 1960s who now lives in the United States]. He said to me, "Zhenya, you believe in socialism with a human face, but that kind of socialism isn't possible." I told him that without a human face it isn't socialism. Some people say that all the tragedies and crimes in our history show the true face of socialism. I think those events were a betrayal of socialism.

We aren't going to ask you to retell your autobiography, especially since you published a brief account of it, A Precocious Autobiography, way back in 1963. As is often said, you may be the most famous living poet in the world today. Certainly in the West you are one of the Soviet Union's best-known citizens. But we do have one biographical question. A great many people in the Soviet Union, and several people in our book, refer to you as the poet of the Khrushchev thaw, or the poet of the generation of the Twentieth Party Congress. Is that how you see yourself?

In one of the first speeches I made to a writers congress I said, "We are all children of the Twentieth Party Congress." The congress was enormously important. I remember how everybody read Khrushchev's so-called secret speech—in factories, at the Writers Union. Even nonparty people like me read it. Many people cried and hung their heads. They were shocked. But I already knew most of the things Khrushchev said at the congress. I had learned them from my family in Siberia. I was just shocked that a party leader said them.

For me, Stalin's funeral in March 1953 was more of a formative event than the congress. I went to the funeral on Trubnaya Square. I'll never forget it. People were crushed to death by mobs and trucks that squeezed them against the walls. I remember that we screamed at the soldiers, "Get those trucks out of here." They said, "We can't. We have orders to be here." Many people died. I spent all night there. There was a huge mountain of discarded clothes—shoes, boots, fur hats. It was an absolutely surrealistic landscape. I wrote two stanzas of a poem called "Stalin's Funeral," but I only managed to finish it a few years ago. Not because of cowardice, but because I couldn't find an ending. But many of us understood instinctively after Stalin's death the need for change and for democratization.

I got those instincts from my parents and my grandparents. My father was a geologist in Siberia, where I grew up. He died rather young, at sixty-four, but he taught me a lot about poetry and politics. My mother was also a geologist, but she became a singer during the war. She gave so many concerts from the back of trucks, sometimes fifteen a day, she lost her voice. After the war, she divorced my father and married again, but her new husband left her with a baby in a cradle. She sang in moviehouses with her broken voice until I made her stop. People would sit there drinking vodka and mocking this singer with the broken voice. Then she worked as an administrator of children's concerts to support me and my younger half-sister on her very small salary. Now she's almost eighty and works everyday in her newspaper kiosk in Moscow. She refuses to retire.

I loved both of my grandfathers very much. One was an intellectual, a mathematician. The other was a peasant—a self-made man, a diamond in the rough, a real revolutionary. Both of them were arrested in the 1930s. One died in a labor camp. The other was released in 1948 but died soon after. Even though I was only a boy, my father's sister, who was politically sharp, told me what had happened to them. I was shocked, but then I understood. That's why later I didn't believe people who said they hadn't known anything about the crimes of the Stalin period. They were lying. I was only a child and I knew.

While Stalin was still alive, my father's sister told me an anecdote about this. One day the director of a mental hospital told the inmates that an inspector was coming from Moscow. He warned them, "If you have any complaints, just remember that the inspector will be here for one day, but I'll be with you forever. I advise you that if he asks you any questions, just quote Stalin's slogan, 'Life is getting better every day.' " So when the inspector came and asked the inmates for their complaints, they all shouted again and again in unison, "Life is getting better every day." The inspector noticed that only one man was silent and asked him why he wasn't shouting. "Comrade Inspector, I'm not crazy. I'm the doctor." Remember, I was only a twelve-year-old child and I understood this anecdote. So when people tell you today they didn't know, they are distorting their biographies. They are covering up. We weren't blind.

As a leading voice for change in the Soviet system under Khrushchev and under Gorbachev, and as a participant in so many political events since the 1950s, you must have strong opinions about what has happened in your country over the last three decades. Looking back, for example, what are your feelings about Khrushchev? It was during his rule that you rose to fame.

Khrushchev did wonderful things. When he made his speech to the Twentieth Congress, he took a heroic step that not only Russia but all humanity will never forget. He released so many innocent people from the concentration camps. He also reduced the Cold War as much as he could. He opened the borders of our country to foreigners. For example, he organized the first youth festival in Moscow. He will go down in history in a positive way.

But Khrushchev was also full of contradictions. He was a child of Stalin's era, one of the party leaders of that time. Churchill said that Khrushchev was a man who tried to jump across an abyss in two leaps and fell into it. It was a daring act when he indicted Stalin at the Twentieth Congress. He risked his career and even his life. He did it because his conscience tormented him. But having roused the genie of democracy, he tried to shove it back in the bottle. After his overthrow, about a month before he died in 1971, Khrushchev said something strange to me. "I am a child of two epochs. One man inside me understood something and the other shouted something completely different."

I think that's a good image because Khrushchev was a Stalinist and an anti-Stalinist. He was a rebel against himself. Gorbachev and our new generation of leaders are completely different. They are more educated and they understand more. And they weren't involved in those tragic crimes. This is my generation. The poets of my generation help prepared these new leaders.

What do you mean "prepared" them?

Don't think that glasnost or perestroika dropped from the sky or that it was given to us by the Politburo. It was many years in preparation. The new generation of leaders absorbed the spirit of our literature. They were students when we began reading our poems in the 1950s. They squeezed onto the balconies of our poetry readings without tickets.

My generation of poets did a lot to break down the Iron Curtain. We cut up our bare hands assaulting that curtain. Sometimes we won, sometimes we lost. Sometimes there were tactical retreats and sometimes we lay on the ground after a hail of insults. But our literature didn't come as a gift from the so-called upstairs. We worked for it. We forged it for ourselves and for future generations. We didn't know that we would produce new kinds of people. But it has happened. Poetry plays a great role in the Soviet Union. I am very happy that we didn't struggle for our poetry in vain. Now the people who are taking charge in all fields—newspapers, factories, party committees—are people without guilt for Stalin's crimes. They don't have bloodstains on their consciences. They don't feel guilty because they aren't.

Are you saying that the poetry of your generation, of the 1950s and 1960s, contributed to the political views of the Gorbachev leadership?

·I don't want to exaggerate our role. The need for perestroika and glasnost began even before my generation arrived on the scene. What is now happening is a historical necessity. When something is necessary, eventually a leader will come along to embody that need. Gorbachev is a man of our generation. He was one of those students who crowded in to hear the poetry readings and political debates of the 1950s. We poets were the first to attack Stalinism, bureaucracy, anti-Semitism, and all the restrictions in our lives. When the newspapers were still silent, literature embodied the conscience of the people.

Writers and poets protected ideals and conscience like two hands protecting a candle against the wind. We began to transform those candles into big torches. The poetry of our generation was the cradle of glasnost. At that time, in the late 1950s and early 1960s, Sakharov was still working on the hydrogen bomb, Solzhenitsyn hadn't published anything yet, and there wasn't any dissident movement. We began the glasnost or openness of that time. Hidden glasnost had always existed in Russian literature, which is the literature of conscience. Our best writers preserved those ideals and fragments of conscience. And we kept doing it, sometimes in times of gloomy cynicism and corruption, amid pools of blood. We were beaten up and insulted, but we kept doing it because we didn't face a mortal danger. Our generation didn't face the threat of death that earlier generations faced under Stalin. So we kept speaking on behalf of the voiceless people.

Poets weren't the only people of your generation who tried to keep their ideals alive during the Brezhnev years. Don't other intellectuals also deserve credit for preparing perestroika and glasnost?

Of course. You see, it was like building a tunnel. When you dig a tunnel from both ends, you work in virtual darkness. Sometimes you don't even know if there's anyone working on the other side until you hear their drill. Sometimes you get desperate and become convinced that no one is working on the other end. That you are only hearing your own drill. But then there is a breakthrough and you meet each other. We saw each other's faces. I knew many, many people who were digging tunnels in other areas of Soviet life.

But I knew the writers best. Look at Vladimir Dudintsev. Let history decide if he is a great writer or not, but he is a heroic man. They covered him with mud in 1956 because of his novel *Not by Bread Alone*. They attacked him again later, but he didn't give up—not even in the 1970s, the time of so-called stagnation. He wrote a great novel, *White Robes*, during those years. It was only published in 1987. He worked almost hopelessly in hopeless times. When such a person does that he becomes society's hope. Glasnost would not have happened if there hadn't been people like Dudintsev who believed in such change and kept working. Anatoly Rybakov is another example. He sat during those years and wrote his novel *Children of the Arbat*. And Anatoly Pristavkin wrote his beautiful novel *The Little Golden Cloud That Spent the Night*, which wasn't published until 1987. Much of what is being published now was written during the period of stagnation. We have enough work from that period to fill our journals for another two or three years.

But for some of us the new situation is difficult because we grew accustomed to fighting censorship every day. I'm used to writing about forbidden topics. Now you can write about almost anything and get it published. I've never experienced this degree of freedom. Under Khrushchev, censorship was like an accordion. It kept being expanded and folded up. He was impulsive, and so there was no stability. Now it's different. Now I have to get accustomed to all this freedom. For example, in the past many poets had to invent a kind of metaphorical language in order to get anything with a political content published. When I was in England in 1987, someone asked me a good question: "Mr. Yevtushenko, will glasnost kill metaphorical poetry?"

Let's talk some more about what people like you did or didn't do between the fall of Khrushchev and the rise of Gorbachev. You speak of people who were tunneling toward perestroika during all those years, but in the West they were not visible.

And so the West thought everybody was a conformist. In the United States they had a very false theory of official and nonofficial Soviet culture. The theory was that if something was published or produced in the Soviet Union, it couldn't be honest art. They called it official art. If something wasn't published in the Soviet Union but published abroad, they called it nonofficial art, which is not true. You can't separate the two so simply. We have completely different systems. We have political censorship, you have commercial censorship. Even during the years of stagnation, some good books and poetry were published. And there was some good theater. But you preferred artists who left the Soviet Union.

Do you think that artists who left should have stayed to dig tunnels and wait for perestroika?

I don't have any right to judge them. I only know that it is a tragedy for a writer to be abroad, out of his own range. I couldn't imagine myself in exile. It would be the worse punishment.

You can't generalize about all the emigrés. They're all different. For instance, Joseph Brodsky is a very good poet—the best Russian poet living abroad. When he was in forced exile inside the Soviet Union, I helped him and he knows it. I wrote a letter defending him. Then he got to the United States and began to say—not in newspapers but in private circles—that I was guilty of something. I heard about this. You know America, like Russia, is a big village. Later he asked my forgiveness. I asked him why he had said such things. He told me, "I'm sorry, Yevgeny, when you are an emigré sometimes you force yourself to find someone to blame." That was a sincere answer.

It only makes me angry when some emigrés, who are full of ignorance and hatred, allow themselves to become part of your anti-Sovietism. They don't want mutual understanding between the United States and the Soviet Union. Their ignorance is dangerous to themselves. If they work against mutual understanding between our two great peoples, they are working for their own death.

What are your feelings about Aleksandr Solzhenitsyn, who was deported in 1974 and has lived in the United States since 1976.

He played a very important role not only in our literature but in Russian history. He did a lot to fight against the revival of Stalinism in the 1960s. Solzhenitsyn wrote some very good books and stories, *One Day in the Life of Ivan Denisovich*, "An Incident at Krechetovka Station," and many other short stories. I think his best novel is *The First Circle*, and *The Gulag Archipelago* is a very important account of things that happened. There are too many primitive pages in his later works because when a writer hates something too much he ceases being a great writer. Hatred is a kind of blindness. A writer must have open eyes to see life.

I defended Solzhenitsyn many, many times, until the moment he was arrested and sent abroad. I am very grateful to him for his books condemning the Stalinist past. But in fighting fanaticism, unfortunately he became a fanatic. He put himself into a cage of his own design, a procrustean bed of his own schemes. But if it were up to me, I would give him the opportunity to travel to the Soviet Union. In fact, I am a cochairman of the executive council of the Memorial Society, which wants his books published here.

You mentioned that Brodsky had criticized you. A number of your critics, particularly in the United States, charge that you conformed during the Brezhnev years to the extent that the authorities tolerated you while persecuting some other Soviet writers.

Part of the American press always accuses some Russian writers of not being rebellious enough, of being conformist, et cetera, et cetera. They accuse me of this because I was not put in prison or in a mental hospital. But I already told you, I did everything that was possible for a poet to do. I'm not God. Nobody is God—not even God.

It's like this. You have the toreador and you have the spectators— the public or the Western press. At bullfights I've seen the spectators become unhappy when the toreador professionally and skillfully slips away from the bull's horns. They even accuse some wonderful toreadors of being cowards, just because they didn't want to be killed by the bull. But they aren't cowards. They are fighters. Unfortunately, many people, watching from a safe distance, thirst for blood.

Let's go from the past to the present. As someone who feels he helped prepare the way, what does perestroika mean to you?

A chance to realize all of our not-yet-realized hopes. We are potentially one of the richest countries in the world. We have incredible natural resources and an absolutely incredible cultural and spiritual past. But over the years we've been like a hunter who set so many traps he got caught in one of them. Now our country can be saved only by millions of hands, not by one pair of hands. That means democracy, even though some people here are trying to frighten us with specters of anarchy.

Economic and political democracy. State and private enterprise should compete in a completely open and equal way. Let's see which survive. We have some wonderful economic writers, like Nikolai Shmelyov, but we also need great managers. If private enterprises survive, okay. Probably we'll end up with state, cooperative, and private enterprises. Open and equal competition will improve all of them. In agriculture we must fulfill the promise of the October Revolution—land to the peasants. Agriculture canot be successful until land is in private hands. Forced collectivization was a terrible mistake, a war against the people, and a betrayal of socialism. Now we must have open competition between collective farms and private farms. I would make only one exception to this economic competition. Military-industrial enterprises should not be in private hands. If they are, the profit motive will be all that matters.

And what kind of political democracy do you have in mind?

Okay, not American democracy in Russia. It's your democracy and sometimes it becomes "demockracy," a word I made up for what happened to Gary Hart. And maybe not a multiparty system. I can even imagine a society without any parties. Why not? What do they really mean? Look at our Communist Party. Americans think it is a faceless monolith. It's nothing like that. There's all sorts of people in there. But there has to be democracy inside the party if there's going to be democracy outside the party. Party members are going to have to be able to express their own opinions and criticize each other.

Did you read my article in *Moscow News* on what I call the party of nonparty people—people who are not members of the Communist Party? It could not have been published even a few years ago. I defended all the independent fronts and groups that are springing up. The Communist Party can't win the struggle against bureaucracy and against the lines in front of shops without the support of the party of nonparty people. They are more numerous than Communist Party members, but their force hasn't been recognized. Nonparty people should be given high state positions alongside party members. And why, for example, is Sergei Zalygin, the editor of *Novyi mir*, the only nonparty editor of a major journal or newspaper?

The bureaucrats are scared of nonparty members. They think they are uncontrollable. But a person who can be controlled by bureaucracy is not a patriot because bureaucracy is a war against the people. People who are controlled only by their own conscience are the real party of the people, whether they are members of the Communist Party or not. The Communist Party has moral people and it has scoundrels. The real dividing line today isn't between Communist Party members and nonmembers but between the fighters for perestroika and the saboteurs of perestroika. Not all Communist Party members are members of the party of perestroika. The saboteurs were behind the so-called letter by

Nina Andreyeva, behind the effort to ban the film *Repentance*, behind the attacks on the cooperatives. Quietly, they bless the anti-Semitism of the Pamyat Society, which now appears at public meeting with its filthy anti-Jewish slogans while some party officials and extreme nationalist official editors look on with tacit approval. The saboteurs fight against glasnost because it might reveal our biggest state secret—their mediocrity and lack of talent.

And why shouldn't religious believers who aren't members of the Communist Party be part of the party for perestroika? Is it really impossible to believe in God and socialism at the same time? The country's churches fought for the war effort in 1941–45, and they fight for peace today. We need their ideals and faith for perestroika. Religious persecution has to stop. I hate people who spit in the face of believers. They insult people who collect money in front of churches, the kind of people who raised me. I had two childhood heroes—Jesus and Don Quixote. Both fought injustice. The real danger isn't people who believe in God but people who don't believe in anything. Perestroika and glasnost are a rehabilitation not just of the victims of repression but of the nation's ideals. We need all of the country's idealists, not just those who happen to be members of the Communist Party.

The Memorial Society, the movement to honor the victims of Stalin's repression, is an example. I wrote a manifesto for the organization when it formalized itself in 1988. The idea of building monuments to the victims goes back to the Twentieth Party Congress in 1956. Later, at the Twenty-Second Party Congress in 1961, Khrushchev even proposed such a monument in his public speech. But nothing came of it. His proposal was obliterated. The idea cropped up again in 1987. Young people, Komsomol members and nonmembers, party members and nonparty members, collected tens of thousands of signatures on petitions across the country—in the streets, subway stations, parks. The movement came from below, from a band of Don Quixotes, who were harassed and sometimes even arrested by local authorities. People rallied around this idea, like streams flowing into a mighty river. I remember when writers from the Urals first came to me with the idea seeking support. Then came workers, doctors, students—party members and nonparty people. Opposition also formed everywhere, but the people won. Gorbachev endorsed the idea himself at the Nineteenth Party Conference in 1988. Memorial formed itself into a national organization at its constituent conference in January 1989. Andrei Sakharov was elected its honorary chairman, and I one of its four co-chairmen. Several unions supported us from the beginning, including Klimov's Filmmakers and Ulyanov's Theater Workers, but not the Writers Union.

Now we have a nationwide Memorial Society. We want to build monuments to Stalin's victims across the country but also create a permanent center to research and document everything that happened— the names of the victims and the criminals, the heroic feats of opposition and mercy, the spiritual cleanliness of those nonparticipants who just watched. We aren't after revenge or the persecution of those who took part in these bloody crimes. The Memorial Society is organizing a perestroika of the nation's memory. Yuri Afanasyev is one of the Society's most active leaders in this respect. Our opponents say it is a rejection of socialism. We say it is the purification of socialism. We do it for the sake of justice, to cleanse the nation's conscience and to be clean in the eyes of our children.

The importance of anti-Stalinism as a driving force of perestroika is absolutely clear. And even though the anti-Stalinist movement has been on the scene since the Khrushchev era, it is very significant that it now has a nationwide organization in the form of the Memorial Society. But some younger perestroika activists, particularly leaders of some of the new socialist clubs, complain that the anti-Stalinist movement, and even perestroika itself, is being monopolized by people of your generation. They argue, for example, that like your literature, your conception of historical justice was formed back in the 1950s and 1960s and though admirable, it doesn't focus enough on contemporary injustices. Some of them prefer Tatyana Zaslavskaya's emphasis on present-day social injustices in the Soviet system.

I have no quarrel with those young people. As I said, they gave birth to the Memorial movement by collecting signatures at a time when local authorities and the militia were hostile to the idea and harassed them. Stalinism is still part of our system, so anti-Stalinism is also a struggle against all the other injustices as well. Workers can't eat glasnost. We have to end all the deficits and shortages in their lives. The entire population is humiliated and debased by having to scramble and scrounge for every imaginable kind of goods, from diapers and clothes to furniture, refrigerators, medicine, and fruit. None of these things can be bought normally. It's no accident that people don't speak of "buying" goods but of "obtaining" them. Our nonconvertible ruble is our greatest patriot. It never sells itself to the enemy. The coupon system that makes scarce goods available to privileged officials is a national disgrace.

All these shortages are not just deprivations but an ocean of national humiliations. It is humiliating to have to beg things from our service industries for our children. It's humiliating to chase after foreign rags because we don't make decent clothing of our own. It is humiliating to lack medical supplies for our people. The shortage of good books is humiliating to the human spirit. The shortage of computers is humiliating to a country that prides itself on being modern.

And when you speak of social injustices, you have to start with judges. They should be above party and state influence. Not even Gorbachev should be able to influence a judge's decision. But we all know how some regional party secretaries still call Moscow to help their friends or convict their enemies—it's called "telephone justice." It's terrible and it must be abolished. And then there's the injustice of our internal passport, which registers people in towns where they must live, and our closed borders. Freedom of movement is supposed to be guaranteed by our constitution. I know we can't abolish the internal passport tomorrow. If we did, 25 million people would immediately move to Moscow. But we must prepare for its abolition. It's an element of slavery. Closed borders, on the other hand, ought to be opened tomorrow. Anyone who wants to leave should be able to. It's humiliating to keep people here against their will. And anyone who just wants to travel abroad also ought to be able to do so. Everybody understands that all this is shameful.

You began by saying that you are a "poetician, not a politician," so let's talk about the deficit, or former deficit, that most interests poets—glasnost. You spoke earlier about censorship in the 1970s. Has four years of glasnost put an end to censorship for poets and other writers?

Ninety percent of censorship has been abolished, but it still exists. The situation now is completely different. Earlier we had censorship by censors. Now we have to worry about censorship by editors, because they have been given the authority to make these decisions. The situation has changed since the earlier days of Gorbachev in 1985. At first, to safeguard themselves, editors still sent the most controversial political manuscripts to the Central Committee for a decision. Now the Central Committee sends them back. It tells editors, "Why bother us? You're paid to be an editor. You do the work." I know that Aleksandr Yakovlev does this, for example. Some editors don't like the new system and resist it.

Let me tell you the story of my long narrative poem "Fuku," which appeared in *Novyi mir* in September 1985. It was an icebreaker and maybe the last major battle between an editor and the formal censorship, Glavlit. In the context of 1985, the poem was very controversial. It had a chapter against Stalin and the terror, a chapter about our homegrown young Russian neofascists and their demonstration on Pushkin

Square, and some other sharp things. The editor of *Novyi mir* got a call from Glavlit saying, "This poem will never be published." He called an editorial board meeting and they decided to go ahead and publish the poem anyway, but they knew that without the censor's stamp the printer wouldn't print it. So *Novyi mir* asked the Writers Union for help and the union secretariat asked me to collect letters from prominent writers expressing support for the poem. In two days I collected forty letters from very different types of people, from the anti-Stalinist Rybakov to the novelist Ivan Stadnyuk, who admires Stalin.

You look surprised that I went to Stadnyuk. A friend who knows him advised me to go. Stadnyuk wrote a supportive letter for me, explaining it like this. "Zhenya, you have a right to express your opinion about our history and I have my right. Later, history will decide who was correct. I think you're wrong about Stalin's time because you are not well informed. But your poem is beautiful and I'll support it. I hope you'll support my writing if things become difficult for me." I told him that I would.

Anyway, *Novyi mir* took the poem and the letters to the cultural department of the Central Committee. Very quickly *Novyi mir* got permission to publish my poem. It was a major conflict between the censorship and editors. That's why I say "Fuku" was an icebreaker. Now it is up to editors to decide.

But a censor still sits in the editorial offices of Moscow News. *Yegor Yakovlev pointed him out to us. Isn't there one in* Novyi mir's *offices?*

Maybe they are at the newspapers, but I've never seen them in the editorial offices of journals.

In practice, what does it mean that "it is up to editors to decide?" Don't they still have to negotiate controversial manuscripts with the Central Committee?

Sure, sometimes.

In the United States, we would call that political censorship.

America's a different society.

The publication of Rybakov's Children of the Arbat *in 1987 was another major stage in the evolution of glasnost. You played a role in that event. Tell us what happened.*

It was a very difficult struggle. Rybakov's case was special, not only because he portrayed Stalin at the center of the terror. He accused Stalin of killing Sergei Kirov. That's an enormous accusation because millions of people died as a result of that event and Rybakov had no proof. I advised him to use my procedure of collecting letters from important representatives of the intelligentsia. He collected about seventy letters supporting his novel. The Central Committee finally permitted Rybakov's novel, but I don't think it could have been published without this support from below.

But what kind of glasnost is this, if the publication of every controversial manuscript requires a major campaign?

Those episodes were at the beginning of glasnost. We are far beyond that now, though the struggle over glasnost continues. You can see it in our press. Censorship by censors has ended. Now we are fighting censorship by editors and by social attitudes. If you can show me one country where some kind of censorship doesn't exist, I'll kiss you.

That's another question. Let's stay with Soviet glasnost. Is it possible that editors will turn out to be worse censors than the censors?

A few of them, but you can make the rounds. For instance, one editor refused to publish one of my very strong anti-Stalinist poems, "Monuments Not Yet Built." This was in 1987. He said he believed in Stalin. Okay, I went to another editor who liked the poem and put it in proofs. But a few days later he was attacked in some newspaper for publishing too much against Stalin, so he told me he couldn't publish my poem. Then I took it to Korotich at *Ogonyok* and he published it. And you know the history of my poem "Bukharin's Widow," which I wrote many months before Bukharin was rehabilitated in February 1988. I couldn't get it published until March 1988, when *Izvestia* finally ran it.

But don't overlook what is most important. Today we have more freedom to publish, more freedom of the press, than we've ever known. More at least since the 1920s. I mean, just imagine, they've published Vasily Grossman's *Life and Fate* and George Orwell. Nobody would have believed it. And that's only part of it. What used to be only kitchen glasnost, what we talked about only at home, now is public discussion in the press. We're openly discussing the most painful issues. We are criticizing very high-ranking officials—members of the government. For the first time, newspapers are publishing signed editorials. This is wonderful. It means people are taking personal responsibility, expressing personal points of view. It's part of the struggle against facelessness. This means there are more possibilities for talented people and fewer possibilities for mediocre ones—for one-sided minds and the knights of inertia. This is incredible glasnost.

I don't mean there aren't many opponents of glasnost. Many people don't like it, even some writers and artists. And we saw plenty of opposition to glasnost expressed by regional party secretaries at the Nineteenth Party Conference. If they are against it, you can imagine the struggle.

As a writer, can you understand why other writers might be against glasnost?

Not just against it. They fight it. Don't you remember what the novelist Yuri Bondaryev said at a meeting of the Russian Writers Union? He compared glasnost to the Nazi threat at Stalingrad and said we needed a new Battle of Stalingrad to defeat the civilized barbarians of glasnost who are threatening Soviet culture.

Why does glasnost make such writers so nervous? For biological, not ideological, reasons. After the appearance of important novels like *Children of the Arbat, The Little Golden Cloud That Spent the Night*, and other literature that had been suppressed for as long as fifty years, they know people are less and less interested in their books. I overheard an editor of a magazine say, "Comrades, what is going on? Today people don't want to read quiet, normal literature." These editors and writers are losing readers for their quiet literature. They are biologically afraid because they know their own quality and talent are minimal. They attack other writers politically, but it is really a biological fear of open competition.

Censorship gave these writers a special privilege: It made them look better than they really are. Now their work is being criticized, and they're like spoiled children fighting for their right to be mediocre and rich. Even our mediocre writers are richer than our best filmmakers. Some of them were actually gifted writers, but they lost faith in their talents. The easy life made them weak. They are terribly afraid. So you get an abnormal situation where some writers virtually demand a return of censorship.

But you know as well as I do that this isn't a peculiarity of the Soviet system. You can find a mortal struggle between mediocre people and talented people in all countries. Mediocre people have comfortable, soft armchairs under their asses. In my opinion, they don't really have ideologies. Their main ideology is their armchairology.

And it isn't just our writers. Glasnost is a kind of disaster for mediocre people in all walks of Soviet life. Now that people can say what's on their minds, it turns out that some people have nothing to say. It's a very sad discovery. At so many meetings people just speak nonsense and say petty things. When they hear other people speak or write sharp things, they say, "Oh, that's in the past, why repeat it?" Or, "Why must they put salt on open wounds? We just rehabilitated the wound so it could heal." My view, and the view of a majority of our writers, is that to put sugar on open wounds is even more dangerous. Ever since ancient times, professional seamen have cured their wounds with salty water. Honest salt is more helpful than dishonest sugar.

Now's a time for summing up in Russia. Summing up all of the positive and negative lessons of our historical experiences. To be fearless builders of the future is possible only if we are fearless social archeologists of our past. We must not only put salt on open wounds, we must dig into them as deeply as possible because there is still some infection that keeps us from being absolutely healthy. Literature must be like acupuncture. We mustn't be afraid to put needles into the most sensitive points of our conscience. It's painful, it's unpleasant, but it might save you. That's why I don't like the so-called quiet, pleasant art.

So we have all these people I call the comrades-but-what-if. They fight change by shouting, "But what if this happens, what if that happens." At the first signs of progress, they build barricades out of their wooden minds. They won't give up quickly or easily because they know they will lose their privileges. They will fight for them. But they are a minority. The majority wants glasnost and perestroika.

Not all of the people we have talked with are so certain that the majority of Soviet citizens are ready for perestroika or even want it. Some social scientists, for example, worry about Russia's undemocratic political culture. And your own account of a mortal struggle between mediocrity and talent in all walks of life isn't exactly an optimistic prognosis.

Look, our main disease is social passivity. It's a product of our history. People have been deceived so often that they are afraid to believe in anything, to have ideals. They're afraid of being disillusioned again. They're instinctively self-protective. It doesn't mean they are cynical—just socially passive. They want to believe in perestroika, but they can't. This is more dangerous than bureaucracy.

It's also true that our political culture is very low. People are very bitter and always attacking each other. We insult each other too much. We still don't know the art of insulting each other politely—the art of polemics. We are trying to learn democracy day by day, but sometimes we're not so successful. Gorbachev understood this problem when he complained that some people are using glasnost to settle scores. It's true. It's part of our backward political culture. We have almost no tradition of democracy.

What hope, then, is there for any kind of democracy in the Soviet Union? Why should anyone take Gorbachev's democratization program seriously? It seems like he is trying to build a factory without any bricks.

Sometimes certain traditions can be created very quickly. After all, with the Revolution Russia jumped from a feudal society to a socialist structure, though we brought along all our old bedbugs, fleas, and lice from the wooden huts of feudalism. That's why our socialism has feudal characteristics. But why shouldn't we build democracy here? Tsarist Russia was the last European country to abolish slavery, but it did it. Our constitution isn't perfect, but it isn't bad. If we lived up to it, we'd have more democracy and fewer injustices. And even though we may never have had democracy, we have a very long tradition of fighters for democracy. Of course, we have all sorts of people here. While democratization gives fighters for democracy and the most gifted and progressive people room, unfortunately it also makes room for the development of very reactionary forces. We are seeing many of our dangerous microbes—all societies have them—like chauvinism and anti-Semitism. But the fighters for democracy will win this time.

Klimov and Ulyanov have suggested that their creative unions are playing a leading role in democratization, even building a democratic model for society. Both of them say that the Writers Union is lagging behind in this respect. And you pointed out that it did not give Memorial any early support. You now are one of the secretaries of the Writers Union. What is going on there?

Cautiously speaking, I'd say the unions of Klimov and Ulyanov are only about a quarter of the way to democracy—optimistically speaking, about halfway. When the Writers Union elected a new leadership in 1986, I proposed a completely new model. It was rejected. My plan recognized that we have to have a permanent staff. There are thousands of writers in the union and its branches in the republics. Writers have a lot of everyday problems that we have to take care of. The union also has a lot of money from profits earned by the magazines it publishes. I think we have about 120 million rubles.

So we need a bureaucracy, but my plan called for a flexible, antibureaucratic bureaucracy. We also need good writers as leaders of the

Writers Union. But if a good writer serves five years as the first secretary, he's lost to literature. He sacrifices all his time to petty things like meeting with foreign delegations. But if we have mediocre writers as first secretary, they'll blow themselves up into prizewinning authors and tyrannize the rest of us.

My plan was to establish a kind of rotation system to avoid the danger of petty tyranny, to eliminate permanent bureaucracy, and to save the good writers. I wanted to elect five coequal secretaries. They would take turns being first secretary for a year each and they'd meet or talk by telephone to solve major problems and make collective decisions. It was a good idea and it got some support, but the majority rejected it. They elected Vladimir Karpov first secretary for five years.

Are you sure you didn't plagiarize the idea from Lenin's State and Revolution, *where he argues that everybody should serve as a bureaucrat temporarily so that nobody can become a permanent bureaucrat?*

I'd better reread it. Maybe we should all reread it. But it was my idea for the Writers Union.

Let's end our talk by returning to the generational theme. You are widely regarded as the poet of the generation that came to public life under Khrushchev. You argue that your generation, including Gorbachev, was formed by the reform politics, anti-Stalinism, and glasnost-like thaw of the late 1950s and early 1960s. Do you think that the generation growing up now, under Gorbachev and in the atmosphere of perestroika, will be similar in outlook to your generation?

Probably, but I think they have one advantage over us. We were naive fish who easily swallowed false bait. This new generation doesn't want to get hooked on false bait. They have a wonderful sense of smell, a real nose for falsity. That's their advantage, but it is also their weakness. They are terribly afraid to believe in things, especially something as big as perestroika. But I think that they'll take their places in the struggle as perestroika continues. They'll understand that if perestroika is suffocated, the only alternatives are either a semi-suffocation in the country or some kind of fascism like neo-Stalinism.

That's why I'm so worried when I'm in America and see that many Americans don't understand perestroika. Just like our reactionaries, your reactionaries need the image of a bogeyman. By the way, I was there during your 1988 presidential election. You are an odd people. You love our liberals, like Andrei Sakharov, but you don't like your own liberals. You should support your local liberals, too. And you should also understand that perestroika is in your interest. It means pluralism, tolerance, more liberal people in Russia. If perestroika fails and we end up with a form of neo-Stalinism, it will be dangerous for you as well. We may all end up together in a third world war. If perestroika fails, it will be very sad for all of us—for humanity.

You seem to be optimistic, but you also see a lot of obstacles.

What is it you used to say in America? We shall overcome.

LEN KARPINSKY

The Autobiography of a "Half-Dissident"

OUR CONVERSATION WITH Len Vyacheslavovich Karpinsky (born 1929) *differs from the other interviews. It is largely the story of a man who fell from being a potential leader of the Soviet Communist Party in the early 1960s to being an outcast by the mid-1970s—a dissident in the eyes of officialdom, a "half-dissident" in his own eyes. So far as we know, it is the only such account ever published. Karpinsky's readmission to the party in October 1988 illustrates one of the doors opened by Gorbachev's policies. Along with Andrei Sakharov, Roy Medvedev, and Karpinsky, many lesser-known and formerly persecuted nonconformists have returned from prison, internal exile, and other forms of banishment to play public roles in Soviet political life. There still are "dissidents" in the Soviet Union, but it has become much harder to know who or what the word means. Not even activists on the remote frontiers of glasnost can agree where perestroika ends and dissent begins. A gentle man with an ironic outlook on politics and on his own life, Karpinsky is among the most radical thinkers in the perestroika movement, which is one reason he believes that "some people at the top still don't fully trust me." On the other hand, he appears in this book along with one of the most important leaders of the Soviet Union, Aleksandr Yakovlev. Few leaders grant a long interview without first knowing where and in what context it will appear. That Yakovlev did not object to being in a book with Len Karpinsky tells us something significant about the "architect of glasnost."*

UNLIKE IN YOUR COUNTRY, the word "career" has a pejorative or dubious connotation here in the Soviet Union. It implies that a person has done something unethical or compromising in order to climb the ladder of success. Because there are so few unofficial ladders to success in our system, for too many of our people making a career in this sense of the word has been a way of life. But I believe that a person's life can have two trajectories. One is his public climb up the career ladder. The other is his internal intellectual or spiritual evolution, an ascent that has usually been hidden from public view. For some people, these two developments may take place at the same time and eventually collide. That is how it was with me. My career took me near the top of the Soviet political system and my internal ascent took me almost to the bottom, when I was expelled from the Communist Party.

Both my mother, who died in 1940, and my father, who lived to the age of eighty-five, were old Bolsheviks. My father, Vyacheslav Karpinsky, was a professional revolutionary and an associate of Lenin before 1917. In fact, he named me Len in honor of Lenin. Father joined the party in 1898 and was an organizer of the Marxist movement in Kharkov. He soon was arrested and sent into internal exile. In 1904 he made his way to Switzerland, where he met Lenin and worked closely with him until the Revolution. My father worked on a number of party newspapers in emigration and even copy-edited some of Lenin's articles. With Lenin's encouragement, he began to write articles of his own, which is how he became a well-known party journalist and much later, under Khrushchev, the first journalist to be awarded the title Hero of Socialist Labor. By then, of course, he was one of the very few surviving old Bolsheviks. Most of the others had been killed by Stalin.

After the Revolution, father stayed in touch with Lenin and helped him with some personal matters. Lenin entrusted him with gathering his personal and party archives from where he had left them in emigration and bringing them back to the Soviet Union. Father was very close at this time to Lenin's wife, Nadezhda Krupskaya. In 1918 Lenin had father appointed editor of the popular peasant newspaper *Bednota* [The Village Poor], which was published in Moscow. Lenin asked father to collect for him the most interesting letters written by peasants to the newspaper. Lenin read the selection, which played a significant role in his decision in 1921 to end the party's policy of grain requisitioning and to introduce the New Economic Policy.

During the NEP years, father was head of the propaganda department of the national soviet and, until 1927, a member of *Pravda*'s editorial board, which was headed by Bukharin. My father continued to work in these general areas until the second half of the 1930s. In 1936–37 he was a consultant to the Central Committee's propaganda department. By then he had written books on the Soviet political system, including several that were used as textbooks. Tired of journalism and politics, he accepted a position at the Academy of Pedagogical Sciences, where he remained until he died in 1965. During his lifetime my father was awarded three orders of Lenin, a very high honor.

As a child of the party elite, you must have enjoyed very special privileges, especially in the 1930s, when there was so much general deprivation in the country, even famine.

I was born in 1929 so I was only a child. At the time I didn't think of them as privileges. I thought that all Soviet people lived as we did. Later I realized that I had had very great privileges. We lived in Moscow's famous house on the embankment, the home of many high party and state officials. It was an apartment building for families of the country's ruling elite. I was friends with Stalin's nephews Seryozha and Sasha Alliluyev, who lived there. Two or three of my friends in the building were children of state ministers, and all the children in the building went to a special school, No. 19. An armed uniformed guard sat at the door of our building behind a big table with a telephone on it. Nobody could enter before calling to an apartment. This was very unusual. In 1941, when the Germans approached Moscow and families had been evacuated, the guards robbed the apartments. They were the same guards who had bowed and scraped before the tenants, even before us boys.

We also had access to special nutritional foods and medicines. My father had a car and a driver when he was working at the Central Committee, and they let him keep it when he retired. On the orders of Vyacheslav Molotov, who then was prime minister, my father was given an excellent piece of land for a dacha. Father put up the money, but the dacha was built by a state or party construction agency and the materials were very inexpensive. I have the dacha now. It is in a beautiful, prestigious place next to the dacha of the late Pyotr Kapitsa, the Nobel Prize-winning scientist.

My family, or at least we children, didn't sense the famine and deprivation in the country in the early and mid-1930s. We had a special dining hall in Moscow, which was very good, and we often went to a resort for leading officials called Nagornoye. It was very luxurious, like a prerevolutionary paradise on earth. There were long tables with every imaginable kind of food and drink, magnificent halls, billiard rooms, a movie theater—everything.

As we know from many accounts, including Yuri Trifonov's famous novel House on the Embankment, *Stalin's terror of the late 1930s swept through your apartment building like a tornado. The building became known as a house of fear. Were you aware of this at the time?*

Though I was only seven or eight years old, I remember that there were arrests all the time. I never saw one happen except the night they took my aunt—my mother's sister—from our apartment. She was the director of a kindergarten and unmarried. They accused her of being a friend of an enemy of the people in Leningrad. My aunt's two brothers were also arrested. The older one was chief prosecutor for the transportation industry in 1937. He was shot. My aunt served eighteen years in prison and exile. She now lives in my father's apartment in the house on the embankment. Her younger brother, Pavel, served ten years and also returned. They gave him back his party card. He's still alive and working.

When the arrests began, when your aunt and uncles disappeared, did you ask your parents what was happening?

I asked, but they didn't tell me the truth. They'd say that our relatives and neighbors had been transferred to a different job in another town, or something like that. Later, of course, I learned what really had happened. In addition to my relatives, many close friends of my father and mother were arrested, and my father sometimes got letters from them asking for help. He constantly tried to help them by sending packages of food and clothing. Even though it was dangerous, I vividly remember how he refused to turn his back on anyone. He never believed they were enemies of the people. He knew the situation was hopeless. He couldn't do anything except try to help them with money and packages. But who knows if any of those things actually reached them. Later, after Stalin died and some of the arrested people began to return, father did a lot to help them. And as you and I know from Bukharin's widow, Anna Larina, who also survived prison and camps, he was one of only a handful of surviving old Bolsheviks willing to sign her 1964 petition for Bukharin's rehabilitation. The majority of those still alive refused to sign. They still were afraid.

It seems a miracle that your father wasn't arrested. As an old Bolshevik who had been close to Lenin and who knew so much about the pre-Stalinist history of the party, he would seem to have been a typical victim of Stalin's terror.

It's also a mystery to me. And he never explained it to me. I don't think he knew himself.

Didn't you ask him, or didn't he ever talk about it with you?

I never asked him, and he never talked to me about it.

Not even after Stalin's death?

By the time Stalin was criticized at the Twentieth Party Congress in 1956, I was already working in the city of Gorky. I worked there until the late 1950s and rarely came home. After I returned to Moscow, we never talked about the period of the terror in any direct way. We'd talk about the country's economy and other things, but not about that. We still had a good relationship, but there was a certain distance between us.

It's hard to understand why you didn't ask him these questions about what happened and how he had survived.

I don't know exactly why I didn't ask him, but I think I know why he wasn't arrested. I figured it out much later. There seems to have been a pattern. Stalin and the NKVD arrested people who were still prominent and active politically in the 1930s or people with ties to ideological and organizational centers in the party's history. By then, father was already in his sixties and working alone mostly as a scholar and writer. He had never belonged to any of the political groups or oppositions in the party. He was a sort of loner. Maybe that's why he was left alone. But it's only my theory.

Were you a Stalinist child? Did you grow up believing in Stalin?

In the 1930s I had a child's kind of faith in Stalin. At school "beloved Stalin" was the central figure in our lives, but father was very reserved about Stalin. In fact, I don't remember any conversations at all about Stalin at home. My father was a Lenin man, so the Stalin cult didn't impress him. I don't think he was personally acquainted with Stalin, though I saw Stalin once. His nephew Sasha had a birthday party at the house on the embankment, and Stalin came by to say hello. That was in 1935 or 1936. He came into the room where we kids were playing, but we hardly paid any attention. Some adult said, "Kids, here's Iosif Vissarionovich." Then we went back to our sweets and games.

Let's talk about your public career. By 1962 you were a national Komsomol secretary and thus one of the highest-ranking political figures of your generation. How did that come about?

During the war I was evacuated to the Urals along with many children from prominent political families. I was a student there for three years and in 1947 I went to Moscow State University to study philosophy. Even before I went to Moscow I was a Komsomol activist—I joined in 1946—and I continued this career at the university. By 1951 I was a member of the Komsomol committee for the entire university. That year I put in two applications—one for membership in the party and one for graduate school. Both were rejected. I can't say either surprised me. Having relatives who had been "repressed"—and you had to write this on your questionnaires and report it orally at meetings—overrode any personal merits a person may have had in the Stalin era. So instead of being able to continue my education in Moscow, they sent me to teach philosophy at a pedagogical institute in Gorky. When I got to Gorky I decided not to tell anyone that my aunt and uncles had been arrested. I didn't lie. I just kept my mouth shut. I was elected secretary of the Komsomol committee at the institute, which began my career as a young apparatchik with a small Komsomol salary.

You began your career at the height of the Stalin cult, but by then you must have had some doubts about Stalin.

Strong doubts. They began at the university in 1948, when the campaign against so-called cosmopolitans—as Jews were being called—got started. One of my best friends, Karl Kantor, was a war veteran and a Jew, a man of great mind and soul. Suddenly, the university party committee viciously attacked him. His friends also turned against him. He wasn't the only one. There seems to have been some sort of mandatory quota—party organizations being told they had to expose a certain number of cosmopolitans. Karl's now a major art historian, a philosopher, a very respected person. But I'll never forget how he was hounded and persecuted by my classmates, including his own best friends.

It was also at that time that I began to talk with older students who had fought in the war. These were private conversations, but I'm surprised we weren't arrested. We asked ourselves candid questions. Why all this idolization of Stalin? We wanted to be serious philosophers, yet we were supposed to worship his primitive writings. At the same time I began to meet other students whose relatives had been arrested. It turned out that many of us had family members and friends who had been shot. I began to realize the dimensions of the terror and to learn things that Khrushchev would tell the congress several years later. You see, many of the students knew more than I did. They had been at the front, and they came from all over the country. Of course, I had been thinking about all these things since I lived in the house on the embankment. But now I understood.

By the way, discussions like this were rather widespread, though secret, in the late 1940s and early 1950s. We took some risks. For example, several of our university classmates were arrested, and I started a fund-raising campaign to help the wife of one of them. The undercurrents of anti-Stalinism were already forming—a growing spirit of disagreement with what was going on in the country.

So by the time I got to Gorky I had certain attitudes. In addition, as a twenty-two year old, I lived my life among young people, not bureaucrats, and worked in a nonbureaucratic way. My wife Ludmilla remembers. She was a student at the institute in Gorky. Those were good, lively times. I had no problems in Gorky, and in 1955, two years after Stalin died, I was accepted as a candidate party member. That year I was also elected a secretary of the Gorky Regional Komsomol Committee. I was put in charge of ideology and propaganda for the entire region. It happened because the head of the national Komsomol organization attended the regional conference where I gave a speech criticizing how we were misleading and even lying to students about the realities of Soviet life. I said this wasn't educating young people but sowing the seeds of disillusionment in them. The Komsomol head liked the speech, and I was made a regional secretary. The following year, after the Twentieth Party Congress, I became first secretary of the Gorky City Komsomol Committee. I was only twenty-seven years old.

What was the impact of Khrushchev's speech at the congress on the party and Komsomol organizations in Gorky?

The speech really wasn't a secret, though I first heard about it through rumors. Soon a representative of the Central Committee came to Gorky and gave us a detailed account of what Khrushchev had said. I wasn't shaken by the speech, but many people were. For me it was more like a galvanizing event that clarified all the doubts of my childhood and all the things I had learned at the university. I was happy the party leadership had finally acknowledged that Stalin was responsible for the deaths of millions of people—that he was an executioner. I was very happy that people were being rehabilitated and allowed to return from the camps. That was the most important thing. But it bothered me that Khrushchev did not touch on the roots of Stalinism. He skimmed the surface.

How did you get promoted to Moscow and the national Komsomol leadership?

One day toward the end of the 1950s, Vladimir Semichastny, then the head of the Komsomol and later chairman of the KGB, came to Gorky. I spent several days with him, touring factories and talking with people. He saw how people related to me and trusted me. About the same time I was a member of a Soviet delegation to Poland, where the situation was very complicated. The delegation included Yuri Voronov, then the editor of *Komsomolskaya pravda*. Under Gorbachev he has been head of the Central Committee's Department of Culture and, since December 1988, editor of *Literaturnaya gazeta*. We had to participate in a number of tense meeting with students in Krakow and though I was sufficiently orthodox, I spoke with the students in a flexible and conciliatory way. This plus my experience with Semichastny in Gorky seemed to have made a good impression in ruling Komsomol circles. In 1959 I was called to Moscow and made head of the Komsomol's Department of Propaganda and Agitation and editor of its journal *Molodoi kommunist* [Young Communist]. A few months later I was elected a secretary of the national Komsomol Central Committee. I was responsible for overseeing almost everything that affected the lives of young people—ideology, culture, the press, the army, physical education. I held the position until 1962.

That year Pavel Satyukov, the chief editor of *Pravda*, asked me to leave the Komsomol and join *Pravda* as a member of the editorial board. I was close to the Satyukov family and *Pravda* was the main newspaper of the Communist Party, so I accepted. I headed the paper's department of Marxism-Leninism until 1967. Considering what later happened, it seems funny, but don't laugh. Anyway, those were the highest posts in my official career—Komsomol secretary and member of *Pravda*'s editorial board. They were high nomenklatura positions.

It's a kind of tradition in America for an organization or newspaper to compose a list of a few dozen people in their thirties who one day are likely to be among the top political leaders of the United States. If some Soviet organization had composed such a list in 1962, would your name have been on it?

Almost certainly. Though I don't want it to sound like bragging, among the generation of rising leaders at that time I was said to have a very promising future. Part of it was the fact that I was a good public speaker. I spoke without a text or notes, and people said that my speeches at congresses and elsewhere impressed them deeply. But I should also tell you that I had been noticed by powerful people. Politburo members and Central Committee secretaries like Mikhail Suslov and Boris Ponomarev knew who I was, originally probably because of my name. I was told that they had said of me, "This is our man and he's doing well." And on the several occasions when I met them they'd say, "Keep up the good work. We've got our eye on you. We are pinning our hopes on you."

Were there other rising stars of your generation whom you knew at the time and who now are playing leading roles in Soviet political life?

Oh sure. I worked with Eduard Shevardnadze, who's now a member of the Politburo and foreign minister. Also Abdurakhman Vizirov, who not long ago was named first secretary of the Azerbaijan Communist Party. They've sent him down there to clean up the mess. Also Boris Pugo, who's now head of the party's Control Committee, and Aleksandr Aksyonov, who until May 1989 was head of Soviet radio and television. I also knew Aleksandr Yakovlev a bit. When I was propaganda secretary for the Komsomol he was at the Central Committee's Department of Propaganda, so naturally we were at meetings together and had some personal talks. I'm not surprised by his reformist views today. I always knew he was an intelligent man and after he was sent away to be ambassador to Canada in the 1970s I also knew he had independent viewpoints. That a man of such intelligent and independent views could rise so high in the party is a result of perestroika.

By the way, I also met Gorbachev once many years ago, probably in 1963, when I was working at *Pravda*. He had come to Moscow on business from Stavropol, where he was a party secretary. A mutual friend invited me to meet him. We went to the room where he was staying and talked for about two hours. Gorbachev was the same person then that he is today—energetic and already advocating perestroika ideas. He told us about agricultural experiments he was trying to undertake in Stavropol, how promising they were, but how many obstacles they faced. In a certain sense he was already a man of perestroika.

I remember being pleased when Gorbachev was brought to Moscow in 1978 as Central Committee secretary for agriculture. I thought it was a good sign. I even wrote him a letter reintroducing myself and asking him to help some friends of mine who were having problems with a useful agricultural-industrial project in the Yaroslavl region. He took care of it very quickly. I saw the letter he wrote.

Were you surprised when Gorbachev became general secretary?

I wasn't surprised, but it made me think about how things turn out in life. It's interesting.

What brought about the fall of Len Karpinsky? Presumably it began with Khrushchev's overthrow in 1964.

Not exactly. Certainly that was not my reaction to the overthrow. In fact, Yegor Yakovlev, my oldest and dearest friend, and I drank some Cognac to celebrate Khrushchev's removal. We thought his impulsive, half-baked decisions had become a brake on the process of reform, even a threat to the process. He had really gotten on our nerves during the preceding two years or so. We believed that Khrushchev had become an obstacle to the program he had initiated himself at the Twentieth Congress. We thought he could no longer lead the process of de-Stalinization and democratization and the new Brezhnev leadership would be better. We didn't realize that Brezhnev and the others got rid of him to stop those reforms. Yegor was deputy editor of *Sovetskaya Rossiya*, and we worked in the same building. I don't remember whether it was in my office or his where we drank to Khrushchev's removal.

Later we realized how wrong we had been. I'll tell you an incident that illustrates how my view of Khrushchev changed. I only met him once while he was in power, briefly at a reception. On his seventy-fifth birthday, when he was living in a kind of forced isolation at his country dacha, a group of us were sitting around at *Izvestia* thinking about him. We decided to call him. I had known Khrushchev's granddaughter Yulia for many years, and also his daughter Rada and his son-in-law Aleksei Adzhubei. By the way, Yulia was married to Nikolai Shmelyov, whom I met only a few years ago. I knew he was a first-rate economist, but I never imagined that he was such a brilliant publicist and fiction writer. What a surprise. Anyway, I called up the Khrushchev family dacha, and they put Nikita Sergeevich on the phone.

When I reintroduced myself, he said, "I don't remember you, but I knew your father very well." Then I told him on behalf of those of us sitting around the telephone the following. Speaking for our generation, I wanted him to know that we were the political children of the Twentieth Congress and of his program. That his achievements were irreversible and that we would fight to prevent anyone from turning back the clock. In congratulating him on his birthday, we wanted him to know that his life had not been in vain and one day it would be clear how great a role he had played in the history of our country.

Khrushchev was deeply touched. He answered me very emotionally. "I have always believed this, and I am very pleased that you and your relatively young generation understand the essence of the Twentieth Congress and the policies I initiated. I am so happy to hear from you in my twilight years." Later, members of his family told me that Khrushchev remained moved by my phone call for several days. No Soviet officials called to congratulate him on his birthday, though the Queen of England and Janos Kadar did. Khrushchev died two years later.

Today, of course, I have a very positive view of Khrushchev. If you talk about his personal qualities, he was nothing like Brezhnev and that gang. Khrushchev was an honest and unbending man. He said what he thought, though what he thought wasn't always so good. Not that he wasn't smart, but his views had been formed in different times. He thought you could solve all problems by working like a bull, storming fortresses, as they used to say in Stalin's time.

Would you agree that without Khrushchev there would have been no Gorbachev?

Absolutely. In a way, that is what I was saying to Khrushchev when I called him on his birthday. That what he had started was irreversible. I would say that Gorbachev is Khrushchev but filled with new knowledge and made wiser by Khrushchev's experience.

When did you first realize that Khrushchev's successors represented a threat to the program of the Twentieth Congress?

It was clear by 1966 from a series of events. Neo-Stalinist articles started appearing in *Kommunist*. References to the Twentieth and Twenty-Second congresses began to disappear from the press. Stalin was being dragged back onto his pedestal. Censorship was being tightened. This was the context in which my own troubles began. In 1967 Fyodor Burlatsky, who also was working at *Pravda*, and I coauthored an article calling for less censorship in the theater and less bureaucratic interference in culture generally. We wrote it for *Pravda*, and the chief editor, Mikhail Zimyanin, told us it was good and he would publish it. When it wasn't published after six months, we gave it to *Komsomolskaya pravda*, telling them our editor liked it. They published it and the trouble began. We got fired, along with the editor of *Komsomolskaya pravda*.

Actually, there might not have been any problems had there not been a Central Committee meeting on that very day. At the meeting the head of the Moscow Party Committee, Nikolai Yegorychev, criticized some situation in the defense industry. Brezhnev, who had once been responsible for defense matters, took this as criticism of him and had

Yegorychev removed. Brezhnev and Suslov came up with the legend that Yegorychev and other former Komsomol leaders were plotting against the old guard—Brezhnev, Suslov, and the others. Brezhnev's aide showed him our article and said it was part of this plot. By the way, poor Burlatsky had never had anything to do with the Komsomol. He was angry about being drawn into this affair for a long time.

Brezhnev's reaction was swift. He ordered that we be removed from *Pravda*. Brezhnev is usually portrayed as a soft, weak-willed man, and maybe he was in regard to some things. But when things had to do with him personally, he hit quick and hard. One person defended me at *Pravda*, Georgi Kunitsyn, who's doing good things today. At the editorial board meeting he said expelling me and Burlatsky from *Pravda* reminded him of the first stages of the terror of the 1930s, when people started denouncing each other. For having defended us, Kunitsyn also was fired from *Pravda*. Burlatsky had a scholarly degree, so he went off to an institute. I was sent to *Izvestia* as a special correspondent.

I worked there for a year and a half, until I complained at an editorial meeting that pro-Stalin items were creeping into *Izvestia*. I said that if the paper thought the Twentieth Party Congress resolution against Stalin had been a mistake, it should say so—not pretend the congress had never happened. I also asked why we never mentioned Khrushchev. Did the editors think they could advocate one outlook on Monday, another on Thursday, and nobody would notice? After I spoke there was complete silence and the meeting broke up. When the editorial board met again a week later, to my great surprise many of *Izvestia*'s writers defended me, including Yegor Yakovlev, who had moved there, and Otto Latsis, who's now deputy editor of *Kommunist*. It didn't matter. Within a few hours the Central Committee decided to remove me from *Izvestia*, but in a peculiar way. They told the chief editor, Lev Tolkunov, let Karpinsky sit in his office but don't let him write anything, not even unsigned editorials. Give him a salary but don't give him a pen.

I sat at *Izvestia* for a while, until our troops invaded Czechoslovakia in August 1968, when I said a few blunt things about the invasion. I wasn't the only one. The *Izvestia* correspondent in Prague, Boris Orlov, saw the tanks and how Aleksandr Dubcek [the Czech party leader of the Prague Spring] was being held at gunpoint, and refused to send reports to the newspaper. Vladimir Krivosheyev, another *Izvestia* correspondent in Prague and now a prominent commentator on television, did the same thing. In fact, he wrote some notes to the Central Committee complaining about Soviet policy in Czechoslovakia.

Anyway, that ended my career at *Izvestia*. I found refuge at the Institute of Sociological Studies, where Burlatsky was deputy director. We started to work together again, but then the institute was demolished by Sergei Trapeznikov, chief of the Central Committee department that oversaw intellectual life under Brezhnev. A great many people were thrown out—people who have become very active and prominent again only with perestroika: Yevgeny Ambartsumov, Burlatsky, Gennadi Lisichkin, and others. They said we were engaged in some covert operation. We resisted for a year, but we had no chance. They demolished us.

My next stop was Progress Publishers, one of our biggest publishing houses. I knew the director from when we worked together at the Komsomol, so he gave me a job as head of the department of scientific communism. Don't laugh. I worked there from 1973 to 1975, when I was called before the party's Control Committee and expelled from the party.

They expelled me on the charge that I was engaged in underground antiparty activity, but it was hardly that. Back in late 1969, while I was at the institute, I had written an essay-length manuscript entitled "Words Are Also Deeds." It set out my theory that despite the bureaucratization of the Soviet system and the betrayal of socialist ideals, a reform movement was forming within the system due to various objective forces at work. One day it could produce new reforms from above. I was arguing against the hopeless mood of stalemate then prevalent among the intelligentsia. It was a private essay. I didn't give the article to anyone except Roy Medvedev, who took a copy to read in 1970. I had known Roy and his brother Zhores for a while. Like me, Roy had been a nomenklatura editor before he became a dissident. I don't know what Roy did with my manuscript. In fact, I was surprised to learn much later that it turned up in a book Steve published [*An End to Silence: Uncensored Opinion in the Soviet Union*] in the United States in 1982. All I knew was that Roy called me in 1970 to say there had been a KGB search at his apartment and they had taken my manuscript along with all his other documents. When I was called to the KGB five years later, they showed me the manuscript and asked if I had written it. I said I had, and they passed the case on to the Control Committee.

The question is how the whole business ended up at the KGB. There's more to the story. Earlier in 1975 I visited Prague on business for Progress Publishers. My old friend Otto Latsis was working there, and he showed me a book manuscript he had written about the history of our system and the need for major reforms. It's being published now, but at that time it clearly could not have been published. So I told Otto, Why leave it lying around Prague? Give it to me. I'm collecting these kinds of unpublishable writings. Someday they'll be needed. When I got back to Moscow I gave Latsis's manuscript to a typist to be retyped. The KGB came to her and took it. Remembering my own manuscript, they decided I had started an underground organization or activity against the party.

When the case came before the Control Committee, four of us were involved—me, Latsis, Igor Klyamkin, whose writings are now being published and stirring much controversy, and Vladimir Glotov, who's now executive secretary of *Ogonyok*. The other three were given reprimands, but I was expelled from the party. The charge was that I had been the instigator and organizer, telling the others to keep writing so that we could build a library for the future, and they had been my victims. I didn't mind that they were treated less harshly. I hadn't even told Latsis, who had to fly back to Moscow for the punishment session, that I was having his manuscript retyped.

Why do you think the party leadership treated you so harshly? After all, it was a delicate matter considering your late father's exalted status in official historiography. He was the subject of official biographies and you were a kind of prodigal son of the party elite.

That's probably the answer. Suslov played a major role in the decision to expel me. Remember what he had told me, "We are pinning our hopes on you." They could forgive people who had made a mistake, but I had betrayed them. They saw me as a traitor from within.

What happened after you were expelled from the party?

I was immediately fired from Progress Publishers. I couldn't get a job for two years. Who was going to hire somebody to teach philosophy or work on a newspaper who had been expelled from the party for antiparty activities? They even kicked me out of the Journalists Union, where I had been head of the publicist department. They didn't even inform me. One day I showed up to renew my union card and a woman told me, "You have been expelled from the union for immoral conduct." They let me back in 1988. Now I'm even head of the Bureau of Veteran Journalists.

But I managed to live, and some old friends continued to help me. After the scandal at Progress Publishers my friend the director was also fired—for letting a dangerous character like me work for him. They said he had sheltered the anarchist Karpinsky. They transferred him to Planeta Publishers, where he and some other friends gave me manuscripts to edit on a free-lance basis, without having me on the staff. That kept me going for two years. Meanwhile, my wife Ludmilla kept her job at Progress; they didn't touch her. In 1977 the daughter of one of my uncles who had been arrested under Stalin got me a job in a state artistic agency that commissioned paintings and statues. When I told the director I had been expelled from the party, he paled and asked if I was a drunk. I said no, "I was expelled for views incompatible with party membership." "Thank God," he replied, "we'll take you." I stayed in this job until September 1987. It was an innocuous position. I traveled around the country taking orders for paintings and monuments. They paid me 92 rubles a month and later 120 a month.

During the decade between your expulsion in 1975 and the beginning of perestroika under Gorbachev, were you what was called a dissident? That's how you were described in several uncensored typescripts circulating in the Soviet Union and by emigré newspapers.

I was a dissident in the eyes of the people who expelled me from the party and perhaps in your eyes. But in my own mind I wasn't a dissident. I didn't participate in dissident groups or help put out underground journals. I was in between. Formally I was expelled from the party, but I remained a party member in my soul. It was the result of my family upbringing and my age. I felt tied to the party.

I guess I would call myself a half-dissident. I didn't break with my Marxist-Leninist views or become an antisocialist like many dissidents. I was more like Roy Medvedev, though he was much more active and influential. Roy represented those of us who fought the deformations in our system but remained faithful to socialist ideals—who believed that we had to start building socialism anew in the Soviet Union. I didn't know many of the dissidents. I was close to the poet-singer Yuli Kim, to Roy, and to the old Communist journalist Raisa Lert. I also knew the young dissident Gleb Pavlovsky, who was one of the editors of the uncensored journal *Poiski* [Quests]. They sent him into internal exile in the early 1980s. Now he's back in Moscow and an editor of the Soviet journal *Twentieth Century and Peace*. My expulsion had the potential of being turned into a criminal case, so I didn't really participate directly in *Poiski*. I just read a few manuscripts for Pavlovsky and gave him my opinion of them.

During your years as a half-dissident, how were you treated by old friends who still were in positions of power or influence?

My friends weren't in very high places at the time. Most of them were in the cultural-scientific intelligentsia, and they remained my friends. They helped me morally and sometimes materially. As for my former associates in the nomenklatura, life had led us in different directions and our paths rarely crossed. But when we did meet they treated me with compassion, though with some reserve, probably because they didn't really understand what had happened to me. You know, there are different floors of life, and sometimes there aren't any stairs between them. They just lived on one floor and I lived on another. But I do know that several of my former associates were angry and bitter when I was expelled. Shevardnadze told one of our mutual friends, "It's a very, very great pity, but I have no power to do anything about it." Nowadays when I meet former friends in high positions, Boris Pugo for example, they greet me with great warmth and happiness.

Looking back, do you think your life and career would have turned out differently if Khrushchev had not been overthrown?

Things would have been different for me, but I'm not sure how different. We are back to the subject we began with—a person's external and internal development. I think that in my soul I was already a half-dissident by the early 1960s, before Khrushchev was removed. The form official Marxism-Leninism was taking no longer satisfied me. I was already moving beyond its official parameters, and eventually I probably would have come into conflict with the prevailing ideology and the system. The conservatism and counterreform policies that followed Khrushchev certainly brought on the conflict much faster, but probably it would have happened anyway.

And if you could relive those years of your life?

I can't answer that venerable question. No one can ever answer it.

But seeing your former associates today at such high levels—Shevardnadze, Pugo, Aleksandr Yakovlev—you must think about it.

I admire those men, but we were different. None of them was shaken as profoundly as I was by the events after Khrushchev's ouster. I can't say they were wrong and I was right. Only that I turned out to be a different kind of person in some respects and my reaction was different. That's why I suspect some people at the top still don't fully trust me, even though I've been readmitted to the party.

Tell us how your return to public life and readmission to the party came about.

Friends helped me, but it took a while. The turning point was my long article in *Moscow News*, "It's Absurd To Hesitate Before an Open Door," in March 1987. Yegor Yakovlev arranged it. Our personal friendship has lasted many years; it's much bigger than politics. I think he is the most outstanding editor of our times—maybe of the century. The Italians recognized this and gave him an award. Yegor has made *Moscow News* a flagship of glasnost. Many people detest the newspaper, but progressive, democratic, cultured people gulp it down.

By the way, I am very happy that Yegor was elected to the Congress of People's Deputies by the Filmmakers Union. As you know, I was one of the people he designated to speak for him on the eve of the election in March 1989. Of the union's ten deputies, Yegor received the most votes. It was a great tribute to his role as a bold fighter for perestroika and as an editor. I hope he will now be elected a member of the smaller Supreme Soviet, which is supposed to be a real standing parliament. It won't be that unless people like Yegor are elected—people who will speak their minds on national issues and not just silently accept any legislation put forth by the bureaucracy. In any event, Yegor's election to the Congress will strengthen his personal and editorial authority against those officials in the party's ideological apparatus who want to limit glasnost.

Of course, Yegor couldn't arrange my return to public life by himself. Falin played a role in having me published in *Moscow News*, and probably Aleksandr Yakovlev helped. Yegor asked me to write the article, Falin and others made some suggestions, I revised it a bit, and it was published. After that I was able to write a few more things for the Soviet press and participate in some roundtable discussions that were published. In 1988 Yuri Afanasyev included a chapter by me in his book *There Is No Alternative*. I hadn't known him before; perestroika brought him to the surface. We are very friendly now and have a lot of mutual undertakings.

In 1987 I also got a better job. You remember Yuri Voronov, whom I've known for many years. I spoke with him in his capacity as head of the Central Committee's Department of Culture. He talked to the minister of culture of the Russian Republic, who, by the way, had worked under me when I was a Komsomol secretary. They found me a research position at a cultural institute. The pay is better and I'm able to think and write.

But my return to the party was more complicated. I appealed for readmission later in 1987, but I was turned down. I had to go before the party's Control Committee, which then was headed by Mikhail Solomentsev [a Politburo member since the Brezhnev era who was removed in 1988]. The functionary who prepared my papers was an elderly and kindly man who kept telling me, "Really, they shouldn't have expelled you. It was not proper." So I went before the Control Committee in that mood, thinking there would be no problem. All of a sudden, Solomentsev came in with this horrible look on his face. For a whole hour he read aloud passages from my 1969 manuscript "Words Are Also Deeds," chastising me for my sins as he went along. Finally he said, "You still have not disarmed ideologically. Nothing has changed in our party. He who was considered a revisionist is still considered a revisionist." Readmission denied.

Did that mean Solomentsev wasn't enthusiastic about perestroika?

Yes. Afterward Falin complained to Aleksandr Yakovlev about the decision. Yakovlev told him that things like this don't get done by themselves and asked why he hadn't been told that the Karpinsky case was coming up for review. Then, in June 1988, a group of leading members of the intelligentsia sent a letter to the Nineteenth Party Conference calling for my readmission to the party. Among the signers were Afanasyev, Shmelyov, Mikhail Shatrov, the publicist Yuri Karyakin, and others. Nothing happened for a while. When queries were made, someone in the apparat said the letter was lost. But my supporters in the Central Committee, who had already criticized us for being poorly organized the first time, had kept a copy and passed it on to Aleksandr Yakovlev. I'm told that Yakovlev talked things over with Pugo, who now headed the Control Committee. At one point Yakovlev's aide called me to tell me to stay in touch and that everything was under control this time. I was reinstated in the party in late October 1988. Yegor did an interview with me about it and published it in *Moscow News*. And in February 1989 he asked me to be a regular columnist for *Moscow News*. I accepted the offer. As I said there, I'm happy to have been readmitted to the party, but I hope that everybody who was treated more harshly—those who were imprisoned—will be fully exonerated, not just amnestied, as most of them have been.

Everywhere we go in Moscow, people are talking about your readmission. Your old friends are very pleased, but so are many young perestroika activists. In fact, you are greatly admired by members of this new genera-

tion, even by ones who don't know you personally. We've often heard them say that Len Karpinsky is a very special figure.

I'm glad to hear that. It means a lot to me. I think some of them were influenced by my 1987 article "It's Absurd To Hesitate Before an Open Door." It was largely an autobiographical article that showed them that my generation, people of the 1960s, did not entirely capitulate in the face of events but tried to fight the advance of conservative forces as best they could.

I wasn't the only person from my generation who resisted, as I've told you. There were many others, including the people in your book. I've already mentioned some of them, but I should say that I also knew Tatyana Zaslavskaya back in the 1960s, when she was working in Novosibirsk. In fact, we were on a trip together in 1968 when Soviet troops entered Czechoslovakia. We talked about it and grieved together. As a scholar, she is one of the very best perestroishchiks. I've also known Aleksandr Bovin for a long time. He's a very intelligent and independent man, as he was when he worked in the Central Committee apparatus. He was so independent they got rid of him. Elem Klimov and I are old friends. I knew him when his beautiful, talented wife, Larissa Shepitko, was alive. We were very close when they were persecuting him and shelving his films. Recently I did a special study of how the bureaucrats treated Klimov's films. It shows—and this was true in the economy as well—that each bureaucrat destroyed culture not mindlessly but for the sake of his bureaucratic career. I don't know Mikhail Ulyanov well, but I know from his speech at the Nineteenth Party Conference that he is a very courageous and persistent fighter for perestroika. They kept interrupting his speech, but he said what he wanted to say. And of course from our generation Yevtushenko is very special. He wrote the poetry of the Twentieth Party Congress. Poetry here is just as important as politics. I was at many of his public readings and remember how he electrified young people. He was the poet-tribune of our generation. He is another one who never gave up.

But the young people today have different attitudes toward my generation. Some of them think we could never carry anything through. Take our mutual friend Valery Pisigin, who organized the Bukharin Komsomol Club in the city of Naberezhnyi Chelny [formerly named Brezhnev] and who also has become head of the interregional cooperative federation. Pisigin called us a generation "with a run but without a jump." I told him that we began the run and his generation will never jump if it doesn't include our run in their run. He now agrees with me. Because it's true, my generation prepared the way for perestroika. Not all of us, of course. Part of my generation was and remains hopelessly lost. That's why Pisigin's generation, people in their late twenties and early thirties, is so important. They are already mature and strong enough for the serious work of perestroika. Just look at Pisigin.

We want to get your views on perestroika itself, on the events from 1985 to 1989, but first a question that you might find awkward. Would you say that you foresaw the coming of perestroika, of such radical reforms from above, many years ago? We ask you this partly because so many experts in the West, and so many people in the Soviet Union, believed that it was impossible.

It would seem immodest if I made such a statement. It is true that this was the essence of my 1969 article—the one that caused all the trouble. I didn't use the words "glasnost" or "perestroika," but the basic ideas were there. I don't want to start shouting that I foresaw perestroika twenty years before the party did. Our party has its pride and it wants to be the pioneer. On the other hand, I was a party member when I wrote that article, and I wasn't the only one in the party thinking like that.

That raises another question. Can you explain where Gorbachev and the present radical leadership came from and how they emerged at the top?

They weren't dropped down here by parachute from abroad. They came from the same place I did—the Communist Party–Komsomol structure, the political-ideological nomenklatura. This structure creates people in its own image, but it also engendered its own opponents— officials who did not accept all the existing absurdities, inefficiencies, inhumanities, and other repulsive features of our system. Such people developed inside the party system along with the mass of careerists and apologists, whose only goals in life were to adapt to the demands of the apparatus and compromise their own consciences.

Party cadres who understood the need for change were produced by the realities of our life, by the natural diversity of people, by the changing of generations. They wanted a more efficient and humane system, but they knew they had to wait until their time came, remain in the apparatus, develop their ideas, seek out like-minded people, and be ready when their hour struck. They are the ones who began perestroika. Now they still are at war with the camp of conformists and careerists.

Don't think it was easy for them over the years. The party apparatus has a self-selection mechanism, and such people were always in danger of being demoted, cast aside, or expelled. They needed patience and maybe cunning to survive with such views. But if you consider that the Communist Party now has 20 million members, I can imagine that a million party members or more were getting ready for perestroika in one way or another. I wasn't the only one who paid with his career.

All this finally took the form of a struggle at the top. Gorbachev is the expression of this process and the initiator of perestroika. Whatever happens in the future, he has already performed a tremendous service to the country and to the world. He wasn't afraid to take responsibility for the reforms on himself. I don't know exactly what happened in 1985, but I'm sure he took a great risk. There were other contenders for the general secretaryship and a struggle for power. Gorbachev is still taking risks. Look at all the conservatives still in high places, still in the Central Committee, still putting the brakes on the reforms. And they're not all of the older generation.

In addition to Gorbachev-like reformers in the party apparatus, did half-dissidents like Karpinsky and fuller dissidents like Medvedev and Sakharov play a positive role in preparing perestroika?

Of course they played a role, more so the full dissidents than the half-dissidents, who mainly sat at home and didn't try to distribute what they wrote or to organize anything. We half-dissidents were timid.

Roy Medvedev played a very large role. His independent written works, circulating in typescript or in editions published abroad, were read by thousands of people. I read all of his historical and political works, and they influenced my thinking. Sakharov fought with different weapons. He wasn't a historian or a philosopher but a moral-intellectual force—an example of honesty and bravery. His disgraceful exile to Gorky became an important mobilizing factor. The flagrant injustice of it was clear. I know many people in scholarly institutes and the intelligentsia who personally protested the treatment of Sakharov. They wrote letters and even went to the Central Committee to protest. So Sakharov played a tremendous role.

Now he is playing an important role in the ideology of democratization and perestroika. If Gorbachev hadn't freed Sakharov from exile, I don't think there would be real trust in perestroika—here or abroad. I participated in a roundtable with Sakharov not long ago, and I pointed to him as an example of how our internal affairs are also world affairs.

Now that the reforms you wanted for so long are actually underway, what is your own understanding of perestroika? What do you hope it will achieve?

We have had a totalitarian bureaucratic regime in which the state was everywhere and for all practical purposes society did not exist apart from the state. Perestroika is an attempt to put the state in its proper place and to bring civil society back to life. That is why democratization and market economic reforms are so important. The former is giving society an opportunity to express its own will—in elections, in the thousands of newly formed political and social associations, and through glasnost. The market reforms are creating new forms of nonstate ownership for urban dwellers and farmers. Perestroika won't reduce the state or eliminate its authoritarianism right away. But beneath the state an independent and active society is being born.

As a person who still is a Marxist-Leninist, do you accept Gorbachev's slogan, "Perestroika means more socialism"?

To be honest, I think it is more of a political slogan than an analytical concept. What does it mean—more or less socialism? Which raises a fundamental question: Do we have, have we ever had, socialism in the Soviet Union? I think we had the beginnings of it in the 1920s, under NEP—embryonic socialism. But I agree with Afanasyev that what happened under Stalin—the Stalinist system—cannot be considered socialism. If we were to say that all that terror and horror and barracks life was socialism, who would have any use for that socialism? Who could believe in it? One would have to conclude that socialism was an illusion that turned out to be a reckless and bloody adventure. As for me, I still believe in socialism.

Afanasyev is right. We have to separate the idea of socialism from Stalinism completely. It isn't enough to say that perestroika can merely scrape the rust off an otherwise healthy socialism. The bureaucratic rust of Stalinism has eaten through the metal into the entire system. All that is left are ideals and some faith in socialism. Many people prefer to cling to metaphorical notions that some kind of socialism existed under Stalin and Brezhnev—prison socialism, barracks socialism, deformed bureaucratic socialism, some kind. These half-baked notions aren't analytical, and they won't lead us to the truth. There is only one way out. To admit it wasn't socialism and start again.

Isn't that a terribly dangerous political statement to the party and to the country more than seventy years after the Revolution? Look at all the attacks on Afanasyev since he said this publicly, and in a somewhat milder way. Even some ardent supporters of a radical perestroika think he went too far and a kind of danger zone is forming around him.

People accuse him of not thinking through his tactics, but the time for tactical caution has passed. We need more people like Afanasyev. We need them most of all. Let him be even bolder and less compromising. We all have to be. If you are afraid of the wolves, you'll never go into the woods.

As for admitting that the system isn't socialism, that is a delicate issue. But as I said, we had the beginnings of socialism in the 1920s, before Stalinism. We had the kind of diverse structures and pluralism toward which we are now striving. In my view, the period since 1985 is like the 1920s. With perestroika we now are beginning socialism again or, if you prefer, moving toward it.

Have you really thought this through? On the one hand, you argue that there can be no socialism without democracy. On the other hand, you draw an analogy between perestroika and the NEP 1920s, when there already was a one-party dictatorship. Are you assuming that democracy is possible in the Soviet one-party system?

I'm not ready to reach a final conclusion about this. I haven't decided. Many intelligent and educated people say that a one-party system is incompatible with democracy. For example, one of our leading experts on political science, Boris Kurashvili, has been expressing that view in the press and on television. I have said all along that we have to reopen this question and think about it. If we don't have a multiparty system, the Communist Party will have to restructure itself so that the equivalent of a two-party system can exist inside it. It will have to allow a permanent opposition, a kind of second party, within its own ranks. And party members, including members of the party apparatus, will have to be free to state their views and take positions without fear of reprisal. The party has to make room for both pragmatists and dreamers. In addition, autonomous political associations and fronts, as are now forming in the country, must be free to criticize the Communist Party. Whether or not all this is possible and how it can be achieved—frankly, I don't know.

You are an outspoken supporter of the political fronts that are emerging across the country, from Moscow to the Baltic republics. Some Soviet observers, including Kurashvili, think that in fact they are the embryo of a Soviet multiparty system.

They have a natural tendency to develop in that direction, but there still are many restraints on their political activities. Moreover, the fronts aren't welcome everywhere in the country. In some areas officials are trying to suppress them. They are most prominent in the Baltic republics of Estonia, Latvia, and Lithuania, where they are playing a very big role. All of us are worried, though, that they will move in undesirable directions—toward secession from the Soviet Union. Of course, we ourselves created this danger by trampling these republics, disregarding their national interests, culture, and language. Our central authorities planted the roots of the emotional explosion of national sentiment we are now witnessing. But these dangers are minimal compared to the positive aspects of the people's fronts.

What is the greatest danger to perestroika?

It is what we call the "braking forces" which are composed primarily of two large social entities. One is the administrative bureaucracy, which doesn't want to lose its income and its means to appropriate the national wealth. The other are the millions of ordinary citizens—office workers, factory workers, collective farm functionaries—who are afraid of a competitive society and prefer wretched stability to perestroika. This is a sociopsychological opposition, not a political one.

That answer doesn't seem fully compatible with your argument in the Soviet press more than a year ago that a bureaucratic ruling class exists in the Soviet Union. That was a very radical assertion. As a Marxist you know better than we do that, for Marxists, where there is a dominant class—bureaucratic or otherwise—there is both economic and political power. If there is such a ruling class in the Soviet system, as you seem to suggest, it raises serious doubts about who Gorbachev represents and who supports his reforms.

Yes, it raises serious, complicated questions. One of them we have already discussed: Where does Gorbachev come from? He comes out of this class and represents its most enlightened and progressive segments. As for who in society supports perestroika, it is everybody who is ready to work creatively, be an individual, and take responsibility. There are millions of such people in the Soviet Union—in the intelligentsia, the working class, the peasantry. Not everybody is afraid of the sea of a competitive society. This is the enormous social stratum that Gorbachev and his allies in the party apparatus are counting on.

As a former member of the nomenklatura, are you confident that a segment of that appointed class is ready for perestroika even though democratization threatens the whole system of appointments?

The nomenklatura is a huge pyramid of positions, offices, and functions. An elective system would strip the nomenklatura of its closed caste character. In this traditional sense, the nomenklatura may cease to exist. We would still have an administrative apparatus, but not one that is dependent only on itself. We would have one dependent on the people and the will of voters. One that instead of ordering people around would take its orders from the people. Even so, I am certain that a significant portion of nomenklatura officials are in favor of perestroika—the capable ones who feel they have the ability and strength to compete. The ones who do not want to spend their entire lives trembling over their privileges and doing nothing.

As in most walks of life, there are two kinds of people who go into our government and administration. There are those for whom elite status, power over others, and flattery are enough. They are like court nobility, preselected, giving orders, and using their power to put down any competitors. Then there are those who see government as a creative profession, as a way to express their abilities, as a way to develop interesting projects, as a way to help the country. I know many people like this and there are more and more of them every day. Now they are in the party leadership, but the battle goes on. Who can say who will win?

What will happen to the country if the anti-perestroika forces win?

It's hard for me to bring myself even to think about it. Maybe 25 percent of the country will say, thank God, things have returned to normal. No more shouters in the street, no more anarchy, no more cooperative and private enterprisers charging an arm and a leg, no more critics telling us that we work badly, no more doubts about our history, no more confusion about our beliefs. Thank God, everything has returned to our normal, vegetablelike existence. But for the majority of the people, who have been awakened and already believe in the necessity of perestroika, the idea of socialism will be buried forever.

As a nation, the collapse of perestroika would be a tremendous blow to our international standing and to the chances of world survival. I think the country would fall into permanent crisis and the government would be extremely aggressive. It would try to win the support of our people by frightening them with external enemies, ideological tensions, and the need for vigilance. The consequences would be catastrophic.

Certainly perestroika is the party's last chance. If perestroika fails, in order not to disappear from history the people will find another political vanguard to lead society out of crisis. It may be another kind of police regime and a very harsh one.

Personally, so long as I breathe, I will be hopeful and optimistic. Perestroika is going to be a lengthy process. We are just emerging from an enormous historical tragedy, from a kind of gigantic historical sabotage of the nation, and we will be paying the price for a long time. It's not like trash in a room that can be swept away with a broom in fifteen minutes and everything will be clean again. It will take decades. I think political authoritarianism will continue to prevail for quite a while in the Soviet Union, but during this time the space for democracy will constantly broaden. Only at the end of the process will there be full democratization.

As for Karpinsky, this is my last chance. Given my age and my health, I'm not going to have another opportunity to finish and publish what I have been thinking for so many years. That is why I was happy to rejoin the party. Even if I have only half a chance remaining, I am going to seize it.

What are your plans for the future?

There are two possibilities. I can reenter political life through the various clubs and forums, television, and the press. I'm not sure I have the strength for that. I don't see myself being able to play much of a political role because I'm used to the fact that in our Communist Party one has to be invited to play such a role. The other possibility is to pursue more academic and theoretical undertakings. For example, I'll be writing about ideological and political issues in my regular articles for *Moscow News*. I see myself behind a desk rather than back on the podium.

Some of the young activists from the political clubs talk about nominating you as a candidate for a local soviet or for some other office.

I don't think it is going to happen, but if I were nominated and elected, I'd participate.

We want to ask you a final question about your life. The theme of repentance for the past is a dramatic feature of perestroika and glasnost. Probably it was framed most vividly in Abuladze's film Repentance, *when the son denounces his father for the evils of Stalinism and then kills himself. But the theme is also discussed regularly in the press in other contexts. It is often asked, for example, who was responsible for what happened to the country after Stalin's death, after Khrushchev's overthrow, under Brezhnev? Explicitly or implicitly, a number of writers are insisting that the people responsible come forward to admit their guilt and repent. As a former high-ranking official, do you feel any sense of guilt or need to repent?*

Up to a certain point, yes. I have to admit that until about 1965 I allowed myself to take some actions for which perhaps I should repent. After that, there were fewer and fewer such actions on my part. But even before 1965, when I still worked in the Komsomol, there were many times when I was criticized myself by higher authorities for letting artists and poets get out of hand, for indulging their free thinking.

Do you look back on your years as a half-dissident as a period of repentance?

No. In those years, above all, I felt no need for repentance. I was convinced that for the most part I was in the right and those who treated me unjustly were in the wrong. But I don't think there is much point in talking about repentance in terms of an individual. All of us who lived in this political system and obediently did much of what we were told to do—all of us ought to repent. A central realization of perestroika, of what is happening in the Soviet Union today, is that we must give moral human values the highest priority. This is so for all of us—Communist Party members and nonmembers. Each individual must turn himself or herself into a moral person. That is what really matters.

GEORGI ARBATOV

"America Also Needs Perestroika"

AS A FULL MEMBER of the Central Committee, Georgi Arkadyevich Arbatov is, along with Yevgeny Velikhov, the second highest ranking political
figure in this book. And as a longtime adviser to Soviet leaders on policy
toward the United States, he is well known to many Americans from his
frequent visits and appearances on television. Less known is that the institute headed by Arbatov—the USA Institute, as it is called in short—has
long been a center of reform thinking about both the Soviet system and
international affairs. Nikolai Shmelyov, whom readers met above, is only
one of a number of iconoclastic scholars gathered together by Arbatov
since the institute opened in 1967. In addition to having been present at
seven of the nine U.S.–Soviet summit meetings since the early 1970s, Arbatov is a well-regarded economist and member of the Soviet Academy of
Sciences, which in 1989 elected him one of its deputies to the new congress.

I REMEMBER VIVIDLY when I decided that I wanted to study international affairs and become a specialist on the United States. It was when I
was a young lieutenant in World War II stationed in the Ukraine. I read
in a newspaper that they had opened the Institute of International Relations. I thought to myself, if I survive the war I'll try to enroll in that
institute. Sixteen of the forty people in my high school class were killed
in the war. It was natural that I wanted to study English and become a
specialist on the United States. We were wartime allies.

I came from an educated family. I was born in 1923. My father had
been a metalworker and a member of the Bolshevik Party. Later he was
director of a cannon factory and then deputy director for administrative
affairs of the Lenin Library in Moscow. He was a very gifted and smart

man. My mother was a schoolteacher. From 1930 to 1935 the family lived in Germany, where my father worked for our Commissariat of Foreign Affairs. For some reason, maybe because we all knew there would be a war, after high school I enrolled in a military school. Actually, it was right on the eve of the war. I joined the party in 1943, at the front, and after I was demobilized in December 1944 I enrolled in the institute. I graduated in 1949. That began my lifelong scholarly study of history, economics, and international affairs.

As a member of the Academy of Sciences and of the party's Central Committee, you have been involved in both scholarly and political activities. But before we talk about that, we'd like to know if the events of the Khrushchev era, the anti-Stalinism generated by his speech to the Twentieth Party Congress, had as great an impact on your life as it did on the lives of other people in our book—Yevtushenko and Bovin, for example.

I'm older than those two, so it may have been a little different for me. Most people my age grew up with a great many illusions about Stalin and his policies, and I shared those illusions. On the other hand, I never worshiped the Stalin cult, as many did. Though I never admitted it to others, and hardly to myself, I couldn't accept the idea of a living god. Also, quite a few of my school friends were arrested. You could hardly find anyone in Moscow who didn't know someone who had been arrested. I knew that all those arrested could not have been guilty. Still, Stalin's death was a very emotional event for me, as it was for most people, but within a few months I understood that things were changing for the better in the country. In this sense I was ready for Khrushchev's congress speech in 1956, though of course it was an enormous event. I think I was struck less by what he said than by the fact that these things were said at a party congress.

The changes that followed in our political life affected me as well. From 1949 to 1957 I had worked at a foreign literature publishing house and a philosophy journal. In 1957 I went to work at our political international affairs magazine, *New Times*. Here's a little-known fact. Otto Kuusinen [a member of the Politburo and Secretariat until his death in 1964] was secretly a member of the editorial board. He wrote under the pen name "N. Baltiski." Kuusinen headed a group preparing a new post-Stalin textbook, *Fundamentals of Marxism-Leninism*. The old one, pardon me, was bullshit. Kuusinen was dissatisfied with the original group of people assigned to work with him and decided to recruit his own people. He had noticed me at *New Times* and asked me to be one of his principal assistants. The book we produced—it came out in 1960—wasn't bad considering when it was written. In fact, there were many interesting things in it.

I then worked for a while at *Kommunist* and in 1960 went off to Prague to write for the journal *Problems of Peace and Socialism*. There were some brilliant people filled with many new ideas at the journal, including the chief editor, Aleksandr Rumyantsev. Some of them now play leading roles in developing perestroika, such as the social critics Yuri Karyakin and Yevgeny Ambartsumov, and Anatoly Chernyaev, who is a personal aide to Gorbachev. I came back from Prague in 1962 to be a department head at the Institute of World Economics and International Relations. In 1964 Yuri Andropov—Kuusinen had introduced me to him—asked me to join his group of advisers at the Central Committee. The group was full of my friends—Burlatsky, Bogomolov, Shakhnazarov, and others. I held various posts at the Central Committee, including head of the USA section of the International Department, until 1967, when I became director of the newly founded Institute for the Study of the United States, under the Academy of Sciences. I was elected a candidate member of the party's Central Committee in 1976 and a full member in 1981.

As you see from the list of people in our book, several of you worked for Andropov as young men. Maybe what you now call "the new thinking" was actually born at that time.

It started then. They were creative and productive years. It's interesting, when there is a need for new ideas, a social demand, people come forward with them out of nowhere. I knew Andropov very well. He was a highly cultured man of the old school. I've known a lot of Western leaders over the years, and I think Andropov was brighter than any of them. Even back then he understood the need for change in our domestic and foreign policies, including the need for detente with the United States.

Did it surprise you when Andropov later became head of the KGB and eventually general secretary?

At that time I thought of him as the party's brightest and most gifted leader. Until the mid-1970s I was certain that he would become general secretary. When he went to the KGB in 1967, I thought it was important to have such a man there, but I don't know if I was surprised.

Are you surprised that a former head of the CIA, George Bush, now is president of the United States?

Maybe it has something to do with the role of national security in both of our countries. But there are big differences between the CIA and the KGB. Moreover, Bush was at the CIA for only one year, while Andropov headed the KGB for fifteen years. But let's talk instead about the institute you have headed since 1967, the Institute on the United States and Canada—or, as it is known in the United States, the Arbatov Institute. Even though you employ scores of people with scholarly degrees who publish many scholarly articles and books, there is an American perception that it isn't really a scholarly institute but a kind of propaganda organ for the Soviet government.

Many people in the United States know better, but that opinion is a reflection of American misperceptions of our system. It was the Reagan administration that really gave wide circulation to this story. From the beginning the Reagan people were tremendously hostile to the institute because they were so public relations conscious. They thought that our appearances in America were relatively effective. People from the institute lectured in the United States, took part in public forums, appeared on television. So the Reagan administration began a campaign against the institute. They tried to discredit us and made it difficult for us to get visas to visit the United States. You know this story and some of the people who were denied visas. But I took all their hostility toward the institute as a compliment. If that administration was so against us, particularly in the early 1980s, could we have been so bad?

Tell us something about your institute's relations with the Soviet leadership over the years. For example, have you advised the leadership on a regular basis about relations with the United States?

The institute was created to improve the general public's knowledge about the United States and the quality of decision making as it relates to the United States. It meant that when we had interesting ideas we always had a means to bring those ideas to the attention of the leadership. Soviet–American relations are the bread and butter of all of us who work in the institute. I have seen a lot of ups and downs in Soviet–American relations since the institute was formed more than twenty years ago. Now we are witnessing major improvements in our relations. The institute has had fruitful and unfruitful years, but I can't complain. I've been lucky. I was present at or witnessed seven of the nine summit meetings between Soviet and American leaders that took place in the 1970s and 1980s. For me it has been an honor—an indication that the institute's work and my own knowledge have been useful.

Let us put the question in a different way. Does the institute conform to what the leadership wants to hear from its experts, or do you try to persuade the leadership of what you think is right or wrong in official policy toward the United States?

I could never work here if it was a conformist institute. Over the years I've told leaders things they didn't want to hear.

Can you give us a few examples?

No, that is confidential. Okay, I'll give you an example. I advised the leadership against participating in the Chautauqua conferences with the United States, which began in 1986. I argued that this was a project of Charles Wick [director of the U.S. Information Agency under the Reagan administration], and why should we help him?

Some Western scholars who have followed your institute's work believe that it was one of the birthplaces of the new Soviet thinking in foreign policy.

Changes in policy thinking don't just happen overnight. They are prepared by people who develop ideas over many years. I can tell you that my institute colleagues and I were not bystanders in this process. If you go back and read what was written by people at this institute—and at a few others, such as the Institute of World Economics and International Relations—you'll find ideas that are now part of the official new thinking. Some of the institutes were absolutely barren, others were not. For example, it was at a few institutes that civilians rather than military people began analyzing security and military issues.

We personally know two or three people who say they had difficulties, even serious political problems, in the 1970s or early 1980s, before you gave them positions at the institute. They express gratitude to you for giving them a place to study and write. Did you go out of your way to help such people?

Having been a member of the Supreme Soviet, I receive many, many letters asking for various kinds of help. People write to me who want to get out of prison, who want to get treatment in a hospital, who need assistance. I can't do a lot, but I do what I can. As for the institute, my policy has been to help bright, decent people advance, whether or not they were in trouble. I can't remember ever bringing in someone who turned out to be of no intellectual use.

In one way or another you have advised every Soviet leader since Brezhnev. In your experience, is there something different about advising Gorbachev?

He is an exceptionally good listener and a very quick learner. He has terrific instincts. I've been with him at several meetings with foreign leaders and senators. I don't remember a single instance when he made a mistake. He is always very well informed.

Did you know Gorbachev before he became general secretary?

Yes. I heard very flattering things about him from Andropov before Gorbachev moved to Moscow. Andropov told me, "There is a brilliant man working in Stavropol." I first met Gorbachev when he used to come to Moscow in the 1970s on business. At the time I was working on economic as well as foreign policy issues. I met with him occasionally, as I did with other regional first secretaries. He made a very good impression on me. He was bright and sensitive and in search of new ideas. Later, when he became national party secretary for agriculture, he was already interested in foreign affairs. His ideas were already formed when he became general secretary.

Since then Gorbachev's personal role has been very important in setting the country on a new course at home and abroad. The choice was stark. Without the kind of reforms that were adopted, the Soviet system would have gone into a long and painful decline. And there was another candidate for the general secretaryship in 1985. When Gorbachev was chosen, he already knew what had to be done and he had a mandate from the party and the people. Even on the eve of becoming general secretary he had this kind of support. Nobody wanted more of what we had had in the preceding years.

People who know you say you were very pessimistic a few years ago. Now you seem to be full of optimism.

Now I am. But in Brezhnev's last years I couldn't help but see how bad things had become. I tried to intervene with people who were close to Brezhnev, but it didn't help. Then there was the upsurge of hope when Andropov became general secretary, but it was so short-lived. A very sad period followed Andropov's death, though maybe that brief period under Chernenko served a purpose. Even people who had doubts about undertaking serious reforms before that were persuaded there had to be real changes—that it was just impossible to go on in the old way. Of course, even now not everyone understands the full dimensions of perestroika and why it is needed.

Personally I share the radical view that perestroika means building a new model of Soviet socialism. We have to go all the way in democratization, glasnost, and economic reforms, not halfway. This bothers some people, but the reasons aren't hard to understand. The Soviet Union is a young country—just over seventy years old. During those years we have lived through so many extraordinary circumstances—the Revolution, the Civil War, Stalinism, the world war, the Cold War— that our structures, psychology, and behavior acquired extraordinary characteristics. It was like growing up under martial law. Even Stalinism was shaped by extraordinary circumstances—the threats of German fascism and Japanese militarism in the 1930s, the burden of the Cold War. So it's not surprising that we haven't yet built the socialist model we intended and believe in.

Now we have to rid ourselves of all those things that arose in those extraordinary times—things in which we used to believe, things we thought were intrinsic to socialism. This isn't easy, partly because many people still believe in all those things but also because the old economic model worked rather well in its time and for certain purposes. If the old economic model had completely failed, if the country had not developed from being a very backward country, it would be easier to change today. It would be easier to give up the obsolete thinking and policies that led the country into a dead end and that had such a negative impact on international relations. I can't think of any other country or government that now is so self-critical and demanding in looking at its own past and learning from the sufferings of the past.

That's why I argue against some of our officials who are guarded or worried about glasnost. The anti-glasnost tradition was imposed on the country during Stalinism, and it has had very negative effects in our domestic policies—but also in foreign policy. In fact, improvements brought by the Twentieth Party Congress back in the 1950s barely touched foreign policy. I don't mean that everything in our foreign policy stagnated in the years that followed. There were achievements— the beginnings of detente, arms control steps, and other things. But the tradition of secrecy, silence, and the absence of glasnost fossilized much of our defense and foreign policy thinking and decision making. When I argue for greater openness, some of our people say that exposing our problems will hurt us abroad. I tell them that the world knew about our problems before glasnost; we can't hide them. Moreover, glasnost has helped us abroad because more people there understand we are serious about our reforms. If there is an attempt to curtail glasnost, it will be harmful and counterproductive.

Bovin gave us an interesting perspective on glasnost. He complains that while openness has spread quickly and broadly in domestic affairs, it still is limited in international affairs. Among other things, he says, journalists who write about world affairs still have to take care not to offend the Soviet Foreign Ministry and various foreign countries. Bovin acknowledges that things are improving, but not fast enough.

I agree that we need more glasnost in the areas of foreign policy and military affairs. We are renouncing the absence of openness in these areas. It caused much harm. But I don't fully agree with Bovin. He's a very gifted man and a very close friend of mine. I think he ought to play a bigger role. But I'm sure that if he were deputy foreign minister and someone at *Izvestia* spoiled his delicate diplomatic game without even knowing what was going on, he wouldn't like it. He'd get upset.

Foreign policy is a serious business. Unfortunately, foreign governments and audiences have gotten accustomed to thinking that what is written by our journalists is the Soviet government's opinion and official line. We are partly to blame for this. As more Soviet journalists express their own opinions, foreign readers will get used to the idea that people here have different opinions. But there is already considerable freedom to write about foreign policy. Bovin is in a hurry. I think he wants to decide overall foreign policy.

But you agree with Bovin that the problem derives from Soviet journalists having spoken in one voice in the past—the voice of the Soviet state?

As someone who participated in this, I can't say that all of us spoke with the same voice, but most journalists did.

And as someone who makes or helps make Soviet foreign policy today, do you agree with Bovin that Soviet journalists should be free to criticize that policy and the Foreign Ministry?

Yes, they should be allowed to express their opinions. But they should be responsible enough to do it in a way that doesn't harm the country's foreign policy.

You sound like many White House spokesmen over the years. They often warn the American media against undermining U.S. foreign policy.

It's just something that can't be avoided. I am in favor of letting journalists speak out. But if you write for a government newspaper like *Izvestia*, as Bovin does, you have to understand that there are certain implications.

One thing about which Gorbachev, the Foreign Ministry, and Soviet journalists seem to agree is that there is an intimate connection between perestroika at home and the new thinking about Soviet policy abroad.

That is absolutely clear. The main priority of our foreign policy is to create the best international circumstances for the reforms going on inside our country. For us, economic and social progress is the most important thing. Of course, there still are some people here who cling to old ideas about the priority of promoting revolutions abroad—people who still think we can work miracles when foreign Marxists ask us for help. But it doesn't work. The best way to influence other countries is by reforming our own system. Perestroika involves a new way of thinking about foreign policy which begins with seeing realities as they are, not as we want them to be. We must face the truth, no matter how bitter it is. Our basic conception of the world has changed. We no longer view it in terms of "we" and "they" but as one humanity that has to live or die together. The nuclear world is too fragile for the use of military force, any kind of serious misbehavior, any geopolitical adventures, or an unlimited arms race. That is a basic principle of our new thinking.

There is a lot of talk here and in the West about "the new thinking," but considerably less clarity about it. Summarize for us, if you can, its main points. Perhaps you can also give us some examples of the old thinking that now have been rejected by the Soviet leadership.

That's a subject for a big article, not a conversation, but I'll try. I should say first that we do not claim to have invented all the ideas of the new thinking. Some of them originated years ago outside the Soviet Union with people such as Albert Einstein, Bertrand Russell, and Olof Palme. We are developing them, along with our own ideas, into a full program for international conduct. To mention just a few of these ideas, we now believe that what unites different countries, their common interests, is more important than the conflicts and differences between them. We also realized that we relied too much on military power for security. Both the Soviet Union and the United States have far more military power than they can use for any reasonable purpose. Militarism on the part of all countries is the real danger. We all must rely for security more on political means—on negotiations, for example. Our mutual task is to reverse the militarization of life. We have no need for all these weapons and huge armies. We also now understand that we cannot obtain national security at the expense of the other side—at your expense—and the same is true for you. This is our concept of mutual security. Our security depends on you feeling secure, and yours depends on us feeling secure. Now we also understand better that the lagging economic development of the Third World is a global problem, and despite our limited resources we have to make our contribution to solving this problem.

More generally, the Soviet Union no longer can live in economic autarchy, isolated from the world economy. Interdependence can only increase. All of these new perceptions make us favor more multilateral efforts, particularly through the United Nations. My own view is that the two superpowers have to be more democratic in their thinking about the world. The Soviet Union and the United States represent only about 10 percent of the world population. We can't and shouldn't try to do everything. And the rest of the world should not be held hostage to U.S.–Soviet relations.

What exactly do you mean when you say the Soviet Union relied too much on military power for its security?

Well, for one thing, we allowed ourselves to chase after every weapons system that you deployed. If you had it, we felt we should have it. Maybe it was inevitable since the arms race began when the United States had a monopoly on nuclear weapons, but we should not have accepted these rules of the game. We have to ask ourselves, what do we need all these weapons for? Fewer and fewer problems can be solved by military power. We don't have to have parity with you in all these weapons. All we need is enough weapons sufficient for our defense.

Is military sufficiency rather than parity now the official Soviet doctrine?

Yes.

What if the United States does not adopt the same doctrine—what if we continue to build weapons for the sake of catching up with the Soviet Union or to achieve military superiority? Will you stick with the doctrine of sufficiency?

Yes.

Even if we continue the arms race, you won't?

We think sufficiency is enough. Of course, we want some kind of equality, but not in numerical terms. We don't have to have as many airplanes as you have. We don't need them. All we need is enough so that you know it would be folly to start a war.

But we have gone beyond this. We want to create a nonnuclear world or a world with very few nuclear weapons. And we understand that we cannot have these major reductions in nuclear weapons without major reductions in conventional weapons. You can see how serious we are about this from Gorbachev's unilateral reductions in our conventional forces. So far as we are concerned, the door is wide open for even larger reductions through negotiations.

Unfortunately, there is a good deal of hypocrisy on your side. Your authorities complain that we have superiority in conventional weapons. Perhaps we do in some categories and we are prepared to build down in these areas. But you've been complaining about this for forty years, despite the fact that the West's GNP is two and a half times bigger than ours. If you really thought we had such superiority, why didn't you catch up? Your automobile and tractor industries are much stronger than ours. Why didn't they build tanks? No, I think you've used this scare about alleged Soviet superiority to hold your NATO alliance together and to justify building an absolutely irrational number of nuclear weapons.

We are arguing that both sides must adopt a new policy to replace the arms race. The side that is ahead in a weapons category should build down rather than the lagging side build up. This is the reasonable way to solve the problem of imbalances. Unfortunately, the human mind has a tendency to lag behind. Politics and diplomacy do especially. Our task is to bring your perceptions into accord with realities, particularly in foreign and military policy. Since 1985 Gorbachev has proposed getting rid of nuclear weapons. We have liberated ourselves from our own old thinking about nuclear and conventional weapons. President Gorbachev and President Reagan made some important progress on nuclear weapons. But our new thinking seems to have put America in an awkward position. Suddenly we start accepting American proposals and you don't know what to do. We're still getting too many negative responses from you.

All this is very interesting, but also very general. Give us some specific examples of old Soviet thinking, of previous foreign policies, that were wrong.

We didn't need to build all those missiles or deploy the SS-20s in Europe. Along with the United States, there was no need to ship so many arms to the Third World. We should stop this poor man's arms race. Another example of the old thinking is our foreign trade policy. This area is dominated by conservatism and stagnation of the worst kind. In many cases, American businessmen were right to complain about our endless red tape, exhausting negotiations, revisions of draft agreements, and the difficulties involved in traveling to the Soviet Union. We are putting an end to these obstacles to normal economic relations. And of course, Afghanistan was a mistake. We've brought our troops home.

Would these examples of wrong-headed policies lead you to conclude that the Soviet Union shares responsibility for the long history of the Cold War between our two countries?

It depends on what period you are talking about. In my reading of the origins of the Cold War, people here at that time saw your dropping of the atomic bomb on Hiroshima and Nagasaki in 1945 as the first shots of the Cold War. Those suspicions on our side were later confirmed by statements by certain American policy makers, Secretary of War Henry Stimson, for example. Some of them wrote in documents and memoirs that the atom bomb would make the Russians play ball by the American rules. I think this shaped the Soviet attitude toward America at that time, though that doesn't mean both sides weren't to blame later.

I think, for example, that President Jimmy Carter's presidency was a period of lost opportunities, when both sides made mistakes. When Carter became president, Brezhnev went out of his way to indicate that we were ready for serious improvements in our relations. Then in 1977 Secretary of State Cyrus Vance came to Moscow with a set of arms control proposals quite different from what had been agreed on. And Washington wouldn't allow him to use any fallback positions. But we shouldn't have rejected them out of hand. We should have said, okay, we have your new proposals, we'll study them and let's meet again in a few months. But we didn't and though we tried later to repair relations, very important time was lost.

Of course, we were not perfect. We have made mistakes, quite a number of them. Some of them serious, some less serious. We've carried a heavy burden of secrecy and suspicion, which can be explained by the extraordinary circumstances in our history, as I mentioned earlier, but this is changing now. We are publishing more economic and military statistics. We have stopped jamming the Voice of America and the BBC. By the way, during a recent vacation I listened to some of the Russian-language broadcasts from abroad. They are absolutely counterproductive. They offend a great many Soviet people and appeal to only a very small intellectual opposition.

If we translate all of Gorbachev's new thinking and new overtures into plain or traditional language, he is proposing a major new detente in Soviet–American relations. One reaction in the United States is that we tried detente in the 1970s and the Soviet Union violated it. In particular, these doubters emphasize the Soviet record on human rights and Jewish emigration, as well as the invasion of Afghanistan.

As I have already said, both sides made mistakes in the 1970s that contributed to the collapse of detente. The United States reneged on many things which had been decided—trade and credit agreements, for example. I think maybe the United States thought that detente meant the capitulation of the Soviet Union. There seems to have been an attitude that you alone had the right to dictate the rules of detente, which always turned out to favor you.

We didn't dictate the rules in Afghanistan. Admittedly, though, there is a dispute about the role of the 1979 Soviet invasion of Afghanistan in the history of detente. Did it kill detente or did it come after detente had already died?

My view is that, had detente not already failed by 1979, Soviet troops may not have been sent to Afghanistan. The decision was taken by a small group of people that did not include me, so I can only try to reconstruct the situation. Why did we suddenly say yes after the Afghan government had asked us twelve or fourteen times earlier in 1979 to send troops to help it? I think the breakdown of detente was one of the reasons. I know for sure that it brought about a different assessment of the situation and nature of the threat in Afghanistan. By 1979 it was clear that the SALT [arms control] process had been derailed. In addition, the United States was so over-involved and overwhelmed by the situation in Iran that it didn't care about anything else. You had concentrated massive naval forces in the area. Everything seemed to have changed from the detente atmosphere earlier in the 1970s. I don't know if this played an 80, 60, or 30 percent role in our decision to send troops to Afghanistan, but it played a role.

But as I pointed out earlier, our new thinking about foreign policy since 1985 repudiates many of our dogmas of the 1970s. Afghanistan involved one such dogma—the notion that such problems can be solved by military force. They cannot. This should be one of the commandments, like Thou shalt not kill: Thou shall not try to solve problems by military force. Now we are out of Afghanistan.

Human rights is another example. I would say that we behaved in a very stupid way by putting human rights in quotation marks or speaking of them as so-called human rights. After all, we made our revolution in 1917 for the sake of human rights. We aren't the only country that has made mistakes in this area. The United States also has made a few. Still, it was a mistake for us to brush aside the issue as a nuisance. On the other hand, the Americans didn't help human rights here by concentrating so much on the dissidents and the Jewish refuseniks. It made it harder for us to deal with the problem. But things have changed greatly since 1985. Can anyone deny our great progress in the area of human rights as a result of perestroika, democratization, and glasnost? And we have only begun.

As for emigration, it is very difficult to discuss this issue with Americans because our traditions are so different. Aside from the Indians, you Americans are a nation of emigrants or descendants of emigrants. Therefore, for you the idea of emigration is perfectly natural. Our experience is different. We had two previous waves of emigration. One immediately after the Russian Civil War of 1918–21—mainly of people who had fought against our revolution and left with weapons in their hands. The other was after World War II and involved many people who had collaborated with Hitler. As a result, the word "emigré" acquired a negative connotation for us. It had the taint of treason, desertion, betrayal.

This is hard for Americans to understand. On the other hand, look at the American reaction to the Arnold Lokshin family, which left Texas to move to the Soviet Union in 1986. They were what you call political emigrés. When they were on one of the Pozner–Donahue television spacebridges programs, the Soviet audience was struck by the hostile attitude of the American audience toward the Lokshins. You treated them like enemies. What would the American reaction be if several Texan families emigrated to the Soviet Union? Americans would feel that those families had rejected or betrayed American ideals and the American way of life. Maybe that gives you some sense of how our people feel about citizens who emigrate from the Soviet Union.

Nonetheless, it is a bad sign when people want to emigrate in large numbers. It means that bad things are happening in the country. Our policy now is to do our best to solve the problems that made so many people so unhappy in this country and caused them to want to leave. Family reunification or religious reasons are different matters. We will solve the problem of family reunification in accordance with the Helsinki Agreement. But we have to analyze why larger numbers of people want to leave.

Approximately 300,000 Soviet Jews were permitted to leave the Soviet Union between the late 1960s and the early 1980s. At the same time, the question of Jewish emigration increasingly became a controversial and disruptive factor in U.S.–Soviet relations. Do you think the Soviet Union should have done something differently in this area in the 1970s?

My personal opinion is that we should not have formulated our policy in a way that made an exception for any single ethnic group or nationality. It exacerbated the emigration question in our country for the reasons I just mentioned. All ethnic groups and nationalities should have the same rights. We shouldn't make exceptions for Jews, Ukrainians, Tatars, Cossacks, or anybody. In time we will open up opportunities for everybody who wants to leave the country, but it will happen when we think the situation is right. Otherwise it will generate new ill feelings inside the country. I think we made a mistake by making exceptions, as in the case of Jews.

In addition, organizations were formed in the West whose purpose was to learn the names and addresses of Jews in the Soviet Union and send them letters of so-called invitation. Much of this was fraudulent. Some of the people they sent letters to turned out to have died years earlier. Some people who received these letters were embarrassed by them. Then there were ties between groups in the West and Jewish groups here. That created a counterreaction or backlash inside the Soviet Union.

A very sad situation developed in the 1970s. It led to bad feelings toward Jews among ordinary Soviet people. I once heard a vice president of a small provincial university say, Why should I admit Jewish boys and girls even if they are more qualified? I only have a few slots, and they will leave the country in a few years. I'd better accept somebody else, he said, because we are educating them at the state's expense. The same pattern began to develop in hiring practices. People became reluctant to hire Jews for competitive or sensitive positions, assuming that one day they would leave the country. It was hard to control such feelings. And of course this made the situation worse for Soviet Jews. That's another illustration of why I am against making exceptions in our emigration policy.

Some Soviet officials argue that limits were and still are put on Jewish emigration because of a so-called brain drain problem.

That's not exactly right, and it doesn't relate only to Jews. The problem is that we pay many of our professional people much less than professionals are paid in the West. And yet the Soviet state pays for their entire education. We don't want to be in the position of training people at the government's expense only to see them leave for the West. Here too the solution is to make radical improvements so that people will want to stay.

So your position is that the Soviet government should have a standard emigration policy that applies to all of its citizens?

Yes, and if we have limitations on emigration, they too should apply to everybody.

If so, there are two possibilities. The Soviet government could adopt a much broader emigration policy that would allow virtually anyone to leave. Or an even narrower one that allowed very few people to leave.

I think we are moving in the direction of a broader emigration policy.

Where Jews are concerned, part of the problem seems to be the fact that the Soviet government considers Jews to be a nationality rather than only believers in a religion. In Soviet internal passports, your basic identity document, "Jew" is a nationality designation, along with Russian, Uzbek, Ukrainian, and the others.

I have no doubts that we made mistakes, but so did the Americans and the West. I think that many of your people now understand that the West's emphasis on the whole emigration problem was counterproductive and that it wasn't humane to tie it to U.S.–Soviet economic relations, as happened back in the early 1970s. In fact, when I was in the United States in 1971 or 1972 I warned that this would create anti-Jewish feelings in the Soviet Union and in the United States if the problem of emigration became an obstacle to detente.

But didn't Brezhnev agree to precisely this linkage in the general detente package negotiated with Richard Nixon and Henry Kissinger?

That's what Kissinger says, but I don't think Brezhnev agreed to this. There were some understandings, but not in such a general way. It was understood that emigration would involve some specific groups of

Soviet Jews living in certain areas, such as the Baltic republics. Later it became a big political war waged by enemies of the Soviet Union and of detente.

But perestroika will end this game by improving things here greatly. Already many more people are going to visit their relatives in the West and returning. And people who left the country are coming to visit their relatives here. Even political emigrés are returning. Procedures for all these comings and goings are being simplified.

I'll tell you something else. Foreign countries will stop being forbidden fruit for many of our people. I know the personal reactions of some of our young people here at the institute when they visited the United States for the first time. They had mixed impressions. They saw good things and bad things, but they already knew about the good things. As for the bad things, they said they had been told about them but they didn't believe what they were told or that some things in the United States were really so bad. They were struck by your ghettos, the poverty of your inner cities, and the provincial attitudes even among educated Americans. Some of our young people were also critical of the loose relations in American families and among American friends, which are so different from the close ties in our country. It is not that they were disappointed. They found everything very interesting but also very complicated. Partly their reaction was a product of our not very intelligent propaganda about the United States. One of the young men here told me that it would be a sound ideological policy to allow everybody to visit the United States. Then they'd have a more balanced view and understand there are no free lunches in America. You work like hell there.

Personally we do not doubt the authenticity or sincerity of these changes in Soviet foreign policy thinking or in actual Soviet policy. But the question remains whether or not these changes are widely accepted in your own political elite. Is there much opposition to the new thinking about the Soviet Union's relations with the outside world?

There has been some opposition among some rather important people. They thought it was wrong or futile to be so conciliatory toward the Reagan administration. They thought that, whatever we proposed, the Americans would reject it. Quite a few people lack trust in the United States. Some of them thought we were making too many concessions. You could find people like that in the Central Committee, but most of them aren't involved in foreign policy. There are quite a few ministers and regional party secretaries who say, "How can you hope to reach agreements with the Americans? Look at what the Americans do." I think Gorbachev's achievements have answered many of those doubts. Who would have thought that we would have reached an INF agreement with President Reagan or that he would visit Moscow?

Of course there are always officials who find it hard to admit they were wrong. For example, we have many specialists who study China and who argued in the late 1970s and early 1980s that the reforms there were serious and opened up new avenues for better relations with China. But for a long time many people opposed a new policy toward China. Now look what we have accomplished under Gorbachev.

You should understand that there also are misgivings about our new policy toward the United States among rank-and-file people. Many of them remember the experience of 1941, when we were suddenly invaded. They are worried that we'll be caught with our pants down again. My colleagues who lecture around the country tell me that during our unilateral moratorium on nuclear testing, which the Reagan administration refused to join, people felt that the Americans were achieving superiority by continuing to test and this was threatening our security. In this respect there was pressure on our leadership. Now that Gorbachev has announced unilateral reductions in our conventional forces, Soviet editorial offices receive many letters saying that the Americans didn't respond positively in the past, so why are we repeating our mistakes? But now that we have published figures on Warsaw Pact and NATO forces, my hope is that people will ask instead, why do we need all these armed forces since we aren't planning any wars against other countries? I think that as perestroika continues and our relations with the West improve even more, people's attitudes will change.

Maybe it is time for us to talk about attitudes in the West. As a frequent visitor to the United States and as a regular reader of American newspapers, you know that we too now are engaged in an important debate about perestroika. Some influential Americans argue that the reforms inside the Soviet Union are dangerous for the United States because they will strengthen Soviet capabilities and make you a more formidable adversary in world affairs. What would you say to these people?

The first thing I would say to them is that perestroika will go on no matter what they think or do. We have undertaken our reforms at home for ourselves, not because you like or dislike them.

I know that some Americans dislike them and I understand why. Since 1945 many American institutions have needed a foreign enemy—

an evil empire. Indeed, the general framework of American foreign policy has been constructed on the premise of this enemy. The Cold War was built on a kind of black-and-white, religious fundamentalism. There was the American paradise and the Soviet hell. When hell disappears, when the enemy image erodes, the whole structure becomes shaky. Some Americans fear this. But they will just have to find ways to live without the image of the Soviet enemy. America also needs perestroika and new thinking of her own.

You seem confident that the enemy image of the Soviet Union is eroding in the United States. Does this mean the American media are doing a good job of reporting perestroika?

It's a very mixed picture. You have a kind of arrogant way of praising us for certain reforms, while forgetting about things like Irangate and your other problems. On the other hand, your media could hardly ignore the dramatic changes here. There is much more coverage now. Your media don't give a fully accurate picture of what is happening here, but some of it comes through. For example, Americans can see that we are changing, our leaders look like normal people, and we have rock and roll.

But, you know, there is so much ideology about us in America. It's a great irony. You've always accused us of being too ideological, but there's no country in the world more ideological than the United States, despite your professed pragmatism. Mr. Reagan's presidency brought this ideological impulse to the fore. We too tended to over-ideologize our foreign policy, but our new thinking is based on realism. For example, that all these weapons are dangerous and useless. Your ideology—or illusions—seem to persist, which is one reason why you can't let go of the enemy image so easily.

Evidently Soviet foreign policy also was formulated around the image of an enemy—the American enemy—for many years.

Yes, it was, but not anymore. We would prefer to have the Americans as a partner, not as an enemy.

Are you saying to dubious Americans that perestroika is good for America?

It depends on what they really want. If they want to make easy money on military contracts and organize Contras against any government they don't like, then perestroika is a tragedy for them. But if they want to solve real problems at home and abroad, perestroika is good for them. If they don't want to squander any more money on surreal military weapons they cannot possibly use, perestroika is a blessing for them. If they want to grapple with real global problems like the environment and the Third World, perestroika is a blessing for them. If they want a stronger world economy, perestroika is good for them. We will be able to buy more American goods and relieve some of the Japanese economic pressure on you by inviting Japan and Western Europe into our markets. So where are the dangers of perestroika for America?

This would all add up to an end to the Cold War.

The Cold War is a living corpse. It died sometime in the 1960s and has been kept alive by political injections of myths and fantasies about the Soviet threat—like a body kept alive on an artificial heart-and-lung machine. It is time to lay it to rest. Neither of us can any longer afford to squander money on fake problems, false stereotypes, and pointless suspicions. Both of us have plenty of real problems at home.

And as an expert on American politics, do you think American political leaders are ready for an end to the Cold War? Would you advise Gorbachev that they are ready?

It worries me that too many of your leaders are wedded to the old international relations that formed after World War II. Even decent people among them seem to be unable to think in different terms. The main danger in America doesn't come from the extreme right but from the foreign policy and military traditionalists—the establishment center. They are so accustomed to the old rules of the game. You have this whole generation of policy makers who were brought up under Cold War conditions. Some of the things they have said and written in the last couple of years are very bad. I hope we can find ways to persuade these people to work with us.

What will happen to your domestic reforms if you cannot persuade them—if Cold War tensions and the arms race continue?

Perestroika will go on. It will be more difficult, but we can manage. We have enough resources for a reasonable defense policy. We have our own scientific research and applied sciences, so if you continue to try to isolate us from world science and technology, we'll manage.

Moreover, not everything depends on the United States. Detente never really died in Western Europe, and now it is flourishing. We are going to have good, normal relations with China. We no longer regard each other as enemies. The world is changing. The United States and the Soviet Union may not be the only superpowers in the world of tomorrow. There is going to have to be a perestroika in the whole system of international relations. The old, existing system is obsolete. It can't cope with global problems or enable either of us to deal with our problems at home. The United States has to decide if it wants to be our partner in this kind of perestroika.

You haven't directly answered the question: Do you think the United States after Reagan is ready to join the Soviet Union in this kind of new thinking?

I'm not confident that you will have new thinking in the United States, but I think your economic problems are going to force a change in your foreign policy anyway. Can you imagine the same amount of military spending and indebtedness over the next eight years? Also, to continue the Cold War you will need a partner. We won't be that partner. So while we may lose valuable time, I think things will be better in the United States.

Does the election of George Bush as president give you confidence that the United States will move in this direction?

I've known George Bush for almost twenty years, and during that time have had many private informal talks with him on my visits to Washington. He is an intelligent and very experienced man. But you never know what is going to happen when a man goes from the No. 2 position to the No. 1 position. Suddenly he has to make the final decisions and take the responsibility. I think Bush will have a more difficult presidency than Reagan had. He lacks Reagan's great popularity—his Teflon effect, as you say.

What would you tell President Bush if you saw him again privately?

I'd tell him that both of our countries face two primary problems. The need to eliminate any possibility of nuclear war. And the need to create favorable international conditions for solving our own internal problems. I'd tell him that President Gorbachev needs a partner and President Bush should be that partner.

Index